OXFORD LABOUR LAW

General Editors
ALAN BOGG, ACL DAVIES, KEITH EWING,
MARK FREEDLAND

Strike Ballots, Democracy, and Law

OXFORD LABOUR LAW

General Editors: Alan Bogg, Professor of Labour Law at University of Bristol Law School; ACL Davies, Dean of the Oxford Law Faculty; Keith Ewing, Professor of Public Law at King's College London; and Mark Freedland, Emeritus Research Fellow in Law at St John's College and Emeritus Professor of Employment Law in the University of Oxford.

This series has come to represent a significant contribution to the literature of British, European, and international labour law. The series recognizes the arrival not only of a renewed interest in labour law generally, but also the need for fresh approaches to the study of labour law following a period of momentous change in the United Kingdom and Europe. The series is concerned with all aspects of labour law, including traditional subjects of study such as collective labour law and individual employment law. It also includes works that concentrate on the growing role of human rights and the combating of discrimination in employment, and others that examine the law and economics of the labour market and the impact of social security law and of national and supranational employment policies upon patterns of employment and the employment contract. Two of the contributing authors to the series, Lucy Vickers and Diamond Ashiagbor, have received awards from the Society of Legal Scholars in respect of their books.

ALSO AVAILABLE IN THE SERIES

Bullying and Behavioural Conflict at Work
The Duality of Individual Rights
Lizzie Barmes

The Concept of the Employer
Jeremias Prassl

The Labour Constitution
The Enduring Idea of Labour Law
Ruth Dukes

The Legal Construction of Personal Work Relations
Mark Freedland FBA and Nicola Kountouris

A Right to Care?
Unpaid Work in European Employment Law
Nicole Busby

Regulating Flexible Work
Deirdre McCann

Welfare to Work
Conditional Rights in Social Policy
Amir Paz-Fuchs

EU Intervention in Domestic Labour Law
Phil Syrpis

Towards a Flexible Labour Market
Labour Legislation and Regulation since the 1990s
Paul Davies and Mark Freedland

The European Employment Strategy Labour Market Regulation and New Governance
Diamond Ashiagbor

The Law of the Labour Market
Industrialization, Employment, and Legal Evolution
Simon Deakin and Frank Wilkinson

The Personal Employment Contract
Mark Freedland

International and European Protection of the Right to Strike
A Comparative Study of Standards Set by the International Labour Organization, the Council of Europe and the European Union
Tonia Novitz

Freedom of Speech and Employment
Lucy Vickers

Women and the Law
Sandra Fredman

Just Wages for Women
Aileen McColgan

Justice in Dismissal
The Law of Termination of Employment
Hugh Collins

The Right to Strike
KD Ewing

Living Wage
Regulatory Solutions to Informal and Precarious Work in Global Supply Chains
Shelley Marshall

Strike Ballots, Democracy, and Law

BREEN CREIGHTON, CATRINA DENVIR,
RICHARD JOHNSTONE, SHAE MCCRYSTAL,
ALICE ORCHISTON

OXFORD
UNIVERSITY PRESS

OXFORD
UNIVERSITY PRESS

Great Clarendon Street, Oxford, OX2 6DP,
United Kingdom

Oxford University Press is a department of the University of Oxford.
It furthers the University's objective of excellence in research, scholarship,
and education by publishing worldwide. Oxford is a registered trade mark of
Oxford University Press in the UK and in certain other countries

First Edition published in 2020

Impression: 1

Published in the United States of America by Oxford University Press
198 Madison Avenue, New York, NY 10016, United States of America

British Library Cataloguing in Publication Data
Data available

Library of Congress Control Number: 2020937992

ISBN 978–0–19–886989–4

Printed and bound by
CPI Group (UK) Ltd, Croydon, CR0 4YY

General Editors' Preface

One of our aims as editors of this series is to encourage labour law scholarship of a wide-ranging and varied nature. We seek to foster high-quality legal research of a theoretical, doctrinal, and empirical nature, drawing on different inter-disciplinary perspectives. The latter might include history, politics, and/or economics. We seek also to promote scholarship that is alive to the international foundations of modern labour law, and sensitive to the importance of comparative study in a shrinking world.

It is in that context that we welcome this latest addition to the series, as an outstanding example of the type of scholarship the editors seek to promote. Principally, this is a study of the law relating to the operation of pre-strike ballots in Australia. But as such the study is set in a broad context, which examines the historical development of strike ballot obligations imposed by the State (mainly in the United Kingdom and Australia), and the international legal framework within which such restraints operate (set mainly by the International Labour Organisation (ILO)).

The authors provide some compelling comparative data about the law relating to strike ballots in a number of jurisdictions, notably the United States and South Africa, as well as Canada and the United Kingdom, before examining in some detail the strike ballot procedures now operating in Australia. These international and comparative dimensions provide a valuable resource for reform proposals to the existing balloting requirements and restraints operating in Australia and the United Kingdom.

In the second half of the book there are three fascinating chapters on the operation of the ballot legislation in Australia. These begin with the authors' analysis of the unique and highly contestable requirement that trade unions must seek the approval of the Fair Work Commission—a State regulator—for authority to conduct a ballot, the granting of which requires certain statutory requirements to be met. An interesting examination of how this requirement operates in practice strengthens the authors' proposal that it should be removed.

The other two chapters in this part examine the operation of the highly complex balloting rules, which have much in common with similar obligations in the United Kingdom, though there are important differences. As in the previous chapter, here the authors draw on a rich seam of data created by interviews with employers and trade union officials about the operation of the law and its impact on industrial action. The reader will encounter a number of important findings for policy-makers in Australia and beyond.

The findings of this study generally tend to undermine the claim that legislatively imposed pre-strike ballots are necessary to promote trade union democracy, and lead to the powerful conclusion with implications for other jurisdictions, namely that 'the mandatory pre-strike ballot requirement under the [Australian legislation] does not foster any form of democracy other than one that simply aggregates preferences—preferences which may not even reflect the genuine views of the members'. Indeed, the authors demonstrate that

> *internal union decision-making* about strike action exhibits the characteristics of participatory forms of democratic practice. Union practices in this context facilitate active participation in decision-making, demonstrate the responsiveness of union leaders to members, appear to tolerate opposing viewpoints, and largely devolve decision-making to those who will be asked actually to take any industrial action. Where, however, balloting occurs through FW Act mandated rules and in public, the process used positively undermines democratic practice, suppresses dissent and debate, and potentially leads to ballot outcomes that are intended not to reflect the genuine wishes of the membership, but to signal (genuinely or otherwise) the readiness of the membership to take industrial action.

The authors emphasize the need to look at balloting obligations in their entirety, noting that 'the aggregate effect of these requirements inhibits employee access to lawful industrial action'. Notable here is what the data tell us about how the balloting obligation is used tactically by both employers and trade unions in collective bargaining, though the balance of advantage—as no doubt intended by governments—has been greatly to empower employers and burden trade unions.

In their powerful conclusion in a text that represents labour law writing at its best, the authors propose changes that would 'provide a basis for meaningful, democratic decision-making in relation to the taking of industrial action'. The thoughtful conclusions—based on detailed research and rigorous analysis—present a challenge to those national governments and international agencies that are prepared to make and accept complex, formalistic, and highly technical laws of the kind examined in this study.

We warmly welcome this book into the Oxford Labour Law Series.

ALB, ACLD, KDE, MRF
16 April 2020

Preface

The origins of this book can be traced to Shae McCrystal's *The Right to Strike in Australia* (Federation Press, Sydney, 2010), where she observed of the pre-strike ballot provisions in the *Fair Work Act 2009* that they imposed a 'significant obstacle' to the capacity of Australian workers to take industrial action to protect and to promote their social and economic interests (at p 81), and quoting earlier research by Orr & Murugesan ('Mandatory Secret Ballots Before Employee Industrial Action' (2007) 20 *Australian Journal of Labour Law* 272), questioned whether there truly was a 'democratic imperative' for the introduction of the ballot requirement.

The purpose of the research upon which this book is based was empirically to investigate whether the ballot requirements in the *Fair Work Act* do impose a significant obstacle to the taking of industrial action, and whether those provisions are indeed impelled by a legitimate 'democratic imperative'.

To test these propositions, Breen Creighton, Richard Johnstone, and Shae McCrystal secured a Discovery Grant from the Australian Research Council in 2013. Catrina Denvir was recruited as a Research Associate in 2015 and was joined by Alice Orchiston in 2016. The research was conducted over a four-year period starting in 2014, and was approved by the University of Sydney Human Research Ethics Committee.

The book is a genuinely collaborative project. Catrina Denvir, and later Alice Orchiston, undertook the bulk of the empirical work—although the other authors did conduct some interviews. All five authors were actively involved in the writing-up process, and in the comparative, international, and theoretical chapters. This was done both through the exchange of drafts and periodic face-to-face team meetings at the University of Sydney.

The book starts from the proposition that virtually all national legal systems, and international law, recognize the right to strike as a fundamental human right. It acknowledges, however, that in no case is this recognition without qualification. Amongst the most common qualifications is a requirement that to be lawful, strike action must first be approved by a ballot of workers. Often, these requirements are said to be necessary to protect the democratic rights of the workers concerned: this is the so-called 'democratic imperative'.

In order to evaluate the true purpose and effect of ballot requirements the book draws upon the detailed empirical study of the operation of the Australian legislative provisions noted above; a comparative analysis of law and practice in a broad range of countries, with special reference to Canada, South Africa, the United Kingdom, and the United States; and the jurisprudence of the Supervisory Bodies of the International Labour Organization.

It finds that in many instances ballot requirements—especially those relating to quorum—are more concerned with curtailing strike activity than with constructively responding to the democratic imperative. Frequently, they also proceed from a distorted perception of what 'democracy' could and should entail in an industrial context. Paradoxically, the study also finds that in some contexts ballot requirements can provide additional bargaining leverage for unions. Overall, however, the study confirms our hypothesis that the principal purpose of ballot requirements—especially in Australia and the United Kingdom—is to curtail strike activity rather than to vindicate the democratic imperative, other than on the basis of a highly attenuated reading of that term.

We believe that the end result constitutes an important study of the practical operation of a complex set of legal rules, and one which exposes the dichotomy between the ostensible and true objectives underpinning the adoption of those rules. It also furnishes a worked example of multi-methods empirical, comparative, and doctrinal research in law, which we hope will inspire similar approaches to other areas of labour law.

The empirical research upon which this book is based would not have been possible without the cooperation of the Fair Work Commission (FWC), which provided the authors with access to all pre-strike ballot applications that were lodged during the Study period. We thank the President of the FWC, the Honourable Justice Iain Ross, Bernadette O'Neill, and Murray Furlong for facilitating access to these data.

We would also like to express our thanks to the Australian Electoral Commission (AEC) for agreeing to discuss the AEC's process for conducting ballots with us.

Thanks are also due to Stephen Smith from the Australian Industry Group and Trevor Clarke from the Australian Council of Trade Unions who helped to encourage their members and affiliates to cooperate with the conduct of the Study. This greatly facilitated access to potential interviewees.

We would also like to express our appreciation to the employer and employee representatives who agreed to be interviewed in the course of the Study. They are necessarily anonymous, but the project would not have been possible without them. The same is true of the stakeholders from the FWC, trade unions, industry groups, and the AEC who gave their time in the course of the research, and who provided many invaluable insights. The end result is much the richer for their generosity.

We owe thanks to many colleagues who provided advice, assistance, and information in the course of our research. They include: Kevin Carey (RMT), Alexander Colvin, Bill Ford, Anthony Forsyth, John Hendy QC, Pat O'Malley, David Peetz, Tonia Novitz, Joellen Riley, John Tuck, Eric Tucker, and Margaret Wilson.

From OUP, we would like to thank Alan Bogg, ACL Davies, Keith Ewing, and Mark Freedland, the editors of the Labour Law Monograph Series for seeing the potential in this project; Jamie Berezin for shepherding us through the review process; and Brianne Bellio for her thoughtful work putting the final product together.

As noted above, the funding for this project was provided through an ARC Discovery Project, ARC DP140100902, which was based at the University of Sydney Law School. We would like to thank Terry Carney and Pat O'Malley for their feedback on the early drafts of the grant application, Julia Robertson for assistance in putting the grant application together, and for grant administration, and Umeya Chaudhuri who worked on the project as a research assistant. Some parts of the book incorporate material which has been published as part of a number of journal articles although the material has been substantially reworked, and the authors acknowledge the agreement of the publishers of the journals concerned to the further use of the material concerned. This material has been variously published in:

Creighton, B, Denvir, C, Johnstone, R, McCrystal, S, & Orchiston, A, 'Pre-Strike Ballots and Collective Bargaining: The Impact of Quorum and Ballot Mode Requirements on Access to Lawful Industrial Action' (2019) 48(3) *Industrial Law Journal* 343–76 (aspects of this article are reproduced in Chapter 5);

Orchiston, A, Creighton, B, Denvir, C, Johnstone, R, & McCrystal, S, 'Pre-Strike Ballots and Enterprise Bargaining Dynamics: An Empirical Analysis' (2019) 42(2) *Melbourne University Law Review* 593–631 (aspects of this article are reproduced in Chapters 5 and 6);

Creighton, B, Denvir, C, Johnstone, R, McCrystal, S, & Orchiston, A, 'The Role of the "Genuinely Try to Reach Agreement" Requirement in the Protected Industrial Action Regime under the Fair Work Act 2009' (2019) 31 *Australian Journal of Labour Law* 279–304 (aspects of this article are reproduced in Chapters 5 and 6);

Creighton, B, Denvir, C, Johnstone, R, & McCrystal, S, 'Protected Industrial Action Ballots: An Empirical View' (2018) 60(1) *Journal of Industrial Relations* 53-76 (aspects of this article are reproduced in Chapters 4 and 5).

Breen Creighton
Catrina Denvir
Richard Johnstone
Shae McCrystal
Alice Orchiston
18 June 2020
Sydney, Melbourne, Brisbane

Contents

1

Strikes, Ballots, Law, and Democracy

Introduction

Strike action by workers and their unions is one of the most interesting and controversial issues in the field of industrial relations.

There are many reasons why workers take such action. The most common is to promote their occupational interests in the context of collective bargaining with employers. Other drivers of strike action can include reactions to events at work, such as threats to workers' health and safety; abusive exercise of managerial power; and perceived failure by employers to honour their legal commitments in matters such as wages, overtime, or working hours. A third set of drivers of strike action includes considerations of a more political nature, where workers seek to protect or to promote their broader social and economic interests—for example by protesting government policy and/or by trying to persuade governments to adopt remedial measures in relation to some social or economic ill.

Strikes by their nature are disruptive and their social, economic, and political impact can be significant. Indeed, taking strike action is largely pointless unless it has the capacity to inflict a measure of pain upon those to whom it is directed. The enterprise of the employer is of course directly impacted, but other enterprises that are connected with the employer (through, for example, domestic or transnational supply chains) may also be impacted. This in turn may have significant economic and social effects. In enterprises that provide services to the public, for example, the provision of those services may be disrupted with adverse consequences for the community at large. Governments too may face adverse consequences either through one or more of disruption of services, public disaffection, or economic dislocation.

These potential consequences inevitably mean that those who organize or participate in strikes come into conflict with the law, and also that all strikes are, to a greater or lesser extent, political in character. That in turn means that the manner in which they are regulated is contested. For example, business interests will often urge governments to legislate to control strike action

Strike Ballots, Democracy, and Law. Breen Creighton, Catrina Denvir, Richard Johnstone, Shae McCrystal, Alice Orchiston, Oxford University Press (2020). © Breen Creighton, Catrina Denvir, Richard Johnstone, Shae McCrystal, Alice Orchiston.
DOI: 10.1093/oso/9780198869894.001.0001.

through measures designed to restrict the ability of workers lawfully to take strike action and/or to reduce the impact of strike action when it does occur. Unions, on the other hand, will almost invariably oppose the adoption of such measures, and instead will urge governments to protect, and to enhance, their capacity to take strike action.

One of the measures most commonly used to regulate strike action is a requirement that the action first be authorized in a ballot of the workers who will participate in it. Employers and governments commonly justify the introduction of such requirements by reference to the rhetoric of 'democracy'. In doing so, they urge that workers should not be 'taken out on strike' unless they have first had an opportunity to exercise their 'democratic will' as to whether they wish to do so. Such rhetoric has obvious attractions. It is, after all, hard to argue that 'democracy' is a 'bad thing'.

The rhetoric of democracy can, however, be misleading in this context. One of the central themes of this book is that pre-strike ballot requirements that are ostensibly about promoting democracy are, in reality, the antithesis of democracy—in the sense that they are directed at inhibiting strike action rather than promoting or protecting democracy in any real sense. This theme is developed in the context of a detailed study of pre-strike ballot provisions both in international law and in national legal systems, with particular reference to the operation of the elaborate and intrusive ballot requirements in the Australian *Fair Work Act 2009* (Cth) (FW Act).

The comparative study shows that many, but by no means all, countries in both the developed and developing world have adopted provisions that require the conduct of a pre-strike ballot as a precondition for the taking of lawful strike action. In most instances, ballot requirements operate as a qualifier to worker access to the capacity lawfully to take strike action, and as such inevitably have an impact on the practice of taking strike action. Under such provisions, for a strike to be lawful the workers and union(s) concerned must first decide to go to ballot. The ballot will then be used either to permit the taking of strike action without further deliberation, or to authorize the taking of strike action in the sense that it enables the union and its members to decide to take strike action at a later time of their own choosing. In either case, it may be necessary to comply with some additional requirements, such as giving advance notice to the employer and/or the public authorities of the timing, character, and (perhaps) duration of the proposed strike. All of this will commonly occur in the context of contest on the part of an employer and/or a regulator, and, in countries where the capacity lawfully to take strike action is limited to active collective bargaining negotiations, will inevitably impact the conduct of those negotiations.

What is a strike?

In 1939 the American economist, JI Griffin, described a strike as 'a temporary stoppage of work by a group of employees in order to express a grievance or enforce a demand'. Thus defined, a strike can be seen to consist of five elements:

- a *stoppage* of work;
- by *workers* in the sense of persons who sell their labour to another, whether as 'employees' as that term is understood at common law, independent contractors, or persons engaged under some other kind of work arrangement;
- acting *in concert*, with the logical inference that an individual worker cannot engage in strike action unless they are doing so jointly with at least one other worker;
- for the *purpose* of protecting or promoting some perceived interest of the strikers—usually this will be *vis-à-vis* the employer of the strikers, but as appears below, on occasion the target of the strike may be government or some other social, political, or economic actor; and
- that is intended to be *temporary* in character—in other words, that both the strikers and (almost invariably) the employer envisage that when the strike has run its course the strikers will return to work with the employer.[1]

In both legal and common parlance, the term 'strike' is also used to encompass a range of other forms of concerted action intended to protect or to promote the interests of the workers concerned, and which may be engaged in as a substitute for, or as a complement to, a strike in the strict sense. *Creighton & Stewart's Labour Law* lists seven such activities:[2]

- *work bans*, whereby workers refuse to do certain types of work, or impose other restrictions on the performance of work;

[1] Griffin 1939: 20. Jacobs 2014: 736 adopts a similar formulation: 'a strike is a collective temporary cessation of work by employees in defence of their economic and social interests'. See also ILO 2018: [783].

[2] Stewart et al 2016: 918–19; footnotes in original omitted.

- *boycotts*, involving a refusal to deal with goods or services bound for, or emanating from, a particular source;
- a *go-slow* or withdrawal of cooperation;
- *work-to-rule*, which involves working to the letter of the contract of employment and commonly includes a ban on voluntary overtime or other 'extra' activities;
- *picketing*—a common and highly visible accompaniment to other forms of industrial action . . . which can range from a small group standing at the entrance to a workplace and endeavouring to get their message across to those entering or leaving the premises and to passers-by, to a mass demonstration which seeks entirely to bar access to the workplace;
- *occupation* of the workplace; and
- coordinated acts of *industrial sabotage*.[[3]]

As discussed in Chapter 2, the Supervisory Bodies of the International Labour Organisation (ILO) have taken the view that such activities are protected as part of the internationally recognized right to strike, so long as the activities themselves, and any strike action that they are intended to support, remain peaceful.[4] Many, but not all, national systems also adopt a reading of 'strike' which would include forms of action other than a stoppage of work.[5] Except where otherwise indicated, the more inclusive usage is adopted throughout this book.[6]

The purposes of strike action

As noted earlier, the purpose of strike action is conventionally described in terms of protecting and promoting the collective interests of workers—most often in the context of collective bargaining between workers and/or their representatives on one side and employers and/or their representatives on the other. Put simply, employees and/or their representatives may use the capacity to take strike action as a means of exerting pressure upon employers in

[3] This can range from deliberately causing plant or equipment to malfunction to coordinated absence from work ostensibly on grounds of illness (in Australian parlance, 'blue flu')—see, eg, *Hillsbus Co Pty Ltd v Gurdev Singh Bajwa & Ors* [2018] FWC 6861.

[4] See ILO 2018: [784] and [936]–[941]; ILO 2012a: [126] and [149].

[5] Note, however, that despite the fact that the Constitutions of France and Italy formally recognize the right to strike, this does not extend to action short of a strike. See Wedderburn 1991: 287–9; Jacobs 2014: 759–60.

[6] When discussing the legislative regimes of the United Kingdom and Australia in detail, the formal language used within those jurisdictions ('industrial action') is used throughout.

support of their claims for improved terms and conditions of employment, or as a means of resisting employer attempts to alter terms and conditions to the detriment of the workers.

Viewed in these terms, the right to strike can be seen to constitute an important means of redressing the power imbalance between individual units of labour and those to whom they sell their labour which is seen by many as an inevitable incident of the capitalist mode of production:

> Except in the most mechanical sense, there is nothing like parity or a possible equilibrium between an individual employer and an individual worker. The concentrated power of accumulated capital can only be matched by the concentrated power of the workers acting in solidarity.
>
> Effective collective bargaining is impossible where the workers do not have the freedom to stop work collectively, and trade unions cannot exist and function if effective collective bargaining is impossible. Quite clearly, to suppress the freedom to strike means to undermine the existence of trade unions.[7]

Whilst the 'equilibrium' factor points to the principal purpose of strike action, such action may be impelled, wholly or in part, by a number of other factors. As noted earlier, prominent among these are what might be termed 'political' considerations.

Purely political strikes—in the sense of strikes the purpose of which is to effect a change of government or to overturn the established constitutional order—fall outside the internationally recognized concept of the right to strike. However international standards in this area do recognize that in certain circumstances workers may legitimately take strike action in order to promote or to protect their broader interests—for example to protest government initiatives which the workers consider will adversely affect their economic or social interests, or to persuade government to adopt legislative or other measures that the workers consider would promote those interests. In 1983 the ILO's Committee of Experts on the Application of Conventions and Recommendations (CEACR) put the matter thus:

> The Committee considers that the right to strike is one of the essential means available to workers and their organisations for the promotion and protection of their economic and social interests. These interests not only have to do with obtaining better working conditions and pursuing collective demands of

[7] Kahn-Freund & Hepple 1972: 6, 53. To the same effect, see Bellace 2016: 43–4; 2018: 528–30.

> an occupational nature, but also with *seeking solutions to economic and social policy questions and to labour problems of any kind which are of direct concern to the workers* [emphasis added].[8]

It should be noted, however, that not all national legal systems afford protection to strike activity that is engaged in for purposes other than collective bargaining or the protection or promotion of occupational interests. For example, as discussed in Chapter 3, s 219 of the *Trade Union and Labour Relations (Consolidation) Act 1992* (UK) (TULRCA) affords protection only to action that is taken 'in contemplation or furtherance of a trade dispute'.[9] This can clearly include strike action associated with collective bargaining, and also with broader interests, so long as they fall within the scope of the definition of 'trade dispute'. The FW Act adopts a more restrictive approach in that it provides protection only in respect of 'industrial action for a proposed enterprise agreement'.[10] In neither country is there protection for strike action for what might broadly be termed 'political' purposes such as protesting government policy or supporting legislative or economic reform. In this sense, law and practice in both countries is inconsistent with the international standards described in Chapter 2. Other countries do, however, provide protection for at least some such action[11]—including, for example, promoting or enforcing the human rights of the strikers or other persons outside the workplace or even the jurisdiction.[12]

Amongst other potential drivers of strike action is the enforcement function:

> The strike may . . . be used as an alternative or as a substitute for legal sanctions; as an alternative where it is felt to be more effective and speedier than a possible recourse to law, as a substitute in those numerous cases in which rights in industrial relations exist outside the law.[13]

By way of illustration, unions may resort to strike action where an employer fails to adhere to either the procedural or substantive terms of an existing agreement, or to observe the terms of relevant work health and safety

[8] ILO 1983: [200]. See also ILO 2018: [758]–[759], [763], and [766].

[9] This form of words can be traced back to s 3 of the *Conspiracy and Protection of Property Act 1875* (UK). It has been pivotal to protection against legal liability in respect of strike action for over 140 years, and has been characterized as the 'Golden Formula' of British Labour Law—see Wedderburn 1986: 520–1. The term 'trade dispute' is now defined in s 244 of TULRCA.

[10] FW Act Part 3-3. See further Stewart et al 2016: 971–3, 989; McCrystal 2010: 149–60.

[11] See further Jacobs 2014: 748–9.

[12] See further Ewing 2004: 50–2.

[13] Kahn-Freund & Hepple 1972: 6.

legislation. Strike action to enforce existing agreements can be a particularly significant factor in situations, such as that in Britain, where collective agreements are not normally legally enforceable between the collective parties.[14] It can also be used as an enforcement mechanism in situations where the relevant regulator is unwilling or unable to take appropriate enforcement action, or where a given issue falls outside the scope of the formal regulatory system. For example, in Australia, before the adoption of formal provision relating to unfair dismissal at the federal level in 1993, it was common practice for unions to take, or threaten, strike action in support of workers whom they considered to have been unfairly dismissed. If and when the union took or threatened strike action in support of the worker in question, the dispute would in many instances be referred to the relevant industrial tribunal which would deal with what was, in effect, an unfair dismissal claim in its 'good offices' jurisdiction, even though strictly speaking it lacked the capacity to do so.[15]

A further factor identified by Kahn-Freund & Hepple as a driver of strike action is the need, conscious or otherwise, for an 'escape valve' in the workplace: 'the strike is sometimes a necessary release of psychological tension, especially where [people] have to work under physical or psychological strain'.[16] As the authors themselves acknowledged, it is hard to know how much weight should be accorded to this factor, but it seems reasonable to suppose that it would be of real significance on occasion—for example, where workers have been denied a wage increase over an extended period in consequence of an employer's refusal to negotiate in good faith.

Significant as factors such as enforcement of industrial norms or psychological release may be in some instances, in the final analysis:

> [T]he imperative need for a social power countervailing that of property overshadows everything else. If the workers are not free by concerted action to withdraw their labour, their organisations do not wield credible social force. The power to withdraw their labour is for the workers what for management is its power to shut down production, to switch it to different purposes, to transfer it to different places.[17]

The role of strike action as a social power countervailing that of property is central to understanding why employers and governments seek to regulate

[14] See TULRCA s 179(1), (2). See also Deakin & Morris 2012: 68–73, 904–6.
[15] See further Creighton, Ford, & Mitchell 1983: 166–8.
[16] Kahn-Freund & Hepple 1972: 8.
[17] Kahn-Freund & Hepple 1972: 8.

the exercise of labour's power to strike. Strike action is essentially an exercise of countervailing power which disrupts the smooth operation of capital and which seeks to increase the share of profit and control over work processes accorded to workers. This establishes worker access to lawful strike action as a site of contest between stakeholders as too much strike action may be perceived to tip the balance too far in favour of workers, whilst too little may make it unduly difficult for workers to safeguard and to promote their interests.

Strike activity, like trade union membership, is at historically low levels throughout the developed world. The reasons for this are many and varied.[18] Nevertheless, the *capacity* of workers to take strike action is still of the utmost importance as a means of protecting and promoting the interests of workers—especially in terms of helping redress the power imbalance between capital and labour. The perceived need to limit labour's capacity to tilt the balance in its favour is clearly reflected in persistent efforts by governments in many countries—notably in Britain and Australia—to limit workers' and unions' capacity lawfully to take strike action. One of the preferred means of doing this is by imposing evermore rigorous ballot requirements as a precondition for lawfully taking strike action. Furthermore, in using the law to try to control strike action, governments are acting in a manner that is entirely consistent with historical precedent—even though the weapon of the mandatory ballot is a relatively new one.

Strikes and the law

Jacobs helpfully describes the evolution of the legal response to the emergence of trade unions and the use of strike action in terms of three phases: repression, toleration, and recognition.[19] During the first of these:

> [S]tate policy is to suppress the agents of modern industrial relations, notably the trade unions, to prosecute their leaders and to thwart methods of collective regulation such as strikes and collective agreements. The instruments of power the state can utilise are manifold: prohibitions of the criminal law; police measures such as arrest; dissolution of meetings, seizure of pamphlets, and so on. In many cases, the repression may be openly directed towards

[18] See, eg, Peetz 2016: 153; Tucker 2014: 471–2.
[19] Jacobs 1986: 194–5.

the trade union movement; in others, repression may come in more subtle guises.[20]

By Jacobs' account, such repressive responses were common throughout Europe in the eighteenth and first part of the nineteenth centuries, although there were, of course, many variations as between different countries and at different times. The British experience is, however, of particular interest. As the first country to adopt large-scale industrial capitalism, Britain was the first to respond to more-or-less stable organizations of workers, as opposed to medieval craft guilds or *ad hoc* groupings of workers in particular sets of circumstances.[21]

In the British context, *repression* found expression in a number of ways.[22] First, participation in strike action would almost invariably constitute a repudiatory breach of the individual servant's contract of service with her or his master, thereby rendering the servant liable to summary dismissal.[23] Second, a striking servant would very likely be subject to criminal prosecution under master and servant legislation.[24] Third, individual workers and/or their organizations could be subject to criminal liability under statutory provisions specifically directed against 'combinations',[25] or statutory provisions of general application that were called in aid to curtail the activities of organized labour.[26] These latter furnish an excellent illustration of Jacobs' 'subtle guises'. Fourth, workers and organizations were liable to prosecution for common law offences such as obstruction, molestation, intimidation, and, above all, conspiracy to commit such offences. This was a particularly significant factor in the nineteenth century in relation to the activities of industrial pickets.[27]

[20] Jacobs 1986: 194.

[21] See, eg, *R v Journeymen Tailors of Cambridge* (1721) 8 Mod 10 (88 ER 9).

[22] For overviews of these exposures, see Orth 1991; Deakin & Morris 2012: 6–13.

[23] It is now more usual to refer to the relationship of *employer* and *employee*, as governed by a *contract of employment*. Nevertheless, the old terminology is still sometimes used, and the common law continues to draw a distinction between a *contract of service* (governing the relationship of employer and employee) and a *contract for services* (governing the relationship between principal and independent contractor). On strike action as a repudiatory breach of the contract of employment, see the discussion accompanying n [65], below.

[24] See Simon 1954: 160–200. In the Australian context, see Merritt 1982; Quinlan 1989: 25–49 (see also the sources cited at footnote 1 therein).

[25] See especially the *Combination Acts 1799* and *1800* (UK).

[26] For example, in the case of the 'Tolpuddle Martyrs', where a number of English farm labourers were sentenced to transportation to Australia for administering unlawful oaths under the *Unlawful Oaths Act 1797* (UK)—a measure that had originally been enacted in consequence of a naval mutiny during the Napoleonic Wars. See further Evatt 1937, 2009; Marlow 1971.

[27] See, eg, *R v Druitt* (1867) 10 Cox CC 592.

Finally, from 1875 onwards both individuals and (especially) unions were increasingly exposed to liability in tort in respect of actual or potential damage inflicted upon employers and other persons in consequence of organizing or participating in industrial action,[28] and to the issue of injunctions to restrain them from engaging in tortious conduct.[29] This was a particularly potent factor in light of the decisions of the House of Lords in *Quinn v Leathem* and *Taff Vale Railway Co v Amalgamated Society of Railway Servants*.[30] The first of these recognized the existence of the tort of 'simple' conspiracy whereby liability derived from the simple fact of acting, or agreeing to act, in concert with the intention of injuring another person, irrespective of whether the conspiracy involved the commission of any independently unlawful act.[31] The second recognized that unions could be liable in tort in their own right in respect of the acts of their members or officials.[32]

After 1824, the United Kingdom entered what Jacobs would term a *toleration* phase, with the various common law and statutory disabilities gradually being stripped away so that by the time Parliament adopted the *Trade Disputes Act 1906* (UK) workers and unions in a very real sense enjoyed the capacity to 'draw up their constitutions and rules, to elect their representatives in full freedom, to organise their administration and activities and to formulate their programmes'.[33] This paved the way for a *recognition* phase that extended from the early part of the twentieth century through to the early 1970s.

During this recognition phase the State positively encouraged the development of both public and private sector collective bargaining by use of a number of non-statutory techniques: most notably through support for the establishment of Whitley Councils and Joint Industrial Councils,[34] and through the application of various iterations of the Fair Wages Resolution.[35] The State also

[28] See, eg, *Bowen v Hall* (1881) 6 QBD 333; *Temperton v Russell* [1893] 1 QB 715; *South Wales Miners' Federation v Glamorgan Coal Co* [1905] AC 239.

[29] See *Springhead Spinning Co v Riley* (1868) LR 6 Eq 551.

[30] Respectively [1901] AC 495 and [1901] AC 426.

[31] This was, in effect, a civil form of the criminal liability adverted to by Brett J in *R v Bunn* (1872) 12 Cox CC 316.

[32] Sometimes with local variations, these tort liabilities were transported to the British colonies in the nineteenth century, including those in Australia and New Zealand. In the Australian context see, eg, *Martell v Victorian Coal Miners' Association* (1903) 9 ALR 231; *Brisbane Shipwrights Provident Union v Heggie* (1906) 3 CLR 686; *Southan v Grounds* (1916) SR(NSW) 274. See also Portus 1958; Sykes 1982: 185–6.

[33] Freedom of Association and the Right to Organise Convention, 1948 (No 87), art 3(1). As appears below, this is the principal juridical basis for ILO standards relating to the right to strike.

[34] See Davies & Freedland 1993: 38–43; Deakin & Morris 2012: 17–18. Whitley Councils operated in the public sector; Joint Industrial Councils in the private sector. This system has largely disappeared—for proposals for rejuvenation, see Ewing, Hendy, & Jones 2016: ch 3; 2018: ch 3.

[35] The first such Resolution was adopted in 1891, and the most recent in 1946. These Resolutions were intended to ensure that businesses that entered into contracts with government and public authorities observed the 'going rate' for the industry in the relevant locality. The 1946 Resolution was rescinded at

provided legislative support for collective bargaining: for example by legislating to reverse the effect of what were perceived to be adverse court decisions such as that of the House of Lords in *Rookes v Barnard* in 1964,[36] and by establishing statutory minimum wage-fixing machinery in sectors of the economy where collective bargaining was weak or non-existent.[37] Furthermore, starting in the early 1960s, successive governments adopted statutory minimum employment standards which applied to all employees irrespective of whether they were union members and/or covered by collective bargaining.[38]

By the early 1970s, however, change was in the air. In 1971 the Heath (Conservative) Government introduced an *Industrial Relations Act* (UK) (IR Act) which at the time seemed to constitute a radical break with the regulatory pattern that had been established over the previous sixty years. The key provisions of the IR Act were helpfully summarized by Weekes et al in the following terms:[39]

> [F]irstly, workers were given the right to belong to a registered trade union or not to belong to a registered or unregistered union. Secondly, collective agreements were to be legally enforceable unless a disclaimer clause was inserted . . . Fourthly, the IR Act provided for the registration of trade unions and employers' associations. Only registered trade unions in general were to have legal rights and to enjoy certain legal immunities. Continued registration was to depend on the organisation concerned having rules which specified, among other things, how, when and by whom authority was to be exercised, especially concerning the taking of industrial action. The IR Act also sought to encourage the reform and formalisation of collective bargaining arrangements . . . legal machinery was set up to deal with recognition, multi-union and procedural problems. As a last resort enforceable court orders were

the behest of the Thatcher (Conservative) Government in 1983. For detailed analysis of the operation of the various iterations of the Resolution, see Bercusson 1978. On the rescission of the 1946 Resolution, see Davies & Freedland 1993: 539–41. For Australian and ILO perspectives on fair wage resolutions, and cognate mechanisms, see Creighton 2012a: 350–60.

[36] [1964] AC 1129. The *Trade Disputes Act 1965* (UK) limited the effect of this decision, although it did not address some of its wider implications. See further Wedderburn 1986: 45–7.

[37] Most notably through a system of Trade Boards established under the *Trade Boards Act 1909* (UK). These Boards were later renamed as Wages Councils (see *Wages Councils Act 1945* (UK)), and were abolished by the Major (Conservative) Government in 1993. See further Davies & Freedland 1993: 542–5, 2007: 27–8, 182–5; Deakin & Morris 2012: 306–7.

[38] See, eg, *Contracts of Employment Act 1963* (UK) (minimum notice of termination); *Redundancy Payments Act 1965* (UK) (redundancy payments); and *Industrial Relations Act 1971* (UK) (protection against unfair dismissal). See further Davies & Freedland 1993: 142–64, 194–211, 376–80.

[39] Weekes et al 1975: 3–4.

> available. Further, certain unfair industrial practices were proscribed either because they undermined rights or because they were considered harmful to 'orderly' arrangements. The Act provided for the first time that a worker under a normal contract of employment could receive compensation for unfair dismissal . . . The Act also gave the government certain emergency powers to deal with industrial disputes which were considered especially damaging to the national economy. Lastly, the Act provided for the introduction of a code of 'good' industrial relations practice.[40]

Notably, the IR Act did not impose a ballot requirement as a precondition for the taking of lawful industrial action, but many of the other initiatives that were enshrined in that measure formed the basis of legislative provisions adopted by the Thatcher Government in the 1980s.

In the event the IR Act had only a limited practical impact.[41] To a significant extent this can be attributed to a campaign of 'civil disobedience' on the part of the labour movement: in particular, unions refused to operate within the norms of the legislation or to cooperate with its institutions.[42] The IR Act was repealed by the Wilson (Labour) Government in 1974. The principle of legislative promotion and protection of employment rights was, however, retained and expanded—notably in the form of the *Employment Protection Act 1975* (UK). This measure also included a potentially effective form of mandatory trade union recognition mechanism.[43]

The 1975 Act can properly be seen as the high-water mark of the recognition phase in Britain.[44] Since the election of the Thatcher (Conservative)

[40] On the origins etc of the IR Act, see Davies & Freedland 1993: chs 6–7; Thomson & Engleman 1975: ch 2.

[41] For detailed studies of the impact of the IR Act, see Weekes et al 1975; Thomson & Engleman 1975. See also Davies & Freedland 1993: ch 7.

[42] In particular, they refused to register under the Act. In many respects, this placed them beyond the reach of the legislation, and rendered significant parts of the legislation redundant in practical terms. This provides an interesting contrast to the situation in Australia between 1904 and the mid-1990s, where registration was of fundamental importance to unions in providing them with access to the traditional system of conciliation and arbitration, and where unions preferred to pay the price for that access in terms of a very high degree of external regulation of their internal affairs and (theoretically at least) of severe curtailment of the right to strike. Although of diminished significance in light of the radical changes to the system over the last quarter century, registration is still of great significance to the capacity of unions to operate and to represent their members under the FW Act. See further Chapter 4 at 92–3 and Chapter 7 at 193.

[43] See further Davies & Freedland 1993: 385–96. For discussion of current provision in this area, see Deakin & Morris 2012: 805–7, 873–99; Collins, Ewing & McColgan 2019: 587–632.

[44] It should be noted that even during the recognition phase there were occasional reversions to limited toleration (eg during and after the two World Wars—see Davies & Freedland 1993: 77–95) or even to repression (see, eg, the *Trade Disputes and Trade Unions Act 1927* (UK) which was adopted in the aftermath of the General Strike of 1926, and which was repealed in 1946 by the Attlee (Labour) Government—see Wedderburn 1986: 667).

Government in 1979 the drift away from recognition that was apparent in the IR Act has accelerated to the point where positive recognition has been replaced by a form of grudging toleration—with a limited reversion to recognition following the election of the Blair (Labour) Government in 1997.[45]

The shift away from recognition has been marked by, *inter alia*: a winding back of the scale and efficacy of protective legislation;[46] the adoption of legislative provisions ostensibly directed to protecting 'freedom of association', the true intent and effect of which was to weaken collectivization;[47] the narrowing of the scope of statutory protection against common law liability for industrial action;[48] and, of particular significance in the present context, the adoption of mandatory pre-strike ballot requirements in 1984.[49] These requirements have been retained by successive governments, and have been 'strengthened' on a number of occasions—most notably in 2016.[50]

A similar developmental pattern can be discerned in industrializing countries in Western Europe, North America, and Australasia in the later part of the nineteenth and early twentieth centuries, albeit with many local variations—especially in relation to the nature and extent of recognition.[51]

In the Australian context, the various colonial legislatures adopted localized versions of remedial provisions such as the *Trade Union Act 1871* (UK) and the *Conspiracy and Protection of Property Act 1875* (UK).[52] They did not, however, follow the lead of Westminster in repealing the local iterations of master and servant legislation.[53] On the contrary, several jurisdictions retained their versions of the English legislation until well into the twentieth century, with Western Australia finally repealing its remaining provision in 1995.[54]

[45] See Davies & Freedland 2007: 42–104, 110–14.

[46] See now *Employment Rights Act 1996* (UK), as amended. It should be noted, however, that the traffic has not all been one way—as exemplified by the introduction of a national minimum wage in 1998 (see further Davies & Freedland 2007: 182–90).

[47] See TULRCA, ss 137–167. For comment, see Deakin & Morris 2012: 816–55; Collins, Ewing, & McColgan 2019: ch 12.

[48] See further Wedderburn 1986: 530–2; Auerbach 1990: chs 3–9; Davies & Freedland 1993: ch 9; Dukes 2010; Deakin & Morris 2012: 32–3.

[49] See further Auerbach 1990: 133–52; Davies & Freedland 1993: 486–8.

[50] See TULRCA, ss 226–234. For comment, see Ewing 1999; Davies & Freedland 2007: 114; Deakin & Morris 2012: 1072–89. As to the position following the changes effected by the *Trade Union Act 2016* (UK), see Ford & Novitz 2016; Novitz 2016; Bogg 2016a; Dukes & Kountouris 2016; Collins, Ewing, & McColgan 2019: 725–43.

[51] See further Jacobs 1986, 2009; Rood et al 1986. On Australia, see Macintyre & Mitchell 1989; Bennett 1994.

[52] On the 1871 and 1875 Acts, see Brodie 2003: 21–5; Curthoys 2004: chs 7–9. On the reception of these measures in Australia, see Sykes 1982: 111–15; Creighton, Ford, & Mitchell 1993: 1147–8; Stewart et al 2016: 51–2.

[53] This was effected by s 17 of the *Conspiracy and Protection of Property Act 1875* (UK).

[54] Merritt 1982 shows that the New South Wales legislation was used extensively up until the 1960s. The New South Wales provision was repealed in 1980, whilst the Western Australian provision had been entirely unused for many years prior to its repeal.

With one limited exception,[55] the various Australian jurisdictions also failed to follow the lead of Britain in terms of introducing statutory protection against common law liability in relation to industrial action. This can largely be attributed to the fact that by the time the British Parliament adopted the 1906 Act, both the States and the Commonwealth had embarked upon a very different approach to industrial regulation from that which operated in Britain. This involved various forms of conciliation and arbitration mechanism whereby an independent public tribunal had the capacity to make 'awards' to prevent or settle industrial disputes irrespective of the wishes of the parties.[56] At federal level, the relevant provisions exhibited zero tolerance towards strikes (and lockouts). In the words of one of the founding fathers of the federal system, the 'New Province for Law and Order' constituted by the system of conciliation and arbitration was intended entirely to displace 'the rude and barbarous processes of strike and lockout'.[57] This reasoning was reflected in the fact that ss 6 and 6A of the *Conciliation and Arbitration Act 1904* (Cth) (C&A Act) made participation in strike action, or a lockout, a criminal offence punishable by fine or imprisonment.[58] This outright proscription of strikes and lockouts was repealed in 1929, but Australian industrial legislation had, and in many respects continues to have, an uneasy relationship with the capacity of workers to take strike action to protect and to promote their interests.[59] It is true, however, that the criminal law plays little active role in industrial relations in Australia, other than in the context of picketing.[60]

As concerns protection against liability in tort, it was not until 1993 that the Commonwealth Parliament, for the first time, provided statutory protection against common law liability for strike action. The relevant provision was set out in the *Industrial Relations Reform Act 1993* (Cth),[61] and was introduced in

[55] Queensland adopted an attenuated version of the British Act of 1906 in 1915. See further Sykes 1960: 180–1. The then-current iteration of the protective provisions was repealed in 1976 at the initiative of a (populist) Country Party Government.

[56] The Commonwealth, New South Wales, South Australia, Queensland, and Western Australia all adopted essentially similar conciliation and arbitration models. Victoria and Tasmania adopted rather different 'wages board' systems, which were somewhat similar to British Wages Councils. By the 1980s, however, both States had, in effect, moved to the conciliation and arbitration model. On the origins of the Colonial/State systems, see Mitchell 1989; Mitchell & Stern 1989, and on the Commonwealth system, see Markey 1989; Macintyre 1989.

[57] Higgins 1913: 13–14.

[58] For an isolated example of a prosecution under s 6, see *Stemp v Australian Glass Manufacturers* (1917) 23 CLR 226.

[59] For an overview of this rather fraught relationship, see Creighton 1991, and the sources cited therein. For descriptions of current statutory exposures in relation to unprotected industrial action, see McCrystal 2010: ch 6; Stewart et al 2016: 922–41. On the enforcement of current provision, see Hardy 2018.

[60] See further McCrystal 2010: 99–102; Stewart et al 2016: 937–9. On other potential criminal liabilities, see Creighton, Ford, & Mitchell 1993: 1146–58; McCrystal 2010: 108–9; Stewart et al 2016: 939–41.

[61] See further McCarry 1994.

the context of a shift away from 'compulsory' conciliation and arbitration in favour of determination of terms and conditions of employment by means of enterprise-level collective bargaining.[62] The protections, which are now set out in Part 3-3 of the FW Act, were narrowly drawn from the outset, and reflected the bare minimum that could credibly be said to give effect to Australia's obligations in international law concerning the right to strike.[63] Initially, however, they did not include a mandatory pre-strike ballot requirement. Such a requirement was not introduced until 2006.[64]

It is important to note that the forms of toleration of strike action that were adopted in both Britain and Australia were, and still are, framed in purely negative terms. That is, neither the TULRCA nor the FW Act creates or recognizes a positive right to strike for individuals or collectivities: rather they provide 'immunity' or 'protection' against a liability that is presumed still to exist. They do not abolish the underlying liabilities. This has the logical consequence that any conduct that falls outside the scope of the statutory protections would still leave those organizing or participating in the action exposed to the grant of injunctions and the award of damages at common law—and in some instances also to liability under statute.

It also remains the case that in most, if not all, instances, participation in strike action would constitute a repudiatory breach of contract on the part of the striking worker,[65] thereby rendering them liable to summary termination and/or to actions for damages.[66] The harshness of this principle is somewhat mitigated by statutory unfair dismissal and anti-victimization provisions in Britain and Australia,[67] but that does not alter the fact that the starting point

[62] See Gahan & Pekarek 2012; Stewart et al 2016: 61–74, and the sources cited therein. Enterprise bargaining and direct statutory regulation have now entirely displaced conciliation and arbitration at both Commonwealth and State level—although the FWC does retain a form of arbitral function in limited circumstances, such as those contemplated in Divisions 6 and 7 of Part 3-3 of the FW Act (read with Division 3 of Part 2-5).

[63] See further Creighton 1997: 43–6; McCrystal 2010: 240–56. Initially, the Constitutional validity of the protections depended largely upon the external affairs power in s 51(xxix) of the Constitution of Australia. This was upheld by the High Court in *Victoria v Commonwealth* (1996) 187 CLR 416, 546–7 on the basis that they gave effect to art 8(1)(d) of the ICESCR. The Court did not, however, express any decided view upon whether they could be supported by art 3 of Convention No 87 or by the Constitution of the ILO. The Constitutionality of the current protections rests principally upon the corporations and referral powers in ss 51(xx) and (xxxix) respectively—see further Stewart et al 2016: ch 5.

[64] See Chapter 4 at 96–100.

[65] For interesting suggestions to the contrary, see Elias 1994: ch 11; Bogg 2016b: 104–7. The more conventional view is helpfully explored in Ewing 1991: ch 2.

[66] The consequences of engaging in action short of an outright stoppage of work may be less drastic—see, eg, Ewing 1991: 9–14. For rare examples of an employer suing employees for damages for breach of contract in respect of participation in industrial action, see *Ebbw Vale Steel, Iron & Coal Co v Tew* (1935) 79 Sol Jo 593 and *National Coal Board v Galley* [1958] 1 WLR 16—for comment see Ewing 1991: 18–20.

[67] In the United Kingdom, the interplay between Part X of the *Employment Rights Act 1996* (UK) and s 238A of TULRCA is such that an employee who is dismissed because of participation in protected

for the legal response to strike action in both countries is the antithesis of any notion of a *right* to strike. Rather than recognizing a *right* to take strike action, the law affords those workers and organizations that choose to participate in strike action a rather grudging and severely circumscribed measure of *protection* or *immunity* against the legal consequences of taking such action.

This approach stands in marked contrast to that which has been adopted in countries such as France, Italy, Spain, Japan, and South Africa where the national Constitution contains a positive affirmation of the right to strike,[68] and where participation in strike action has the effect of suspending the individual employment relationship,[69] rather than providing a basis for terminating it.[70] Even where there is no constitutionally recognized right to strike, non-common law legal systems generally recognize the concept of suspension rather than repudiation.[71]

Despite important differences between national legal systems as to the means by which the right to strike is accorded recognition, and as to just what is recognized, it is clearly the case that 'the right to strike has overwhelmingly acquired the status of a fundamental right in all democratic industrialised market economies'.[72] The right of workers and unions to take strike action to protect and to promote their social and economic interests also finds significant levels of protection in international law as explored in Chapter 2.

Rationale for ballot requirements

This book is based on the assumption that taking, or threatening to take, strike action is the most powerful weapon available to organized labour in seeking to protect and to promote the interests of individual workers in

industrial action is entitled to protection against unfair dismissal, whilst s 237 of TULRCA has the effect of depriving employees who participate in 'unofficial' industrial action of such protection—for comment see Deakin & Morris 2012: 520, 1132–52; Collins, Ewing, & McColgan 2019: 779–96. In Australia, see FW Act, ss 340–342, 346–347—for comment, see McCrystal 2010: 150–1; Stewart et al 2016: 951–2. For an unsuccessful attempt to challenge the fairness of a dismissal because of participation in unprotected industrial action, see *Petrunic v Q Catering Limited* [2019] FWC 3981.

[68] See further Jacobs 2014: 733. The Constitutional entrenchment of the right to strike is examined in greater detail in Chapter 3.

[69] See further Jacobs 1986: 239–40, 2014: 735–6, 774–80; Wedderburn 1991: 280–3.

[70] For a (vain) attempt by Lord Denning MR to introduce the concept of suspension in English law, see *Morgan v Fry* [1968] 2 QB 710. For discussion of the practical difficulties associated with this proposal, see Wedderburn 1986: 192 and the repudiation of Lord Denning's proposed approach in *Simmons v Hoover Ltd* [1977] ICR 61. See also Forster 1971; Ewing 1991: 5–7.

[71] See Jacobs 2014: 775–80. This is also the approach favoured by the CEACR—see ILO 2012a: [152].

[72] Jacobs 2014: 735.

negotiations with employers. Recognition of the capacity to do so is an essential element of the transition from repression to toleration and recognition described in the previous section, and continues to be the case, even in the face of the precipitous decline in levels of strike action, trade union membership, and bargaining coverage in almost all developed countries over the last twenty years.[73]

The fact that the threat to take strike action is now only rarely acted upon undoubtedly reflects, and is perhaps a cause of, the recent decline in the power of organized labour. It may be, however, that declining levels of strike action can, to some extent at least, be attributed to the fact that employers are increasingly anxious to avoid the disruption associated with such action in a highly competitive global environment, and are in consequence more prone to make concessions in bargaining in the face of credible threats of strike action, rather than suffering the pain associated with it actually taking place. Paradoxically, therefore, provisions that are intended to reduce levels of industrial disruption through the imposition of ballot requirements may actually enhance workers' bargaining power by virtue of the fact that once strike action has been approved by ballot it becomes a more real and present threat than might be the case in the absence of such a requirement.[74]

Implicit in this analysis is the reality that strike action can lead to significant social and economic disruption. In some instances, it can—intentionally or otherwise—help bring down governments.[75] As noted earlier, recognizing a right to strike—especially in common law jurisdictions—entails a derogation from the legal rights of those adversely affected by the strike action. Permitting such derogation is a significant step,[76] and it is not entirely surprising that governments should want to ensure that what some would see as derogations from the rule of law should be subject to appropriate regulatory and democratic controls.[77]

[73] See further Peetz 2012a.

[74] See further the discussion in Chapter 6.

[75] For example, it is widely assumed that strike action by British coal miners in 1973 and 1974 helped precipitate the fall of the Heath (Conservative) Government in 1974, and that public sector strikes during the so-called 'Winter of Discontent' in 1978–9 helped bring about the fall of the Callaghan (Labour) Government in 1979 and the election of the Thatcher (Conservative) Government in the same year—see further Sandbrook 2010: chs 3, 15, and 16; Sandbrook 2012: chs 30–3.

[76] The eminent constitutional lawyer, AV Dicey considered that the passing of the *Trade Disputes Act 1906* (UK) meant that 'the rule of equal law is in England now exposed to a new peril', Dicey 1964: 204. Meanwhile, a distinguished commentator on the law of torts opined that 'the Legislature has thought fit by the *Trade Disputes Act 1906*, to confer extraordinary immunities on combinations both of employers and of workmen, and to some extent on persons acting in their interests. Legal science has evidently nothing to do with this violent empirical operation on the body politic . . .', Pollock 1908: v.

[77] For continuing judicial unease at the grant of the 'privilege' of immunity from suit, see the opinion of the majority of the High Court of Australia in *Esso Australia Pty Ltd v The Australian Workers' Union*

Pre-strike ballots have obvious attractions as a means of achieving this objective.[78]

Pre-strike ballots have the further attraction for their proponents that they appear to provide protection against the possibility that workers may be suborned or misled into taking strike action by militant, politically motivated union officials in circumstances where the workers concerned do not wish to engage in such action or where it is (in the opinion of government) contrary to their interests to do so. A ballot requirement is seen as a means to guard against this by ensuring that the workers have the capacity to express their preferences in a polling place or in the privacy of their own homes.[79]

There is a singular lack of evidence to suggest that workers are, to any significant extent, suborned or misled into taking strike action against their wills and/or better judgement.[80] The suborned workers argument has been persuasively challenged by numerous commentators on both practical and theoretical grounds.[81] Nevertheless, as noted earlier, governments of all political complexions regularly invoke the 'democratic imperative' to justify the introduction of ballot requirements at national, state, provincial, or cantonal level.[82]

Not infrequently, the democratic imperative is little more than a thinly veiled pretext for trying to reduce levels of industrial disputation and/or to compromise the effectiveness of strike action by delaying its commencement (thereby enabling employers more effectively to try to persuade employees not to support the proposed action and/or to take effective measures to mitigate the effects of the strike if/when it does occur). In some instances this may be driven by a genuine desire to avoid the economic and social disruption that may accompany strike activity. In other instances, it seems to be little more than a crude attempt to curtail the power of organized labour.[83]

[2017] HCA 54, [453]. Cf the dissenting opinion of Gaegler J at [103]–[104]. See further McCrystal 2019: 295–7.

[78] See, eg, Department of Employment 1983: [1], [67].

[79] See Donovan 1968: [426].

[80] See Anton 1961: 151–2; Donovan 1968: [428]; McCallum 1976.

[81] See, eg, Fredman 1992; McCrystal & Novitz 2012; Ford & Novitz 2016; Dukes & Kountouris 2016.

[82] See, eg, Department of Employment 1983: [1]. In the Australian context, see Minister for Workplace Relations and Small Business 1998: 2–7.

[83] There is certainly reason to suppose that this was an important factor in the introduction of ballot requirements in Australia in 2006 (see Minister for Workplace Relations and Small Business 1998; Creighton, Denvir, & McCrystal 2016: 167–70), New Zealand in 2012 and 2014 (see Wilson 2016: 203–6), and the United Kingdom in 2016 (see Novitz 2016).

There are significant practical objections to pre-strike ballot requirements. One such objection turns on the fact that in the great majority of cases ballot outcomes overwhelmingly favour the taking of strike action. This inevitably raises the question of whether any useful purpose is served by requiring industrial participants to go to the time, trouble, and expense of what is, in most instances, a rubber-stamp exercise. As demonstrated in Chapter 5, where ballots fail, it is almost invariably for technical reasons, such as failure to achieve quorum, rather than a principled rejection of the proposed strike action by the workers concerned.

A further potential objection to ballot requirements resides in the fact that once strike action has been approved by a ballot it may in practical terms become more difficult to resolve the underpinning dispute. This may be partly because workers feel more strongly committed to a particular course of action in consequence of having approved it in a ballot, and partly because negotiators' freedom of manoeuvre may be constrained by the basis upon which the ballot was conducted.[84]

There are also telling philosophical objections to ballot requirements. First, by definition they constitute an interference with the organizational autonomy of trade unions—either by interfering with the content of their rules, or by constraining the manner in which they conduct negotiations. Second, such requirements may sit uneasily with the notion of the right to strike as an enforceable 'right':

> [A ballot requirement] entails the exercise of the individual's right to strike being conditional upon the wishes of hundreds or thousands of other people, and is like saying there is a human right but only if its exercise has been approved in any particular case by others. It would be difficult to contemplate circumstances where it would be considered acceptable to make the exercise of any other human right conditional upon the wishes of others. Imagine if the right to freedom of expression were conditional upon the newspaper proprietor having to seek the views of his or her shareholders voting in a secret ballot. The objections to the right to strike being conditional on a ballot are clearly more pressing where the ballot obligation is imposed by the state . . . by legislation, rather than by the trade union through the contract of membership.[85]

[84] This factor clearly weighed upon the Donovan Commission in deciding (Donovan 1968: [430]) not to recommend the introduction of ballot requirements in the United Kingdom at that time.

[85] Ewing 2004: 54. For other critiques of ballot requirements, see Wedderburn 1986: 624–34; Davies & Freedland 1993: 483–8.

Such objections notwithstanding, there is widespread acceptance that it is not inconsistent with international standards concerning the right to strike to make the exercise of the right to strike conditional upon approval in a ballot conducted for that purpose. This can be done either by requiring that the rules of unions contain provision for the approval of strike action by ballot,[86] or by imposing a general statutory requirement that to be lawful all strike action must first be approved by secret ballot.[87] Not only are such requirements acceptable in international law, it is clear from Chapter 3 that many governments in both developed and developing economies have adopted more or less rigorous pre-strike ballot requirements—although it is important to bear in mind that by no means all governments have gone down this path, and that none have adopted such complex and intrusive requirements as Australia and the United Kingdom. Furthermore, the Supervisory Bodies of the ILO stipulate that any such requirements must be 'reasonable', and must not be such 'as to place a substantial limitation on the means of action open to trade union organisations'. International standards in this area are explored in greater detail in Chapter 2.

How pre-strike ballots can affect strike action

While mandating pre-strike ballots to further democratic objectives has obvious attractions as a political catchcry, and indeed as a matter of philosophical principle, the manner and form of regulation used to implement ballot provisions can have a range of practical consequences that may be at variance with the seemingly benign principle. In particular, ballot regimes can be implemented in a manner that has little to do with democracy and more with social control. For example, the CEACR has repeatedly warned that there is a real risk that the form and content of such regimes may be so complex as significantly to impede workers' ability to strike to protect or to promote their legitimate interests.[88] Two case studies—one from the United Kingdom, and one from Australia—helpfully illustrate the point.

[86] This is the approach adopted in New Zealand and in Apartheid-era South Africa—see respectively, Wilson 2016: 203 and Benjamin & Cooper 2016: 213, and the discussion of these jurisdictions in Chapter 3.

[87] This is the approach adopted in both the United Kingdom and Australia, see Chapter 3.

[88] See, eg, ILO 1983: [219]; ILO 1994: [170].

English railways 2017

With some 83,000 members, the National Union of Rail, Maritime and Transport Workers (RMT) is the largest union in the rail transport sector in the United Kingdom. In 2017, in the context of industrial disputes with a number of rail franchise holders in England and Wales, the RMT asked its members to approve both 'strike action' and 'industrial action short of a strike' in ballots conducted in accordance with the TULRCA.[89]

As discussed in Chapter 3, for industrial action to be lawful in Britain, the industrial action must be official union action authorized in a pre-strike ballot, in which at least 50 per cent +1 of those entitled to vote cast a valid ballot, and a majority of those who do so must vote in favour of the proposed action. As a consequence of amendments to the TULRCA in 2016,[90] railways are characterized as 'important public services'.[91] This means that for proposed industrial action to be lawful, not only must at least 50 per cent +1 of those entitled to vote cast a valid vote, at least 40 per cent of those *entitled* to vote must vote in favour of the proposed action.

In July/August 2017 the RMT conducted ballots of 'Guards and Commercial Guards' employed by the South West Trains franchise to ascertain whether they wished to approve both 'strike action' and 'industrial action short of a strike'. Of the 769 employees entitled to participate in the two ballots, 386 cast valid votes. This represented 50.2 per cent of those entitled to vote, which meant that it passed the 50 per cent +1 requirement. Furthermore, 72.3 per cent of those who cast valid ballots voted in favour of the proposed strike action. However, this constituted just 36.3 per cent of those entitled to vote rather than the requisite 40 per cent, with the consequence that the proposed action was not approved.

In contrast, 89.8 per cent of employees who returned valid voting papers in the 'industrial action short of a strike' ballot voted in favour of the proposed industrial action. This represented 44.9 per cent of those entitled to vote, comfortably in excess of the 40 per cent requirement. Ironically, however, the total number of employees who cast valid votes represented only 49.9 per cent of the total entitled to vote, with the consequence that this ballot also was unsuccessful.

[89] For more detailed discussion of the UK ballot requirements, see Chapter 3.
[90] *Trade Union Act 2016* (UK). For comment, see Ford & Novitz 2016; Bogg 2016a; Novitz 2016.
[91] TULRCA s 226(2E)(d) and Important Public Service Regulations 2017 (UK).

Later in the same year, the RMT balloted 1,849 individuals who were employed by Virgin Trains East Coast. In this instance 811 individuals returned valid votes in both the 'strike' and 'industrial action short of a strike' ballots. In both instances this represented 44 per cent of those entitled to vote. This meant that the ballot failed to meet the 50 per cent +1 requirement. The 'strike' ballot also failed to meet the 40 per cent requirement, despite the fact that 82.4 per cent of those who cast valid votes supported taking strike action. Meanwhile, 92.6 per cent of individuals who cast valid votes in the 'industrial action short of a strike' ballot approved the proposed action. This represented 40.5 per cent of those entitled to vote, but of course failed because it did not meet the 50 per cent +1 threshold.

In all four instances, clear majorities of those who returned valid ballots expressed support for both strike action and for industrial action short of a strike. Because the outcomes of the ballots failed to satisfy the technical requirements of the relevant legislation, the workers concerned were denied the right lawfully to take strike action to protect and to promote their interests. This sits somewhat uncomfortably with the 'democratic imperative' which is commonly used to justify the imposition of ballot requirements.[92]

Australia Post 2009

Australian compulsory pre-strike ballot provisions are found in the FW Act.[93] Although there are many similarities between the British and Australian ballot requirements, they do differ in some important respects. These include the fact that the British provisions focus primarily on how the union must conduct the ballot whereas the Australian provisions stipulate that any union and employees that wish lawfully to take strike action must first apply to an independent tribunal, the Fair Work Commission (FWC), for a Protected Action Ballot Order (PABO). Once a PABO has been made, the ballot itself must be conducted by an independent ballot agent (not the union) in accordance with the terms of the PABO and of the FW Act. Lawful strike action can occur only where at least 50 per cent of the employees on the electoral roll cast a valid ballot, and at least 50 per cent of that number vote in favour of the proposed action.

[92] This issue is discussed at greater length in Chapter 7.
[93] See further Creighton, Denvir, & McCrystal 2016: 154–9, and Chapter 4.

In 2008 and 2009, Australia Post was engaged in negotiations with one of the principal unions in the industry, the Communications, Electric, Electronic, Energy, Information, Postal, Plumbing and Allied Services Union of Australia (CEPU), for a new collective agreement to cover employed workers across the corporation. One of the matters at issue in the negotiations was CEPU's demand for inclusion of a clause in the proposed agreement that would restrict Australia Post's capacity to use independent contractors to carry out a range of functions that would otherwise be performed by employees.[94] In seeking inclusion of this clause, CEPU was attempting to shore up the position of employee staff of Australia Post, by preventing the use of independent contractors to undercut the wages and conditions won through collective bargaining.

At a certain point in the negotiations, CEPU decided that it wanted to take strike action in support of its bargaining position. In accordance with the applicable statutory provisions, this meant that they first had to obtain a PABO from Fair Work Australia (FWA).[95] Amongst other things, this meant that it had to satisfy the relevant jurisdictional pre-requisites, and to demonstrate that it was 'genuinely trying to reach an agreement' with the employer.[96]

A complicating factor for CEPU in this instance was the fact that there was some doubt as to whether the contractor clause it was seeking could lawfully be included in an agreement made under the FW Act. This in turn raised questions as to whether CEPU could be said 'genuinely to be trying to reach agreement'.[97] The uncertainty surrounding this issue, together with the time required to satisfy the ballot pre-requisites, resulted in a delay of several months before any ballot could be conducted.

CEPU first sought a PABO in August 2009, whereupon Australia Post sought, and obtained, leave to intervene on the hearing of the application.[98] After hearing evidence from both CEPU and the employer, Senior Deputy President Drake made a PABO. In doing so, her Honour was satisfied that CEPU was no longer actively pursuing claims that could not be included in an enterprise agreement and as such had met the threshold requirement for an order.[99]

[94] McCrystal 2012: 141–2.
[95] FWA was re-badged as the FWC with effect from 1 January 2013.
[96] FW Act s 443. For further discussion, see Chapters 4 and 5.
[97] For further discussion of restrictions on the content of agreements, see Harris 2006; Stewart el al 2016: 365–9, and the sources cited therein.
[98] *CEPU v Australian Postal Corporation* [2009] FWA 136 [6]. See further the discussion of the intervention issue in Chapter 4.
[99] *CEPU v Australian Postal Corporation* [2009] FWA 136: [24].

The employer immediately sought leave to appeal to a Full Bench of FWA. In September, leave was granted, and the decision at first instance was quashed on the ground that CEPU had not satisfied the genuinely trying to reach an agreement requirement by reason of the fact that it had been pursuing a claim for content which could not be included in an enterprise agreement. In the view of the Full Bench, CEPU had not abandoned that claim at the time of the application.[100]

Subsequent to this decision, CEPU made a number of alterations to its bargaining claims and in late October 2009 it re-applied to FWA for a PABO.[101] Again, Australia Post intervened to oppose the making of an order on the grounds that CEPU was still pursuing claims relating to content that could not be included in an enterprise agreement. Commissioner Roberts found that some of the claims that CEPU was pursuing could be construed as claims for the inclusion of impermissible content, and denied the application.[102] Commissioner Roberts also noted that had he not concluded that CEPU was pursuing claims for impermissible content, the union would have been found to have been genuinely trying to reach agreement.[103]

Having made more amendments to its claims, CEPU lodged a further application for a PABO early in the following month.[104] It argued that these changes meant that it now satisfied the genuinely trying to reach agreement requirement.[105] Australia Post again opposed the making of an order, arguing that CEPU's amended claims still fell outside the scope of what could lawfully be included in an agreement.[106] On this occasion, FWA found in favour of CEPU and made the order sought.[107]

As in August, Australia Post immediately sought leave to appeal the decision to a Full Bench of FWA. The Full Bench granted the requisite leave, but dismissed the appeal on 23 November.[108] In doing so, the Full Bench determined that while there might be ongoing questions over the status of some of CEPU's claims, the FW Act provided that CEPU could be said to be genuinely trying to reach an agreement if it had a reasonable belief that the claims could be included in the agreement.[109] In reaching this conclusion,

100 *Australian Postal Corporation* [2009] FWAFB 599.
101 *CEPU* [2009] FWA 878.
102 *CEPU* [2009] FWA 878: [27].
103 *CEPU* [2009] FWA 878: [28].
104 *CEPU* [2009] FWA 998.
105 *CEPU* [2009] FWA 998: [4].
106 *CEPU* [2009] FWA 998: [24].
107 *CEPU* [2009] FWA 998: [31].
108 *Australian Postal Corporation v CEPU* [2010] FWAFB 344.
109 FW Act s 409(1)(a).

the Full Bench found that the history of the matter demonstrated that CEPU was trying to reach an agreement, was trying to formulate a claim that could be included in an agreement, and had a reasonable belief that its claims were lawful.[110]

After four full months of attempting to obtain an order for a ballot of its members, including three FWA applications, and two appeals to the Full Bench, CEPU was finally permitted to have a pre-strike ballot. It is true that the employer was eventually unsuccessful in its attempts to prevent the ballot going ahead, but in a real sense the employer had achieved its objectives. It had ensured that the union was tied up in complex and costly litigation for four months; delayed its capacity to take, or threaten or take, strike action; and diverted union resources and energy away from bargaining. This in turn very likely contributed to fatigue on the part of both members and officials of CEPU, thereby making members less likely to engage in protracted and extensive strike action even after it became lawful to do so. Critically, the employer's tactics had also ensured that CEPU and its members were unable lawfully to take strike action at the time of year when their bargaining leverage could be expected to be at its peak: that is, in the period leading up to Christmas.

The ballot results approving the proposed action were declared on 7 December 2009,[111] and by the time notice requirements were also complied with,[112] the earliest CEPU could have engaged in strike action was 13 or 14 December. This would still allow time to impact the Christmas rush, but meant that to maximize the impact of strike action, CEPU would have had little choice but to resort to all-out strike action—thereby significantly inconveniencing, and very likely alienating, the general public. In contrast, had CEPU been able to impose work bans and/or engage in sporadic strike action in the lead-up to Christmas in October through to late December it could still have exerted significant pressure on the employer, but with much less public inconvenience.

Unlike the English rail workers discussed earlier in this chapter, workers at Australia Post were at least able, eventually, lawfully to take strike action. Their capacity to do so was, however, significantly circumscribed by the fact that their representatives had to seek approval from a public tribunal before

[110] *Australian Postal Corporation v CEPU* [2010] FWAFB 344: [58]–[59].

[111] AEC Declaration of Result, Protected Action Ballot, *CEPU; Australian Postal Corporation*, Matter No B2009/10982, 7 December 2009, available at https://www.fwc.gov.au/documents/documents/industrialballotsresults/cepu/cepu_200910982.pdf.

[112] See Chapter 4 at 120.

they could even ask their members whether they wanted to take such action, let alone actually take it. This was a process rendered more onerous by the capacity of a litigious and well-resourced employer to exploit a range of technical issues to delay the taking of strike action and to dissipate the resources and energies of workers and their union. Having cleared the obstacles associated with the PABO requirement, CEPU and its members then had to confront the challenges posed by a complex balloting process (described in Chapter 4) which, amongst other things, incorporates a quorum requirement which itself serves as a significant inhibitor to taking strike action—albeit one that is less onerous than that faced by workers in so-called 'important public services' in the United Kingdom.[113]

The Australia Post dispute helpfully shows how an employer can intervene and delay a pre-strike ballot through the use of intervention before an industrial tribunal (which can subsequently find its way into the courts, although that did not happen in this instance). This is also a feature of the British system of pre-strike ballots where, according to Davies & Freedland, enforcement of the pre-strike ballot regime has been shifted to employers.[114] There are numerous examples in the British context of pre-strike ballots being challenged before the courts by employers on the basis that the union concerned had not complied with the legal technicalities.[115] The involvement of employers as enforcers of pre-strike ballot regulation in what is essentially an internal union decision-making process is discussed further in Chapter 3. The role of employer litigation in the Australian system, where employers are able to object to an applicant union being permitted to conduct a ballot, is discussed further in Chapters 4 and 5.

These case studies are not atypical. They illustrate the difficulties routinely faced by unions operating in these two models of pre-strike ballot regulation. The legal complexity and delays associated with the application of the Australian and British balloting requirements raise significant questions as to the compatibility of the respective legislative regimes with the democratic imperative which ostensibly constitutes the rationale for those regimes. This tension between rhetoric and reality is the central theme of this book, and the next section of this chapter reviews the literature on 'democracy' and previous empirical studies on the effects of pre-strike ballots.

[113] On the impact of the quorum requirement under the FW Act, see Chapter 5.
[114] Davies & Freedland 1993: 487.
[115] See, eg, Gall 2017; Simpson 2013; Evans 1987.

Democracy at work

As noted earlier, the introduction of pre-strike ballot requirements is frequently justified by reference to the alleged need to ensure that unions conduct their affairs in a 'democratic' manner. This rhetoric has the attraction for its advocates of harnessing the language of democracy, with its associated positive connotations.

It is important to recognize, however, that what constitutes 'democracy', and what it should encompass in practice in any given situation, are contested terrain. In the political context, the notion that elections and ballots necessarily produce democratic outcomes has long been challenged.[116] Furthermore, just what 'democracy' requires in organizations like trade unions is very much open to debate given the inevitable tension between the objective of organizational autonomy and a set of legal rules that, ostensibly at least, is intended to promote democratic outcomes.

It is not possible in the present context to do justice to the rich and voluminous literature on democratic theory. Instead a very brief review of the more important strands of such theory must suffice.

A useful starting point in this context is the work of Novitz who identifies three strands of theory that frame consideration of what constitutes democracy in the industrial context: representative, participatory, and deliberative.[117]

In representative democracy individuals are represented in decision-making processes through representatives who are elected to represent the interests of that electorate in those processes. A basic minimum principle is majority rule, where each vote is equal, and where the rights of minorities are separately protected and guaranteed against possible majority abuses.[118] Representative democracy is generally contrasted with direct democracy, in which all citizens are involved and participate directly in discussions and decision-making.

The aim of participatory democracy is to ensure that citizens are empowered to participate in decision-making, and in that process receive education on the issues involved so that they are better able to understand and accept collective decisions.[119] Participatory democracy can be practised by individuals and through representatives where the plurality of interests in society are recognized through different interest groups and associations being provided with

[116] See, eg, Dahl 1956: 131; Schumpeter 1942: 252–3.
[117] Novitz 2003: 17–20.
[118] Novitz 2003: 17.
[119] Mantouvalou 2014: 218. As to deliberative democracy more generally, see, eg, Habermas 1996; Bohman & Rehg 1997; Bessette 1980.

the opportunity to participate directly in making decisions of relevance to their stakeholders.[120]

Deliberative democracy focuses on reaching consensus through discussion and debate: the idea of rational discourse is elevated above bargaining in decision-making.[121] A wide range of civil society actors are given the opportunity to deliberate on political decisions, with groups reaching consensus on outcomes. The central idea is that all those affected by a decision should have a right to participate in making that decision both through hearing the views of others and by providing reasons for their own position.[122] In contrast to participatory democracy, the aim is 'consensus led' decision-making, such that 'those participating are expected to engage reflectively with their own vested interests and prejudices and to be persuaded potentially to act in opposition to these'.[123]

Participatory democracy and deliberative democracy emphasize the need for engagement and participation in decision-making by all those affected by decisions—while differing in practice on how those decisions are ultimately reached. What is rejected by these models is the idea that democracy is achieved through the simple aggregation of votes. For example, Mantouvalou observes '[t]o suggest that any decision reached by a majority is democratic' reflects 'a crude and inadequate view of democracy',[124] whilst McCrystal & Novitz note that democratic theory has undergone certain profound developments of such a nature that in the twenty-first century majoritarian democracy is not by itself adequate.[125] In a similar vein, Fredman argues that the 'notion that democracy is exhausted by periodic ballots' is questionable, challenging the idea of 'protectionist democracy' whereby ballots act only to restrain the power of leaders without more extensive forms of participation being involved.[126]

These democratic theories developed largely in the political sphere. When the focus shifts to the industrial context the application of democratic theory is complicated by consideration of the purpose and functions of trade unions. In part the need for unions to adhere to democratic principles in their internal decision-making stems from the fact that for unions to be effective as representatives of their members, those members must sacrifice a degree of individual autonomy: an essential *quid pro quo* for that surrender of autonomy

[120] As to participatory democracy more generally, see, eg, Pateman 1970; Mansbridge 1980; Hilmer 2010.
[121] McCrystal & Novitz 2012: 125.
[122] Mantouvalou 2014: 218.
[123] Bogg & Novitz 2012: 334–5.
[124] Mantouvalou 2014: 217.
[125] McCrystal & Novitz 2012: 121.
[126] Fredman 1992: 29.

must be democratic control of its exercise by those to whom it is surrendered. Of course, individual workers also surrender a significant degree of autonomy to their employers, and the need for redress for that surrender of autonomy is an important part of the rationale for industrial democracy in a more general sense—notably, through the right to form, join, and be represented by trade unions. These perceptions of 'democracy' help explain why the (real or apparent) sharing of power between governments, employers, and workers (tripartism) is such a critical part of the structure, governance, and operation of the ILO, and why organizational autonomy is such an important focus of ILO Convention No 87 and of the principles of freedom of association, respect for which is inherent in the fact of membership of the Organization itself.

Viewed in these terms, the democratic imperative can be illustrated at a number of levels.

First, unions act as representatives of their members in their working lives and in what are frequently conflictual relationships with their employers. In particular, this has led to the development of the idea of 'industrial democracy', popularized by the Webbs at the end of the nineteenth century, in which unions are the avenue through which workers exercise collective voice and agency at work, and that this is done primarily through collective bargaining.[127] On this reading, trade unions enable workers to participate in a democratic manner in decisions that affect their daily working lives. In particular, as Elias has pointed out, collective bargaining functions as an expression of industrial democracy—allowing workers to participate in the formation of the rules and practices that govern their workplaces.[128] If workers are represented by trade unions in this process, the union itself must provide an avenue for their participation in the decision-making processes of the union.

Second, as associations of citizens, unions are civil society actors pursuing the interests of working people in the broader democratic processes and institutions of society. They possess legal rights and privileges necessary to carry out their functions. This supports the argument that unions themselves should be democratically run given their status in society and the legal rights and privileges they obtain. Whether this is appropriate, how such democracy should be achieved, and the role of law in this context is a matter of debate. Legal requirements for pre-strike ballots of union members need to be evaluated in this context. The imposition of pre-strike ballot requirements reflects a belief that it is necessary to impose democracy on trade unions, and that the internal

[127] Bogg & Novitz 2012: 324.
[128] Elias 1990: 32.

processes that govern the making of strike decisions should not be left exclusively to unions to determine for themselves.

Respect for the autonomy of trade unions as self-governing associations of working people requires respect for the internal governance decisions of those unions, which are often institutionalized though the union's rules.[129] Further, one of the principal purposes for which unions are established, to engage collectively with labour purchasers over working conditions and terms of engagement of the members of the union, also informs the internal decision-making processes of trade unions. As Howard has observed, democratic practices in trade unions 'can do much to inhibit the tactical effectiveness of unions confronting employers'.[130] In particular, the processes of collective bargaining require the exercise of 'experience, judgement and expertise', and democratic processes may not be the best way to ensure that union members are represented at the bargaining table by the most qualified officials.[131] Members may not understand the law or the intricacies of bargaining tactics, and democratic processes may slow decision-making, reducing the tactical advantages from delegating decision-making to those with appropriate responsibilities. Davis summarizes the argument another way: that unions may be compared to armies, which 'need discipline, not democracy'.[132] However, Elias & Ewing also observe that successfully to undertake collective bargaining on behalf of members, unions need to be both accountable and democratic.[133]

In contrast, the justification for imposing democratic processes on trade unions through external legal means rests on the position of trade unions with respect to their members, employers, and the public. The 'rights and privileges' conferred on unions are claimed to justify public concern with how unions are governed to ensure that such rights and privileges are used appropriately.[134] In particular, this relates to the potential impact of union actions (such as strikes or support for a political party) on employers and the general public.[135] Concerns are also raised about the rights of individual union members and the need to protect them against oppressive conduct on the part of the majority.[136]

Where democracy is to be externally imposed on the internal decision-making processes of trade unions, there are differing views on what that

[129] See Chapter 7 for an analysis of whether and how the internal governance rules of Australian unions address issues of democratic decision-making about strike action.
[130] Howard 1980: 166.
[131] Elias 1990: 30.
[132] Davis 1987: 5 citing Sayles & Strauss 1972: 207–19.
[133] Elias & Ewing 1987: 262–4.
[134] These arguments are usefully summarized in Orr & Murugesan 2007: 281; Fredman 1992: 25–6.
[135] Elias & Ewing 1987: 273.
[136] Elias & Ewing 1987: 260.

democracy should look like, how it can be measured, and whether legal rules actually produce democratic outcomes. Democracy in trade unions is not the same as democracy in the political sphere.[137] Further, trade unions make different kinds of decisions. Some are purely internal to the union itself, requiring no further action on the part of members, for example, as to the election of officials and the delegation of powers and responsibilities to act for the union. Others have external consequences, like decisions to take strike action, the execution of which will necessarily impact members who will be called upon to comply with the outcome of the decision and third parties such as employers and the public affected by the action.

Many observers have expressed scepticism as to the capacity of law to generate democratic outcomes in trade unions beyond preference aggregation. Undy & Martin observe that legislation attempting to drive democratic change in trade unions will 'depend for its effect . . . on the interaction between the method promoted and the union's existing processes of decision-making, both formal and informal'.[138] Fredman's study of the British legislation in the 1980s that was ostensibly enacted to promote democratic practice in unions concluded that the legislation had had the effect of bureaucratizing union processes, concentrating power and decision-making in the hands of those who were able to understand the legal rules, alienating members and subverting democracy.[139] Similarly, Undy et al found that the same legislation had had the effect of centralizing decision-making, concentrating decision-making power, and weakening representative democracy in unions in the United Kingdom.[140]

Legislative pre-strike ballot requirements provide a useful opportunity to study the capacity of the law to generate democratic outcomes, and to regulate industrial behaviour. Because they are most often imposed in the name of democracy, and involve an inherently democratic process (the ballot), it is possible to explore the form of democracy imposed by pre-strike ballot requirements alongside any other intended or unintended consequences. Previous studies of pre-strike ballot regimes in the United Kingdom, Canada, and, to a limited extent, Australia offer helpful insights into the effects of pre-strike ballot regimes in practice.

[137] Fredman 1992: 31; McCallum 1976: 167; Tracey 1985.
[138] Undy & Martin 1984: 209.
[139] Fredman 1992: 33
[140] Undy et al 1996.

Previous studies of the effects of pre-strike ballots

As demonstrated earlier in this chapter, in Britain and Australia the pre-strike ballot rules are set out within statutory frameworks, and unions have little autonomy in relation to the manner in which ballots are conducted. Further, in both countries, the legality of any subsequent strike action depends on compliance with the pre-strike ballot rules. By contrast, in Canada, under the federal statutory regime outlined in Chapter 3, unions are left to provide for the conduct of a pre-strike ballot in their own rules and the lawfulness of any subsequent strike does not depend on the conduct or outcome of the ballot.

One of the earliest empirical studies of the effect of mandatory pre-strike ballots was that undertaken in Canada in 1961 in the Province of Alberta which at the time had both mandatory pre-strike ballots and a requirement for government supervision of the conduct of the ballots.[141] The study concluded that there was little empirical evidence to support the need for mandatory pre-strike ballots to improve democratic practice within trade unions.[142]

That study aside, almost all of the empirical studies on the operation of ballot requirements have been undertaken in the United Kingdom following the introduction of pre-strike ballot requirements in that country in 1984.[143]

Research by Undy, Martin, and colleagues published between 1984 and 1996 examined the impact of balloting requirements on internal union democratic practice, and in that context considered the specific role of pre-strike ballots, using case study analysis of the rules and practices of a range of unions.[144] They found that British unions had largely absorbed compulsory pre-strike ballots into their 'repertoire of bargaining tactics',[145] such that pre-strike ballots had provided a low-cost mechanism for unions to convey the strength of their members' views and legitimated their decisions in respect of strike action.[146] Pre-strike ballot requirements also appeared to have encouraged unions to adapt their tactics when approaching industrial action, particularly in respect of the requirement to specify proposed forms of industrial action.[147]

The British research also found, however, that rejection of proposed industrial action in a pre-strike ballot had the effect of weakening a union's bargaining power in collective bargaining.[148] It was also clear that the increased

[141] *Labour Relations Code*, RSA 2000, c L-1, s 73; Anton 1961: 151; see further Chapter 3 at 73.
[142] Anton 1961.
[143] The history of these legislative developments is outlined in Elgar & Simpson 1996: 1.
[144] Undy & Martin 1984; Martin et al 1991; Undy et al 1996.
[145] Martin et al 1991: 207.
[146] Martin et al 1991: 198, 202; Undy et al 1996.
[147] Undy et al 1996: 230.
[148] Martin et al 1991: 202.

regulatory burden had impacted union processes around pre-strike decision-making. In particular, it was found that unions sought strictly to comply with the legislative requirements for pre-strike ballots, with the complexities of the law producing more risk-averse practices.[149] Unions centralized decision-making concerning industrial action by introducing increasingly bureaucratic processes which had the effect of encouraging more 'oligarchic' processes over 'democratic' ones.[150] As concerns pre-strike ballot success, unions achieved better results in voter turnout and strong mandates for industrial action in enterprises with strong labour–management relationships, but fared less well in enterprises where the relationship with employers was antagonistic and/or where workplace organization was less well-developed.[151]

These findings were supported by research conducted by Elgar & Simpson which found that during the 1980s unions had progressively internalized mandatory ballot requirements,[152] and in the 1990s continued to comply with the legal rules around balloting, even as they became more complex.[153] There was also evidence that unions were using pre-strike ballots 'constructively' as part of industrial campaigns, enhancing the credibility of threats to take industrial action.[154] However, Elgar & Simpson also found that in some instances pre-strike ballots compromised the capacity of unions to react quickly to issues arising in bargaining; that they imposed cost and delay on the process of taking industrial action;[155] and that the legal complexities provided increased opportunities for employers to challenge the legality of ballot outcomes.[156] They concluded that while compulsory ballot requirements had some advantages from a union perspective, their overall effect had been to 'provide fertile ground' for employers to challenge the legality of ballots,[157] and to require unions to divert considerable resources to ensure that they remained within the 'parameters of legality'.[158]

As outlined in the discussion of the 2017 English railway disputes, the balloting rules in the United Kingdom were amended in 2016 to include new quorum and majority requirements. These have not yet been the subject of empirical study, but in the lead up to their introduction Darlington & Dobson

[149] Undy et al 1996: 228, 230.
[150] Undy et al 1996: 230.
[151] Undy et al 1996: 229.
[152] Elgar & Simpson 1993: 103.
[153] Elgar & Simpson 2017: 16.
[154] Elgar & Simpson 2017: 25.
[155] Elgar & Simpson 2017: 20.
[156] Elgar & Simpson 2017: 13.
[157] Elgar & Simpson 2017: 16.
[158] Elgar & Simpson 2017: 22.

examined 158 ballots conducted between 1997 and 2015 and found that only 50 per cent would have met the quorum requirement had it been in place at the time.[159] The introduction of the 2016 changes is also notable for a subtle shift in the political rhetoric accompanying the introduction of the amendments. While the need for unions to be more 'democratic' remained part of the political discourse,[160] according to Novitz, the rationales underpinning the amendments also reflected a 'particular kind of explicit economic pragmatism',[161] in which a key objective was to ensure that industrial action was used only as a last resort and to avoid the potentially far reaching effects of strikes in public services.[162]

In Australia, where pre-strike ballots have been compulsory since 2006, there have not previously been any dedicated studies of the pre-strike ballot regime. There have, however, been small-scale studies of the operation of the ballot requirements, carried out for purposes of two reviews of the operation of the FW Act. Overall these studies concluded that in the majority of cases pre-strike ballots led to the authorization of industrial action, and that where action was not authorized it was usually because of failure to achieve quorum, rather than because of worker opposition to authorizing the proposed action.[163] In submissions to both reviews, stakeholders reported high levels of cost and inconvenience associated with complying with the balloting rules, and a significant impact—in terms of the time needed to authorize industrial action—on the capacity to deploy it.[164] One of the Australian reviews also found that more aggressive forms of action (such as a strike) were proposed with the same frequency as lower impact action (such as partial work-bans).[165] This is consistent with what happens in Britain where unions often ballot for strike action and for 'industrial action short of a strike'.[166]

The evidence concerning the impact of pre-strike ballot requirements on rates of strike action is not entirely clear. Pre-strike ballots were introduced in countries like Britain and Australia at a time of rapidly declining rates of strike action.[167] A variety of economic, social, political, and cultural factors have driven this decline globally, and the role of the law in this process appears

[159] Darlington & Dobson 2015.
[160] Dukes & Kountouris: 348.
[161] Novitz 2016: 236.
[162] Novitz 2016: 239. See also Dukes & Kountouris 2016: 339.
[163] Edwards, McCallum, & Moore 2012: 180; Productivity Commission 2015: 871.
[164] Edwards, McCallum, & Moore 2012: 180; Productivity Commission 2015: 875–6.
[165] Productivity Commission 2015: 872. This is not consistent with the findings described in Chapter 4. It is also at variance with the British research described at Undy et al 1996: 230.
[166] This occurred, eg, in the 2017 railway disputes described earlier in this chapter.
[167] Tucker 2014: 458–61.

to be marginal at best.[168] Peetz has suggested that oppressive procedural requirements accompanied by pre-strike ballots will generally influence strike patterns by making it harder to take action.[169] However, he qualifies this conclusion by reference to the greater impact on patterns of strike action of underlying economic and institutional forces—a finding also echoed by Tucker.[170] There is also research focused exclusively on the private sector that suggests that pre-strike ballots do not have any significant effect on strike incidence, but do appear overall to reduce the duration of strike action.[171]

The existing empirical research indicates that compulsory pre-strike ballot requirements have an impact on internal union decision-making and the wider bargaining environment, and the effects are not necessarily those expected by legislators. Positive effects for unions include the internalization of compulsory balloting processes and the adoption of better record-keeping and administrative processes. Unions have also embraced the opportunity to use pre-strike ballots as a signalling device to employers and the public in respect of the legitimacy of proposed strike action. Increasingly detailed legal regulation of pre-strike ballots in Britain has, however, provided employers with opportunities to seek interlocutory injunctions against strike action by arguing that balloting rules have not been complied with.[172] Further, the risk of non-compliance with the legal requirements appears to have led to some bureaucratization of internal union processes, slowing access to strike action, thereby making it more difficult for unions to respond quickly to changing circumstances.[173] As noted earlier, all of this has occurred in the context of a broader trend of decreasing rates of strike action across the developed world, such that rates of strike action remain at historically low levels.[174]

As will appear in subsequent chapters, however, politicians globally continue to assert a need further to tighten the rules in respect of strike action, and in particular pre-strike ballots, as a way of curbing allegedly anti-democratic practices or poor industrial behaviour by trade unions. These arguments, unsupported by evidence, were canvassed in Australia in 2014 when the Abbott (conservative Coalition) Government unsuccessfully tried to amend the law to prevent access to pre-strike ballots if union claims in bargaining were

168 Peetz 2016: 153; Tucker 2014: 471–2.
169 Peetz 2016: 153.
170 Peetz 2016: 153; Tucker 2014: 455.
171 Campolieti, Hebdon, & Dachis 2014; Cramton, Gunderson, & Tracy 1999.
172 Evans 1987; Gall 2016; Simpson 2013.
173 Undy et al 1996: 228–30.
174 Stanford 2018; Peetz 2016: 150–2. For more general discussion, see Gall 2012; Veldon 2007.

considered to be 'manifestly excessive',[175] and in Britain in 2016 when the new quorum and majority requirements were adopted.[176]

Missing entirely from these debates is a detailed analysis of the impact of pre-strike ballot requirements in the context of the collective bargaining negotiations to which they relate, the possibly negative effects on union processes of evermore stringent legal requirements that force unions to centralize decision-making in respect of balloting their members over possible industrial action, or whether it is legitimate to give any role to employers in respect of whether pre-strike ballot requirements have been met.

Also missing from the debates is any consideration of the purposes for which strike action can lawfully be taken. As noted earlier, in Australia such action can be taken for one purpose only: the negotiation of enterprise agreements applying to a single enterprise. There is, in other words, no capacity in Australia to take strike action for any of the broader purposes identified by Kahn-Freund & Hepple in 1972. The position in Britain is very similar, but is perhaps slightly less restrictive in that it is possible to take any form of action that can be seen to be 'in contemplation or furtherance of a trade dispute'. This appears to reflect a rather broader conception of industrial action than that contemplated by the FW Act. In both countries, however, the scope of permissible action, and the associated balloting requirements, fall some significant way short of the relevant international standards which are described in Chapter 2.

Introduction to the Study

This book draws on empirical research of Australian pre-strike ballot regulation in order to provide a comprehensive and sophisticated analysis of the impact of mandatory pre-strike ballots on union and collective bargaining practice (the Study).[177] The book also places that research in international and comparative context.

The primary research question for the Study was: how do compulsory pre-strike ballot requirements affect the processes and practices of collective

[175] In the Fair Work Amendment (Bargaining Processes) Bill 2014, Schedule 1; The Government referred to 'irresponsible unions' using industrial action capriciously as a 'first resort' tool in bargaining—Senator Matthias Cormann, *Parliamentary Debates*, The Senate, 10 February 2015, 339. See also 100–1.

[176] See above at 82–5. These arguments also surfaced in New Zealand when a pre-strike ballot requirement was introduced in 2012—*Employment Relations (Secret Ballots for Strikes) Amendment Act 2012*. According to Wilson these amendments were justified by reference to the supposed need to protect and to promote 'democracy', and in particular to protect union members from 'intimidation' when voting—Wilson 2016: 204.

[177] A detailed explanation of the research methodology used in the Study is set out in Appendix 1.

bargaining between unions and employers, and the relationship between unions and their members?

To address this question, the Study examined three sub-questions:

1. Do pre-strike ballot requirements inhibit the ability of unions and their members to take strike action in support of their claims during collective bargaining?
2. How do pre-strike ballot requirements impact upon the internal democratic processes of trade unions? and
3. What impact do mandatory pre-strike ballot requirements have on associated collective bargaining negotiations?

These questions are explored through a mixed methods case study of the pre-strike ballot regime in the FW Act. The Study used two primary research methods to address the sub-questions.

First, it included a quantitative statistical analysis of 1,302 pre-strike ballot applications during the period 1 July 2015 to 30 June 2016 (the Study period), including data on the formal process of applying for a ballot; the content of the ballots themselves; the decision of the FWC and subsequent order; whether a ballot was held; and the ballot result where the matter proceeded to ballot. Statistical analysis of these data provided a quantitative overview of the practical operation of the pre-strike ballot requirement during the Study period and provided a picture of how the requirement operates to impede access to strike action in practice.

Second, to explore the second and third sub-questions considering the impact of ballot procedures on internal union democracy, and the effect on associated collective bargaining negotiations, interviews were conducted with a range of participants in the system including PABO applicants, employer respondents, and stakeholders. Interviewees were drawn from those applications analysed in the quantitative study, allowing triangulation with findings from the quantitative analysis and further exploration of particular issues arising out of those data. In all, there were seventy-four in-depth semi-structured interviews with PABO applicants and respondents exploring their experiences making PABO applications and in conducting associated negotiations arising during the Study period. In semi-structured interviews, participants were asked to share their experiences of engaging with the regulatory framework. The questions were designed to explore:

- factors influencing decisions to apply for PABOs;
- perceptions of the state of negotiations at the time of the application;

- perceptions of why applications and consequential pre-strike ballots are successful or unsuccessful; and
- factors influencing the time between an application to the FWC, the conduct of a pre-action ballot, and any subsequent strike action.

Additional qualitative data were drawn from thirteen interviews with stakeholders including representatives of employer and employee peak councils, members of the FWC, and Australian Electoral Commission (AEC)[178] staff with responsibility for industrial elections. The interview questions were designed to explore issues relating to the PABO regime, drawing on respondents' specific expertise.

The interview data were coded thematically using a modified grounded theory approach.

The structure of this book

This chapter has examined the nature and purposes of strike action, and its interaction with the legal process. In broad terms strikes are seen as a means of protecting and promoting the social and economic interests of workers—especially, but not exclusively, in the context of collective bargaining concerning terms and conditions of employment.

The chapter has outlined the relationship between strikes and the law in historical terms—tracing the transition from repression through toleration to recognition of union organization in general, and the capacity to take strike action in particular. It also noted a more recent shift away from recognition back to a form of reluctant toleration.

It noted that nowhere is the capacity to take strike action entirely unqualified: rather, it is commonly limited in one or more of a number of ways. These include restrictions on the organizations and/or individuals that can lawfully take strike action, the forms of strike action that can legitimately be taken, the matters in relation to which it is permissible to take strike action, and the procedural requirements to which it is necessary to adhere in order lawfully to take strike action.

One of the most common of these procedural constraints is a requirement that any proposed strike action must be authorized by some kind of

[178] The AEC is an independent statutory body which has responsibility for the conduct of ballots in a range of contexts, including federal elections, by-elections, and referenda.

pre-strike ballot. The chapter outlined the rationale for such requirements—with particular emphasis on the so-called 'democratic imperative'. Using case studies of disputes in English railways in 2017 and the Australian postal service in 2009 it identified some of the important theoretical and practical issues that emerge from the detailed empirical study of the ballot requirements contained in the relevant Australian legislation that forms the centrepiece of this book.

Underpinning Chapter 1, and the entire book, is the assumption that the right to strike to promote or to protect the individual's economic and social interests is a universally recognized human right, either standing on its own, or as part of the principle of freedom of association. This is reflected in the fact that the right to strike is recognized, directly or indirectly, in major international standard-setting instruments, and in the constitutions of many nation states. The international recognition of the right to strike is outlined in Chapter 2, as is the approach to pre-strike ballot requirements that has been adopted by the supervisory bodies of the ILO.

Even where not afforded constitutional protection, the right to strike is accorded statutory recognition virtually everywhere, and in many instances that recognition is conditioned by a requirement that to be lawful, strike action must be authorized by secret ballot. The comparative review in Chapter 3 describes the principal forms of pre-strike ballot requirements that have been adopted around the world. It shows that they can range from 'light touch' provision to the effect that union rules must contain provision requiring the conduct of pre-strike ballots but attaching no consequence to failure to do so beyond those normally attaching to breaches of a union's rules, through to highly prescriptive requirements which can have the effect of making it exceedingly difficult lawfully to take strike action.

Chapter 3 goes on to describe the approaches to pre-strike ballot requirements that have been adopted in four jurisdictions: the United States, where there are no formal pre-strike ballot requirements; South Africa, where formerly stringent ballot requirements were replaced by light touch regulation in 1995; Canada, where there are formal requirements for the conduct of pre-strike ballots, but where they appear to be of only very marginal inconvenience to trade unions; and Britain, which has adopted exceedingly complex provisions which betoken an almost obsessive desire to regulate the circumstances and manner in which strike action can lawfully be taken. The chapter also points to the case of Australia, which has adopted an approach that is, in many respects, similar to that in Britain—albeit with some significant differences. The similarities are such that the detailed study of the operation of the

Australian provision affords many insights into the operation of the British provisions, and into the role of law as a means of regulating industrial behaviour more generally.

Chapter 4 provides a detailed description of the Australian pre-strike ballot provisions, and includes the history and development of the provisions, and a detailed description of their current operation in practice. It contends that the Australian pre-strike ballot provisions are overelaborate, and that they need to be examined in their totality in order properly to understand how they operate, and their impact on industrial relations processes.

Chapters 5 to 7 explore critical aspects of the operation of the Australian provisions based on the findings of the Study: the impact of the pre-strike ballot requirements on the capacity of trade unions to organize and take strike action (Chapter 5); the ways in which pre-strike ballot requirements provide bargaining leverage to unions and (to a lesser extent) employers (Chapter 6); and the extent to which the pre-strike ballot requirements give effect to the so-called 'democratic imperative', that is, the proposition that the imposition of such requirements is justified in order to vindicate the democratic rights of individual workers and the public interest in ensuring that the exercise of industrial muscle is based on democratic decision-making (Chapter 7).

The final chapter addresses three issues: it outlines the overall impact of the pre-strike ballot provisions in Australia, and the implications of the empirical findings for the development of legislative policy; examines stakeholder perceptions of the Australian provisions; and considers possible alternative approaches to the highly prescriptive and ideologically driven provisions that have been adopted in Australia and the United Kingdom.

Appendix 1 contains a detailed explanation of the research methods used for the empirical component of the Australian case study, and Appendix 2 sets out the coding framework used for qualitative analysis of the interview data.

2

The Right to Strike and Pre-Strike Ballot Requirements in International Law

Introduction

In Chapter 1 reference was made to the fact that the capacity of workers to take strike action in order to protect and to promote their social and economic interests is recognized as a fundamental human right both in international law and in many national legal systems. The purpose of the present chapter is to examine in more detail the protection accorded to the right to strike in international law—notably in the International Covenant on Economic, Social and Cultural Rights of 1966 (ICESCR), and in international labour standards adopted under the auspices of the International Labour Organisation (ILO)—and in particular the extent to which it is permissible in international law to make exercise of the right to strike conditional upon the conduct of a pre-strike ballot.[1] In doing so, it provides a point of reference for the detailed examination of the provisions relating to pre-strike ballots that have been adopted in Australia (and to a lesser extent the United Kingdom), and their practical operation, in the rest of the book.

As appears below, the internationally recognized right to strike is an expansive one. It is not, however, unqualified. Of particular relevance for present purposes, it is permissible—subject to certain qualifications—to make the exercise of the right to strike subject to prior approval by a ballot of the workers who are to participate in the proposed strike action.

[1] For in-depth analysis of the legal position of the right to strike in international instruments, see Novitz 2003.

Strike Ballots, Democracy, and Law. Breen Creighton, Catrina Denvir, Richard Johnstone, Shae McCrystal, Alice Orchiston, Oxford University Press (2020). © Breen Creighton, Catrina Denvir, Richard Johnstone, Shae McCrystal, Alice Orchiston.
DOI: 10.1093/oso/9780198869894.001.0001.

The right to strike in international law

Universal and regional standards

Explicit recognition of the right to strike as a fundamental human right is to be found in art 8(1) of the ICESCR:

> The States Parties to the present Covenant undertake to ensure:
> (d) The right to strike, provided that it is exercised in conformity with the laws of the particular country.
> 3. Nothing in this article shall authorise States Parties to the International Labour Organisation Convention of 1948 concerning Freedom of Association and Protection of the Right to Organise to take legislative measures which would prejudice, or apply the law in such a manner as would prejudice, the guarantees provided for in that Convention.[2]

In contrast, neither the Universal Declaration of Human Rights 1948 (Universal Declaration) nor the International Covenant on Civil and Political Rights 1966 (ICCPR) makes specific reference to the right to strike. Article 22 of the ICCPR does, however, provide express protection for 'the right to freedom of association . . . including the right to form and join trade unions for the protection of his interests'. In contrast, art 20(1) of the Declaration does not directly refer to freedom of association for industrial purposes, but does stipulate that 'everyone has the right to freedom of . . . association'.

Significantly, art 22(3) of the ICCPR preserves the operation of the ILO's Freedom of Association and Right to Organise Convention, 1948 (No 87) in precisely the same terms as art 8(3) of the ICESCR.[3] This suggests that if it is indeed the case that Convention No 87 protects the right to strike,[4] it must follow that it is also protected by the ICCPR.

Many regional instruments dealing with fundamental human rights also endorse the need to respect the principle of freedom of association. Few of them,

[2] Swepson 2014: 206 suggests that this linkage between an instrument adopted under the auspices of the United Nations and an ILO Convention is 'unique' in international law. On art 8 in general, see Fenwick 2002.

[3] Presumably the fact that art 20(1) of the Universal Declaration does not make direct reference to freedom of association for industrial purposes explains the absence of any reference to Convention No 87.

[4] See the discussion at text accompanying nn 9–14 and 25 below.

however, make express reference to the right to strike. An important exception is furnished by arts 5 and 6 of the European Social Charter 1961:

> 5. With a view to ensuring or promoting the freedom of workers and employers to form local, national or international organisations for the protection of their economic and social interests and to join those organisations, the Contracting parties undertake that national law shall not be such as to impair, nor shall it be applied as to impair, this freedom . . .
> 6. With a view to ensuring the effective exercise of the right to bargain collectively, the Contracting Parties . . . recognise . . .
>   (4) the right of workers and employers to collective action in cases of conflicts of interest, including the right to strike, subject to obligations that might arise out of collective agreements previously entered into.[5]

Article 11 of the European Convention on Human Rights 1950 (ECHR) is silent as to the right to strike. It does, however, provide express protection for the principle of freedom of association for industrial purposes:

> Everyone has the right to freedom of peaceful assembly and to freedom of association with others, including the right to form and join trade unions for the protection of his interests.
>
> No restrictions shall be placed on the exercise of these rights other than such as are prescribed by law and necessary in a democratic society in the interests of national security or public safety, for the prevention of disorder or crime, for the protection of health or morals or for the protection of the rights of others.

On the view of ILO Convention No 87 noted earlier, it implicitly also protects the right to strike. Article 12(1) of the Charter of Fundamental Rights of the European Union 2000 (EU Charter) endorses the principle of freedom of association in very similar terms to art 11(1) of the ECHR, but goes rather further (art 28) in providing that:

> Workers and employers, or their respective organisations, have, in accordance with Union law and national laws and practices, the right to negotiate and conclude collective agreements at the appropriate levels and, in cases

[5] See further Kovacs 2005.

of conflicts of interest, to take collective action to defend their interests, including strike action.[6]

The right to strike and the ILO

It will be recalled that art 8(3) of the ICESCR expressly stipulates that nothing in art 8 authorizes derogation from ILO Convention No 87. That instrument is the centrepiece of ILO standard-setting in relation to freedom of association. Its core protections are set out in arts 2 and 3:

> Art 2 Workers and employers, without distinction whatsoever, shall have the right to establish and, subject only to the rules of the organisation concerned, to join organisations of their own choosing without previous authorisation.
> Art 3 (1) Workers' and employers' organisations shall have the right to draw up their constitutions and rules, to elect their representatives in full freedom, to organise their administration and activities and to formulate their programmes.
> (2) The public authorities shall refrain from any interference which would restrict this right or impede the lawful exercise thereof.

According to art 10, 'organisations' for these purposes means 'any organisation of workers or of employers for furthering and defending the interests of workers or of employers'. Also relevant in this context is art 8:

> (1) In exercising the rights provided for in this Convention workers and employers and their respective organisations, like other persons or organised collectivities, shall respect the law of the land.
> (2) The law of the land shall not be such as to impair, nor shall it be so applied as to impair, the guarantees provided for in this Convention.

Self-evidently, these provisions do not make any express reference to the right to strike. Nevertheless, from the early 1950s onwards the Committee of Experts on the Application of Conventions and Recommendations (CEACR) and the International Labour Conference Committee on the Application of Standards

[6] Express reference to the right to strike is also to be found in the Charter of the Organization of American States 1948 (art 43(2)) and the Protocol to the American Convention on Human Rights 1969 (art 16).

(Conference Committee) have consistently taken the view that the guarantees of organizational autonomy in art 3 of Convention No 87 require respect for the right to strike.[7] This is subject to the art 8(1) qualification that workers and their organizations must observe the law of the land whilst exercising their rights under the Convention—that qualifier must, however, be read subject to the art 8(2) requirement that the law of the land not be such as to impair those rights.

Like Convention No 87, the complementary Right to Organise and Collective Bargaining Convention 1949 (No 98) is silent as to the right to strike. Logically, the guarantee of access to autonomous collective bargaining in art 4 of this Convention would provide support for the capacity to take strike action in the context of collective bargaining. Article 4 is not, however, generally read in this manner—presumably because it could provide support for strike action only in relation to 'demands of an occupational nature', whereas art 3 of Convention No 87 can credibly be read so as to protect action directed to finding 'solutions to economic and social policy questions and to labour problems of any kind which are of direct concern to the workers'.

The legitimacy of the principles developed by the CEACR and the Conference Committee in relation to the right to strike has increasingly been called into question in recent years, most notably by employer members of the Conference Committee in 2012 in the context of its consideration of the 2012 General Survey of the CEACR:

> As the Employers' group had consistently highlighted year after year, they fundamentally objected to the Committee of Experts' opinions concerning the right to strike being received or promoted as soft law jurisprudence. There was no mention of the right to strike in the text of Convention No 87, and the determinative body to decide such rules recognised by the ILO was the Conference, not the Committee of Experts. Under article 37 of the ILO Constitution, only the International Court of Justice (ICJ) could give a definitive interpretation of international labour Conventions. The situation was exacerbated because General Surveys were important and were published and distributed worldwide without any [prior approval by the Conference Committee] . . . The Employer members therefore objected in the strongest

[7] On the supervision of Standards generally, see Servais 2015: 302–6; 2019b. For the CEACR's approach to the interpretation of arts 3 and 8 of Convention No 87, see ILO 2012a: [117]–[122], and for a summary of the Committee's views on the substance of the right to strike, see ILO 2012a: [123]–[161]. For commentary, see Novitz 2003: chs 11–14; Gernigon et al 2000; McCrystal 2010: 27–45; Creighton 2014: 351–7; Servais 2015: 107–10.

terms to the interpretation by the Committee of Experts of Convention No 87 and the right to strike, to the use of the General Survey with regard to the right to strike and to being placed in such a position by the General Survey.[8]

With respect, these comments of the Employers' Group were somewhat disingenuous. The Employers' Group had fully acquiesced in the development of the jurisprudence on the right to strike during the Cold War period—presumably to provide a basis for criticism of the lack of respect for the right to strike in Eastern Bloc countries. With the end of the Cold War, that imperative disappeared and the Employers' Group became increasingly critical of the jurisprudence of the Committee in this area. This culminated in their refusal to agree to the selection of 'cases' to be discussed by the Conference Committee in 2012 in the absence of an express disclaimer to the effect that the CEACR's report was not 'an agreed or determinative text of the ILO tripartite constituents'. In effect, they went on strike in order to repudiate the principles that had developed, with their support, in order to protect that right in an occupational context![9] Not surprisingly, the Workers' Group refused to agree to the insertion of any such disclaimer, with the result that—amidst great tension and ill-feeling—the Conference Committee was largely non-functional at the 2012 Conference.[10]

As frequently happens in international organizations, subsequent discussions and meetings took some of the heat out of the situation, and the Conference Committee has operated on a more normal basis in subsequent years, although there are also indications that the employer attack upon the legitimacy of the principles relating to the right to strike has shifted from the Conference Committee to the Governing Body's Committee on Freedom of Association (CFA).[11] Interestingly, despite earlier enthusiasm for referral of the question of whether art 3 of Convention No 87 extends to protecting the right to strike to the International Court of Justice under art 37(1) of the ILO Constitution, the Employers' Group have more recently rejected this proposal. They have also rejected the idea of establishing a special tribunal 'for the expeditious determination of any dispute or question relating to the interpretation of a Convention' in reliance on art 37(2) of the Constitution.[12]

[8] ILO 2012b: [81] and see also [46]–[52] and [153].

[9] For further exploration of employer views on this issue, see, eg, Wisskirchen 2005; Hornung-Draus 2018.

[10] See further La Hovary 2013; Swepson 2013; Bellace 2014, 2016, and 2018.

[11] Bellace 2018: 529.

[12] See Bellace 2018: 501–4; Le Hovary 2017. On art 37(2), see Valticos & von Potobsky 1995: [124]; Servais 2015: [143]–[145].

The centrality of respect for the principles of freedom of association to the functioning of the ILO is reflected in the fact that the ILC has, over the years, adopted six further standard-setting instruments dealing with various aspects of freedom of association or with freedom of association in certain occupational contexts.[13] It should be noted, however, that, like Conventions Nos 87 and 98, these instruments make no reference to the right to strike. On the other hand, art 1(d) of the Abolition of Forced Labour Convention 1957 (No 105) does accord some degree of formal recognition to the right to strike in that it proscribes the use of forced labour 'as a punishment for having participated in strikes'.[14] Meanwhile, paras 4 and 6 of the Voluntary Conciliation and Arbitration Recommendation 1951 (No 92) suggest that if an industrial dispute has been referred to conciliation or arbitration the parties should be 'encouraged' to 'abstain' from strikes or lockouts whilst the conciliation or arbitration is in progress: this is, however, subject to the qualification (para 7) that 'no provision of this Recommendation may be interpreted as limiting, in any way whatsoever, the right to strike'. Finally, the Resolution Concerning Trade Union Rights and Their Relation to Civil Liberties 1970 is clearly based on the assumption that the right to strike constitutes part of 'matters concerning freedom of association and trade union rights and related civil liberties falling within the competence of the ILO'.[15]

The importance of respect for the principle of freedom of association for the effective operation of the ILO is also reflected in the fact that 'recognition of the principle of freedom of association' was singled out in the Preamble to the original Constitution of the Organization as one of the means of improving the conditions of labour 'involving such injustice, hardship and privation' which were afflicting large numbers of people to such an extent as to 'imperil the peace and harmony of the world'. Similar reasoning is reflected in art I of the

[13] These include the Right of Association (Agriculture) Convention 1921 (No 11); the Right of Association (Non-Metropolitan Territories) Convention 1947 (No 84); the Workers' Representatives Convention 1971 (No 135); the Rural Workers' Organisations Convention 1974 (No 141); the Labour Relations (Public Service) Convention 1978 (No 151); and the Collective Bargaining Convention 1981 (No 154). For summaries of their content, see Valticos & von Potobsky 1995: 92–104; Creighton 2014: 322–6; ILO 2019c: 33–8.

[14] See further ILO 2012a: [313]–[315].

[15] Paragraph 15 of the Resolution invited the Governing Body of the ILO to instruct the Director General 'to undertake further comprehensive studies and to prepare reports on law and practice . . . with a view to considering further action to ensure full and universal respect for trade union rights in their broadest sense' with particular reference to, *inter alia*, the right to strike. Paragraph 15 did not lead to the adoption of any new standard dealing with the right to strike, but the 1970 Resolution, and para 15 in particular, has been relied upon by both the CFA (see ILO 2018: [68]) and the CEACR (see, eg, ILO 1994: [143], [149]; ILO 2012a: [262]) as part of the conceptual underpinning of their oversight of national law and practice in the field of freedom of association in general, and the right to strike in particular.

Declaration of Philadelphia which was appended to the Constitution in 1944, and which affirms the fundamental principles on which the Organization is based, including that 'freedom of expression and of association are essential to sustained progress'.

More recently, the ILO Declaration on Fundamental Principles and Rights at Work 1998 (1998 Declaration) states that:

> [A]ll Members, even if they have not ratified the Conventions in question, have an obligation arising from the very fact of membership in the Organisation to respect, to promote and to realise, in good faith and in accordance with the Constitution, the principles concerning the fundamental rights which are the subject of those Conventions, namely:
>
> (a) freedom of association and the effective recognition of the right to collective bargaining . . .

The 1998 Declaration does not name the specific Conventions observance of which it enjoins. It can safely be assumed, however, that they would include Convention No 87—although there is some suggestion that the obligations imposed by ratification of that Convention are not necessarily the same as those imposed by the 1998 Declaration.[16]

Ten years later, the Conference adopted the ILO Declaration on Social Justice for a Fair Globalization (2008 Declaration) which, by art IA(iv), recognizes the importance of 'freedom of association and effective recognition of the right to collective bargaining' in attaining the strategic objectives of the Organization. In the following year, in response to the Global Financial Crisis, the Conference adopted a resolution entitled 'Recovering from the crisis: a Global Jobs Pact', art 14(1)(ii) of which was to the same effect as art IA(iv) of the 2008 Declaration.

Most recently, in 2019 the Conference adopted the ILO Centenary Declaration for the Future of Work (Centenary Declaration), art II(A) of which declares that:

> In discharging its constitutional mandate, taking into account the profound transformations in the world of work, and further developing its human-centred approach to the future of work, the ILO must direct its efforts to:
>
> . . .

[16] See Alston 2004, 2005; Alston & Heenan 2004. For contrary views, see Langille 2005; Maupin 2005. See also Bellace 2016: 37–9, 2018: 521–3.

> (iv) promoting workers' rights as a key element for the attainment of inclusive and sustainable growth, with a focus on freedom of association and the effective recognition of the right to collective bargaining as enabling rights.

To help achieve this (art IV(B):

> All Members should work towards the ratification and implementation of the ILO fundamental Conventions and periodically consider, in consultation with employers' and workers' organisations, the ratification of other ILO standards.

Like its forerunners, the Centenary Declaration is entirely silent in relation to the right to strike.

It was noted in Chapter 1 that respect for the principle of freedom of association is an integral part of the version of the democratic imperative that is the cornerstone of the ILO as a tripartite organization.[17] The fact that the principle is accorded such significance in the Preamble to the Constitution, and in core affirmations of principle such as the Declaration of Philadelphia, the 1998 Declaration, the 2008 Declaration, and the Centenary Declaration serves again to emphasize the centrality of respect for that principle to the effective functioning of the ILO as a tripartite body. Without respect for the principle of freedom of association, there cannot be independent and democratic trade unions, and without the existence of free and democratic unions there cannot be meaningful tripartism. As also discussed in Chapter 1, respect for the right to strike is an essential element of respect for the principle of freedom of association. It follows that any unwarranted interference with the right to strike compromises the principle of freedom of association, and with it the foundational principles of the ILO. This premise is an important element in the conceptual underpinning of the discussion in this book.

The references to freedom of association in the Preamble to the Constitution and in the Declaration of Philadelphia help provide the juridical basis for two special procedures that have been established for the express purpose of dealing with alleged failures on the part of Member States to ensure respect for the principle of freedom of association.[18] These consist of the Fact-Finding and Conciliation Commission on Freedom of Association

[17] See Chapter 1 at 29.
[18] See further ILO 2018: 1, 307–8; Valticos & von Potobsky 1995: 295; Novitz 2003: 188–99; Servais 2015: 50. On the follow-up mechanism for the 1998 Declaration, see Novitz 2003: 203–6.

(FFCC) and the CFA.[19] Both of these Committees have consistently adhered to the view that the fact of membership of the ILO carries with it an obligation to respect the principles of freedom of association, and that those principles include the right to strike.[20] For all practical purposes, the principles of freedom of association as developed by the CFA and the FFCC are the same as those applied by the CEACR and the Conference Committee.[21] The source of the obligation to respect the principles is, however, different: in the case of the CFA/FFCC it is the Constitution of the Organization itself, whereas in the case of the CEACR/Conference Committee it is the fact of ratification of Convention No 87.[22]

If it is indeed the case that the principle of freedom of association that is protected by the Constitution of the ILO and by Convention No 87 encompasses the right to strike, then, as indicated earlier, it can credibly be said that other international instruments such as art 20 of the Universal Declaration of Human Rights and art 22 of the ICCPR that purport to protect the principle of freedom of association also implicitly protect the right to strike.[23]

Conditioning the right to strike

The principle

As noted earlier, there is universal agreement that the 'right' to strike as recognized in international law is not an unqualified one. In particular, it is clear that it is permissible, subject to certain qualifications, to make its exercise subject to prescribed procedural and/or substantive conditions. As appears below, this is implicit in art 8(1) of Convention No 87, and in the qualifier in art 8(2); in

[19] See Servais 2015: 307–10. See also ILO 2018: ch 1 and Annex 1.

[20] See ILO 2018: [751]–[757]; Gernigon, Odero & Guido 2000: 11–12; Bellace 2018: 516.

[21] The decisions of the CFA are digested in ILO 2018. The principles relating to the right to strike appear at ch 10 of that publication. The decisions of the Committee are also described and analysed in Gernigon, Odero, & Guido 2000, whilst the impact of its work over its first fifty years is discussed in Gravel, Duplessis, & Gernigon 2001.

[22] The great majority (as at June 2020—155) of the ILO's 187 members have ratified Convention No 87. Convention No 98, meanwhile, has attracted 167 ratifications. Ratifying States include almost all developed countries, with the conspicuous exceptions of South Korea and the United States.

[23] Over the years there has been considerable debate as to whether the 'right' to take strike action should be regarded as a 'right' in the sense of a positive, enforceable right to strike to protect and to promote the legitimate social and economic interests of individuals and their organizations, or as a 'freedom' in the sense of the capacity lawfully to take strike action to protect and to promote those interests without being subject to legal sanction. For an excellent summary of this debate, see Novitz 2003: ch 2. See also the contributions of Ben-Israel 1988; Mthombeni 1990; Ewing 1991: ch 2; Leader 1992: 180–210; Leary 1996; Fudge 2007; and Novitz & Fenwick 2010.

art 8(1)(d) of the ICESCR; in art 28 of the EU Charter; and in the principles developed by the Supervisory Bodies of the ILO. It is explicit in art 31 of the European Social Charter:

> The rights and principles set forth in Part I when effectively realised, and their effective exercise as provided for in Part II,[24] shall not be subject to any restrictions or limitations not specified in those parts, *except such as are prescribed by law and are necessary in a democratic society for the protection of the rights and freedoms of others or for the protection of public interest, national security, public health, or morals.* [emphasis added][25]

All of the other international instruments noted above that, directly or indirectly, protect the right to strike require that the exercise of that right be subject to the law of the land—but with the (explicit or implicit) qualification that the law of the land must 'not be such as to impair' and must not be 'so applied as to impair' the guarantees provided by the instrument in question.[26]

In other words, there is universal recognition that the exercise of the right to strike can properly be made subject to a measure of legal constraint—provided those constraints are not of such a character as unduly to interfere with the right to strike itself. As Jacobs has it: 'reasonable limitations on the right to strike are not in contradiction to the right to strike as a fundamental right'.[27]

Permissible constraints upon the right to strike fall into two broad categories: substantive and procedural. It is important to appreciate, however, that none of these constraints are mandatory: that is, none of the international instruments under consideration positively require that the right to strike be made subject to any of the permissible constraints—whether substantive or procedural. The point is that such constraints are not regarded as inconsistent with the relevant principles of international or (where applicable) constitutional law if they are in fact imposed, so long as they are consistent with the terms of the instrument concerned.

[24] This would include the guarantees set out in arts 5 and 6 of the Charter.

[25] Article G of Part III of the 1996 Revision of the European Social Charter is in identical terms. Both art 11(2) of the ECHR and 22(3) of the ICCPR are to the same effect, although, as noted earlier, neither instrument makes express reference to the right to strike.

[26] See ICESCR art 8(1)(d) and 8(3); ICCPR, art 22; ILO Convention No 87, arts 3, 8 and 10; and EU Charter, art 28.

[27] Jacobs 2014: 796.

Substantive constraints

Permissible substantive constraints can include requirements that the purpose of strike action not be 'political' in character—bearing in mind the CEACR's view that strikes can properly be used to protect and to promote workers' economic and social interests, including 'seeking solutions to economic and social policy questions and to labour problems of any kind which are of direct concern to the workers'.[28] It would not, therefore, be permissible to stipulate that the purpose of strike action can only be occupational in character,[29] but it would be permissible to proscribe strikes which had purely 'political' objectives, such as the overthrow of the existing constitutional order or to effect a change of government.

Permissible substantive constraints may also include requirements that whilst strike action is permissible in the context of negotiating for a collective agreement, further strike action in respect of matters regulated by the agreement is not permissible during the life of an agreement once made. In other words, the law can legitimately draw a distinction between disputes of right (where strike action is not permissible) and disputes of interest (where strike action is permissible).[30] The capacity to take strike action in certain circumstances—such as times of acute national or local crisis may also be restricted, but only 'for a limited period and to the extent necessary to meet the requirements of the situation'.[31]

Restrictions, within prescribed limits, upon the groups of workers who may lawfully take strike action are also permitted, for example many countries forbid the taking of strike action by members of the police or armed services, and by public servants 'exercising authority in the name of the State' (such as judicial officers, senior civil servants). The exclusion of members of the police and armed forces is clearly consistent with the fact that both categories of workers can legitimately be denied access to the protections provided by both Conventions Nos 87 and 98.[32] Although art 6 of Convention No 98 contains an express exclusion for public servants engaged in the administration of the State, there is no such provision in Convention No 87. Nevertheless, there is general agreement that

[28] ILO 1983: [200].

[29] This suggests that the requirement that industrial action must be in contemplation or furtherance of a *trade dispute* as defined in s 244 of the TULRCA, and the 'permitted matters' stipulation in s 172(1) of the *Fair Work Act 2009* (Cth) (FW Act), are highly problematic in terms of compliance with ILO standards relating to the right to strike. See further Ewing & Rees 1984; McCrystal 2010: 240–2; Novitz 2010: 184 and the sources cited therein.

[30] See ILO 2012a: [142].

[31] ILO 2012a: [140].

[32] Articles 9(1) and 5(1) respectively.

workers such as judicial officers and very senior public servants can legitimately be denied the right to strike, or that it can be severely curtailed.

There is also widespread agreement that workers in 'services the interruption of which would endanger the life, personal safety or health of the whole or part of the population' can legitimately be denied the right to strike. There is, however, rather less agreement as to just which workers can legitimately be regarded as engaged in such services.[33] In its 2012 General Survey, the CEACR noted that (footnotes omitted):

> In practice, the manner in which strikes are viewed at the national level varies widely: several States continue to defined essential services too broadly, or leave too much discretion to the authorities to unilaterally declare a service essential; others allow strikes to be prohibited on the basis of their potential economic consequences . . . or prohibit strikes on the basis of the potential detriment to public order or to the general or national interest. Such provisions are not compatible with the principles relating to the right to strike.[34]

More specifically (footnotes omitted):

> [T]he ILO supervisory bodies have considered that it should be possible for strikes to be organised by workers in both the public and private sectors in numerous services, including the following: the banking sector, railways, transport services and public transport, air transport services and civil aviation, teachers and the public education service, the agricultural sector, fuel distribution services and the hydrocarbon, natural gas and petrochemical sector, coal production, maintenance of ports and airports, port services and authorities and loading and unloading services for ships, postal services, municipal services, services for the loading and unloading of animals and of perishable foodstuffs, EPZs, government printing services, road cleaning and refuse collection, radio and television, hotel services and construction.[35]

On the other hand, the Supervisory Bodies have determined that (footnotes omitted):

> essential services in the strict sense of the term may include air traffic control services, telephone services and the services responsible for dealing with the

[33] See ILO 2012a: [129]–[141]; ILO 2018: [824]–[906].
[34] ILO 2012a: [132].
[35] ILO 2012a: [134]. See also ILO 2018: [842].

> consequences of natural disasters, as well as firefighting services, health and ambulance services, prison services, the security forces and water and electricity services. The Committee has also considered that other services (such as meteorological services and social security services) include certain components which are essential and others that are not.[36]

It is important to appreciate that the notion of 'essential service' is not absolute. On the contrary, the CEACR has made clear that 'a non-essential service may become essential if the strike exceeds a certain duration or extent, or as a function of the special characteristics of a country (for example, an island state)'.[37] Furthermore:

> In situations in which a substantial restriction or total prohibition of strike action would not appear to be justified and where, without calling into question the right of the large majority of workers, consideration might be given to ensuring that users' basic needs are met or that facilities operate safely or without interruption, the introduction of a negotiated minimum service, as a possible alternative to a total prohibition of strikes, could be appropriate.[38]

A further, somewhat controversial, restraint upon the capacity to take strike action has attracted some support in recent years. This arises in circumstances where strike action may be thought to be *disproportionate* to the objectives sought to be achieved by the action, or to have 'a disproportionate effect on the rights of others'.[39] This concept was endorsed by the Court of Justice of the European Communities in a number of cases in the 2000s,[40] and has been a source of concern to the CEACR.[41] Nevertheless, neither the CEACR nor the CFA has yet expressed a decided view on whether such restrictions are or are not compatible with ILO principles concerning the right to strike.[42]

It is also important to appreciate that not all permissible restraints will be acceptable in all circumstances: rather, the acceptability of any given constraint

[36] ILO 2012a: [135]. See also ILO 2018: [840].

[37] ILO 2012a: [131].

[38] ILO 2012a: [136]. See also ILO 2018: [866]–[906].

[39] The terminology is Ewing's—2004: 56–57.

[40] See Case C-438/05 *International Transport Workers' Federation and Finnish Seaman's Union v Viking Line ABP* [2007] ECR I-10779; Case C-341/04 *Laval un Partneri Ltd v Svenska Byggnadsarbetareforbundets* [2007] ECR I-11767. For detailed discussion and analysis of these decisions, see Freedland & Prassl 2014.

[41] See ILO 2012a: [128].

[42] See further Servais 2017: 385; Bellace 2018: 530. For an employer perspective on this issue, see Wisskirchen 2005.

will depend upon the precise terms of the constraint, and the context in which it is imposed. For example, prohibition of strike action during the life of an agreement is acceptable in terms of ILO standards only where the processes by which the agreement has been made are themselves consistent with the principles of freedom of association. This includes that there be compensatory mechanisms such as 'recourse to impartial and rapid arbitration machinery for individual or collective grievances concerning the interpretation or application of collective agreements'.[43] It can also safely be assumed that it would not be consistent with the principles of freedom of association to curtail workers' capacity to take strike action during the life of an agreement in circumstances where the workers concerned did not have adequate access to the capacity to take strike action whilst negotiating for the agreement in the first place.

Even where it is permissible to deny a particular group of workers the right to take strike action—for example because they are engaged in essential services or are public servants engaged in the administration of the State—the Supervisory Bodies insist that the workers concerned be 'afforded adequate protection so as to compensate for the restrictions imposed on their freedom of action'. Such protection should include: 'impartial conciliation and eventually arbitration procedures which have the confidence of the parties'. Such procedures should include the involvement of workers and their organizations, and any arbitration awards 'should be binding on both parties and once issued should be implemented rapidly and completely'.[44]

Procedural constraints

Of principal relevance in the present context are procedural constraints: that is, procedural requirements that must be satisfied for proposed strike action to be lawful.

According to the CFA:

> The conditions that have to be fulfilled under the law in order to render a strike lawful should be reasonable and in any event not such as to place a substantial limitation on the means of action open to trade union organisations.

[43] ILO 2012a: [142], 2018: [768]. Interestingly, the CEACR has taken the view that even where strike action can legitimately be constrained during the life of an agreement, workers should retain the capacity to strike 'against the social and economic policy of the Government' during the life of the agreement (ILO 2012a: [142]). See also Novitz 2003: 283–4.

[44] ILO 2012a: [141]. See also ILO 2018: [853]–[863].

> The legal procedures for declaring a strike should not be so complicated as to make it practically impossible to declare a legal strike.[45]

Within these parameters, permissible procedural requirements can include:

- that strike action first be approved by a ballot of the workers involved in the proposed action;
- that workers and unions that are proposing to take strike action give notice of that intention to the public authorities and/or the employer(s) concerned in advance of commencement of the action;
- that prior to taking strike action the parties have exhausted attempts to reach an agreed outcome, perhaps including recourse to compulsory conciliation or mediation. Sometimes, such requirements may consist of an obligation to engage in good faith bargaining; and
- that parties first observe a cooling off period before the commencement of strike action.

The most common of these procedural requirements, and the one that is of chief importance for the purposes of this book, is the requirement that a proposed strike first be approved by a ballot of the workers concerned.

The issue that is most likely to cause ballot requirements to be found to be inconsistent with the internationally protected right to strike is the imposition of quorum requirements: that is, a requirement that either a specified proportion of the workers concerned cast a valid ballot and/or that proposed strike action be approved by a specified proportion of the 'electorate' (including those who do not cast a ballot).

It is important to appreciate that a quorum requirement would not in itself be inconsistent with the principles of freedom of association.[46] Where difficulties may arise is when the requirement is of such a character as to place a substantial limitation upon the capacity of workers to take strike action. For example, the CFA has determined that requirements that at least half of eligible voters vote in a ballot, or that an absolute majority of eligible voters approve proposed strike action, are inconsistent with the right to strike.[47]

[45] ILO 2018: [789] and [790] respectively.
[46] ILO 2018: [809].
[47] ILO 2018: [806]–[807].

Ballot requirements can also raise compliance issues where the relevant legislation imposes restrictions upon who can be included on the 'electoral roll' for a pre-strike ballot—for example, by mandating or permitting the exclusion of particular categories of workers, or workers in a particular geographical or organizational unit, who could be expected to favour the taking of strike action. Equally, compliance issues could arise where the law mandates or permits the inclusion on the roll of workers, most obviously members of management, who could be expected to oppose the taking of strike action.

Excessively onerous rules relating to the manner in which a strike ballot is to be conducted can also give rise to compliance problems in this context. For example, a requirement that a ballot be conducted between 9.00am and 5.00pm could be found to be non-compliant where part of the workforce worked on night-shifts, or a requirement that a ballot be conducted at a particular geographical location could be found to be non-compliant in circumstances where all or part of the workforce worked at scattered locations and/or were 'on the road' for all or most of the time.

Even where procedural requirements are not unreasonable or excessive taken in isolation, their cumulative effect and/or their complexity may be such 'as to make it practically impossible to declare a legal strike'.[48] The British and Australian provisions that are described in Chapters 3 and 4 sail very close to the wind in this respect, although as appears below they have not formally been determined to be inconsistent with either Convention No 87 or the principles of freedom of association on this ground.

The CEACR does, for example, appear to have sent somewhat 'mixed messages' in relation to the quorum provisions in the British Government's Trade Union Bill 2015, and in the Act of 2016. Essentially, it seems to have regarded a 50 per cent quorum as within the 'limits of reasonableness' for purposes of compliance with Convention No 87. However, it considered that the requirement that 40 per cent of all employees in 'important public services', which is equivalent to a requirement for 80 per cent approval on a 50 per cent voter turnout, vote in favour of strike action was not consistent with the Convention to the extent that it applied in services that were not 'essential services' in the strict sense of the term (namely, primary and secondary teaching and transport services).[49] It has not, however, expressed any direct concerns at any stage about the complexity

[48] ILO 2018: [790].
[49] See ILO 2016: 153–4, 2017: 178–9.

issue in its communications with the British Government. On the other hand, in a 2019 Observation it did: (i) request the Government to keep it informed as to progress (or, more accurately the lack thereof) in permitting electronic balloting;[50] (ii) note 'with regret' that the Government was not prepared to change its position in relation to the 40 per cent requirement in teaching and transport services; and (iii) 'once again' request the Government 'to review section 3 of the *Trade Union Act* with the social partners concerned and take the necessary measures so that the requirement of support of 40 per cent of all workers for a strike ballot does not apply to education and transport services'.[51]

As concerns Australia, the CFA in *Case No 2698 (Australia)* was clearly not entirely comfortable with the complexity of the ballot provisions in Division 8 of Part 3-3 of the *Fair Work Act 2009* (Cth) (FW Act), although it stopped short of finding that they were inconsistent with the principles of freedom of association on that ground.[52] Interestingly, the CEACR has not made any comment on the complexity issue in its communications with the Government of Australia at any time since the requirements were introduced in 2006.[53]

Conclusions

The 2012 General Survey, the observations of the CEACR, and the decisions of the CFA all serve a useful purpose inasmuch that they set some parameters for the form and substance of pre-strike ballot requirements. It must be said, however, that they also suggest that the Supervisory Bodies have lost sight of the wood in their concern to tend the trees in this context. In particular, neither the CFA nor the CEACR appear to have taken adequate account of the fact that in many contexts the real problem with the imposition of ballot requirements resides in the fact of their existence, rather than in their detail. That is, the imposition of any kind of ballot requirement constitutes an impermissible interference with the organizational autonomy of bodies which are by their very nature intended to be voluntary, democratic organizations of workers. Proper respect for the principles of freedom of association, and the guarantees provided by arts 2 and 3 of Convention No 87 and the other standard-setting instruments discussed in this chapter, requires that such organizations should be

50 See further the discussion in Chapter 3 at 80.
51 ILO 2019a: 175.
52 ILO 2010a: [225] and [229(f)]. See also McCrystal 2011: 170–1.
53 See further the discussion in Chapter 8 at 241.

free to determine whether and when they will engage in strike action to protect and to promote the legitimate social and economic interests of their members. As appears below in Chapters 7 and 8, current British and Australian provision concerning ballot requirements do not meet these criteria. That remains the case even (or especially) where those requirements are cloaked in the rhetoric of 'democracy'.[54]

[54] See further the discussion of this issue in Chapters 1, 5, and 7.

3
Pre-Strike Ballots in Comparative Perspective

Introduction

As has been described in the previous two chapters, pre-strike ballot requirements are a conditioning mechanism that may be imposed as a preliminary measure to regulate the lawfulness of any subsequent strike action. This is also recognized by the International Labour Organisation (ILO), provided that the pre-strike ballot requirements are not overly burdensome in practice. This chapter examines the prevalence of pre-strike ballot provisions, the nature of the regulatory provisions adopted in countries that have pre-strike ballot requirements, and the rationale behind their introduction and use. Like the analysis of the relevant principles of international law in Chapter 2, this analysis provides a context within which to understand the experience of pre-strike ballot regulation in the United Kingdom and Australia, and other countries that utilize them.

The chapter begins with consideration of pre-strike ballot requirements in seventy-six national labour law systems on the basis of a survey of entries in the International Encyclopaedia for Labour Law and Industrial Relations (IELLIR). It then examines the history and development of ballot requirements in the United States, South Africa, Canada, and the United Kingdom as four exemplars of differing approaches to the regulation of decisions by unions and workers to take strike action. As noted in Chapter 1, Australian provision in this area shares many features of the UK legislation, and notable features of the Australian law will be outlined here before the Australian system is described in detail in Chapter 4. This will show the extent to which Britain and Australia exemplify a distinctive approach to pre-strike ballot legal requirements. This approach, which includes complex levels of regulation of internal decision-making, along with employer and State-based enforcement of those decisions, casts the United Kingdom and Australia as outliers when considered in the context of the regulatory approaches adopted in other jurisdictions.

Strike Ballots, Democracy, and Law. Breen Creighton, Catrina Denvir, Richard Johnstone, Shae McCrystal, Alice Orchiston, Oxford University Press (2020).
DOI: 10.1093/oso/9780198869894.001.0001.

Pre-strike ballots in international context

The IELLIR was used as the basis for a comparative survey of the existence and scope of pre-strike ballot requirements in national labour law systems on the grounds that it is the most comprehensive and accessible English language source available.[1] The survey excluded any countries whose entries had not been updated since January 2000, which resulted in the inclusion of seventy-four countries in total.[2] The material derived from the IELLIR was supplemented by reference to *The Right to Strike: A Comparative View* edited by Bernd Waas.[3] This publication reviews the laws of thirty-one countries, including two (Colombia and Ecuador) that are not covered by the IELLIR. This brings the total number of countries surveyed for purposes of this Chapter to seventy-six.

Where available, additional secondary sources on specific countries were also consulted. Some countries surveyed are federal States, some of which have differing pre-strike ballot requirements as between the constituent parts of the federal entity. For purposes of the survey, the predominant approach taken in those countries was taken into account.[4] The term 'strike action' is used in the initial survey to include both strike action and action short of a strike. Differences between the nomenclature used and conduct covered between the various jurisdictions are not noted for the sake of clarity.

The decision to take strike action was regulated by a ballot requirement of some kind in just under half (thirty-five) of the seventy-six countries surveyed.[5] This indicates that the external regulation of decisions by workers and

[1] Hendrickx 2018. There are, however, limitations in relying upon the Encyclopaedia. First, not all entries are up to date and/or do not provide comprehensive commentary on the issue of strike ballots. For example, with respect to South Africa, the text dates from 2001 but refers to the pre-strike ballot requirement that applied under s 65 of the *Labour Relations Act 1956* (South Africa). This measure was repealed in 1995 as part of the enactment of the *Labour Relations Act 1995* (South Africa). As concerns New Zealand, the pre-strike ballot requirement introduced in 2012 in s 82A of the *Employment Relations Act 2000* (New Zealand) is not discussed in the entry for that country. Second, while some entries explore the practical application of the law in the jurisdiction concerned, not all do so. This means that there may be significant gaps in the information available in respect of law and practice in some of the countries covered by the survey.

[2] This total includes two countries—Tuvalu and Vanuatu—that are dealt with as part of the entry for 'South Pacific' in the Encyclopaedia.

[3] Waas 2014a.

[4] For example, as discussed below, almost all US jurisdictions do not require pre-strike ballots. However, there are some ballot requirements in six of the State jurisdictions which apply to a very small number of workers. See below n 46. For the purposes of the survey, the US was identified as a country which does not have pre-strike ballot requirements.

[5] These countries are: Australia, Belarus, Bulgaria, Canada, Chile, Colombia, the Czech Republic, the Dominican Republic, Ecuador, Ethiopia, Greece, Iceland, Ireland, Kazakhstan, Lithuania, Malaysia, Nepal, New Zealand, Nigeria, the Philippines, Poland, Portugal, Romania, the Russian Federation, Singapore, Slovakia, Slovenia, South Korea, Thailand, Turkey, Tuvalu, the United Kingdom, Vanuatu, Vietnam, and Zambia.

their unions to take strike action is relatively common, although by no means universal. Countries with a common law background are more likely to have mandatory ballot requirements than those with a non-common law background, although the two categories are by no means mutually exclusive.

As noted in Chapter 2, compulsory pre-strike ballot requirements may be seen as an interference with the rights of trade unions to manage their internal affairs in a manner that is inconsistent with respect for the principles of freedom of association. This might suggest that mandatory pre-strike ballots would be less common in countries where the right to strike and principles of freedom of association are constitutionally entrenched than in jurisdictions where there is no such constitutional protection. In fact, no such correlation was found across the countries surveyed. Express constitutional protection of the right to strike was identified in forty-four countries,[6] twenty of which had procedural limitations on the exercise of the right to strike, including regulation of the decision to take strike action through a pre-strike ballot.

While there was no clear correlation between constitutional protection of the right to strike and the absence of pre-strike ballot requirements, this combination was more prevalent in continental European countries. For example, in France, Italy, and Spain, the right to strike is constitutionally entrenched as a right accruing to workers as individuals, but can be exercised only on a collective basis.[7] In these countries the recognition of the right to strike as an individual right militates against the imposition of limitations on the right to strike in the form of strike ballots because such requirements could have the effect of denying individuals the right to act collectively by force of the decision of a

[6] Those countries are Argentina, Belarus, Brazil, Bulgaria, Costa Rica, Croatia, Cyprus, the Czech Republic, the Dominican Republic, Ecuador, France, Georgia, Ghana, Greece, Hong Kong, Hungary, Iceland, Italy, Japan, Kazakhstan, Latvia, Lithuania, Malta, Mexico, Norway, Panama, the Philippines, Poland, Portugal, Romania, the Russian Federation, Serbia, Singapore, Slovakia, Slovenia, South Africa, South Korea, Spain, Sweden, Switzerland, Turkey, Uganda, Uruguay, Venezuela, and Vietnam. This survey is not comprehensive as constitutional protections were not discussed in every entry, and countries where constitutional protection of the right to strike is implicit rather than express were not included. For example, Canada is not included in this list, but recent changes in the interpretation of the constitutional protection of the principles of freedom of association have led to Canada's Supreme Court recognizing a limited right to strike in that country. See further Fudge & Jensen 2016. Similarly in Germany, the right to act collectively is protected as part of the broader constitutional protection of the principles of freedom of association—see Waas 2014b: 236. By contrast, in Ireland, the explicit Charter protection of freedom of association is considered unlikely to extend to protection of the right to strike—see Kerr 2014: 305. The likelihood that the survey understates the number of countries with constitutional protection of the right to strike is borne out by the fact that, as noted in Chapter 2, the CEACR in 2012 identified ninety-three ILO Member States that had constitutional protection of the right to strike.

[7] Despax, Laborde, & Rojot 2017: 367–8 (France); Treu 2016: 239 (Italy, and see further Pascucci 2014: 335). As to Spain, see Baylas 2010: 112. This is also the case with respect to South Africa, see Benjamin & Cooper 2016: 218.

majority.[8] For example, in Italy a proposal to impose balloting requirements on workers in essential services to prevent strikes arising out of 'micro conflicts' where employees disagree with union decisions was strongly opposed as an excessive limitation on the individual right to strike.[9] Even more tellingly, in Sweden, all union rules provide that the power to call union members out on strike is vested in the executive committee of the union.[10] Pre-strike ballots, where used, can be for 'consultative' purposes only.[11]

Three of the countries surveyed—South Africa, Spain, and Germany—formerly had pre-strike ballot requirements, but at the time of writing those requirements had been substantially pared back or removed. In South Africa, pre-strike ballots were a pre-condition for taking lawful strike action from 1924 to 1995.[12] The right to strike was constitutionally entrenched in 1996,[13] after the *Labour Relations Act 1956* was amended in 1995 by the *Labour Relations Act 1995* (LRA 1995) to give effect to the pending Constitution, including removal of all previous pre-strike ballot provisions.[14] The LRA 1995 requires that union rules provide for a pre-strike ballot, but does not make the lawfulness of strike action conditional upon the conduct of a ballot, and does not (as had been the case under the previous dispensation) give employers the capacity to challenge the legitimacy of strike action on the basis of compliance with this requirement.[15]

In Spain, a legislative requirement that a strike 'be the will of a majority of workers' was struck down by the Constitutional Court in 1981 on the grounds that it was contrary to the constitutional protection of the right to strike.[16] In reaching this conclusion, the Court observed that only unions themselves can impose such conditions on the exercise of the right to strike by their members.[17] In contrast, Germany has no constitutional protection of the right to strike: rather, the laws pertaining to strike action are derived predominantly from case law.[18] In the 1970s the German courts had required pre-strike ballots as a condition of legality for strike action as part of the 'principle of proportionality',[19] but jurisprudential developments in the late 1980s mean that 'ballots

[8] Despax, Laborde, & Rojot 2017: 367–8 (France); Treu 2016: 246 (Italy). As to Spain, see Baylas 2010: 112.
[9] Treu 2016: 246.
[10] Adlercreutz & Nystrom 2015: 176.
[11] Adlercreutz & Nystrom 2015: 176.
[12] See further below at text accompanying nn 54–61.
[13] *Constitution of the Republic of South Africa Act 1996* s 23(2)(c).
[14] *Labour Relations Act 1995* (South Africa) s 1.
[15] Benjamin & Cooper 2016: 220.
[16] Olea, Rodriguez-Sanudo, & Guerrero 2018: 150–1; Baylas 2010: 113.
[17] Baylas 2010: 113.
[18] Deinert 2010: 55.
[19] Weiss & Schmidt 2008: 203;

are no longer a pre-condition to a lawful strike', even though in practice they are widely used by trade unions on a voluntary basis.[20]

Leaving to one side those countries without mandatory pre-strike ballot requirements, the survey suggests that countries that have pre-strike ballot requirements can be divided into four groupings. The first group have adopted the most light-touch form of pre-strike ballot requirement. It includes South Africa (as discussed above), Nigeria, and Vanuatu. In these jurisdictions, the relevant legislation simply provides that union rules must provide for decisions about strike action to be made by ballot,[21] but leaves the form and implementation of those rules to the union acting in accordance with its rules. In all three cases, non-compliance with the rules does not impact the lawfulness of any subsequent strike.

The second group comprises Portugal and Slovenia. Both of these jurisdictions have different rules in place for strikes called by unions and those called by groups of employees (which is permissible under the laws of both countries). Where a strike is called by a trade union, there is no ballot requirement. However, in Portugal where the majority of workers in an enterprise are not represented by a union or unions, a strike decision may be taken by an 'employee assembly'.[22] Such an employee assembly can be convoked by at least 200 employees or 20 per cent of the employees of the enterprise, and any proposed strike action must be approved by a ballot in which a majority of employees in the enterprise participate, and a majority of those who vote approve the strike.[23] Similarly in Slovenia, where unorganized workers seek to strike, the decision must be taken by a majority of the employees at the relevant enterprise.[24]

The third grouping consists of just one jurisdiction: Turkey. In that country, a pre-strike ballot requirement is activated only if 25 per cent of employees in an enterprise make a request to the relevant authority for a ballot to be held.[25] Where that happens, a ballot is conducted by an independent authority, and the strike cannot lawfully proceed if a majority of employees engaged at the relevant enterprise take part in voting, and a majority of those who vote are opposed to the strike.[26] While it has been suggested that the provision is designed to mitigate the adverse effects of strikes on those who choose not to

[20] Weiss & Schmidt 2008: 206; Deinert 2010: 72.

[21] Agomo 2016: 110 (Nigeria); Brooks 2017: 149 (South Pacific). As to South Africa, see Benjamin & Cooper 2016: 220.

[22] Gomes & Carvalho 2011: 161.

[23] Gomes & Carvalho 2011: 161.

[24] Vodovnik, Korpic-Horvat, & Ticar 2018: 318 and 321.

[25] Dereli 2015: 376.

[26] Dereli 2015: 376.

strike, together with the employer and other stakeholders, in practice it has been found to lead to employees being pressured by employers to seek a strike ballot and then to vote no in the ballot itself.[27] This suggests that the requirement operates more as a reaction to the declaration of a strike in order to try to stop the strike proceeding rather than as a test of the wishes of the workers.

In the fourth, and largest, group, pre-strike ballot requirements are made a precondition of the lawfulness of strike action. The legislative preconditions vary. Some jurisdictions simply require a decision by a simple majority of those voting.[28] Others impose requirements in relation to issues such as: how ballots are to be conducted (eg by post or other means);[29] that ballots be secret;[30] voter turn-out requirements (quorum);[31] qualified majorities;[32] and the content of ballot papers.[33] Further, some countries impose ballot mandate periods such that the ballot must be conducted again after a specified period.[34] Almost all countries allow trade unions to conduct pre-strike ballots themselves, although there are some jurisdictions where the ballot must be conducted by an independent party[35] or conducted under supervision of some kind.[36]

[27] Dereli 2015: 376–7.

[28] As in Bulgaria (Mrachkov 2017: 286), Thailand (Suttawet 2018: 92), and Zambia (Kalula & Zulu 2009: 60).

[29] As in the United Kingdom which requires all votes to be conducted by post (Butler 2018: 303).

[30] As in Australia (Creighton, Denvir, & McCrystal 2016: 163); various jurisdictions in Canada (Carter et al 2000: 343); Chile (Morgando-Valenzuela 2015: 269); Greece (Douka & Koniaris 2015: 341); Iceland (Blondal & Sigurdardottir 2012: 122); Ireland (Costello 2015: 250); Lithuania (Nekrosius & Andriuskeviciute 2007: 167); Malaysia (Arudsothy 2001: 114); Nepal (Mathur 2008: 188); New Zealand (Wilson 2016: 203; *Employment Relations Act* (New Zealand) s 82A); the Philippines (Macaraya 2017: 192); Romania (Dimitriu 2016: 206); Singapore (Chandran 2017: 82); South Korea (Lee & Ko 2015: 250); Tuvalu (Brooks 2017: 186); the United Kingdom (Butler 2018: 303); and Vanuatu (Brooks 2017: 149).

[31] Quorum requirements vary remarkably. For example, in Iceland there is no quorum requirement for postal ballots, but a one-fifth voter turn-out requirement is imposed for attendance ballots (Blondal & Sigurdardottir 2012: 122). In Belarus, on the other hand, two thirds of voters must cast a vote for the ballot to be valid (Kryvoi 2017: 139).

[32] Again, majority requirements vary from simple majorities of those who vote (where a minimum number of voters may or may not be required), to absolute majorities (where 50 per cent +1 must vote in favour) or, in some cases even higher majorities are required as in Nepal where 60 per cent must vote in favour (Mathur 2008: 188), or Tuvalu and Malaysia which require a 2/3 vote in favour (Brooks 2017: 186 (Tuvalu); Arudsothy 2001: 115 (Malaysia)).

[33] For example in Chile, the ballot paper must simply give voters one of two options: 'Last offer of employer' or 'strike' (Morgando-Valenzuela 2015: 269). In New Zealand, the *Employment Relations Act 2000* s 82B states that the 'question to be voted on in a secret ballot . . . is whether the member of the union is in favour of a strike'. In the United Kingdom, there are extensive rules as to the content of the ballot paper, including the 'health warning' quoted at text accompanying n 157 below (see also Butler 2018: 304–5 and the discussion below at text accompanying n 157).

[34] For example, in Malaysia the mandate of the ballot lasts for ninety days, Arudsothy 2001: 114.

[35] For example, in Australia the ballot must be conducted by an 'independent ballot agent' which must be either the Australian Electoral Commission (which otherwise conducts political ballots) or an agent appointed for this purpose—see Creighton, Denvir, & McCrystal 2016: 163, and Chapter 4 at 112–17.

[36] For example, in the United Kingdom while the union conducts the ballot, it must appoint an independent scrutineer if the ballot will involve fifty-one or more union members, Butler 2018: 304; Novitz 2010: 195, n 105.

There are many differences as between the countries surveyed in relation to the composition of the electoral roll for purposes of pre-strike ballots. In some instances, it consists of members of the relevant trade union who are affected by the strike decision, whilst in others it consists of all employees of the relevant enterprise, whether union members or not. This second approach is particularly common in countries like Canada where in its various jurisdictions the union is the sole bargaining agent of all employees irrespective of whether or not the individual is a member of the trade union.[37] The notion that all employees should have a right to vote may seem to accord with basic democratic principles—however, there are some instances where such a requirement appears to reflect a policy of making it more difficult to authorize strike action. By way of illustration, in the Russian Federation the ballot rules were changed in 1995 from requiring a vote of just the members of the relevant union, to a majority vote of 'all employees of the organisation'.[38] It has been suggested that this change has made it significantly harder for unions to authorize proposed strike action.[39]

The survey highlights a stark difference between, on the one hand, those countries where there are pre-strike ballot provisions but it is a matter for the trade union concerned to pursue in accordance with their own rules as to methods of voting and majority requirements, and on the other, those countries where pre-strike ballot requirements are subject to detailed regulation often associated with opportunities for employers to interfere or challenge the lawfulness of strike action on the basis of a failure to comply with the pre-strike ballot requirements. The United Kingdom furnishes a particularly clear example of this latter category, with the relevant legislation combining a high level of pre-strike ballot regulation with opportunities for employers to obtain injunctions against proposed strike action on the basis of a failure to comply with the rules.[40] Other examples include Ireland and apartheid-era South Africa. In Ireland, the courts are able to grant a labour injunction where threatened strike action has not been properly approved by a ballot and the action is otherwise unlawful at common law.[41] In South Africa, prior to 1995, employers routinely sought and obtained injunctive relief in respect of proposed strike action, often on the basis of failure to comply with pre-strike ballot rules.[42] In

[37] Carter et al 2000: 262.
[38] Gorbacheva 2019: 182.
[39] Gorbacheva 2019: 183. In practice this problem may be more apparent than real as in 2014 Nikita Lyutov observed that there had been no official strikes in the Russian Federation 'during the last years' but frequent 'unofficial protests', see Lyutov 2014: 465.
[40] See Novitz 2010: 173–212 and the discussion below at 80, 84–5.
[41] Costello 2015: 250; Kerr 2014: 305. See further, Kerr 2013: 232–4.
[42] Piron & Le Roux 2001: 137.

Canada, by contrast, the imposition of mandatory pre-strike ballots has not led to significant difficulties for trade unions or operated as a significant obstacle to strike action, perhaps because of a lack of opportunities for employers to intervene in the process.[43]

This overview of pre-strike ballot requirements suggests that they are a relatively common pre-requisite for taking lawful strike action. There appears to be no direct correlation between constitutional entrenchment of the right to strike and pre-strike ballot requirements, although vesting the right to strike in individual workers rather than workers as a collective may tend in practice to militate against the presence of mandatory balloting rules. This is to ensure that the capacity of individuals to exercise the right (even if required to be exercised collectively) is not constrained by the will of the majority.

There is marked variation in mandatory pre-strike ballot requirements across the jurisdictions surveyed. However, they appear to cause little difficulty in practice where the relevant provisions are intended wholly or mainly to ensure that sufficient support has been demonstrated for strike action amongst those called upon to take it, particularly if parties external to the actual making of the strike decision (employers; regulators; the public) lack the capacity to interfere in that decision. In contrast, where the relevant provisions have been designed with the purpose of reducing strike action, they may seek to achieve their objectives by a number of means, such as: including voters on the electoral roll who are not members of the union or represented by the union; imposing high quorum and/or high majority requirements; providing for state supervision of ballot procedures; making detailed provision for the balloting process; and providing opportunities for parties external to the decision itself, most notably employers, to challenge the legality of the ballot. This distinction will be explored further in the next section of this chapter.

Ballot requirements in selected national jurisdictions

To explore the themes identified in the survey, this section examines pre-strike ballot regimes in four jurisdictions which serve as exemplars of different approaches to pre-strike ballot regulation. The discussion starts with the United States. This is a country where mandatory pre-strike ballot requirements have been adopted in only a very small number of state jurisdictions, and not at all at federal level. Nevertheless, in practice, unions routinely use ballots to

[43] See Slinn & Tucker 2016.

authorize proposed strike action even though they are not legally required to do so.[44] The second of the four jurisdictions is South Africa. As noted earlier, this is a country where mandatory pre-strike ballot requirements were substantially removed in circumstances where they had previously been a source of extensive legal challenge to the exercise of the right to strike. In Canada, the third jurisdiction, all of the Provinces and the national Government have had pre-strike ballot requirements for many years, but those requirements appear not to have been a source of difficulty for unions seeking to exercise the right to strike. Finally, the United Kingdom furnishes an example of a jurisdiction where the level of pre-strike ballot regulation has continued to increase over the last three decades, and where it has caused significant difficulties for unions in taking strike action. Reference will also be made to the Australian legislation in this context which has similarly prescriptive regulation of pre-strike ballots, although the relevant provisions will be examined in detail in Chapter 4.

The United States

The United States stands out amongst the jurisdictions under consideration because it does not have a mandatory pre-strike ballot requirement. In the twentieth century, most jurisdictions in the United States adopted legislation providing for collective bargaining and permitting strike action as a legitimate tool of economic coercion. In the federal jurisdiction the *Norris-La Guardia Act 1932* (US) expressly barred the courts from issuing labour injunctions in labour disputes, whilst the *National Labour Relations Act 1935* (US) (Wagner Act) established the structures of collective bargaining including union recognition for the purposes of bargaining, good faith requirements, and express recognition of the right of workers to engage in concerted activity.[45]

Since the passing of the Wagner Act, mandatory pre-strike ballot requirements have not been a feature of labour legislation, either federally or, with very limited exceptions, at State level.[46] However, in practice, unions in the United States typically include requirements for pre-strike ballots in their constitutions, and their use to authorize strike action is frequent.[47] Referring to

[44] The situation in Japan and Mexico is essentially the same as in the United States—see respectively Kuwamura 2014: 354; Sanchez Sanchez 2014: 406–7.

[45] Colvin 2016: 245.

[46] The exceptions include State laws in Colorado, Michigan, Minnesota, and Wisconsin (in all of which the relevant provisions are of very little practical relevance) and laws impacting public servants in Alaska and Illinois—Colvin 2016: 248–9.

[47] Colvin 2016: 252.

this as 'order without law', Colvin argues that voluntary use of pre-strike ballots by United States unions reflects the fact that they operate along strongly democratic lines, and find value in being able to demonstrate member support for proposed strike action.[48]

The absence of mandatory pre-strike ballots in the United States is perhaps surprising in light of many employers' strong resistance to union organization campaigns, and the potential for pre-strike ballots to add to the organizational burdens of trade unions.[49] However, Colvin notes that if the real goal of pre-strike ballot regulation is to reduce strike action rather than ensure union democracy, employers in the United States have not needed further legal assistance in this respect due to the fact that they have the capacity permanently to replace striking workers.[50] The threat of termination of employment enables employers to resist recourse to strike action much more effectively than could be achieved by use of mandatory pre-strike ballots.[51] As Colvin has it: 'with the waning of American union strike power and the availability of permanent replacements as an alternative legal weapon against strikes, there has been a lack of need to turn to strike ballots as a mechanism for limiting industrial conflict'.[52]

South Africa

South Africa appears to be one of only two countries where mandatory pre-strike ballots have been introduced by the legislature, and subsequently repealed.[53] The relevant provisions existed in the *Industrial Conciliation Act 1924* and the *Labour Relations Act 1956* (LRA 1956), applying from 1924 to 1995, and were repealed as part of the introduction of a new constitutional protection of the right to strike in 1995–96.

Under the LRA 1956, employees and their unions could strike free from liability at common law, provided they complied with a number of statutory

[48] Colvin 2016: 254.

[49] Colvin 2016: 251; Craver 2014: 582.

[50] Colvin 2016: 251–2.

[51] Cf Craver 2014: 582 who notes that in practice employers rarely resort to hiring permanent replacement workers. That, of course, may be because the mere existence of the capacity to do so, or to threaten to do so, is sufficient to achieve their objectives.

[52] Colvin 2016: 255.

[53] The other country is Spain, which as noted above at 63–4, had to remove a legislative requirement imposing a pre-strike ballot when it was found to be incompatible with the constitutional protection of the right to strike.

pre-requisites.[54] Of principal relevance for present purposes, s 65 of the LRA 1956 required approval of the proposed strike action by a majority of affected union members in a secret ballot administered in accordance with the constitution of the trade union concerned. Failure to conduct a ballot, or to adhere to the procedures set down for the conduct of a ballot in the union's rules, meant that upon application by an employer the courts could interdict (issue an injunction against) the strike, effectively preventing it proceeding on pain of possible proceedings for contempt of court.[55]

The pre-strike ballot requirement in the LRA 1956 was the source of extensive litigation by employers who frequently challenged compliance by unions with their own rules.[56] As Benjamin & Cooper point out this meant that South African courts 'frequently curtailed the exercise of power by trade union parties by interdicting strikes on the basis of non-compliance with ballot requirements'.[57] Rycroft further notes that the 'onerous guidelines' on strike ballots set down by the courts made it 'almost impossible to comply . . . giving employers further opportunities to challenge the legality of a strike'.[58] In particular the courts found that irregularities in holding a pre-strike ballot made any associated strike action unlawful, an approach which led to a 'formalistic and strict approach to determining the legality of a strike'.[59] In considering whether to grant an interdict the courts were 'in the main, narrowly trained on a rigid and formal observance of every aspect of the balloting process',[60] and on occasion imposed requirements on the conduct of ballots that went beyond the legislative guidelines. For example, in one case a court held that a pre-strike ballot was not lawful because the employer should have been invited to send an observer to the balloting, despite the fact that this was not required by either the union rules or the relevant statute.[61]

The adoption of a new Constitution in 1996 which guaranteed the right to strike for every worker was preceded by new labour legislation.[62] The LRA 1995

[54] For a substantial period this only applied in respect of the white minority. Strike action by non-whites was unlawful until 1981—see Benjamin & Cooper 2016: 211, note 4.

[55] Benjamin & Cooper 2016.

[56] Piron & Le Roux 2001: 137. The authors also point out that there was considerable litigation by employers with respect to unions that had made no attempt whatsoever to comply with the pre-strike ballot requirement. See also Rycroft 2015a: 7–8.

[57] Benjamin & Cooper 2016: 214.

[58] Rycroft 2015b: 115.

[59] Benjamin & Cooper 2016: 215 and 216.

[60] Benjamin & Cooper 2016: 215 and 216. The authors note that failures in respect of the number of scrutineers, casting ballots in the presence of other persons, or failure to sign an attendance register were factors that were used to interdict strikes.

[61] Benjamin & Cooper 2016: 216.

[62] See Cheadle 2015.

governs the exercise of the constitutional right to strike. While the LRA 1995 contains both procedural and substantive limitations on strike action, it does not mandate pre-strike ballots beyond a requirement that the rules of a union provide for conducting a strike ballot.[63] However, in contrast to the former laws, failure to conduct such a ballot has 'no bearing on the legality of the strike and the protection afforded to strikers'.[64] Remedies for failure to comply with the rules of a union are provided to union members,[65] including removal of the right of a union to discipline or expel a member who refuses to go on strike where the union constitution has not been complied with in respect of pre-strike ballots.[66] The rights formerly accorded to employers to seek interdicts in consequence of a failure to adhere to pre-strike ballot rules no longer apply.[67]

The removal of the mandatory pre-strike ballot requirement in 1995 reflected an awareness that if the Constitution guaranteed the right to strike to all workers, whether unionized or not, it would be incongruous to require majority support for the exercise of an individual right where the individuals concerned were union members but not to require it where they were not.[68] Further, in discussing the role of employers and labour injunctions, the Explanatory Memorandum for the Labour Relations Bill in 1995 noted that pre-strike ballots 'provide fertile soil for employers to interdict strikes and to justify the dismissal of strikers in strikes that are technically irregular but otherwise functional to collective bargaining'.[69] This was seen to justify the removal of any role for employers in this respect.

In 2012, the Government of South Africa introduced in Parliament amendments to the LRA 1995. The proposed amendments sought to require unions to produce a certificate of 'proof of compliance' with the balloting rules from an independent body with the power to issue such certificates.[70] The introduction of the proposed changes coincided with a wave of strike-related violence associated with unofficial minority strikes.[71] The Government expressed the view that 'minority strikes are more prone to intimidation and violence than those based on a majority vote' implying that 'a trade union supervised ballot allows for such [minority] strikes', suggesting that external supervision was necessary.[72] Here the Government was drawing on well-worn justifications

63 LRA 1995 s 95(5)(p).
64 Rycroft 2015a: 8–9.
65 LRA 1995 ss 95(5)(q), 158(1).
66 Rycroft 2015b: 116.
67 LRA 1995 s 67(7).
68 Benjamin & Cooper 2016: 220. See further Cheadle 2015: 71.
69 Benjamin & Cooper 2016: 220.
70 Labour Relations Amendment Bill 2012 (South Africa).
71 Rycroft 2015a: 2; du Toit 2014: 492.
72 Benjamin & Cooper 2016: 222–3.

for pre-strike ballot requirements, that unions cannot be trusted to manage their internal governance, and that majority requirements subject more radical union leaders to the wishes of their supposedly more moderate members.[73] Ultimately the provisions did not become law as a result of vigorous opposition from the trade union movement.[74]

Canada

Under Canadian law and practice there is no express right to strike except to the extent that the constitutional protection of the principles of freedom of association have been interpreted to so extend.[75] Instead, strike action is regulated under the labour relations statutes in the various jurisdictions. In particular, all jurisdictions prohibit the declaration or authorization of a strike by a trade union unless the union has conducted a strike vote in accordance with the relevant statutory requirements.[76] The role of the common law is, however, largely confined to policing strike-related activity such as picketing, but is not used directly to control strike activity even in circumstances where it might, theoretically, have some application.[77]

Canada is a federal state, with overlapping responsibility for industrial matters between the federal and provincial legislatures, although primary responsibility rests with the provinces. The discussion will examine the federal jurisdiction which was the last Canadian jurisdiction to adopt pre-strike ballots. This jurisdiction primarily covers the federal public sector, and other industries with a cross-jurisdictional character such as the post, shipping, radio broadcasting, banking, and airline industries.[78]

In the federal jurisdiction, a Wagner Act-style collective bargaining system was implemented shortly after World War II. Pre-strike ballots were not a feature of the legislation, although during World War II the federal Parliament had imposed wartime measures requiring the conduct of pre-strike votes and

[73] See further the discussion in Chapter 1 at text accompanying nn 81–4.

[74] This is explored in Ngcukaitobi 2013.

[75] See Fudge & Jensen 2016.

[76] *Canada Labour Code*, RSC 1973 (Canada) c L-2, s 87; *Industrial Relations Act*, RSNB, 1973 c 1-4, s 94; *Labour Act* RSPEI 1988, c L-1, s 41; *Labour Code*, RSQ, c-27, s. 20.2; *Labour Relations Act*, Ontario, 1995, c 1, Sch A, s 79; *Labour Relations Act*, CCSM, c L10s, s 93; *Labour Relations Act*, RSNL 1990, c L-1, s 119; *Labour Relations Code*, RSA 2000, c L-1, s 73; *Labour Relations Code*, RSBC 1996, c 244, s 59; *Trade Union Act*, RSNS 1989, c 475, s 47; *Saskatchewan Employment Act*, SS 2013, c S-14.1, s 6-31-34. For a useful table outlining the key features of the pre-strike ballot requirement in each Canadian jurisdiction see Slinn & Tucker 2016: 184–9.

[77] Carter et al 2000: 319; Adams 1993: paras 11.320–11.372.

[78] As to the exact scope of the federal jurisdiction see *Canada Labour Code*, RSC 1973, c L-2, s 2.

their supervision.[79] Although some of the provincial jurisdictions adopted pre-strike ballots in the post-war period,[80] the issue was not seriously considered again in the federal context until the late 1960s.

In 1966, in the wake of a major strike in the railways,[81] the then-federal Government established a Task Force under the chairmanship of HD Woods to look into 'the whole question of labour disputes'.[82] At the time, rates of strike action in Canada were rising,[83] and the available evidence suggested that pre-strike ballots were already common practice in accordance with the constitutions of many trade unions.[84] Earlier empirical research into the need for pre-strike balloting commissioned by the Canadian Government had found no clear prima facie case in favour of the imposition of mandatory ballots.[85] Anton observed that the assertions of union leaders that 'strike voting is an internal affair of the union which is adequately supervised and provided for by most union constitutions' were valid.[86] When faced with the same question, the Woods Task Force Report rejected the imposition of pre-strike ballots, finding that there did not appear to be a significant problem to be addressed through making them mandatory.[87] However, the existence of public interest in the conduct of pre-strike ballots was also noted and it was proposed that where unions do ballot, the ballot should be secret, maximum access to the ballot should be provided, and employers should have a fair opportunity to make their case known to the voters.[88] It was also recommended that strike votes should not be taken until after the other pre-conditions for lawful strike action had been met, to ensure that the ballot did not cause difficulties with respect to ongoing collective negotiations or act as a bargaining chip for the union.[89]

In 1996, the Canadian Government established a Task Force chaired by Andrew Sims to make recommendations to modernize federal Canadian labour laws.[90] In its 1996 Report the Task Force recommended the introduction of mandatory pre-strike ballots in the federal jurisdiction. In doing so, the Task

[79] Anton 1961: 10–11; Slinn & Tucker 2016: 174–5.
[80] Alberta adopted pre-strike ballot requirements at the end of World War II, and Nova Scotia and British Columbia adopted them shortly thereafter—Slinn & Tucker 2016: 175–6.
[81] Woods 1967: 131.
[82] Woods 1968: appendix A, 219.
[83] Sturmthal 1969: 490.
[84] Palmer 1969: 148–9 cited in Slinn & Tucker 2016: 180.
[85] Anton 1961: 151.
[86] Anton 1961: 152.
[87] Woods 1968: 152–4.
[88] Woods 1968: 154.
[89] Woods 1968: 153–4.
[90] Vaillancourt 2000: 760.

Force appealed to internal union democracy, noting the signalling function of internal democratic practice in trade unions:

> Unions, as democratic organizations, customarily take their mandates from their members, particularly on crucial questions like the decision to take industrial action. A visible and proximate reaffirmation of that fact is healthy because it reinforces the legitimacy of the union's position in the eyes of the employer, the employees and the public at large.[91]

The Report of the Task Force noted the existence of widespread support for mandatory ballots amongst employers.[92] It also noted the complication raised by the nature of representation under the Canadian model where a certified union acts as the sole bargaining representative for all members of a bargaining unit irrespective of whether they are union members. This raised concern over union strike votes that only included members, not all employees represented in bargaining, given that all employees were part of the bargaining unit.[93] Finally, the Task Force expressed concern that unions were conducting strike votes too early in the collective bargaining process, thereby allowing the outcome of the vote to be used as a strategic bargaining tool.[94]

The recommendation in the Sims Report for mandatory pre-strike ballots was subsequently implemented by the Federal Parliament in the *Canada Labour Code*, and the relevant provisions are now to be found in the *Canada Labour Code*, RSC 1973, c L-2, s 87.3. According to Slinn & Tucker, the debates accompanying the legislative amendments made it clear that 'concern about economic harm from work stoppages and fear of wildcat strikes strongly influenced legislators'.[95]

Under the current provision, a trade union may not authorize any strike unless that strike has been approved in a secret ballot vote within the previous sixty days (or any longer period if agreed between the employer and the union in writing).[96] 'Strike' in this context is extended to include action short of a

[91] Sims Task Force 1996, cited in Slinn & Tucker 2016: 180.
[92] Sims Task Force 1996, cited in Slinn & Tucker 2016: 180.
[93] Sims Task Force 1996, cited in Slinn & Tucker 2016: 180.
[94] Sims Task Force 1996, cited in Slinn & Tucker 2016: 180. See Chapter 6 at 164–8 where the role of pre-strike ballots as leverage in collective bargaining in the Australian workplace relations system is discussed.
[95] Slinn and Tucker 2016: 181.
[96] *Canada Labour Code*, RSC 1973 (CLC) c L-2, s 87.3(1). An exception applies if the union is acting in response to a lawful lockout by an employer, in which case no ballot need be held. As appears in Chapter 4 at 103, the same is true in Australian law.

strike designed to restrict or limit output.[97] The electoral roll for the strike ballot includes all employees in the relevant bargaining unit (including non-union members).[98]

In conducting the ballot, the union must ensure that those employees who are eligible to vote are given a reasonable opportunity to participate in the vote and to be informed of the results.[99] The vote must be secret, and the proposed strike action must be approved by a majority of those who vote in the ballot.[100]

Standing to enforce the pre-strike ballot rules is given to any employee member of the bargaining unit alleging irregularities in the ballot.[101] An application for a declaration of invalidity must be brought to the Canada Industrial Relations Board within ten days of the announcement of the results of the vote, ensuring that any concerns over the conduct of the ballot are dealt with expeditiously.[102]

The strike ballot provisions in the Canada Labour Code are minimal, leaving the conduct of pre-strike ballots to unions, and matters of enforcement to aggrieved employees. These light touch provisions are reflected in all other Canadian jurisdictions apart from Alberta, which has more complex rules requiring state supervision of pre-strike ballots.[103] Slinn & Tucker observe that the 'strike ballot laws in Canada have not developed primarily as tools of strike suppression but rather as a manifestation of light regulation of union practices designed to ensure that strikes don't occur without majority support'.[104] This may go some way to explaining why, in practice, the Canadian provisions create few difficulties for unions and almost none of the complex litigation that arises in the United Kingdom and Australia.

The United Kingdom

As noted in Chapter 1, strike action by British unions and their members (and all other employees) is unlawful as a breach of the individual employee's

[97] CLC s 3(1) definition of strike: '*strike* includes a cessation of work or a refusal to work or to continue to work by employees, in combination, in concert or in accordance with a common understanding, and a slowdown of work or other concerted activity on the part of employees in relation to their work that is designed to restrict or limit output'. A similarly broad definition of 'industrial action' appears in s 19(1) of the FW Act.

[98] CLC s 87.3(1).

[99] CLC s 87.3(3).

[100] CLC s 87.3(1).

[101] CLC s 87.3(4).

[102] CLC s 87.3(4).

[103] *Labour Relations Code*, RSA 2000, c L-1, ss 75–77; see further Anton 1961: ch 4.

[104] Slinn & Tucker 2016: 183.

contract of employment, and for the collectivity as one or more of the economic torts. However, immunity against tort liability may accrue to trade unions and individuals provided certain preconditions are met.[105] One of these is that the proposed action be approved by a pre-strike ballot conducted in accordance with ss 226–235 of the *Trade Union Labour Relations Consolidation Act 1992* (UK) (TULRCA). Furthermore, an individual worker will be protected against dismissal from employment for twelve weeks from the commencement of strike action provided that the relevant strike action is immune from liability under the TULRCA and has been officially endorsed by the relevant trade union.[106]

The content of the pre-strike ballot requirements in the United Kingdom are famously complex and are the subject of an extensive literature.[107] The following discussion explores the background to the introduction of pre-strike ballots, the rationales for the introduction of pre-strike ballot requirements in 1984, the debate sparked by the imposition of new quorum and majority requirements in 2016, and a brief outline of the provisions themselves.

Mandatory pre-strike ballot requirements had been considered in various contexts in the United Kingdom prior to 1984. As early as 1958 the imposition of mandatory pre-strike ballots was rejected in a pamphlet produced by Conservative Party lawyers titled 'A Giant's Strength'.[108] While expressing concern at the power of trade unions and the economic impact of strike action, the pamphlet noted that the introduction of mandatory pre-strike ballots could: encourage union members to support strike action; make negotiators more intransigent; and lead to an increase in unofficial strikes to avoid statutory balloting.[109] The practicalities of mandatory ballots were also considered a significant obstacle, as was the potential for abuse of the system through 'the wording of questions'.[110] However, the pamphlet did recommend the introduction of balloting at the request of a defined proportion of union members seeking to stop strike action.[111]

These themes were further ventilated in the 1968 Report of the Donovan Royal Commission on Trade Unions and Employer's Associations.[112] The Royal

[105] This immunity is enacted in s 219 of the TULRCA. For further discussion of these provisions, see Chapter 1, text accompanying n 9.

[106] TULRCA ss 237–238A.

[107] See, eg, Collins, Ewing, & McColgan 2019: 725–43; Davies & Freedland 1993: 486–8, 2007: 114; Elgar & Simpson 1996; Undy et al 1996: ch 6; Simpson 2002, 2005; Novitz 2010; Dukes 2010; McCrystal & Novitz 2012; Darlington & Dobson 2015; Bogg 2016a; Novitz 2016; Dukes & Kountouris 2016; Elgar & Simpson 2017.

[108] Cited and discussed in Fairbrother 1984: 10.

[109] Fairbrother 1984: 10.

[110] Fairbrother 1984: 10.

[111] Fairbrother 1984: 10.

[112] Donovan 1968.

Commission was tasked with considering the 'problems of disorderly and inefficient industrial relations' and the potential role of the law in limiting the 'power of organised labour'.[113] As noted earlier, the Commission ultimately rejected mandatory pre-strike ballots.[114] The Commission gave a number of reasons for this, including that: 'a law forbidding strike action before the holding of a secret ballot could not be enforced in the case of small-scale unofficial stoppages, which make up the overwhelming majority of the total number of strikes';[115] the absence of evidence that 'workers are less likely to vote for strike action than their leaders';[116] the possibility that 'once a vote has been taken and has gone in favour of strike action, the resulting stoppage may delay a settlement by restricting union leaders' freedom of action';[117] and the difficulties associated with the framing of questions for the purpose of conducting ballots.[118]

While the Donovan Commission did not consider pre-strike ballots to be the solution to the 'strike problem', the then Labour Government produced a white paper later in the same year proposing the imposition of pre-strike ballots on unions where doubt existed as to the support of their members for proposed strike action.[119] This met with strong resistance from the union movement,[120] and legislation to give effect to the White Paper had not been introduced into Parliament by the time the Wilson (Labour) Government lost office to the Conservative Party under Edward Heath in 1970. The new Government's *Industrial Relations Act 1971* (UK) (IR Act) enabled the Secretary of State for Employment to apply to the Industrial Court for an order requiring a strike ballot of members of a union where emergency circumstances existed or there was a threat to the livelihood of workers within an industry, and in either case there was reasonable doubt that the action had the support of the workers involved.[121] This provision was used only once in the context of a high profile dispute in the railways. The Government obtained an order for a strike ballot, which when carried out resulted in a vote in favour of further strike action by a majority of five to one.[122] The dispute settled shortly afterwards, with an increased pay offer for the workers. This incident was widely assumed to have

[113] Davies & Freedland 1993: 255.
[114] Donovan 1968: [430].
[115] Donovan 1968: [427].
[116] Donovan 1968: [428].
[117] Donovan 1968: [429].
[118] Donovan 1968: [429].
[119] Department of Trade and Industry 1969.
[120] Davies & Freedland 1993: 271; Fairbrother 1984: 15.
[121] *Industrial Relations Act 1971* (UK) ss 141–145.
[122] Fairbrother 1984: 11; Davies & Freedland 1993: 297; Department of Employment 1983: 18. See also Chapter 1 at 12.

confirmed the assumption that strike ballots could encourage militancy among union members.[123]

The question of mandatory pre-strike ballots remained dormant for the remainder of the 1970s, but was raised again in 1983 with the publication of the Thatcher (Conservative) Government's Green Paper 'Democracy in Trade Unions'.[124] The Green Paper laid the blame for economic and industrial instability at the door of the trade unions, pinpointed internal union processes as the source of many problems, and saw the reform of those processes as the solution to the problem thus conceived.[125] In particular, it was asserted that unions were unresponsive to their members with 'strike decisions being taken by a show of hands at stage-managed mass meetings to which outsiders may be admitted and where dissenters may be intimidated'.[126] The 'immunities and privileges' afforded to trade unions in the conduct of industrial relations were considered to justify the imposition of greater controls on the internal affairs of trade unions so that both the public and union members could be assured that unions were properly conducted.[127] The primary mechanism proposed to ensure that this was the case was internal union democracy as reflected in balloting for important union decisions, including those involving taking strike action.[128]

While the language of the Green Paper emphasized 'democracy', numerous observers discerned the existence of a rather different rationale: reducing both union power and the incidence of strike action.[129] Ensuring that decisions were made by ballot was seen as a way to slow down union decision-making, and to subject union leaders to the democratic will of their allegedly less militant members.[130] Auerbach has observed that the then Government sought to 'encourage union members to adopt an individualistic rather than a collective or membership approach to voting in ballots' so as to 'enhance the likelihood of predominantly negative ballot results'.[131] Interestingly, at the time this proposal

123 Fairbrother 1984: 11; Davies & Freedland 1993: 297.

124 Department of Employment 1983.

125 Department of Employment 1983: 1, 17.

126 Department of Employment 1983: 17.

127 Department of Employment 1983: 1. See also the discussion of derogation from the rule of law at text accompanying nn 76–8 in Chapter 1.

128 Department of Employment 1983: ch 3.

129 Davies & Freedland 1993: 485–7; Hutton 1984: 226: 'Behind the Secretary of State's broad appeal to democracy there lies a partisan assessment of how to reduce the number of strikes'.

130 Elias 1990: 48 observes that the Conservative Government's approach was based on a strong concern at levels of industrial action and its economic impact, the assumption underpinning the legislative changes being that 'union officials are in general unrepresentative of and will adopt a more militant posture than their members'.

131 Auerbach 1990: 198.

was put forward, research into the internal conduct of trade unions in Britain suggested that a large number of unions already engaged in democratic practices, using strike ballots, or engaging in consultation with their members, in relation to strike decisions.[132] This supports the proposition that the introduction of mandatory balloting and detailed proscription of the form and conduct of ballots was motivated by other concerns.

The Green Paper proposals concerning pre-strike ballots were subsequently given legal effect by ss 10–11 of the *Trade Union Act 1984* (UK). These provisions had the effect that conduct of a pre-strike ballot was a pre-requisite of immunity from tort liability for a union in respect of strike action. Any strike action which did not meet this pre-requisite could be the subject of an injunction or (in Scotland) interdict at the initiative of the employer(s) concerned. Furthermore, individual workers who participated in such action would not be protected from dismissal from their employment and the union could potentially be pursued for damages in tort. Davies & Freedland suggest that in introducing these provisions the Conservative Government was meeting employer demands 'for control over industrial action' by effectively turning employers into enforcers of internal union democracy in decisions about strike action.[133] To a significant degree this constituted a reversion to the pre-1906 approach to regulation of industrial conflict.[134] It also broke new ground by identifying stakeholders other than union members as having an interest in how internal union decisions were made.

The trade union movement responded to the introduction of compulsory pre-strike ballots by internalizing the pre-strike ballot process and adapting to the new dispensation by seeking to ensure that they acted lawfully when taking strike action.[135] Further, the use of pre-strike ballots had a number of effects which were not necessarily anticipated by the Government that introduced them, although some of these had been flagged by the Conservative Party Lawyers Group and the Donovan Report in the 1950s and 1960s. In particular, balloting appeared to lend democratic legitimacy to decisions to take strike action; to give notice of the seriousness of the intent behind any proposed action; and to demonstrate the level of member support for proposed

[132] Fairbrother 1984: 48–9. The Green Paper did acknowledge that the rules of some trade unions already provided for strike ballots, however evidence of democratic practice in trade unions was ignored in favour of the view that union powers were being 'exercised irresponsibly' and 'by leaders who are out of touch with their members' views' using methods of consultation with members that were 'totally inadequate'—Department of Employment 1983: 17.

[133] Davies & Freedland 1993: 487.

[134] See further the discussion of the transition from tolerance to recognition in Chapter 1 (text accompanying nn 19–38).

[135] Martin et al 1991: 198 and 207; Elgar & Simpson 1996: 16; 2017: 10.

action to employers, third parties, and the public.[136] These effects, together with the relative ease with which unions adapted to the new requirements, led successive governments to amend the legislation so as to make it more difficult for unions lawfully to take strike action.[137] Furthermore, significant numbers of employers had recourse to the pre-emptive weapon of the injunction against strike action where they could identify any defect in the conduct of a pre-strike ballot.[138]

In 2016 the Parliament adopted extensive changes to the balloting regime, including the introduction of new quorum and majority requirements.[139] To support these changes, the Cameron (Conservative) Government resorted to rhetoric that clearly harked back to the 1983 Green Paper, emphasizing the need to make unions 'more democratic', and painting a picture of 'aggressive, even violent' union leaders, intimidating or bullying union members 'into taking part in industrial action despite their better judgement'.[140] As debate on the legislation progressed, it also placed increasing emphasis upon the need to control and reduce industrial conflict, and to make access to strike action a 'last resort' option rather than a legitimate industrial tactic to be deployed by unions during the normal course of collective bargaining.[141]

At the time that the changes were adopted, the British Government committed itself to investigate whether electronic balloting would be authorized for pre-strike ballots. Following this commitment, in December 2017, a report on electronic balloting was commissioned, and in due course, that report was released.[142] It recommended that a trial of electronic balloting be considered before any wider implementation was undertaken. At the time of writing, however, electronic balloting as an alternative to postal balloting for pre-strike ballots has not been implemented in the United Kingdom.[143]

The pre-strike ballot provisions presently set out in ss 226–35 of the TULRCA are highly restrictive in their own terms, and are exceedingly complex. As such they are replete with technical pitfalls. Along with the Australian provisions which are described in detail in Chapter 4, they possibly constitute

136 See Elgar & Simpson 1993: 83; Novitz 2016: 234.

137 See, eg, the introduction of a requirement that ballots be conducted by post by the *Trade Union Reform and Employment Rights Act 1993* (UK) s 4, and the increasingly prescriptive approach to the conduct of ballots in the period prior to the election of the Blair (Labour) Government in 1997.

138 See Gall 2016; Simpson 2013; Evans 1987.

139 The *Trade Union Act 2016* (UK) amending the TULRCA. For discussion of the amendments, see Ford & Novitz 2016; Bogg 2016a; Dukes & Kountouris 2016; Novitz 2016.

140 Dukes & Kountouris 2016: 348.

141 Ford & Novitz 2016; Novitz 2016.

142 Knight 2017.

143 See https://www.gov.uk/industrial-action-strikes/holding-a-ballot.

the most complex pre-strike ballot regime in the world. Detailed analysis of the relevant provisions is available elsewhere;[144] the following outline is intended to provide a basis for comparative analysis.

For a trade union to be able to establish immunity for industrial action undertaken in contemplation or pursuance of a trade dispute,[145] or for an employee to enjoy even limited protection against dismissal for participation in industrial action, the industrial action must be official union action authorized in a pre-strike ballot,[146] and the union must not have sought participation by its members in industrial action before the date of the ballot.[147]

The electoral roll for the ballot consists of every member of the union whom it is reasonable to believe at the time of the ballot will 'be called on to break or interfere with their contracts of employment' and no one else.[148] The inclusion of those who are not entitled to vote, or the exclusion of any person who should have been included, can lead to the ballot being declared invalid.[149]

A minimum of seven days prior to the conduct of the ballot, the union must take reasonable steps to ensure that all employers who will be subject to the proposed industrial action receive notice of the ballot and the date on which it will commence, a sample ballot paper, and a detailed list of the categories of employees concerned, the workplaces where they work, and the numbers of employees overall and in each category.[150]

The ballot itself must be secret, conducted by post,[151] and every voter must be allowed to vote without any 'interference' or 'constraint' from the union, its officials, or its members, and so far as is reasonably practicable, without incurring any cost.[152] The union can conduct the ballot itself, but for ballots involving fifty-one or more members it must also appoint an 'independent

[144] See, eg, Butler 2018: 302–7; Novitz 2016; Deakin & Morris 2012: 1072–89; Prassl 2014: 557–8. Note, however, that none of these sources takes full account of the provisions set out in the *Trade Unions Act 2016* (UK), in relation to which see Ford & Novitz 2016; Dukes & Kountouris 2016; Elgar & Simpson 2017; Collins, Ewing, & McColgan 2019: 725–43.

[145] The existence of a 'trade dispute' in these cases can be a matter of contention and if the conduct does not fall within the definition of trade dispute in s 244 of the TULRCA, the action will not be protected—see Simpson 2002 and Chapter 1 at 6, n 9. As to the legal consequences of unlawful strikes, see Deakin & Morris 2012: 1040–60; Prassl 2014: 560–3.

[146] TULRCA s 226(1).

[147] TULRCA s 233(3)(a).

[148] TULRCA s 227(1). There are also complex rules in respect of multiple workplaces and whether unions can aggregate votes across workplaces or are required to obtain approval in separate ballots at each workplace for the separate workplaces to participate in the industrial action—TULRCA ss 228, 228A.

[149] TULRCA s 227(2).

[150] TULRCA s 226A.

[151] TULRCA ss 230(2), (4).

[152] TULRCA s 230(1).

scrutineer' to report on the conduct of the ballot within four weeks of completion of the ballot.[153]

The ballot paper must ask one of two questions (or both): is the voter prepared to take part in a strike?; and is the voter prepared to take part in action short of a strike?[154] If both strike action and action short of a strike are proposed, they must be subject to separate questions—that is, they cannot be rolled up together.[155]

The ballot paper must include a range of other information including:[156]

- a summary of the matter or matters at issue in the trade dispute to which the proposed action relates;
- if action short of a strike is proposed, the type or types of action must be stated;
- the period or periods within which the action is expected to take place;
- who, in the event of a vote in favour of industrial action is authorized to call upon members to take part in the action;
- the name of the independent scrutineer if there is one;
- the address to which, and the date by which, the voting paper is to be returned; and
- a 'health warning' which reads as follows:

> If you take part in a strike or other industrial action, you may be in breach of your contract of employment. However, if you are dismissed for taking part in strike or other industrial action which is called officially and is otherwise lawful, the dismissal will be unfair . . . [157]

Approval of the proposed industrial action in the ballot requires that at least 50 per cent of those who are entitled to vote have voted in the ballot, and that a majority of that number have voted in favour of the proposed action.[158] This means that any proposed industrial action must have a minimum of 25 per cent +1 of the employees on the electoral roll voting in favour of the action (50

[153] TULRCA ss 226B–226C.
[154] TULRCA s 229(2). There are further complexities relating to the form etc of ballot questions. Failure to comply with these can lead to invalidation of ballots—see further Butler 2018: 304–5.
[155] This can be contrasted with the situation under the FW Act where the union or group taking industrial action makes the decision whether to ask a single rolled up question or a series of questions. See Chapter 4 at 113–14.
[156] TULRCA s 229.
[157] TULRCA s 229(4).
[158] TULRCA ss 226(2)–(2A).

per cent +1 must vote, and a majority of those must vote in favour). Where the employees voting in the ballot are classified as being employed in 'important public services',[159] then at least 40 per cent of those who are entitled to vote must vote in favour of the proposed industrial action.[160] This means that in addition to achieving the quorum of 50 per cent actually voting, at least 40 per cent of the entire voting cohort must vote in favour of the proposed action.[161] The difficulty of the important public service requirement was illustrated in Chapter 1 in the description of disputes on the English railways where a ballot of 'Guards and Commercial Guards' met the quorum requirement, had a 72.3 per cent majority voting for strike action, but only 36.3 per cent of those entitled to vote had voted yes, so the ballot failed.[162] Not surprisingly, the Supervisory Bodies of the ILO found this requirement unacceptable, at least so far as it applied to certain categories of workers in 'important public services'.[163]

Once the results of the ballot have been determined, notice of those results must be given to all persons entitled to vote and all relevant employers as soon as reasonably practicable.[164] The mandate of the ballot once conducted will last for six months, or up to nine months by agreement between the union and the employer, after which time another ballot must be conducted.[165] There are also notice provisions that must be complied with when taking industrial action, and any failures in implementing the notice provisions can lead to employers obtaining injunctive relief.[166]

The degree of statutory regulation of every aspect of the pre-strike ballot process in the TULRCA clearly constitutes a very high level of external interference in the conduct of the internal affairs of trade unions—allegedly, justified on the basis of 'democratic' imperatives and protection of individual union members against their supposedly more militant leadership. What is

[159] Employees in the following services may be decreed by the Secretary of State to work in an 'important public service': health services, education of those aged under 17, fire services, transport services, decommissioning of nuclear installations and management of radioactive waste; and border security—TULRCA ss 226(2B)–(2EA).

[160] TULRCA s 226(2C).

[161] By contrast, in ballots outside of an important public service, at least 50 per cent must vote, but only a majority of those who actually vote must be in favour of the proposed action, totalling at minimum 25 per cent + 1 of the total voting cohort where quorum is only just met.

[162] See Chapter 1 at 21–2.

[163] See Chapter 2 at text accompanying nn 49–50.

[164] TULRCA ss 230, 231A. The matters that must be included in the notice are: the number of individuals entitled to vote in the ballot; the number of votes cast; the number of individuals answering yes and no to the question (or each question); the number of spoiled or otherwise invalid voting papers returned; whether the 50 per cent turnout requirement was met; and in the case of important public services, whether the 40 per cent majority requirement was met.

[165] TULRCA s 234(1).

[166] See further Novitz 2010: 197–8.

particularly notable about the current British regime is the extent to which enforcement of the pre-strike ballot prescriptions is vested in the employers of those union members balloted. The information that must be provided to employers at every step of the way impacts this process in two distinct ways. First, it gives employers advance notice of everything the union plans to do, thereby giving them plenty of time and scope to deploy their resources to persuade employees not to participate in the ballot[167] or to vote no, and to mitigate the effects of future industrial action if it does go ahead.[168] As Simpson points out, these provisions have the effect that trade unions can lawfully organize industrial action only 'if they give employers of the workers concerned the information necessary for them to first, influence members' votes in the ballot which unions must hold and second, to take action necessary to reduce the effect of any industrial action which does occur, thereby reducing both the impact of the action and the unions' bargaining power'.[169]

Second, the provisions on notice provide employers with ammunition to find an error or omission on the part of the union which can then form the basis for an application for injunctive relief to prevent the proposed action taking place, thereby reinforcing employers' role as enforcers of rules ostensibly designed to protect union members from their own associations.

It seems clear that the design of these provisions owes very little to legitimate concerns about proper union practice and democracy. Instead they bear witness to an almost obsessive level of legal prescription intended to make it as difficult as possible for unions and their members effectively to take strike action. Commenting on the rhetoric used to support the 2016 amendments, Novitz observed that democratic values were less prominent than had formerly been the case, giving way to justifications that were largely pragmatic and economic in character, seeking to limit strike action to a 'last resort tactic' and thereby to minimize economic harm associated with such action.[170] The intrusive and highly prescriptive character of the legislative regime was seen by Novitz not as a function of a desire to increase member control of union decisions, but

[167] In a system with voter turn-out requirements, abstention from voting may operate more effectively to prevent the proposed action from being approved than a no vote (because the no vote will count towards the quorum). See Darlington & Dobson 2015: 9. The impact of abstentions on the outcome of pre-strike ballots in the context of quorum requirements is discussed further in Chapter 5 at 133–5 and Chapter 7 at 205, 210.

[168] Similarly, under the FW Act in Australia, employers are entitled to be 'heard' on an application for a pre-strike ballot order by a bargaining representative. This means that the employer will be privy to all of the relevant information in respect of the proposed ballot, has advance notice of the intentions of the union, and an opportunity to campaign against the proposed action.

[169] Simpson 2005: 337.

[170] Novitz 2016: 236–8.

unequivocally as a mechanism which makes it harder for workers in the United Kingdom to strike.

Australia

The other country with pre-strike ballot requirements that match those in the United Kingdom for complexity is Australia. The relevant provisions are now to be found in Part 3-3, Division 8 of the *Fair Work Act 2009* (Cth) (FW Act). The history and substance of these provisions are described in Chapter 4 and tell a similar story to that in Britain, whereby the rhetoric of union democracy is used to justify the imposition of complex regulation in which employers and the State emerge as enforcers of the legality of internal union decision-making. The brief comparative overview in this section highlights the essential characteristics of the Australian model to illuminate the degree to which Britain and Australia emerge as exceptional in the international context as jurisdictions where levels of regulation have created significant difficulties for unions lawfully to take strike action.

In common with the British provisions, any industrial action taken by employees in Australia will be protected against legal liability under the FW Act only if the action is first authorized in a pre-strike ballot of those who may be called upon to take action.[171] For industrial action to be authorized for these purposes: an independent ballot agent must be used; a secret ballot must be conducted (either by electronic, postal, or attendance (workplace ballot) means);[172] a majority of those entitled to vote in the ballot must cast a valid vote; and a majority of those who did cast a valid vote must have voted in favour of the proposed industrial action.[173] There are also rules governing the wording that must be set out on the ballot paper and requirements in respect of the questions asked.[174] Each form of industrial action authorized by the ballot must commence within thirty days of the declaration of the ballot result, or the continued mandate of the ballot ceases to apply to that particular form of action.[175] On the other hand, provided the action is taken within that initial period, the ballot mandate is of indefinite duration—that is, there is no equivalent to the British six-month mandate limitation period.

[171] FW Act s 409(2).
[172] FW Act ss 450, 451.
[173] FW Act s 459(1)(d).
[174] Fair Work Regulations 2009 r 3.16 and Sch 3.2.
[175] FW Act s 459(1)(d) and see further Denvir & McCrystal 2017.

While the ballot process in Australia functions in a similar manner to the balloting processes in Britain, there are notable differences in the rules specifying when a union can go to ballot and how any ballot is to be conducted. Under the FW Act, a pre-strike ballot can be conducted only if an industrial tribunal, the Fair Work Commission (FWC), has first made a 'protected industrial action ballot order' (PABO).[176] Employers may be heard by the FWC in response to an application for any such order:[177] in particular they may oppose the making of an order on a number of technical grounds some of which are described below; or they may seek changes to the ballot itself; or seek an extension of the notice that must be given before any industrial action that has been approved is actually taken.[178] Further, employers are able to seek tribunal orders against any particular course of industrial action if they believe that the ballot process or the ballot outcome has not been complied with,[179] or court orders are made to redress other errors in the process. The FWC itself is also empowered to act *on its own motion* if it forms the view that industrial action will be taken that has not complied with the balloting requirements.[180]

An important element in the jurisdictional basis for the grant of a PABO under the FW Act is that bargaining for an enterprise agreement has commenced and the applicant for the PABO is, and has been, genuinely trying to reach agreement with the employer(s) of the employees seeking to take the action.[181] Alleged failure to satisfy this criterion is frequently used by employers to challenge the making of a PABO, as was seen in the discussion of the Australia Post dispute in Chapter 1.[182] Where a PABO is ordered by the FWC, the ballot must be conducted by an independent ballot agent. The independent ballot agent most commonly used is the Australian Electoral Commission (AEC) which is the independent statutory agency responsible for the conduct of political elections, whose services are provided to unions for this purpose at no cost to them. If a different independent ballot agent is used, the union bears the full cost.[183]

It is clear from this outline of the Australian provisions that Australia and Britain share a similar approach to regulation of pre-strike ballots which, under the guise of democratic principle, imposes a significant burden on

[176] FW Act s 443.
[177] *Australian Postal Corp v CEPU* (2009) 189 IR 262.
[178] See Chapter 4 at 109, n 98 and Chapter 5 at 126.
[179] FW Act s 418.
[180] FW Act s 418.
[181] FW Act s 443. As to the requirement genuinely to reach agreement, see further Creighton et al 2019a.
[182] Chapter 1 at 22–6.
[183] See further Chapter 4 at 112–13.

unions when seeking to take strike action. In Britain, the provisions incentivize employers to act as enforcers of internal union decision-making, and in Australia the provisions shift this burden both to State agencies and to employers. In both countries, union members are effectively ignored as potential actors in ensuring that their own unions act democratically and accountably. It also emerges that, in comparison with other countries' approaches to pre-strike ballots, Britain and Australia are outliers in their approach to regulation, with no other country surveyed adopting anything like the level of detailed regulation found in these two countries, or, with the exception of the historical position in South Africa, providing so many avenues for employer interference in internal union decision-making.

Conclusions

The discussion in this chapter shows that there are significant variations in the labour laws and practices of different countries that have adopted pre-strike ballot requirements. However, where such requirements have been adopted, there is a high degree of commonality in the ostensible rationale provided for doing so. Pre-strike ballots are presented as a means of achieving appropriate levels of democratic practice by ensuring that all workers who are called upon to take strike action have an opportunity to vote in the decision as to whether or not to do so. Where the decision is made by a union, the coercive power of strikes is used to justify imposing external controls on ostensibly private worker organizations. If workers want the right lawfully to take strike action and inflict economic harm on others, they must be willing to adhere to proper democratic practice before doing so. Equally important, but generally only implicit in the motivations for pre-strike ballot regulation, is the desire to reduce levels of industrial conflict and strike action. This in turn is generally based on the assumption that union members are less militant than their leadership—despite the singular lack of evidence to support this proposition in any jurisdiction.

What is equally striking about pre-strike ballot requirements is the extent to which the form of regulatory intervention affects union practice and access to lawful strike action. In many countries such requirements are relatively straightforward; require only minimal knowledge, planning, or expertise; and generally reflect good democratic practice exercised by trade unions irrespective of whether there is any formal requirement to ballot. However, in the United Kingdom and Australia, pre-strike balloting requirements are overly complex, highly prescriptive, and almost impossible to understand and comply with without detailed legal knowledge and expertise. In both countries the almost obsessive levels of prescription that characterizes the relevant provisions appears to give the lie to the notion that these provisions are simply about ensuring that workers 'have a say' in strike decisions.

In countries that have adopted pre-strike ballot requirements, the most important factors that affect unions' capacity lawfully to engage in strike action are: the consequences of failing to meet the statutory requirements and the identity of the party/ies that have responsibility of enforcing the rules. In jurisdictions where a failure to comply with rules governing strike ballots means that any subsequent strike is unlawful, the stakes are much higher for unions than in those where failure to conduct a ballot constitutes nothing more than a breach of the rules of the union concerned. Further, if the capacity to challenge the validity of a strike ballot vests in parties other than the members of the union, pre-strike ballot rules become a significant obstacle for unions in the exercise of the right to strike. This has been seen to be the case in Britain, Australia, and in South Africa prior to the changes effected in 1995. Employer access to injunctive relief to police the internal decision-making of unions seeking to take strike action appears to be one of the most significant factors that can turn pre-strike ballot laws into a mechanism for strike-breaking rather than a pre-requisite for democratic practice.

Finally, the chapter reveals a consistent tendency to try to justify the adoption of mandatory ballot requirements by reference to the 'democratic imperative'. As noted in Chapter 1, democratic arguments are very difficult to counter in the context of the regulation of decision-making—ballots are an inherently democratic process in that they are a mechanism through which individual stakeholders are given the opportunity to influence the outcome of a decision. However, it is also clear from Chapter 1 that while ballots in and of themselves are inherently democratic, the processes that surround the conduct of any ballot, and in particular the opportunities for informed debate about the merits or otherwise of proposed action, will fundamentally affect the quality of that democracy. What emerges from this survey of the law and practice of a range of countries is that where policy-makers are genuinely concerned only with facilitating the exercise of a democratic vote prior to strike action, a form of light touch regulation is generally used, requiring a ballot but leaving enforcement of the rules up to those directly affected (the voting cohort). The Canadian systems are exemplars of this model. However, where other motivations are in play, much more detailed and formal regulation tends to emerge, and third parties are given a role in the enforcement of that regulation. Of the countries that have taken this more formal approach to regulation, the United Kingdom and Australia are outliers, with by far the most detailed, intrusive, and heavy-handed regulation of pre-strike ballots of any of the countries considered in the survey.

As indicated in Chapter 1, the British pre-strike ballot regime, which dates back to 1984, has been considered at length in other studies, both doctrinal and empirical. The Australian model is of more recent origin, having been introduced in 2006, and its history and contours are examined in depth in the next chapter.

4
Pre-Strike Ballot Regulation in Australia

Introduction

The Australian pre-strike ballot provisions were outlined in Chapter 3 and compared with those in the United Kingdom, Canada, South Africa, and the United States. That overview highlighted the highly intrusive forms of pre-strike ballot regulation that have been adopted in both Australia and Britain. In both countries the relevant statutory provisions were seen to be complex, highly prescriptive, and requiring quite a sophisticated level of legal expertise to enable compliance. They were also seen to have many features in common—although there were also important differences between the Australian and British regulatory regimes. Among the common features is the fact that in both jurisdictions employers have the capacity to interfere in the pre-strike ballot process to enforce compliance by unions with the statutory requirements.

As noted in Chapter 1, there is an extensive academic literature on the British provisions, and on their practical operation between 1984, when they were first introduced, and the adoption of new quorum and voting rules in 2016. The Australian provisions are of more recent origin, and have so far generated a less extensive literature than their British counterparts. The discussion in this chapter and the next three chapters will focus upon the Australian provisions as a case study of the issues identified in the book so far, along with consideration of relevant British provisions where appropriate. As previously indicated, the Study is based on a large-scale empirical examination of the Australian pre-strike balloting laws and their impact on trade union decision-making, and draws upon both quantitative statistical analysis and qualitative grounded theory analysis of interviews with a range of stakeholders in the Australian system.

To set the context for the chapters that follow, this chapter sets out the history and development of the Australian provisions, along with a detailed description of their current content and practical operation.

Strike Ballots, Democracy, and Law. Breen Creighton, Catrina Denvir, Richard Johnstone, Shae McCrystal, Alice Orchiston, Oxford University Press (2020). © Breen Creighton, Catrina Denvir, Richard Johnstone, Shae McCrystal, Alice Orchiston. DOI: 10.1093/oso/9780198869894.001.0001.

The pre-strike ballot requirements in Division 8 of Part 3-3 of the *Fair Work Act 2009* (FW Act) involve three stages: a bargaining representative—usually a trade union—that wishes to take protected industrial action under the FW Act must apply to the Fair Work Commission (FWC) for a Protected Action Ballot Order (PABO); the tribunal is then required to make an order if the statutory requirements are satisfied; and an order having been made, the ballot must be conducted in accordance with the statutory requirements.[1] For the employees and their representative to be able lawfully to take industrial action, at least 50 per cent of the employees concerned must vote, and a simple majority of that majority must vote in favour of the proposed action. The bargaining representative must then decide whether and when the employees will take industrial action. In doing so, it must comply with other requirements relating to notice etc, and any action must commence within thirty days of the declaration of the ballot (extendible to sixty days with the agreement of the FWC).

The chapter clearly bears out the earlier proposition that the Australian pre-strike ballot regime is over-elaborate. It also argues that the elements of that regime cannot be considered in isolation, but must be looked at in totality in order to understand their full effect. It shows that the interaction of the various components of the system creates difficulties in terms of authorizing industrial action that are of such a character as to raise significant concerns about Australia's compliance with the international labour standards that were described in Chapter 2. The discussion also raises questions about the motives for the introduction of the ballot requirements in 2006, and their subsequent retention. The chapter shows that despite the rhetoric of democracy as justification for their introduction, the statutory requirements in fact limit access to ballots to applicants that can demonstrate that they are bargaining in a manner that is acceptable to a regulator, and that enables employers to intervene and challenge all aspects of compliance by a bargaining representative with the process. A central theme of the chapter is that a truly democratic regime would leave these matters to the bargaining representative, most usually a union and its members, to determine. Importantly, the chapter also highlights a number of aspects of the regulatory regime where the impact of the law in practice is uncertain, and in doing so flags the discussion of the practical operation of the legislation in the chapters that follow.

[1] It is, of course, permissible for an applicant to decide not to proceed with a ballot even after a PABO has been made, and indeed the Study data show that this did occur on occasion—see further Table 4.1.

History of pre-strike ballot regulation in Australia

Australia is a federal state, with a constitutional division of powers between the federal and State levels of government. In the federal jurisdiction, mandatory pre-strike ballots were introduced only in 2006. There is, however, a much longer history of balloting requirements in the federal and State jurisdictions which forms part of the historical context for the subsequent introduction of mandatory pre-strike ballots.

For most of the twentieth century, Australian industrial relations were dominated by ostensibly 'compulsory' conciliation and arbitration systems which operated at both federal and State levels.[2] Under these regulatory arrangements, trade unions that registered under the relevant legislation became institutional actors within highly centralized systems for the collective determination of wages and conditions: indeed, the various systems can properly be said to have been designed 'to promote unions to the status of *joint regulators* of industry'.[3] While registration was voluntary, the rewards for doing so were significant. Registered unions were 'granted legal status, and guaranteed organizational security and preference for their members in employment',[4] and, most important, were recognized for the purposes of dispute resolution before arbitral tribunals. Consequently, registered unions were able to initiate industrial disputes and refer those disputes to arbitration in order to achieve binding wages and conditions outcomes through arbitrated awards that were applicable to both union and non-union members.[5]

The trade-off for Australian trade unions in becoming 'joint regulators of industry' was twofold.[6] First, their capacity to take industrial action to promote and to protect their interests as organizations, and to protect and to promote the interests of their members, was severely circumscribed. Sections 6 and 6A of the original *Conciliation and Arbitration Act 1904* (Cth) (C&A Act) made engaging in strikes or lockout punishable as a criminal offence. Even after the

[2] The introduction of compulsory conciliation and arbitration in the Australian jurisdictions is discussed in detail in the essays collected in Macintyre & Mitchell 1989. The federal system was 'compulsory' in the sense that its procedures were mandatory once it had been activated by one or both parties to a 'dispute'—however parties always had a choice as to whether to activate the system. As noted in Chapter 1, at n 56, Victoria and Tasmania adopted a rather different approach from the other States, although by the 1980s they had arrived at much the same position as the other States.

[3] Creighton, Ford, & Mitchell 1993: 923. Portus 1958: 115 refers to union status in the conciliation and arbitration systems as 'semi-official'.

[4] Creighton, Ford, & Mitchell 1993: 923. For discussion of preference arrangements, see Weeks 1995: chs 3 and 4.

[5] Healey 1972 provides a helpful historical outline of the operation of conciliation and arbitration and the role of unions within it.

[6] See also the discussion of this issue in Chapter 7, at text accompanying nn 17–19.

repeal of these provisions in 1929, the system remained deeply hostile to organizing or participating in industrial action. This is evidenced by the extensive range of statutory restrictions on taking industrial action that, in some instances, remain in place today,[7] and by the fact that it was not until 1993 that the Commonwealth introduced any form of statutory protection against common law liability for industrial action.[8]

The second element in the trade-off for the benefits of conciliation and arbitration was an extraordinarily high degree of external scrutiny of unions' internal affairs, and in particular their relationship with their members.[9] When compared to British unions,[10] registered trade unions in Australia gave up 'their status as private and voluntary bodies',[11] effectively becoming public organizations.[12] For example, in return for rights of preference in hiring,[13] trade unions surrendered some control over the basis on which they admitted new members and dealt with existing members. They could lose registered status and access to preference arrangements if their membership rules were burdensome, oppressive, unreasonable, or if they were found to have acted unfairly or unjustly to their members in matters of preference.[14]

The first Australian jurisdiction to legislate mandatory pre-strike ballot provisions was the State of Queensland in 1916.[15] Under this legislation, for industrial action to be 'lawful' it had to be 'authorized' by a trade union, and was not regarded as having been so authorized until all members affected by the strike had the opportunity of participating in a ballot taken at a general meeting constituted in accordance with the rules of the union, and a majority voted in the ballot to support the strike.[16] Where a meeting could not be organized, the

[7] See further McCrystal 2010: chs 3 and 6.
[8] *Industrial Relations Reform Act 1993* (Cth). See further Creighton 1991; McCarry 1994.
[9] Creighton, Ford, & Mitchell 1993: 923 observe that Australian trade unions were regulated 'in a process of registration, in the prescription and enforcement of union rules, through the government of membership entitlement, through the supervision of democratic procedures for the election of office bearers, and in many other respects'.
[10] Arguably, British unions are now subject to a level of external regulation that is not dissimilar to that of their Australian counterparts.
[11] Creighton, Ford, & Mitchell 1993: 889, and see also 923–5.
[12] McCallum 1976: 168.
[13] C&A Act s 40. See too *Conciliation and Arbitration Act 1947* (Cth) s 8, introducing what later became s 56 of the C&A Act.
[14] Weeks 1995: 54.
[15] As noted in Chapter 1, at n 55, Queensland was the first, and only, State to introduce an equivalent to the *Trade Disputes Act 1906* (UK)—*Trade Union Act 1915* (Qld). The protection was repealed by the Bjelke-Petersen (populist) Government in 1976—*Industrial Conciliation and Arbitration Act (No 2) 1976* (Qld), s 4. See further Sykes 1960: 180–1; McCrystal 2010: 68–70.
[16] *Industrial Arbitration Act 1916* (Qld) 1916–1946 s 65(1); 1946–1961 ss 51, 51A; *Industrial Conciliation and Arbitration Act 1961* (Qld) 1961–1975 s 98. For discussion of the provisions from 1916 to 1949, see Matthews 1946.

provisions allowed for the conduct of a postal ballot, or for the motion to be put to members at a series of meetings. This requirement was ultimately repealed in 1975, in favour of a provision that allowed for a minimum number of affected employees to seek the imposition of a strike ballot from the Queensland industrial registrar.[17] Sykes suggests that the change occurred because 'in many cases the conducting of a union ballot was in practice difficult or impossible'.[18]

The State of Western Australia introduced pre-strike ballot requirements in 1979, making strike action an offence unless first approved in a secret ballot.[19] To administer such a ballot, the union concerned had first to obtain permission from the Western Australian Industrial Relations Commission (WAIRC), which was not obliged to provide it.[20] While over time the provisions were substantially expanded and became increasingly prescriptive in relation to the conduct of pre-strike ballots,[21] they appear largely to have been ignored in practice, and were eventually repealed in 2002.[22] However, the broader significance of the WA ballot provisions lies in their signalling effect, especially for the Liberal-National Party (conservative) Coalition in the 1990s and early 2000s. In particular, the requirement that permission to ballot be obtained from an industrial tribunal appears to have been influential in respect of the adoption of the federal requirement that a PABO be obtained from the FWC (and its predecessors).[23]

In the federal sphere, the first provisions providing for pre-strike ballots were introduced in 1928, in response to a lengthy period of industrial unrest.[24] As noted earlier, there was no rational role for such provision whilst ss 6 and 6A of the C&A Act remained on foot, and it is slightly curious that the 1928 provisions preceded the de-criminalization of strikes and lockouts by a year. The 1928 amendments provided that any ten members of a trade union could request that the union conduct a ballot of its members in respect of an election, resolution, or question affecting the union, including a decision to take strike action. If the request was refused, the federal tribunal could order that a ballot

[17] *Industrial Conciliation and Arbitration Amendment Act 1975* (Qld) s 12 which repealed existing s 98 and replaced it with new s 98.

[18] Sykes 1982: 117.

[19] *Industrial Arbitration Act 1979* (WA) s 97.

[20] *Industrial Arbitration Act 1979* (WA) s 75.

[21] See, eg, the *Industrial Relations (Pre-strike Ballot) Regulations 1997* (WA) and the *Industrial Relations (Pre-Strike Ballot Expenses) Regulation 1997* (WA) both of which were repealed in 2002. Notably, the latter provided for reimbursement of strike ballot expenses by the WA Registrar provided the relevant strike did not contravene the legislation. This provision may constitute a precursor to the payment of ballot expenses by the Government in the federal jurisdiction.

[22] *Labour Relations Reform Act 2002* (WA) s 194.

[23] Stakeholder Interview 12.

[24] Oxnam 1971: 27; McCallum 1984: 183.

be held.[25] Further, the tribunal could act on its own motion to order a secret ballot of union members if it was seized of an industrial dispute and wished to ascertain the views of the union membership about any aspect of the dispute.[26]

While the provision allowing ten or more members of a trade union to request a ballot was repealed in 1930,[27] the federal tribunal's powers to order ballots where it was dealing with an industrial dispute remained in place until 2006.[28] In practice, the provision was rarely used for disputes involving strike action. From 1928 to 1976 only four ballot orders were made,[29] generally in cases where the federal tribunal had taken the view that industrial action was proposed or being taken contrary to the views of the members concerned.[30] Research in the 1950s on the effect of this provision in practice suggested that the attitude of the union to the ballot substantially affected the outcome. Where unions did not oppose a ballot, the outcome was more likely to oppose proposed industrial action; but where the union opposed a ballot, then members would more likely support the proposed action.[31]

The *Industrial Relations Act 1988* (Cth) replaced the much-amended C&A Act, and introduced very limited provisions permitting collective bargaining to operate alongside a (slightly) refurbished conciliation and arbitration system. While retaining the federal tribunal's powers to order a ballot in dispute situations, the 1988 Act also included new provisions designed, according to the then Labor Government, to ensure that the affairs of registered trade unions were conducted along more democratic lines. This included a provision enabling union members to request a pre-strike ballot.[32]

Under this provision, a group of members of a trade union who were directed or requested by the union to take industrial action could apply to the federal tribunal (which at the time was the Australian Industrial Relations Commission (AIRC)) for the conduct of a secret ballot to ascertain whether the affected members supported the proposed industrial action.[33] The AIRC

[25] *Conciliation and Arbitration Act 1928* (Cth) inserting new ss 56A–56G into the *Conciliation and Arbitration Act 1904* (Cth).

[26] *Conciliation and Arbitration Act 1928* (Cth) inserting new s 56D into the *Conciliation and Arbitration Act 1904* (Cth).

[27] *Conciliation and Arbitration Amendment Act 1930* (Cth).

[28] At the time of the repeal of these provisions, they were located in the *Workplace Relations Act 1996* (Cth) (WR Act) s 135.

[29] McCallum 1976: 171.

[30] Creighton, Denvir, & McCrystal 2016: 155.

[31] Portus 1958: 229.

[32] Commonwealth of Australia, *Commonwealth Parliamentary Debates*, House of Representatives, 14 May 1987, p 3170, The Honourable Ralph Willis (Industrial Relations Bill 1987 (Cth), Second Reading Speech—note that this was not the Bill that was ultimately passed by Parliament, but the strike ballot provision was retained in its original form).

[33] *Industrial Relations Act 1988* (Cth) s 136.

could then use the results of the ballot to assist in resolving the underlying dispute, and if the majority of voting members did not approve the proposed action, union members were not required to obey any rules of the union that bound them to follow union instructions to engage in or support the relevant industrial action.[34] These provisions were little used in practice, with only one application for a ballot being made to the AIRC during the period from July 2001 to June 2005, whilst over the same period eight applications were made to the AIRC under what was then s 135 of the WR Act for a ballot in respect of an industrial dispute.[35] Whilst none of the ballot provisions, dating back to 1928, were used on other than a very occasional basis the fact of their inclusion in the legislation over an extended period did signal more broadly that the concept of union members voting on industrial decisions was not unacceptable in either policy or practical terms.[36]

The *Industrial Relations Reform Act 1993* (Cth) amended the *Industrial Relations Act 1988* (Cth) in a number of important respects. Relevantly for present purposes, it decisively shifted the focus of the federal system away from conciliation and arbitration and in favour of enterprise-level collective bargaining, and for the first time formally recognized that such bargaining could lawfully be supported by industrial action.[37]

Under the new dispensation, industrial action taken in support of collective negotiations was lawful if: the committee of management of a union authorized the industrial action; the union complied with its own rules; and, if applicable, a simple majority of members of the union voted in favour of the action in any secret ballot ordered by the AIRC under its dispute-settling power.[38] The Explanatory Memorandum to the 1993 amendments asserted that the statutory pre-requisites for taking lawful industrial action were reasonable, and that the ability of the federal arbitral tribunal to submit the decision of a union to take industrial action to a ballot of employees was 'considered by the expert International Labour Organisation (ILO) Supervisory Bodies to be consistent with the right to strike'.[39]

Following the 1996 federal election a Liberal-National Party Coalition Government under the Prime Ministership of John Howard took office. This

[34] *Industrial Relations Act* ss 139, 140(1). In some ways this provision was otiose, given that since 1971 unions had been prohibited from imposing, or threatening to impose, a penalty, forfeiture, or disability of any kind on a member or an organization because the member has refused or failed to join in industrial action. See further the discussion in Chapter 7 at 194.

[35] AIRC 2005: 61–2.

[36] Stakeholder Interview 12.

[37] See McCarry 1994.

[38] *Industrial Relations Act 1988* (Cth) (as amended in 1993) ss 170PJ, 170PK.

[39] Parliament of the Commonwealth of Australia 1993: 63.

new Government was motivated by a strong individualist and anti-union ideology, and quickly introduced significant changes to the federal industrial relations system, although its ambitions were somewhat curtailed by the fact that it did not have control of the Senate (the upper house of the Australian Parliament).

The Coalition's reform programme included the introduction of mandatory secret ballots for proposed industrial action by trade unions. Despite introducing amendments providing for mandatory pre-strike ballots on no fewer than four occasions,[40] the Government was unable to effect this change until after it secured control of both Houses of the Parliament at the 2005 federal election. The proposed ballot requirements duly became law as part of the radical series of legislative reforms enshrined in the *Workplace Relations Amendment (Work Choices) Act 2005* (Cth) (Work Choices).[41]

Neither the Second Reading Speech nor the Explanatory Memorandum to Work Choices provided an adequate explanation of the rationale for the scheme of compulsory pre-strike ballots that was included in the legislation. However, because the amendments had been proposed four times previously, various justifications for imposing pre-strike ballots can be derived from the supplementary materials associated with the earlier unsuccessful Bills.

In 1998, the then-Workplace Relations Minister Peter Reith released a Ministerial Discussion Paper on pre-strike ballots. Amongst other things, the Paper claimed that mandatory pre-strike ballots could 'strengthen the accountability and responsiveness of unions to their members', 'facilitate freedom of choice by allowing employees to express individual preferences freely', and ensure that only industrial action with 'the genuine support of the employees concerned' was legitimized.[42] Further, it was claimed that pre-strike ballots would 'protect both employers and employees from capricious industrial action, *particularly where it is initiated by persons outside the workplace*'.[43] Here, 'persons outside the workplace' was a reference to trade unions, and illustrated the way in which the Government of the day tended to characterize trade unions as 'third parties' to work relationships.

The other substantive discussion of the proposed ballot regime was in a Senate Committee Report on the Workplace Relations Amendment (More

[40] See: Workplace Relations Legislation Amendment (More Jobs, Better Pay) Bill 1999; Workplace Relations Amendment (Secret Ballots for Protected Action) Bill 2000; Workplace Relations Amendment (Secret Ballots for Protected Action) Bill 2002 Nos 1 and 2.

[41] See further McCrystal 2006: 203–4.

[42] Reith 1998: 2–7.

[43] Reith 1998: 6 (emphasis added).

Jobs, Better Pay) Bill 1999. The Government members of that Committee argued that secret ballot provisions would ensure that employees 'and not their union officials' decided 'whether industrial action is necessary to further claims for a workplace agreement'.[44] In response, the Labor members of the Committee observed that while they agreed that strike decisions should be made democratically, no evidence had been presented to the Committee to show that employees in Australia were regularly being forced into taking industrial action against their wishes, and that no case had been made that the existing provisions were inadequate.[45]

There is also some reason to suppose that an important driver of the introduction of the mandatory balloting requirements was 'Australia's reputation as a high strike prone country', and a perception that the proposed requirements could be portrayed as addressing this problem and 'as part of a move towards greater degrees of industrial democracy'.[46]

A further significant background factor in the adoption of the mandatory ballot requirements was the adoption of such provision by the Thatcher Government in the United Kingdom in 1984, and their retention by the Blair Labour Government after 1997. In the debates on the Coalition's various attempts to introduce mandatory ballots, Government Ministers were not averse to taunting the Labor Opposition with reminders that 'if it is good enough in the United Kingdom for Tony Blair and the Labour Party to have secret ballots, why can the Labor Party in Australia not allow workers to enjoy that basic right'.[47]

Under the Work Choices amendments, the existing balloting provisions were replaced by provision for compulsory pre-strike ballots administered by the AIRC. Under the amended legislation, any union or group of employees wishing to take protected industrial action had first to obtain the permission of the AIRC for the conduct of a ballot to authorize proposed industrial action.[48]

[44] Senate Employment, Workplace Relations, Small Business and Education Legislation Committee 1999: 125.

[45] Senate Employment, Workplace Relations, Small Business and Education Legislation Committee 1999: 254–5.

[46] Stakeholder Interview 12.

[47] Commonwealth of Australia, *Parliamentary Debates*, House of Representatives, 30 August 2000, p 19655, The Honourable Peter Reith MP, and see further p 19657. Other examples include Commonwealth of Australia, *Parliamentary Debates*, House of Representatives, 30 August 2000, p 19633, 17653–4; Commonwealth of Australia, *Parliamentary Debates*, Senate, 31 August 2000, the Hon Ian Campbell, p 17038; Commonwealth of Australia, *Parliamentary Debates*, House of Representatives, 4 March, 2003, p 12130, 12133–8, 12143.

[48] *Workplace Relations Act 1996* (Cth) (WR Act) (as amended in 2005) s 451. While there was no restriction on applications by unions, a group of non-unionized employees could bring an application only if they met a threshold requirement that they could demonstrate that a specified number of employees supported the application—WR Act (as amended 2005) s 451(4). According to s 450 the prescribed number ranged between 4 employees for agreements covering fewer than 80 employees, 5 per

The AIRC could give such permission only where the application met the requirements of the Act, and where the applicant could demonstrate that it had been, and continued to be, genuinely trying to reach an agreement with the employer of the employees to be balloted.[49] Employers were party to the application, and were entitled to make submissions to the AIRC in relation to the application.[50] Once an order was made, the ballot had to be conducted by either the AEC or an authorized ballot agent.[51] For subsequent industrial action to be lawful, a majority of those entitled to vote in the ballot were required to have cast a valid ballot, and a majority of those who had done so were required to have voted to approve the proposed action.[52] The Government did not offer any explanation as to why unions had to apply to the AIRC for permission to conduct a pre-strike ballot, although Minister Reith did refer to the need to ensure that industrial action take place only as part of a 'genuine bargaining process' in 'genuine pursuit of a negotiated agreement'.[53]

In 2007, the Coalition Government lost office and the newly elected Labor Government in due course introduced new workplace relations legislation that became law in 2009 as the FW Act. This measure repealed the WR Act in its entirety, but retained significant portions of Work Choices—including those dealing with industrial action in general, and pre-strike ballots in particular—with little or no change.

Prior to the 2007 election the Labor Party had promised that industrial action would only be allowed in accordance with 'clear, tough rules',[54] and in relation to pre-strike ballots, had asserted that 'no one should be asked to take industrial action without having had the opportunity of a democratic vote', in a 'fair and simple' ballot process.[55] The new provisions retained the obligation that had applied under the WR Act that permission for a ballot could not be granted unless the applicant could show that they were genuinely trying to reach agreement at the enterprise in respect of which negotiations were taking place. This was justified in the Explanatory Memorandum to the Fair Work Bill 2008 as necessary to ensure that industrial action only occurs during

cent of the workforce where between 80 and 5,000 employees were to be covered, and 250 where more than 5,000 employees were to be covered.

[49] WR Act (as amended in 2005) s 461. An additional requirement, that the applicant not be engaged in 'pattern bargaining', was largely defunct in practice. See further McCrystal 2009: 151–2.

[50] WR Act (as amended 2005) s 450 (definition of 'party').

[51] WR Act (as amended 2005) s 480.

[52] WR Act (as amended 2005) s 478.

[53] Reith 1998: 7–9.

[54] Rudd & Gillard 2007: 16.

[55] Rudd & Gillard 2007: 16.

'genuine bargaining and not for spurious reasons', and to make parties focus on agreement-making before applying for permission for a pre-strike ballot.[56] Such changes to the ballot provisions as were effected by the 2009 Act were minor in character and intended to streamline the operation of some aspects of the balloting regime.[57]

Following a change of government at the federal level in 2013, the newly elected Coalition (conservative) Government proposed amendments to the pre-strike ballot regime to make it even more difficult for unions to obtain a PABO.[58] The amendments would have prevented the tribunal from making such an order if it found that a union had made claims that were 'manifestly excessive' or which would 'have a significant adverse impact on productivity at the workplace'. Ultimately, the Government was unable to win sufficient support in the Senate to secure passage of the proposed amendments and the Bill lapsed.

The changes proposed in 2013 were justified on the alleged basis that it was 'irresponsible' for unions to seek to take industrial action in support of claims in bargaining that were 'extreme, unreasonable or unrealistic' or 'fanciful',[59] and referred to the 'capricious' use of industrial action by unions as a 'first resort' tool in bargaining.[60] The Government did not provide any evidence in support of these assertions, but the underlying trope is familiar. Unions must be more radical than their members if they seek to persuade their members to take industrial action in support of claims that cannot be won or justified. This rhetoric also conveniently ignores the concept of 'ambit'—that is, the practice of asking for more than can realistically be expected to be obtained—which is a time-honoured feature of the Australian system of conciliation and arbitration, and indeed of all collective bargaining systems.[61]

[56] Parliament of the Commonwealth of Australia 2008: lix and lxiv. At lxiv the Explanatory Memorandum also raises an economic argument for the retention of the genuinely try to reach agreement pre-requisite for ballot applications—that the Government will not fully fund secret ballots for industrial action which will be unprotected at the time of the application because the applicant is not genuinely trying to reach agreement. Under the *Fair Work Act 2009 (Cth)* (FW Act), 100 per cent of the cost of a protected action ballot is borne by the Commonwealth if the ballot is carried out by the AEC. See further the discussion of this issue in Chapter 5 at 138–9.

[57] Eg the requirement that employee applicants for a ballot had to show a threshold of support (above n 48) was removed. See further McCrystal 2012: 114–34.

[58] Fair Work Amendment (Bargaining Processes) Bill 2014, Schedule 1.

[59] Commonwealth of Australia, *Parliamentary Debates*, The Senate, 10 February 2015, 339, The Honourable Mathias Cormann MP.

[60] Commonwealth of Australia, *Parliamentary Debates*, The Senate, 10 February 2015, 339, The Honourable Mathias Cormann MP.

[61] For constitutional reasons the concept of ambit had a particular significance under the traditional system of conciliation and arbitration, and is a concept with which all participants in that system would be familiar. See further Creighton, Ford, & Mitchell 1993: 646–50.

The changes that were proposed in 2013 also made explicit what had formerly been implicit in the Coalition's agenda—the desire to influence and shape the manner in which unions bargain and the claims that they can support through industrial action. In seeking to subject union claims to an assessment of whether they were 'excessive' or would adversely affect 'productivity', it is clear that access to the pre-strike balloting provisions was to be restricted to circumstances where the claims made by unions were pre-vetted by the FWC by reference to statutory criteria which would (presumably) reflect the Government's preferences as to the circumstances in which industrial action could be used, and the claims it could be used to support. Under such provision the ballot itself might have continued to be a 'democratic' measure, but one that was to be available only where other aspects of the position of the union were acceptable to the Government as expressed in statute.

This history of Australian regulation of pre-strike ballots highlights that policy-makers and politicians in Australia have been motivated by similar concerns and objectives to their counterparts in Britain. The rhetoric of democracy and union militancy has consistently been used without an adequate evidentiary foundation to justify provisions aimed at making access to strike action more difficult in practice. Regulators have also sought to restrict access to strike action to a narrow range of circumstances, and to take decisions about proceeding to ballot and the conduct of the ballot itself out of the control of trade unions. In the 2013 proposals it was clear that the Australian Government's motives extended to restricting access to pre-strike ballots to unions that engaged in bargaining in a manner that was consistent with the Government's agenda. This reflects a similar shift in express policy objectives to those in Britain where, as Novitz has shown, the 2016 amendments to the *Trade Union Act* reflected the Cameron Government's desire to make access to industrial action a 'last resort' option, and to limit the economic harm flowing from strike action.[62]

As the following discussion will show, the end result is that in both Australia and Britain, unions and their members are subject to high levels of external regulation of their decision-making in relation to strike action—including interference in decision-making at the behest of the employers against whom the industrial action is to be directed.

[62] Novitz 2016.

The legal framework and its practical operation

The remainder of this chapter examines the current Australian regulatory regime. It explains the legal context for the pre-strike ballot provisions and describes their content. It then goes on to provide an empirical profile of their operation in practice.

As noted in Chapter 1, under Australian law, industrial action that is undertaken without statutory protection can expose those who organize or participate in such action to liability at either or both of common law and statute.

Unprotected action will almost invariably constitute a breach of contract on the part of the employees concerned, with potential implications for tenure in employment and (theoretically at least) exposure to actions in damages. For unions, unprotected action may involve the commission of one or more of the so-called economic torts, leaving the union and its members and officials exposed to potential injunctive relief and/or awards of damages for the losses inflicted by the action.[63] There are also various statutory liabilities that may arise from unprotected industrial action, as for example if it: is undertaken during the currency of an existing enterprise agreement;[64] is taken in contravention of an order of the federal tribunal;[65] or constitutes an unlawful boycott for purposes of Division 2 of Part IV of the *Competition and Consumer Act 2010* (Cth).[66]

For the great majority of Australian employees,[67] protection against these various common law and statutory liabilities is available under s 415 of the FW Act, but only if those organizing or participating in the industrial action have complied with a range of statutory pre-requisites, including that the action has been approved in a protected industrial action ballot by those who are to participate in the proposed action.[68] Industrial action by employees in this context is defined to include strike action and other forms of action including bans, go-slows, and work-to-rule,[69] and in practice encompasses almost all forms of

[63] As to the potential liabilities, and the concept of 'protected industrial action', see Stewart et al 2016: ch 26.

[64] FW Act s 417.

[65] Such as an order of the FWC under s 418 of the FW Act directing that unprotected industrial action stop or not occur.

[66] See further McCrystal 2010: 64–6, 102–8; Stewart et al 2016: 963–70.

[67] Most Australian employees are subject to the FW Act and covered by the federal pre-strike ballot provisions with the exception of some State jurisdiction public servants and local council workers, and employees of non-corporate employers in Western Australia—See further Stewart et al 2016: 126–34.

[68] FW Act s 409(2).

[69] See also the discussion of the nature of industrial action in Chapter 1 at 3–4.

action that are likely to be taken by employees collectively in pursuit of their industrial objectives.[70]

The only circumstance in which a ballot is not required is if the industrial action is taken in response to a lockout by an employer.[71] However, employers may lawfully lockout employees only in response to employee industrial action,[72] which means that in the normal course of events a ballot will have been required before lawful employee action could commence, thereby enabling the employer to respond by means of a lockout. Notably, there are no provisions in the FW Act regulating the process by which an employer makes a decision to lockout employees, apart from requirements that the employer give notice of any decision to implement a lockout.[73]

As a preliminary matter, it is important to understand the role of a 'bargaining representative' in the context of the FW Act. The key provisions are found in ss 176–178A, and operate in such a way that it is possible to have a multiplicity of bargaining representatives in negotiations for any particular agreement. This is a significant point of difference between the Australian system of agreement-making and that in virtually all other developed economies.

This unusual situation derives from the fact that under the FW Act each employee to be covered by a proposed agreement is entitled individually to nominate their own bargaining representative (including themselves).[74] Unions are the default bargaining representatives for their members, but only in respect of those members who have not deliberately chosen other, or no, representation. In the context of protected industrial action, only those who are represented by a bargaining representative who has obtained a PABO can vote in the subsequent ballot and take industrial action in reliance upon the outcome of that ballot. Those who have other representation must ballot separately. Those who have no bargaining representative are unable to ballot or take protected industrial action (although they remain entitled to appoint a bargaining representative, who may be themselves, for that purpose at any time).

[70] As to the definition of 'industrial action' in s 19(1) and the ambiguities created by the definition—especially in relating to picketing—see Creighton, Denvir, & McCrystal 2017.

[71] FW Act s 410.

[72] FW Act s 411.

[73] FW Act s 414(5). Note that the FW Act is silent as to the duration of employer notice, but does require that it be in writing and that the employer 'take all reasonable steps to notify the employees who will be covered by the agreement of the action'.

[74] FW Act s 176(1), (4). An enterprise agreement cannot, however, be made with a single employee—FW Act s 172(6).

The legal context for protected industrial action

As explained earlier, it is not possible lawfully to take industrial action unless that action has been approved by a ballot conducted in accordance with Div 8 of Part 3-3 of the FW Act. This in turn requires that the FWC has made a PABO, which can be done only in circumstances where negotiations have actually commenced (the 'notification time'), and where the party applying for a PABO is, and has been, genuinely trying to reach agreement.[75] Furthermore, the claims that can be supported by protected industrial action are limited to those matters that can lawfully be included in an enterprise agreement,[76] and the employees proposing to take protected industrial action must not already be covered by an unexpired enterprise agreement.[77]

Negotiations for a new enterprise agreement do not commence under the FW Act until an employer initiates bargaining with their employees, or is required to initiate bargaining because the employees have obtained a 'majority support determination' (MSD).[78] An MSD is an order of the FWC that a majority of affected employees at an enterprise want to bargain for an enterprise agreement. Importantly, a MSD asks this question of all employees who will be covered by a proposed agreement, not just those who are union members or represented by a particular bargaining representative. This applies even though in subsequent negotiations employees are not required to bargain as a single collective and industrial action is generally taken separately by bargaining representatives and the employees they represent (although they may coordinate their action for maximum impact).

In combination, these provisions have the effect that for most of the time the majority of Australian employees do not have access to the capacity lawfully to take industrial action because either an unexpired enterprise agreement is in place or bargaining for a new or replacement enterprise agreement has not commenced. It should be noted, however, that negotiations for a new

[75] FW Act s 437(2A) provides that an application for a PABO cannot be made unless the notification time has passed. The 'notification time' is the time at which the employer commences agreement-making by issuing to employees notices of the right to be represented under s 173 of the FW Act. For a rare example of a PABO being refused on 'notification time' grounds, see *United Workers' Union v Coles Group Supply Chain Pty Ltd* [2019] FWC 8219.

[76] As to the content that can be included in enterprise agreements, see Stewart et al 2016: 365–82.

[77] FW Act s 417. This reflects the fact that all enterprise agreements made under the FW Act must have a 'nominal expiry date' of no more than four years from the commencement of the agreement (FW Act s 186(5)).

[78] FW Act s 173(2)(a) and (b). Section 173(2) does contemplate two other circumstances in which bargaining may be triggered, but they are not relevant in the present context. See further Forsyth et al 2017 and n 90 below.

agreement *can* commence before the expiry of an existing agreement, but no industrial action in support of a replacement agreement can be taken until that agreement has expired.

The data in the Study show that, during the Study period, negotiations for a new enterprise agreement most often commenced two to six months prior to the nominal expiry date of the existing enterprise agreement (30.3 per cent of all negotiations), meaning that no industrial action was available to those employees for at least the first two months of the negotiating period, and in other cases for longer. If there is no enterprise agreement, or an existing agreement has expired, employees cannot commence the process for taking lawful industrial action if the employer has not agreed to bargain, or the employees have not been able to achieve the numbers required for a MSD to require the employer to commence bargaining. In these circumstances protected industrial action cannot be taken at all.

Protected Action Ballot Orders

Where employees and their bargaining representatives are in a position to take protected industrial action, they must follow the rules for pre-strike ballots set out in Division 8 of Part 3-3 of the FW Act.

The stated object of Division 8 is to 'establish a fair, simple and democratic process to allow a bargaining representative to determine whether employees wish to engage in particular protected action for a proposed enterprise agreement'.[79]

The first step in the ballot process is for a bargaining representative to apply to the FWC for a PABO. This decision is not regulated by the FW Act: rather, it is a matter to be determined by the internal decision-making processes of the union, or of any group of employees who decide they want to access the capacity to take protected industrial action. Without a PABO, protected industrial action cannot take place. This means that a decision not to apply for a PABO will have the effect of denying access to protected industrial action for the workers concerned. Such a decision is, therefore, a matter of considerable importance to those workers, and is an issue that is further explored in Chapter 7.

The decision to apply, or not to apply, for a PABO takes place in the context of collective negotiations, and will necessarily be affected by the progress

[79] FW Act s 436.

of those negotiations. It will also be impacted by the need to satisfy the statutory pre-requisites for making a PABO application and for obtaining an Order. Applying (or not applying) for an Order will also likely have an impact on any negotiations that are on foot, given that the PABO application itself will signal to the employer that their employees are giving serious consideration to the possibility of taking protected industrial action. This potential impact is further explored in Chapter 6.

Most bargaining under the FW Act takes place at the level of what the FW Act terms the 'single enterprise'.[80] While the FW Act does allow for multi-enterprise agreement-making,[81] industrial action cannot be taken by employees or employers in support of their claims in respect of a multi-enterprise agreement. This means that the provisions under discussion are relevant only for negotiations in respect of agreements for single enterprises. This has been an ongoing source of concern for the Supervisory Bodies of the ILO, but successive Governments have not evinced any preparedness to bring Australian legislation into line with Australia's international obligations in this regard.[82]

Although protected industrial action can be taken only in the context of negotiations for a single enterprise agreement, the statutory rules relating to bargaining representatives that were described earlier can have the effect that there are multiple bargaining representatives in respect of any given agreement. Where this occurs, bargaining representatives can apply jointly or severally for a PABO, but any resultant ballot will be conducted separately in respect of the group of employees represented by each bargaining representative.

There are also provisions under the FW Act which enable multiple enterprises to bargain together for a single enterprise agreement, where those enterprises are sufficiently connected for it to be useful for them to bargain as a single employer for a single employer agreement. Such employers are called 'single interest employers'. Under FW Act s 172(5), employers engaged in a joint venture or common enterprise, or employers that are related bodies corporate, are automatically entitled to bargain together as single interest employers. Other employers that do not meet this definition can seek a 'single interest employer authorization' from the FWC[83] or the relevant Minister.[84] Authorizations have

[80] FW Act s 172(2), (5) and ss 247–252. See also the discussion below.
[81] FW Act s 172(3).
[82] Starting in 2001 (ILO 2001: 222) the CEACR has regularly raised this issue with the Government by way of Observations, with the most recent being in 2010 (ILO 2010b: 56–7). The CFA also raised the issue in *Case No 2698 (Australia)*—357th Report of the CFA, [220], [229(d)].
[83] FW Act s 249.
[84] FW Act s 247.

typically been granted for groups of private school employers or franchise operations.[85]

Single interest employers then operate as a single employer for the purposes of collective bargaining and agreement-making. However, the decision of related employers to act as a single entity for these purposes does not bind the employees of those employers, who can still choose to bring separate PABO applications to the FWC, ballot their members separately, and take protected industrial action. From a union perspective, balloting separately has the attraction that the quorum requirement for each ballot will be lower than in the case of a single ballot across all enterprises within that single interest employer group.

The presence of single interest employers can be significant in practice because the negotiation of one single enterprise agreement might generate a large number of PABO applications. For example, during the Study period, there were five single interest employer negotiations, which between them generated more than half of all the PABO applications made in the period from July 2015 to June 2016 (741 applications out of a total of 1,302). Two involved groups of non-government schools, and three involved agreements in the health sector in Victoria. All of the employee groups involved with these single interest employers chose to apply for a PABO and to ballot separately. Of the 1,302 applications in the Study period:

- 496 applications related to the Catholic Employing Authorities Single Enterprise Agreement Collective Agreement—Diocesan Schools of Queensland 2012 negotiation;
- 43 applications related to the Catholic Employing Authorities Single Interest—South Australian Catholic Schools Enterprise Agreement 2013 negotiation;
- 144 applications related to the Nurses and Midwives (Victorian Public Sector) (Single Interest Employers) Enterprise Agreement 2012–2016 negotiation;
- 35 applications related to the Victorian Public Health Sector (Health Professionals, Health and Allied Services, Managers and Administrative Officers) Enterprise Agreement 2011-2015 negotiation; and
- 23 applications related to the Victorian Public Mental Health Services Enterprise Agreement 2012–2016 negotiation.

[85] See eg *Domino's Pizza Enterprises Ltd* [2009] FWA 493; *The Corporation of the Trustees of the Order of the Sisters of Mercy in Queensland and Others* [2009] FWA 1013.

The significance of these single interest employer negotiations becomes apparent when it is noted that the 1,302 PABO applications in the Study arose out of only 397 discrete sets of agreement negotiations.[86] As a consequence, the absolute number of PABO applications at any point in time can give a misleading impression of the number of enterprises where protected industrial action is threatened in the context of enterprise agreement negotiations.

Once an application for a PABO is brought before the FWC, an order must be made if the application has been made in accordance with the Act,[87] bargaining for the agreement has commenced,[88] and the bargaining representative has been, and is, 'genuinely trying to reach an agreement' with the employer of the employees to be balloted.[89]

The first substantive requirement for a PABO order is that bargaining for the agreement must have commenced, as discussed above, meaning that the employer must either have decided/agreed to initiate bargaining or be obliged to do so in consequence of the making of a MSD, or of one of the other eventualities contemplated by s 173(2).[90]

Next, the FWC must be satisfied that the bargaining representative is, and has been, genuinely trying to reach agreement at the enterprise concerned. This requires the FWC to make a finding of fact as to the subjective motivations of the bargaining representative applying for the PABO by reference to the state of the negotiations, and all other relevant circumstances.[91] There is no one type of behaviour or approach to bargaining that will conclusively demonstrate that an applicant has satisfied the requirement: all relevant factors must be considered in each case.[92] In reaching a decision on this issue, the FWC is required to consider the steps taken to reach agreement; the extent to which claims are communicated; the provision of considered responses to claims; and the extent to which bargaining has progressed.[93] Hard

[86] This figure is estimated as it requires an inference to be drawn as to the likely connection between PABO applications that are submitted separately by different ballot representatives or resubmitted by the same ballot representative (eg where two different unions submit PABO applications in respect of the same negotiation). This figure has previously been reported as 399 (see Creighton et al 2018, 2019a, 2019b; Orchiston et al 2019).

[87] FW Act s 443(1)(a).

[88] FW Act ss 173(2), 437(2A).

[89] FW Act s 443(1)(b). See also FW Act s 413(3). As to the meaning of 'genuinely try to reach agreement' see Stewart et al 2016: 982–4; Creighton et al 2019a: 293–300.

[90] The other situations where an employer can be required to commence negotiations for a new agreement are the making of a scope order which extends to employees not previously covered, or the making of a low-paid bargaining determination; see further Stewart et al 2016: 904–13.

[91] *Total Marine Services Pty Ltd v MUA* [2009] FWAFB 368.

[92] *Esso Australia v AMWU* [2015] FWCFB 210.

[93] *Total Marine Services Pty Ltd v MUA* [2009] FWAFB 368. The Coalition Government unsuccessfully tried to codify these elements of the genuinely try to reach agreement requirement through

bargaining is permitted, and parties do not have to compromise on claims in order to show that they are meeting the genuinely trying to reach agreement requirement, although intransigence in bargaining may, depending on the circumstances, suggest a lack of genuineness and lead to the refusal of an Order.[94]

Unlike the position under Work Choices, employers are not automatically a party to PABO applications. However, it was determined at an early stage in the life of the FW Act that employers are entitled to be heard in respect of PABO applications.[95] Employers have frequently made use of this capacity to become involved in proceedings: to argue that the substantive grounds for making a PABO order have not been made out;[96] to seek changes to the questions asked in the ballot;[97] or to ask for a longer period of notice of proposed industrial action should the PABO order be granted and the proposed industrial action be approved.[98]

Employers' capacity to intervene in PABO proceedings—especially on genuinely trying to reach agreement grounds—can serve significantly to prolong the PABO process due to the fact that the FWC must examine in detail the bargaining behaviour of applicants in order to ascertain their subjective intentions in the negotiations.[99] The extent to which employers deliberately use the opportunities afforded by the legal requirements to delay industrial action or cause difficulties for unions in trying to access protected action is an open question. It is clear from the case law in this area, and from the Australia Post example described in Chapter 1, that some employers do take the opportunities presented by the system to try to obstruct union plans. The extent to which this is true more generally is explored in Chapter 5, along with the impact in practice on union approaches to bargaining and strategizing in relation to PABO applications.

proposed amendments in the Fair Work Amendment (Bargaining Processes) Bill 2014. The Bill lapsed with the 2016 dissolution of Parliament, and at the time of writing had not been revived.

[94] See, eg, *Ford Motor Co of Australia Ltd v CEPU* (2009) 190 IR 300; *NUW (NSW) v ACCO Australia Pty Ltd* [2009] FWA 226.

[95] *Australia Postal Corp v CEPU* [2009] FWA 136. Note also the discussion of this case in Chapter 1 at 22–6.

[96] As in *United Voice v Castlemaine Perkins Pty Limited T/A Lion* [2017] FWC 4951 where the application was refused on the grounds that the bargaining representative had not met the requirement genuinely to try to reach agreement.

[97] As in *John Holland Pty Ltd v AMWU* (2010) 210 IR 419.

[98] FW Act s 414 requires a bargaining representative to give an employer three working days' notice of proposed industrial action. This notice period may be extended by the FWC to up to seven working days in the PABO. This is discussed further below at 120, 132.

[99] See, eg, *Esso Australia v AMWU* [2015] FWCFB 210.

In respect of the volume of PABO applications, Table 4.1 demonstrates that the number of applications varies significantly from year to year, but that the FWC generally deals with somewhere between 500 and 1,000 applications annually.

Table 4.1 also shows that PABO applications have a very high success rate, and that even in the face of employer objections, they are rarely refused by the FWC. As the table indicates, the success rate is normally around 90 per cent of applications (column three). Specifically, during the 2015–2016 period, 1,302 PABO applications were made to the FWC covering negotiations in respect of 397 enterprises or ventures.[100] Of these applications:

- 1,253 (96.3 per cent) were approved;[101]
- 6 (0.5 per cent) were not approved;
- 1 (0.1 per cent) was unknown; and
- 42 (3.2 per cent) were withdrawn by the applicant before an order was made.[102]

While the success rate of PABO applications is high, the extent to which employer opposition to PABO applications can be used to improve the employer's position in terms of length of notice or knowledge of the union's position, or to frustrate the bargaining agenda of a union, is considered in Chapter 5.

As Table 4.1 shows, the 2015–2016 year is an outlier in respect of the number of PABO applications lodged (n = 1,302). However, this can be attributed to the single interest employer negotiations outlined above. If the single interest employer ballot applications in this period were counted not as individual ballots for each employer (n = 741), but as a single ballot for each group of employers (n = 5), then the numbers for 2015–2016 come down to 566 applications lodged, 517 ballots approved (91.3 per cent), with 467 votes conducted (90.3 per cent of ballots approved). These rates of approval and votes conducted align more closely with figures reported over the previous six years, suggesting that the 2015–2016 period is less of an outlier than might first appear.

100 The difference between the number of PABO applications made and the number of enterprise negotiations to which these applications related is explained by the presence of multiple PABO applications in a number of single-interest employer enterprise agreement negotiations in the Study as discussed above.

101 In a previous publication this figure was reported as 1,255 (Creighton et al 2018). Due to new information coming to light this was revised to 1,254 in later publications (see Creighton et al 2019b; Orchiston et al 2019). The current figure of 1,253 reflects the fact that one ballot was never approved or withdrawn, and the decision was referred to another Commissioner for determination; however, no record of either withdrawal or approval was found as of November 2018. See further *MUA v Maersk Crewing Australia Pty Ltd* [2016] FWCFB 1894 (B2015/1574) and also Creighton et al 2019a: 289, n 64.

102 This figure was reached based on evidence of a withdrawal order or where no PABO order could be found by the investigators where the FWC confirmed withdrawal during later email correspondence.

Table 4.1 Ballot applications and ballot votes[1]

	Total ballot applications lodged	Total ballot applications where orders are made	% applications where orders are made	Total ballots votes conducted	% orders proceeding to vote
2009–2010	982	714	72.7	662	92.7
2010–2011	759	675	88.9	578	85.6
2011–2012	1,011	914	90.4	796	87.1
2012–2013	915	847	92.6	779	92.0
2013–2014	627	560	89.3	469	83.8
2014–2015	641	574	89.6	501	87.8
2015–2016	1,302	1,253	96.3	1,203[2]	96.0

1. An earlier version of this table was published in Creighton, Denvir, & McCrystal 2016: 166. Sourced from Fair Work Commission 2010, 2011, 2012, 2013, 2014, 2015. Figures relating to total ballot applications are taken from the annual reports of the FWC whilst those relating to applications granted are taken from the FWC's quarterly reports with the exception of data for 2015–2016 which were taken directly from the Study. Data on ballot applications where orders were not made in 2009–2010 and 2010–2011 were provided by the FWC directly to the authors. These figures have not previously been published and although all possible care had been taken to ensure the accuracy of these figures, not every record has been checked for data entry compliance. Applications granted may later be revoked or withdrawn, which explains why not all applications granted proceed to a vote. For illustrative purposes, of the 714 ballot orders made in 2009–2010, 97 were later withdrawn and 27 were later revoked (17.09 per cent overall), the timing of withdrawal may have been before or after conduct of the ballot.

2. Previously reported as 1,204 (see Creighton et al 2018, 2019b; Orchiston et al 2019) which was correct at the time of publication.

The remaining variations evident in the number of applications from year to year can be attributed to a range of factors, including the occurrence, and progress, of bargaining rounds in particular industries in any given year. It is not uncommon for enterprise agreements within the same industry to expire around the same time either as a result of bargaining having been commenced in those industries by design or as a result of historical factors. This means that many industries experience 'bargaining rounds' where multiple employers in the industry are negotiating with their employees at the same time, consistent with the goals of relevant unions to ensure a degree of parity in the pay and conditions of their members working in similar roles in different enterprises. Returning to Table 4.1, the other outlier year is 2011–2012 which is four years prior to the 2015–2016 outlier, and likely reflects an equally high number of single-interest employer agreement negotiations in the same sectors as those that were negotiated in 2015–2016—bearing in mind that the maximum nominal length of an agreement under the FW Act is four years.

Table 4.2 Number of protected industrial action ballots submitted to the FWC July 2015–June 2016[1]

Industry	All applications		Enterprise agreements only	
	N	%	N	%
Health	241	18.5	30	7.6
Food production & manufacturing	60	4.6	41	10.3
Transport	72	5.5	49	12.3
Building, construction, & labour	55	4.2	47	11.8
Manufacturing & engineering	122	9.4	86	21.7
Public services & utilities	103	7.9	58	14.6
Education	545	41.9	7	1.8
Other services	59	4.5	46	11.6
Maritime	10	0.8	7	1.8
Metal, mining, oil, & gas	35	2.7	26	6.5

[1] An earlier version of this table was published in Creighton et al 2018: 61.

The industry effect is illustrated by Table 4.2, which shows the number of PABO applications by industry.

Consistent with the high number of PABOs connected to single interest employer agreement negotiations during the Study period, almost 42 per cent of applications submitted arose in the education sector, followed by just over 18 per cent in health, and just under 10 per cent in manufacturing and engineering.[103]

Conduct of the protected industrial action ballot

Once an order is made by the FWC, the ballot itself cannot be conducted by the applicant bargaining representative but must be conducted by an 'independent ballot agent' in accordance with the terms of the PABO and the detailed requirements of the regulations, discussed below.[104] The independent ballot agent may be either a person or body selected by the bargaining representative

[103] Table 4.2 counts each application individually, and does not remove multiple applications in relation to the same negotiations and/or the same worksite. Industries are taken directly from the PABO application forms and categorized into overarching industry groups.

[104] Fair Work Regulations 2009 (Cth) regs 3.16–3.18.

for that purpose and approved by the FWC, or, in default, the AEC.[105] Where the ballot is conducted by the AEC, the Federal Government bears the whole cost of the ballot, but if another independent ballot agent is used, the bargaining representative must bear the cost.[106] The conduct of the ballot, and the preparation of the electoral roll, is the responsibility of the ballot agent.

The electoral roll for the ballot consists of those employees who are represented by the bargaining representative who applied for the PABO and who will be covered by the proposed enterprise agreement to which the ballot relates.[107] As explained earlier in this chapter, under the FW Act each employee to be covered by a proposed enterprise agreement is entitled to be represented in bargaining by a bargaining representative of their own choosing.[108] This means that the electoral roll for ballots can include a single employee, if they are their own bargaining representative;[109] or employees represented by a union; or a group of employees represented by a single individual.[110]

The form of the ballot paper is prescribed by regulation. In addition to information about the ballot itself (name of bargaining representative and closing date) it must:[111]

- describe the proposed protected industrial action;
- set out the questions for voters, to be marked 'Yes' or 'No';
- contain information for voters including the applicant for the ballot; any agent acting for the applicant; a description of the employees to be balloted; and the name of the ballot agent; and
- contain the following statement in capital letters: 'YOUR VOTE IS SECRET, AND YOU ARE FREE TO CHOOSE WHETHER OR NOT TO SUPPORT THE PROPOSED INDUSTRIAL ACTION'.

The ballot paper may contain a single rolled up question, or may specify a range of different types of industrial action, seeking approval for each. The ballot questions

[105] As noted in Chapter 1 at n 181, the AEC is an independent statutory body which has responsibility for the conduct of federal elections, by-elections and referenda.

[106] FW Act ss 464–465.

[107] FW Act s 453.

[108] FW Act s 176; see further Read 2018: 69.

[109] Two examples of ballots involving electoral rolls of one person are *Dale v Australian Taxation Office* [2015] FWC 5665; *Streeter v BHP Coal Pty Ltd* (FWA, PR510636, 17 June 2011).

[110] As was the case in *Mr Richard Bowers v Victoria Police* [2011] FWA 5789 where Mr Bowers represented himself and 132 of his colleagues.

[111] Fair Work Regulations 2009 (Cth) reg 3.16 and Schedule 3.2. In the United Kingdom, pre-strike ballot papers are required to include a 'health warning', see Chapter 3 at 82.

must describe the action in such a way that the employees are capable of responding to it.[112] Employers have frequently challenged the wording of ballot questions, but the FWC has taken the approach that while ambiguity should be avoided, 'in most cases the drafting of the questions will be a matter for the applicant'.[113]

The ballot must be conducted in secret, and may be carried out by postal, attendance (at or adjacent to the workplace), or electronic means.[114] Where the ballot agent is the AEC, the bargaining representative may have input into the mode of ballot used—however, the final decision rests with the AEC. As discussed further in Chapter 5, while the FW Act permits electronic balloting, the AEC does not currently offer it.[115] Instead, it provides only postal or attendance ballots, with the overwhelming majority of pre-strike ballots being conducted by post. Where a ballot agent other than the AEC is used, the FWC must provide the ballot agent with detailed instructions on a range of matters including the ballot mode.[116] This is presently the only option available where a bargaining representative wants to conduct an electronic ballot, and it means that they will have to bear the cost themselves. In the Study period, ten PABO applicants opted to bear this expense and use an agent other than the AEC.

As noted above, unions may propose that employees have the capacity to take a wide variety of types of industrial action, ranging from strike action through to work bans and other more creative actions (like refusing to wear a work uniform when one is otherwise required). During the Study period, bargaining representatives sought approval of a wide range of potential forms of industrial action, as shown in Table 4.3. The table sets out all PABO applications made during the Study period (n = 1,302) (column 1) and also shows non-duplicate, 'action-unique' applications (n = 480),[117] where adjustments have been made for multiple applications in relation to the same enterprise agreement negotiations (column 2).[118] The table shows that overtime and job function bans

[112] *John Holland Pty Ltd v AMWU* (2010) 194 IR 239 [19].
[113] *John Holland Pty Ltd v AMWU* (2010) 194 IR 239 [19].
[114] FW Act ss 450, 451; the legislative 'guide' to Part 3-3 in s 406 and the 'guide' to Division 8 in s 435 both state that the provisions establish the process for employees to choose 'by means of a fair and democratic secret ballot'.
[115] As to a proposal in the United Kingdom to offer electronic ballots, see Chapter 3 at 80.
[116] FW Act s 450.
[117] This figure is an estimate and was previously reported as 481 in Creighton et al 2018. As explained in n 86, determining unique applications relies on both the classification of a PABO application as unique, as well as correctly determining where linked applications propose unique actions. This is subject to change as new information comes to light linking agreements previously recorded as unlinked.
[118] Multiple applications in relation to the same agreement (as might arise where different unions pursued industrial action jointly) were characterized as 'unique' only if the applications differed in the type of industrial action they proposed. Where industrial action was identical across separate applications in respect of the same enterprise agreement, it was included only once.

Table 4.3 Industrial actions proposed in ballot applications[1]

	All applications			Unique applications		
		As a proportion of ballots	As a proportion of actions proposed		As a proportion of ballots	As a proportion of actions proposed
	N	%	%	N	%	%
One or more type of ban on						
Overtime	675	51.8	10.8	396	82.5	12.3
Job function	1183	90.9	18.9	382	79.6	11.9
Recalls/call-backs/weekend work/shift changes	185	14.2	3.0	146	30.4	4.6
Stop work meetings	21	1.6	0.3	17	3.5	0.5
One or more strike/stop work of						
Less than 1 hour	514	39.5	8.2	63	13.1	2.0
1 hour	592	45.5	9.5	222	46.3	6.9
2 hour	264	20.3	4.2	211	44.0	6.6
3 hour	114	8.8	1.8	93	19.4	2.9
4 hour	516	39.6	8.2	322	67.1	10.0
6 hour	44	3.4	0.7	32	6.7	1.0
8 hour	194	14.9	3.1	159	33.1	5.0
10 hour	16	1.2	0.3	9	1.9	0.3
12 hour	140	10.8	2.2	118	24.6	3.7

Continued

Table 4.3 Continued

	All applications			Unique applications		
		As a proportion of ballots	As a proportion of actions proposed		As a proportion of ballots	As a proportion of actions proposed
	N	%	%	N	%	%
24 hour	989	76.0	15.8	358	74.6	11.2
48 hour	213	16.4	3.4	175	36.5	5.5
72 hour	120	9.2	1.9	100	20.8	3.1
Shift length	21	1.6	0.3	16	3.3	0.5
Indefinite	296	22.7	4.7	251	52.3	7.8
Week long	146	11.2	2.3	126	26.3	3.9
14–28 days	5	0.4	0.1	4	0.8	0.1
Time unspecified	9	0.7	0.1	8	1.7	0.2

[1] This table provides an updated version of the figures reported in Table 3 of Creighton et al 2018 and includes additional data with respect to the following action types: 24-hour, 48-hour, and 14–28-day actions. Unique application percentages also reflect the re-estimate of unique application numbers (from 481 to 480).

were common, with overtime and recall bans being slightly more prevalent as a proportion of overall actions proposed when the duplication arising from multiple ballots submitted in relation to the same enterprise agreement was removed. Looking at unique actions only (column 2) shorter strikes were more often proposed than longer strikes, with 46.3 per cent of unique ballots proposing one-hour strikes, 44 per cent proposing two-hour strikes, and 67.1 per cent proposing four-hour strikes. This may be linked to the fact that unique applications also commonly proposed indefinite strikes (52.3 per cent), and this may have been used instead of specifying longer strikes.[119]

Approval of proposed industrial action

As noted earlier, for proposed industrial action to be approved in a ballot, a quorum of at least 50 per cent of those eligible to vote must cast a valid ballot, and at least 50 per cent of those who do so must vote in favour of the proposed action.[120] Where more than one form of industrial action is proposed in the ballot, each form of action must be separately approved, and if multiple occurrences of the action are proposed, this must be stated. This means that it is possible for a ballot to propose a range of forms of industrial action, but for only some forms of action to be approved by employees in the vote. Once proposed industrial action is approved in the ballot, the balloted employees may take the action provided that they comply with other statutory provisions which are discussed below relating to notice, form of action, and timing.[121]

Rates of approval of industrial action in pre-strike ballots are discussed at length in Chapter 5. Here it is sufficient to note that during the period of the Study, 1,201 ballot results were located. Of these 1,201 ballot results, 922 (76.8 per cent) pre-strike ballots reached quorum and approved at least one form of proposed industrial action. Of the 266 ballots that did not reach quorum, 233 (88 per cent) involved a majority vote in favour of proposed industrial action. There were only thirteen instances where quorum was met but the majority did not vote in favour of at least some form of proposed action. Clearly, therefore, union members did not routinely vote against proposed industrial action—overwhelmingly, where ballots were unsuccessful it was because of a failure to meet quorum, rather than

[119] These figures differ from that reported in Creighton et al 2018, see further Table 4.3, n 1.
[120] FW Act s 459.
[121] See especially FW Act s 414.

because union members voted against the proposed action (except to the extent that an abstention can be equated to a 'no' vote).

Reaching quorum is one of the most critical aspects of success in the FW Act ballot regime. The factors—in particular, the ballot method used—that impact on success in reaching quorum are explored in Chapter 5. The discussion in that chapter will show how a combination of legislative design and regulator choice on the part of the AEC mean that the most common form of ballot used (postal balloting) under the FW Act is also the least effective form of ballot to achieve quorum.

The PABO process itself is a significant obstacle to taking protected industrial action under the FW Act. The discussion in this chapter has shown that there are a number of complex elements to the process, which require a sophisticated understanding of the relevant legal requirements, and involves the potential for employers to intervene and object to the granting of PABO or to the terms of the Order.

One measure of the impact of the PABO requirement on access to industrial action is simply the amount of time the whole process takes. For the PABO applications lodged in the Study period, the average length of time from lodgement to the declaration of the results in the ballot was 37.3 days (just over five weeks).

There are two elements to this timeframe. First, there is the time that PABO applications spend at the FWC between lodgement and the making of a PABO; and second, there is the time that it takes actually to conduct the ballot following the making of the PABO.

PABO applications took, on average, 6.6 days from the date of application to the making of an Order by the FWC. Longer delays occurred when employers objected to PABO applications. In the Study period, the average interval between PABO application and Order was 5.8 days[122] where there was no active contest by an employer, but 7.9 days when an employer did contest the application. This difference is statistically significant.

Ballots took, on average, 31.1 days to complete from the date of the PABO to the declaration of results. However, this average changed when the method of ballot was taken into account. The average length of time to conduct a postal ballot (from order to result declaration) during the Study period was 33.4 days (just over 2 days longer than the average), while the average length of time to conduct an attendance ballot was 19.2 days (just under 12 days shorter than the average). The average is skewed in favour of postal ballots because of the significantly higher number of postal ballots in the sample. The difference is

[122] Average = 6.2 if 'assumed no contest' ballots are included in calculating the mean.

statistically significant and, given the way in which the regulatory model preferences postal ballots, further demonstrates the manner in which the system is characterized by balloting processes which make it more difficult for workers to access strike action in practice.

This analysis indicates that the PABO regime introduces a significant delay between the decision of a union to seek permission to take protected industrial action and the time that the option of taking protected industrial action becomes available to that union. While the delay occurs in all cases, longer delays are produced when employers object to PABO applications, and when postal ballots are used as the method of voting. This discussion shows that the regulatory methods adopted for pre-strike ballot regulation can actively contribute to the extent to which the pre-strike ballot requirement impedes access to industrial action for workers. Crucially, as will be discussed in Chapter 5, it is not simply quorum that must be considered: it is the manner in which all of the different aspects of the balloting regime interact to produce obstacles and delay. The combined effect of these factors in terms of inhibiting access to protected industrial action raises significant issues about the extent to which these provisions are consistent with ILO standards on freedom of association, an issue that is also taken up in Chapter 5.

Taking protected industrial action

Once industrial action has been approved in a pre-strike ballot, protected industrial action may be taken by those employees who are represented by the bargaining representative who applied for the ballot. Other employees of the employer who will be covered by the proposed agreement can only take protected industrial action if their own bargaining representative has had proposed action approved in a separate pre-strike ballot.

Significantly, the pre-strike ballot conducted by the independent ballot agent does not actually involve a decision by the union or employees to take industrial action. Once the ballot results are declared, the legislation requires the bargaining representative of the relevant employees to provide notice of proposed industrial action of at least three working days before any particular form of action that has been approved in the ballot can commence.[123] In other words, having secured authorization through the ballot process, the bargaining

[123] FW Act s 414.

representative and the employees it represents (characteristically a union and its members) must decide whether they want actually to take industrial action, and if so, which of the available forms of action they wish to utilize, and when they want to do so (being mindful of the thirty-day rule discussed below). If they do decide to take action, the bargaining representative must then give the requisite notice to the employer. While the FW Act is highly prescriptive in respect of the ballot itself, there are no rules in respect of how these post-ballot decisions are to be taken by unions and employees. This inevitably raises the question of whether these later decisions, in particular the decision actually to take protected industrial action, are taken in a democratic manner. This is explored in Chapter 7.

Once the decision is made actually to take industrial action, three working days' notice of industrial action to employers is required before action can commence. However, the three days does not include either the day the notice is given to the employer or the actual day on which the action commences, which means that it in reality the action cannot commence until the fifth day at the earliest.[124] A longer period of notice of up to seven days must be given if the FWC so requires,[125] in which case the action cannot commence until, at the earliest, the ninth day. The decision by the FWC to require a longer period of notice is made at the same time as the PABO, on request by the employer. The data in the Study show that a longer period of notice is conceded by a bargaining representative in around 27.5 per cent of cases.

These notice requirements clearly show that the ballot requirements operate in a manner that more severely inhibits workers' capacity lawfully to take industrial action than a plain reading of the legislation might suggest: even the minimum notice period of three days is actually five days, and in many instances is as much as nine days. This can be a particularly significant consideration in light of the 'thirty-day rule'.

Once approved in a ballot, industrial action must be commenced within thirty days (or up to sixty days with the approval of the FWC) of the declaration of the ballot.[126] If the action is not commenced within that time, then the union and its members lose the capacity to take the action, and would need to recommence the ballot process if they wish to regain that capacity. Where action

[124] This arises due the rules as to calculating time under the *Acts Interpretation Act 1901* (Cth) s 36 as it applied on 25 June 2009 (FW Act s 40A—Amendments to the *Acts Interpretation Act 1901* (Cth) made after 25 June 2009 do not apply to the FW Act). In addition, a working day does not include a Saturday, a Sunday, or a public holiday (FW Act s 12). This means, for example, that if three days' notice is given at 9.00am on a Friday, action cannot commence until the following Thursday (seven days later).

[125] FW Act s 414.

[126] For discussion of the 'thirty-day rule' see Denvir & McCrystal 2017: 173–5.

is commenced within the thirty-day period, then that action can again be taken beyond the thirty-day limit—however it is important to appreciate that if the ballot approved multiple forms of action, legal protection extends only to those forms of action that were actually commenced during the thirty-day period.[127] Given that multiple forms of industrial action are frequently authorized in pre-strike ballots (in some cases as many as forty different forms of action may be approved), this means that one of each form of approved action must occur within the thirty days of the declaration of the ballot result.[128] Anything that is not used cannot be taken again without a new ballot. The way in which unions have adapted to this rule is considered further in Chapter 5—especially the way in which it can impact negotiations by in effect forcing unions to take multiple forms of action at an earlier stage than they might otherwise wish in order to keep alive the capacity to take such action at a later stage.

It was not possible to track how many of the successful ballots in the Study period led to industrial action being taken. However, it was possible to follow up whether industrial action took place with respect to forty-nine of the ballots that were discussed in the qualitative interviews.[129] Of these forty-nine ballots, thirty-one were used as the basis for taking some form of industrial action by the relevant employees. While these data are not conclusive, they do indicate that in respect of those ballots that could be followed up, industrial action occurred more often than not.

It also proved possible to ascertain the form of industrial action that was taken in twenty-nine of the thirty-one cases in the qualitative sample where some form of industrial action was taken.[130] This is reflected in Figure 4.1, which shows the forms of action taken as a proportion of the number of ballots where action was taken. It shows that job function bans were the most common form of action with 44.8 per cent of all ballots where industrial action was taken involving this type of action. This was followed by overtime bans,

[127] *United Collieries Ltd v CFMEU* (2006) 153 FCR 543; *Energy Australia Yallourn Pty Ltd v CFMEU* (2014) 218 FCR 316.

[128] In November 2019 the Police Federation of Australia obtained a PABO which invited members to approve the taking of no fewer than fifty-one forms of industrial action in the context of ongoing negotiations with Victoria Police—*Police Federation of Australia v Victoria Police*, 11 November 2019, PR714133. In due course, all fifty-one forms of action were approved by massive majorities in a ballot which attracted a 63 per cent return on a roll of voters with 17,218 names.

[129] This excludes any follow up with the PABOs arising out of single-interest employer authorizations in the Study due to the likelihood that this would skew the data.

[130] Two ballots have been excluded from the analysis. These pertained to the same agreement involving three different unions and one employer. The employer and a bargaining representative for one of the unions were interviewed. As a result it was only possible to confirm the forms of industrial action taken for those members of the union whose representative was interviewed. Although it seems likely that the forms of industrial action were taken across all three ballots, it was not possible to establish with certainty that this was the case.

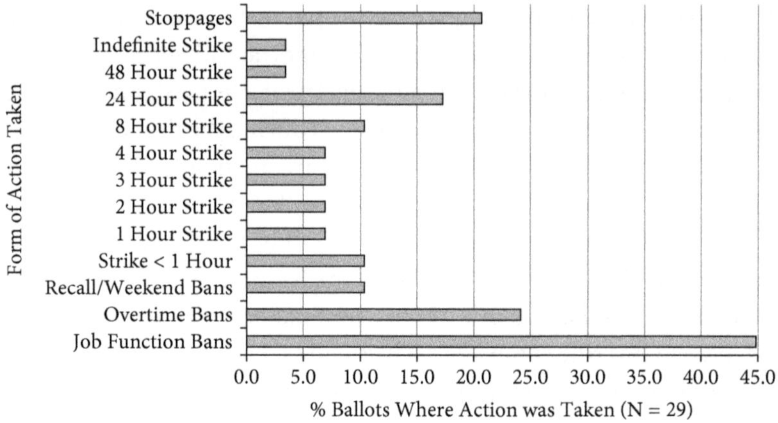

Figure 4.1 Forms of action taken

which accounted for 24.1 per cent of all actions taken, and stoppages, which accounted for 20.7 per cent of all actions taken. Notice was given in respect of three approved ballots where, in the event, no action was taken.

Conclusions

The pre-strike ballot provisions in the FW Act largely replicate those that were introduced by the neo-liberal Coalition Government in 2005. The 2005 provisions were ostensibly motivated by that Government's preoccupations with freedom of choice, preventing 'capricious' industrial action initiated by third parties (ie trade unions), ensuring that industrial action was only taken with the full support of the employees concerned, and making trade unions more responsive and accountable to their members. In contrast, the full rationale for the retention of these provisions by a Labor Government in 2009 was never fully spelled out.

Stakeholder interviews undertaken for the Study suggested that participants in the industrial relations system were also aware of a key underlying motivation for the ballots provisions, particularly when first enacted in 2005: 'to slow down the process by which a union in the course of bargaining could take protected industrial action'.[131]

As the analysis of the 2009 Australian provisions in this chapter demonstrates, those provisions are characterized by a similar level of prescriptive

[131] Stakeholder Interview 12.

detail to their British counterparts. They provide employers with numerous opportunities to challenge the lawfulness of internal union decision-making on industrial action, and place procedural and substantive constraints upon employees' capacity to take industrial action in a timely manner. These include the PABO, independent ballot agent, quorum, and thirty-day requirements

As the discussion has shown, navigating the complex legislative provisions requires a well-developed understanding of the legal regime. In addition, various elements of the balloting rules combine in practice to produce significant delay and to incentivize use of the means of conducting ballots that are least likely to facilitate democratic voice and timely access to the right to strike.

Although the FW Act specifies that the purpose of the provisions for protected action ballots is 'to establish a fair, simple and democratic process',[132] the provisions, as explained in this chapter, are so complex, particularly when viewed as a whole, that they quite possibly contravene ILO standards relating to the right to strike, as discussed in Chapters 2 and 5. As noted earlier, the ILO standards expressly contemplate that pre-requisites (such as compulsory ballots) for taking industrial action may be acceptable, but only so long as they are 'reasonable', and 'are not such as to place a substantial limitation on the means of action open to trade union organisations'.[133] In particular, the CFA has suggested that the quorum provisions may be 'excessive and could excessively hinder the possibility of carrying out a strike, particularly in large enterprises'.[134] The impact of the totality of the provisions in practice on the capacity of workers lawfully to take industrial action is explored in Chapter 5.

Trade union officials interviewed for the Study repeatedly stated that the process of applying for a PABO was extremely cumbersome, 'difficult and tiresome . . . long and hard',[135] 'bureaucratic and . . . takes away resources',[136] and required 'very long days . . . just to make sure you get all the paperwork right'.[137] The process led to significant delays in taking protected industrial action—which were further exacerbated if there were postal ballots, which took 'so many weeks'[138]—and which prevented unions, in many cases, from taking industrial action when it was likely to be most effective.

132 FW Act s 436.
133 ILO 2018: [789].
134 ILO 2018: [806]. See *Case No 2698 (Australia)* 357th Report of the CFA; McCrystal 2010: 263–4, 2011: 171.
135 Interview 28, Union.
136 Interview 62, Union.
137 Interview 32, Union.
138 Interview 51, Union.

Despite this, the complexity and protracted character of the ballot process had some unexpected consequences, which are explored in the following chapters. There are a number of interesting questions about the relationship between industrial action ballots and the associated enterprise bargaining negotiations. Does lodging a PABO application facilitate arriving at an agreed outcome, and if so, in what way? Is a successful vote sufficient to encourage an employer to make bargaining concessions, or is actually taking industrial action the only way to operationalize what might otherwise be seen as an empty threat? These issues are addressed in Chapters 5 and 6.

Chapter 5 explores how pre-strike ballot requirements inhibit the capacity of unions to organize industrial action and have an impact on their capacity to use industrial action in the most strategically effective manner. Chapter 6 examines the ways in which pre-strike ballot requirements can provide leverage to unions in the bargaining context and explores stakeholder perceptions of the operation of the strike ballot provisions.

This chapter has raised issues concerning union decision-making in relation to industrial action—particularly decisions about whether and when to apply for a PABO and when to notify and take industrial action after authorization has been secured through the ballot process. In contrast to the ballot itself, these are entirely unregulated, and the discussion has raised questions as to the mechanisms unions use to make those decisions and the quality of the democratic process they engender. These decisions and associated issues concerning the democratic imperative are explored in Chapter 7.

5

The Impact of Ballot Requirements on Organizing and Taking Strike Action

Introduction

The previous chapter demonstrated how the process for applying to the Fair Work Commission (FWC) for a Protected Action Ballot Order (PABO) is prescriptively regulated by the *Fair Work Act 2009* (Cth) (FW Act). The PABO system gives employers ample opportunity to challenge the legality of union decision-making on industrial action, and includes many procedural and substantive constraints upon employees' capacity to take such action.

Drawing on a combination of qualitative analysis of interview data and descriptive and inferential statistical analysis, this chapter explores in greater detail how these pre-strike ballot requirements inhibit the capacity of unions to organize industrial action and impede their capacity to use industrial action in the most strategically effective manner.

Beginning with the requirement to apply to the FWC for a PABO, the chapter looks at how this requirement can be used by employers to delay the conduct of pre-strike ballots and, by extension, industrial action. It then examines pre-strike ballots themselves to illustrate the difficulties associated with the quorum requirement, and how prescribed methods of balloting can affect the outcome of the ballot seeking to authorize industrial action. It also addresses the administrative burdens incurred by unions in complying with the ballot requirements.

Next, the chapter considers the obstacles to taking industrial action following the making of a PABO and a successful outcome in a subsequent ballot. This analysis of the practical operation of the ballot requirements establishes empirically the interrelationship between different components of the ballot regime and reveals that the aggregate effect of these requirements inhibits employee access to lawful industrial action. Having explored the cumulative impact of the ballot requirements, the chapter examines whether they comply with the relevant International Labour Organisation (ILO) standards.

Strike Ballots, Democracy, and Law. Breen Creighton, Catrina Denvir, Richard Johnstone, Shae McCrystal, Alice Orchiston, Oxford University Press (2020).
DOI: 10.1093/oso/9780198869894.001.0001.

Employer opportunity to contest the ballot application

In Chapter 4 it was noted that although employers are not automatically party to PABO applications, it was determined in the *Australia Post Case* that they are entitled to be heard when an application is considered, and that they are interested parties for the purposes of appeals against the making of PABO orders.[1]

It is clear from the same case that before the FWC can make a PABO it must be satisfied that the applicant has met the statutory requirements in s 443 of the FW Act. These are: that a bargaining representative(s) has made a valid application; that the applicant representative has been genuinely trying to reach an agreement with the employer(s) of the employees to be balloted (GTRA); and that the 'notification time' for the agreement has passed.[2] Employers may challenge the making of a PABO for failure to comply with these statutory requirements, and may also challenge aspects of the proposed order, for example by arguing that the nature of the proposed industrial action was not sufficiently clearly stated,[3] or that the notice period for taking protected industrial action should be extended for anything up to the statutory maximum of seven working days.[4]

Statistical analysis of PABO applications confirms that most are not contested. During the Study period, 1,302 PABO applications were made to the FWC pertaining to negotiations covering an estimated 397 enterprises or ventures.[5] Over this period applications were contested in 279 cases (21.4 per cent), not contested in 312 cases (24 per cent), and assumed not contested in 668 (51.3 per cent) cases.[6] In the remaining forty-three applications (3.3 per cent) it could not be determined whether or not the ballot was contested, as the order or decision relating to the application could not be located or was not made (eg due to withdrawal by the applicant).

Of the 279 contested applications, 228 were lodged in relation to the Queensland Schools single enterprise agreement authorization, and were

[1] *Australia Postal Corp v CEPU* [2009] FWA 136. See also the discussion of this case in Chapter 1.

[2] As to the notification time, see Chapter 4, at n 75.

[3] See, eg, *John Holland Pty Ltd v AMWU* (2010) 194 IR 239.

[4] See *Fair Work Act 2009* (Cth) (FW Act) ss 414(2), 443(5); see further Stewart et al 2016: 976–7.

[5] See Chapter 4, n 86 for an explanation of the difference between the number of PABO applications made and the number of enterprise negotiations to which they related.

[6] Assumed non-contested is the conclusion drawn by the research team when an order for a ballot was made without a decision also being made available. The FWC does not publish a decision when it makes an order in all instances. Whilst some FWC Members will invariably provide a written decision, in other cases decisions are only published where there is a hearing which involved discussions about a change of notice period or where a ballot is contested on some other ground.

directed at the lawfulness of the bargaining representative submitting separate applications for each school involved in the negotiations. The FWC approved all the Queensland Schools applications. A further fifty-one PABOs were contested on one or more of the following grounds:

- failing to notify the employer of the application (n = 2);
- requests for longer notice periods for proposed industrial action (n = 18);
- objection to industrial action question formulation (n = 13);[7]
- good faith bargaining concerns (n = 2);[8]
- failure to meet the GTRA requirement (n = 22);[9] and
- other (n = 10).

From this group of fifty-one contested PABO applications analysed in the Study, one application was withdrawn, one was referred to another commissioner for a decision (the outcome of which could not be traced but was suspected to be 'withdrawn'),[10] six were refused, and the remaining forty-three were approved. This means that only 2.1 per cent of the 279 contested applications were ultimately refused.

Of the six applications that were refused: two were refused because the applicant had not met the GTRA requirement;[11] two were refused because the union failed to comply with the statutory pre-requisites for lodging a ballot application, specifically, failing to notify the employer of the application;[12] and one was refused because the notification time under which agreement-making commences under the FW Act had not passed.[13] It was not possible to

[7] Proposed ballot questions were changed in 1.2 per cent of cases, with 0.5 per cent of changes (n = 6) requested by the employer, and 0.7 per cent of changes (n = 9) occurring at the instigation of the FWC member who was dealing with the PABO application.

[8] *Australian Meat Industry Employees Union v Hirino Pty Ltd* [2016] FWC 2125 (6 April 2016)—the objection was later withdrawn; *Transport Workers' Union v Transdev NSW Pty Ltd* [2016] FWC 1928 (31 March 2016).

[9] See further Creighton et al 2019a, and the discussion in Chapter 4.

[10] In *MUA v Maersk Crewing Australia Pty Ltd* [2016] FWCFB 1894 (B2015/1574) the PABO application was challenged because there had been no notification time for the agreement. Upon adjudication of the notification time issue, the matter was referred to another Commissioner for consideration. No withdrawal notice or decision was later found and the application does not appear to have been the subject of a new PABO application (or 're-application').

[11] *Australian Institute of Marine and Power Engineers v Mermaid Marine Vessel Operators Pty Ltd* [2016] FWC 3495 (31 May 2016); *Construction, Forestry, Maritime, Mining and Energy Union v AGL Loy Yang Pty Ltd* [2016] FWC 4364 (1 July 2016).

[12] *RTBU and Others, Application for a protected action ballot order*, FWC PR581609 (B2016/121), 16 June 2016; *AMWU v Elphinstone Enterprises Pty Ltd* [2016] FWC 1141.

[13] *Construction, Forestry, Mining and Energy Union v AGL Loy Yang Pty Ltd* [2016] FWCFB 2878 (11 May 2016). The CFMEU lodged another PABO in *Construction, Forestry, Mining and Energy*

ascertain the reason for refusal of the sixth application.[14] The small proportion of applications that were successfully contested, and the great majority of contested applications that were approved, suggests that some employers use their capacity to contest applications to delay the grant of PABO even though there are no genuine grounds for doing so.

This is borne out by the qualitative interview findings. It is evident from the interviews with union and employer representatives that some employers object to PABO applications on technical grounds to slow the union's momentum and delay access to industrial action. As an ACTU representative explained: 'every time you go to the Commission, there's an opportunity for the employers, with their resources, to bring the lawyers along and pick arcane, technical fights with you'.[15] According to another union representative, this is a 'frustrating' side-effect of the ballot approval process:

> I find the approval process if the employer wants to challenge really quite irritating. Often I find that often it's misunderstood what grounds you can challenge on and so we'll go to hearings and end up listening to submissions about health and safety impacts and this kind of thing. Often with their legal reps knowing full well they're not grounds but it's just a way to stall the process and it's very frustrating. I feel like the Commission should ask the grounds or for submissions in advance or ask the grounds upon which they are challenging in advance.[16]

Additionally, one union representative commented that the employer's 'delaying tactic' of contesting the ballot application was not only designed to forestall industrial action but was intended to 'provoke' the union members to 'do something silly' such as walking off the job, so that the employer could then pursue the union for taking unprotected industrial action.[17] Another union representative stated that the employer used delaying tactics to cause 'stress' so

Union v AGL Loy Yang Pty Ltd [2016] FWC 4364 (1 July 2016) with this later application being one of the two applications in the Study that were refused on GTRA grounds.

[14] The FWC order in this matter refers to reasons for refusing the PABO outlined in the transcript which could not be found—*Maritime Union of Australia v MMA Vessel Operations Pty Ltd*, PR575512, 24 December 2015 (B2015/1581). The applicant re-applied for a PABO, which the employer unsuccessfully opposed on the basis of GTRA at first instance, and on appeal (*Maritime Union of Australia v MMA Offshore Vessel Operations Pty Ltd* [2016] FWC 2481 (17 May 2016); *MMA Offshore Vessel Operations Pty Ltd v MUA* [2016] FWCFB 3957 (28 June 2016)).

[15] Stakeholder Interview 9.

[16] Interview 41, Union.

[17] Interview 69, Union.

that the union members would 'give up' on their pursuit of protected industrial action.[18]

According to an ACTU representative, using the legal process as a 'delay strategy' is incentivized in specific circumstances:

> [W]here the industrial action proposed is particularly significant . . . the employer's got an incentive if it's a multimillion dollar stoppage, to try and find the loophole. And secondly, if the unions were trying to do something a little bit innovative, that was also a magnet for employer opposition.[19]

Analysis of interviews with employer representatives reveals how employers have adapted to the ballot regime and how they respond to a PABO application to maximize their own strategic advantage. Several of the employer representatives who participated in the Study described taking steps to stall industrial action. For example, one employer representative explicitly acknowledged using technicalities to obtain a bargaining advantage:

> Well, the request to have an extension [of the notice period for industrial action] or to have the period of time extended the ballot's opened for is simply a stall tactic—it buys us more time to be able to continue to have negotiations . . . So initially, you know, requests, and I can't think, one of them might have been 20 days, but, you know, we got 28 days and in fact [the union] have been in discussions with the manager to [extend to] 35 days, so that simply means that obviously the period before they could take protected action is delayed, so that's in our interests.[20]

Another employer representative who discussed using delay tactics offered the following justification:

> Last time we did think there was a heightened threat of industrial action because the fever of where negotiations were at and the militancy was very different and so it was basically, you know, if we can delay this occurring and damaging our business even by 48 hours, and 48 hours, and 48 hours because they have to reapply then it gets, you know, goes back through the registry and all that sort of stuff then that's protecting our business. So that was one

[18] Interview 18, Union.
[19] Stakeholder Interview 9.
[20] Interview 33, Employer. Similar comments were expressed in Interview 35, Employer.

> of the key things last time was well let's make sure that they dot their Is and cross their Ts and hold them to account because that buys us more time as an employer.[21]

Deciding whether or not to oppose a PABO application is ultimately a cost-benefit exercise for employers. Most employer representatives indicated that they did not routinely contest PABO applications because they had no valid basis on which to do so, or because the ballot would likely be granted even if it were opposed. For example, one employer representative said that after having weighed up the 'potential outcomes', they resolved not to contest the application: 'our experience was that . . . they generally get through . . . [even if] you're picking at a certain piece of it that you might have some success on'.[22]

Keeping on the 'good side' of the relevant FWC Member was a guiding consideration for another employer:

> We also wanted to keep in the Commissioner's good graces because if you run an argument that you know is likely to fail you're going to consume a lot of a very busy Commissioner's time, so what we said was that we'll save that time with the Commission and if the vote gets up, instead of asking for three days' notice we'll ask for seven [days' notice] of industrial action. So, that was our company strategy.[23]

The FWC members interviewed observed that a small number of employers strategically challenge PABO applications (while also noting that the majority do not). For example, one member stated:

> Yeah. [Employers game the system] Occasionally. I mean I have one at the moment. I won't identify it, but it's the same law firm that's arguing the same point in relation to this matter as it did six months ago in another matter. Which it failed. The complaint is always about, well bargaining should continue and if it continues then there's a prospect that the agreement will be made and so the union's insistence on taking industrial action is effectively then indicating that they're not genuinely trying to reach an agreement.[24]

[21] Interview 52, Employer.
[22] Interview 25, Employer.
[23] Interview 36, Employer.
[24] Stakeholder Interview 3.

In some instances, employer opposition to a PABO application may stem from a misunderstanding of the legislative requirements rather than a calculated strategy to stall. One union representative recalled a PABO application where the employer opposed the order because 'they wanted to keep talking'.[25] The union representative did not perceive this to be a 'delaying tactic', and said: 'I just think they didn't know . . . They've got a history of doing things like that . . . they don't fully understand processes all the time', and added: 'they always oppose it'.[26]

Irrespective of an employer's motive for opposing a PABO application, the associated delay for the PABO applicant can be greater than the forty-eight hours contemplated by the legislation because a Commissioner may reserve their decision and/or the matter may go to hearing. For example, an employer interviewee recalled opposing a PABO on the basis that the union had not correctly described the relevant employer entities and that there were 'irregularities' with the application. The Commissioner reserved their decision for two weeks and then made the PABO.[27] Basing a challenge on the requirement that the ballot applicant be genuinely trying to reach agreement can lead to a lengthy delay because the FWC must examine in detail the bargaining behaviour of the applicant in order to ascertain their subjective intentions.[28]

The opportunity for employers to contest also has a shadow effect on bargaining behaviour. Due to a perceived risk of contestation in some sectors, driven by decisions of the FWC relating to the notice period, some unions have adopted the practice of consenting to a longer notice period by default. This enables the union to avoid employer opposition and the cost and delay associated with a contested hearing. For instance, one union interviewee recalled that the employer 'asked for an extension to five days' notice', and the union agreed so that the employer 'didn't oppose' the application.[29] The union representative explained that there was a risk that the employer would contest the PABO application by arguing that a longer notice period was in the 'public interest', and therefore it was efficacious to consent to a longer notice period.[30] Another participant from a different union in a different industry described how agreeing to an extended notice period was 'standard' in their sector:

[25] Interview 42, Union.
[26] Interview 42, Union.
[27] Interview 52, Employer.
[28] See, eg, *Esso Australia v AMWU* [2015] FWCFB 210.
[29] Interview 68, Union.
[30] Interview 68, Union.

> Yes [we agreed to extend the notice period]. The minimum is three days, three clear working days, the commission has discretion to order up to seven clear working days' notice, there was a decision from [redacted] dealing with [redacted employees], where it was extensively argued and [the commissioner] said five days' notice . . . That now has formed the *de facto* standard in [our] sector.[31]

Quantitative analysis of a sample of PABO applications confirms that unions regularly agree to a longer notice period of up to seven business days (nine calendar days), the statutory maximum. In 27.5 per cent of PABO applications in the sample (n = 358), employers indicated that they would not challenge the PABO application if the notice period was changed by consent, and such changes were agreed by the ballot applicant in all but eight instances. Where a change was made to the notice period, the mean length of days' notice required was increased from three working days to five working days (min = four, max = seven, SD = 0.4).

While consenting to an extended notice period avoids the cost and delay of having the application contested, an increased notice period provides the employer with greater capacity to prepare for, and therefore ameliorate, the impact of the ensuing protected industrial action, thereby diminishing its effectiveness. This suggests that the practical impact of the legislative provision allowing employers to contest PABO applications is not confined to circumstances where employers formally contest the application; it also drives union behaviour in applications that are not formally contested.

Balloting requirements and associated administrative burdens

Once a PABO is ordered by the FWC, the next stage involves the conduct of the ballot itself—by an independent ballot agent. As discussed in Chapter 4, for industrial action to be approved 50 per cent of eligible voters must cast a valid ballot, and a simple majority of those who do so must vote in favour of the proposed form of action.[32] The conduct of the ballot, and the preparation of the electoral roll, is the responsibility of the ballot agent. The mode of ballot must

[31] Interview 32, Union.
[32] As to the length of the ballot 'mandate' see below at 153.

be secret, and may be carried out by postal, attendance (at or adjacent to the workplace), or electronic means.[33]

Quorum requirement

Consistent with the British research described in Chapter 1,[34] and the English railways case example in that chapter, the findings of the Study show that the FW Act quorum requirement can have a significant impact on ballot outcomes. In addition, the Study confirms that the mode by which the ballot is conducted (attendance, postal, or electronic) has an impact on whether or not the ballot is ultimately successful, and that there is a link between choice of ballot agent used and the mode of ballot.[35] Analysis of qualitative interviews provides a clear picture of how in practice the statutory requirements for balloting impose substantial administrative burdens on unions, which again is in line with union experience in Britain.

The impact of the quorum requirement on the capacity of Australian workers to take protected industrial action can be assessed by identifying the number of pre-strike ballots in the dataset that failed due to a lack of quorum and examining the proportion of non-quorate ballots in which a majority of voters approved proposed industrial action. This shows that abstentions more effectively defeat proposed industrial action than 'no' votes. This is consistent with the findings of Darlington & Dobson's study in the United Kingdom.[36]

Proportion of ballots which reached quorum

Based on the findings of the Study, failure to achieve quorum is the most common reason that industrial action is not approved by voters in a ballot conducted under the FW Act.

During the Study period, 1,253 PABO applications were approved by the FWC, and 1,203 proceeded to ballot.[37] Of the 1,203 ballots (for which 1,201

[33] FW Act ss 450, 451; the legislative 'guide' to Part 3-3 in s 406 and the 'guide' to Division 8 in s 435 both state that the provisions establish the process for employees to choose 'by means of a fair and democratic secret ballot'.

[34] See Chapter 1 at 32–4.

[35] On the choice of ballot agent, see FW Act ss 176–178A and Chapter 4 at 112–13. For comment, see Stewart et al 2016: 878–82.

[36] See Darlington & Dobson 2015. It should be noted that Darlington & Dobson's study was undertaken prior to the introduction of a quorum requirement in that country.

[37] Fifty applications were withdrawn after a PABO was made but before a ballot was conducted, and a further four were withdrawn after the ballot had been conducted. This figure has previously been

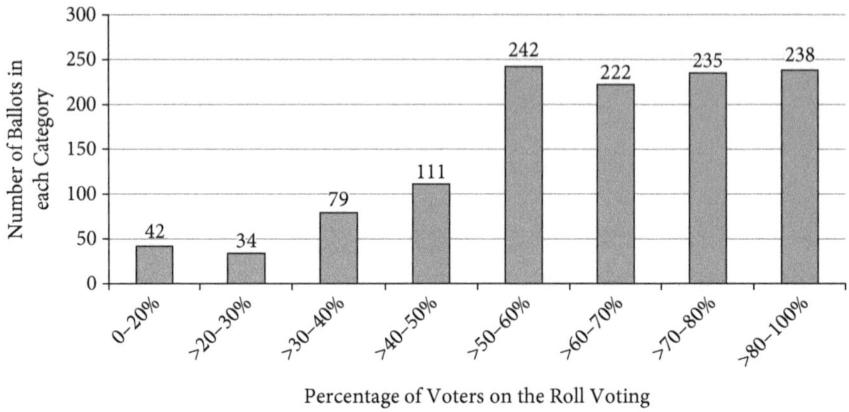

Figure 5.1 Percentage of voters on the roll voting in the ballot[1]

1. This figure presents an update of Figure 3 of Creighton et al 2018 and Figure 1 of Creighton et al 2019b to account for additional ballot results published and clarification of existing results.

results were located) 22 per cent (n = 266)[38] did not achieve quorum, whilst 78 per cent (n = 935) did. Figure 5.1 shows the percentage of voters on the roll voting in a ballot, demonstrating variation in voter turnout.

Of the ballots that reached quorum, the most commonly recorded rate of voter turnout was between 50 and 60 per cent of those on the roll (n = 242 or 20 per cent of all ballots conducted). Some ballots achieved particularly strong turnout, with 80–100% of those on the roll casting a vote (n = 238 or 19.8 per cent of all ballots conducted).

Of the non-quorate ballots, only a small number involved a turnout of 30 per cent or less (n = 76 or 6.3 per cent of all ballots conducted). The majority of non-quorate ballots were within a narrower margin: 111 ballots involved voter turnouts of between >40 per cent and <50 per cent (representing 9.2 per cent of all ballots conducted), and 79 involved voter turnouts of between >30 per cent and >40 per cent of eligible voters (representing 6.6 per cent of all ballots conducted). Of the 111 ballots that achieved a >40 per cent–<50 per cent turnout, the vast majority (98.2 per cent (n = 109)) approved the proposed strike action and so would have authorized that action but for the quorum requirement. In

reported as 1,204 (see Creighton at al 2018, 2019b; Orchiston et al 2019) which was correct at the time of publication.

38 Previously reported as 265 in Creighton et al 2018, which was correct at the time of publication.

other words, abstentions more effectively defeated the proposed industrial action than votes against might have done.[39]

Ballot mode and ballot agent requirements

Political scientists have shown, in the context of political elections, that the design of a balloting system will affect voter turnout.[40] It is therefore logical to assume that in pre-strike ballots the type of balloting system used will affect the ability to reach quorum. The following discussion considers the influence of ballot mode on voter turnout and ballot outcome, comparing the relative benefits of attendance, postal, and electronic ballots.

Relationship between ballot mode and voter turnout

Examining the differences between voter turnout and mode of ballot, Figure 5.2 shows that ballots conducted by attendance and electronic modes were likely to secure a higher voter turnout than postal ballots. For every three postal ballots that reached quorum, one did not. In contrast, 11.8 attendance ballots reached quorum for every one that did not. A similarly high success rate was seen in the small sample of electronic ballots, where quorum was achieved in all nine instances.

Figure 5.2 indicates a relationship between the mode of ballot and reaching quorum. In order formally to test whether there is a relationship between ballot mode and reaching quorum, a multi-level binary logistic regression model was used. This model predicts 'reaching the quorum' (Dependent Variable) on the basis of ballot mode (Independent Variable I), the city in which the ballot application was lodged (Independent Variable II), and the length of the vote in days (Independent Variable III). As there were so few electronic ballots, and none that failed to reach quorum, those ballots were discounted for purposes of the model.[41]

The model confirms that there is a statistically significant relationship between reaching quorum and the mode of ballot used, meaning that reaching quorum does differ according to ballot mode and that this difference cannot

[39] See further the discussion of this issue in Chapter 4 at 117–19.
[40] See, eg, Karp & Banducci 2000; Norris 2005; Kousser & Mullin 2007; Trechsel 2007.
[41] Full model output is available in Appendix 1.

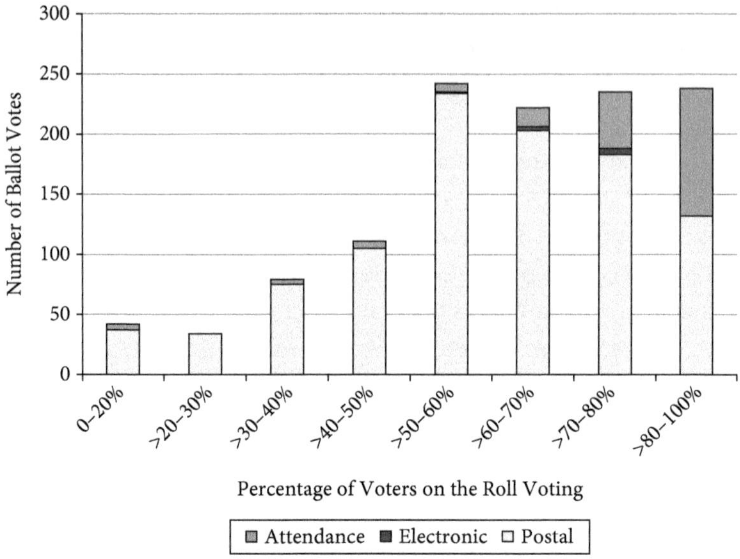

Figure 5.2 Percentage of voters voting by ballot mode[1]

[1.] This figure updates Figure 4 of Creighton et al 2018 and Figure 2 of Creighton et al 2019b to account for additional ballot results published and clarification of existing results.

be attributed to chance. Attendance ballots are associated with a 91 per cent chance of reaching quorum, compared to ballots conducted by post, which are associated with an 80 per cent chance of reaching quorum.

Analysis of the qualitative interviews revealed that unions are aware that ballot mode affects the likelihood of attaining quorum. Participants in the Study commonly considered that postal ballots were associated with a greater likelihood of not reaching quorum. Some union participants raised concerns about postal ballot papers being lost, ignored, or not readily understood by the employees who were invited to participate in the ballot, leading to a poor response rate:

> We have a strong preference for attendance ballots over postal ballots mostly because of the literacy levels of our guys . . . often times people come from non-English speaking backgrounds and it's quite difficult to get people to return postal votes, they just throw them in the bin when they receive them . . . that's a major problem for us given the response rate we need in order to succeed.[42]

[42] Interview 61, Union.

> [A] lot of people, they don't understand the process . . . if they get . . . the home-vote, they just throw it. You know, I say: 'Throw it on top of the fridge—or stick it on the fridge or the mantel piece', and then they forget about it.[43]

However, not all union interviewees expressed a clear preference for attendance ballots. Much depended on the nature of the business and the industry, as one interviewee explained:

> We cover a lot of yards that are shift work, so it's difficult to get coverage, even in a day. They might have different shift patterns, so it might take . . . four or five days for all the employees to come through the business. So, that's why we haven't got an issue with [postal], we usually say postal. If it's a smaller yard, we'll apply for an attendance ballot.[44]

In Australia until 2012, all pre-strike ballots were by post or attendance only. In that year, electronic balloting was introduced as an option as a result of the recommendations by the FW Act Review Committee, which observed that 'allowing electronic voting in appropriate circumstances has the potential to increase voter turnout and potentially reduce delays'.[45] Electronic balloting was seen by some respondents as a means by which to maximize the chance that a ballot would achieve quorum:

> I think it was the organisers that wanted to do that [an electronic ballot] more than anything because then they could go and talk to the members and talk them through it and help them vote at the time rather than going, it's all at your home address so you've got to go home, bring it back and then bring it all in. And then it would cause a multiple stage thing to get the members to actually then vote. So it's a lot easier if you can just do it online.[46]

Support for electronic ballots was, however, industry-specific. Some bargaining representatives from traditionally 'blue collar' unions expressed

[43] Interview 48, Union. Another interviewee remarked 'with postal ballots even with local government elections, for example, people get the papers and they just ignore them and don't vote', Interview 57, Union.
[44] Interview 42, Union.
[45] Edwards, McCallum, & Moore 2012: 183. Note also the discussion of potential for electronic balloting in the United Kingdom in Chapter 3, at 80.
[46] Interview 70, Union. Similar sentiments were expressed by another interviewee: Interview 4, Union.

concerns regarding the accessibility of electronic voting to their members, and the likely response rate:

> [S]ome of them are illiterate and some of them don't even know how to turn on a computer . . . a majority of our membership, if not . . . a great deal of it, would feel disconnected by the whole system if they had to do everything online.[47]
>
> I think attendance ballots are the way to go. I guess in a white collar kind of environment where everyone has access to computers and so on, [electronic voting] might be a better and more feasible option, but not in terms of our worksite, I don't think it would work.[48]

Factors impacting ballot mode selection

Whilst a majority of union participants expressed a clear preference for attendance ballots, only 15.9 per cent (n = 191) of ballots in the Study were conducted by that mode, 83.3 per cent (n = 1,003) were by postal ballot and just 0.7 per cent (n = 9) by electronic ballot.[49] Understanding why this is the case requires consideration of factors that impact the choice of ballot mode.

Under the FW Act, the mode of voting used in any particular pre-strike ballot will depend upon who conducts the ballot—the AEC or another independent ballot agent. Where the ballot is conducted by the AEC, the AEC determines the ballot mode; where the ballot is conducted by an independent ballot agent other than the AEC, the FWC determines the ballot mode. The choice of using the AEC or other independent ballot agent lies with the bargaining representative applying for a PABO.[50]

Almost all ballots during the reference period were conducted by the AEC: of the 1,203 pre-strike ballots in the Study, the AEC conducted 99.2 per cent (n = 1,193) whilst 0.8 per cent (n = 10) involved another independent ballot agent.[51] This raises two connected questions. First, what factors are involved

[47] Interview 20, Union.

[48] Interview 2, Union.

[49] Note that these raw numbers are updated from figures reported in Creighton et al 2019b—this has no effect on reported percentages.

[50] However, a proposed independent ballot agent other than the AEC must be 'a fit and proper person to conduct the ballot' and the FWC can refuse to use the proposed agent if not so satisfied (FW Act s 444(1)(b)). Where a ballot agent other than the AEC is used, the FWC also has the power to appoint an 'independent advisor' for the conduct of the ballot—FW Act s 444(3).

[51] When those ballots that did not go to vote are included, of 1,302 a total of 1,291 specified the AEC and 11 specified non-AEC ballot agents.

in the decision to use the AEC, and second, how does the AEC determine the ballot mode to be used?

According to the union representatives interviewed, there are three principal considerations influencing the choice of ballot agent: cost, convenience, and reputation.

Where the AEC is used, the federal Government bears the full cost of the ballot; where another independent ballot agent is used, the bargaining representative bears the full cost.[52] Many union respondents saw the AEC as a cost-effective, convenient choice, as one union representative explained: 'despite the fact that we've had some difficulties with [the AEC] it's still the quickest and the easiest and the cheapest for us'.[53] Another referred to the AEC as the 'default' option, simply because it is 'free'.[54] Cost considerations were particularly important for unions that were involved in a substantial number of ballots: 'the reason we'd use the AEC is because we don't have to pay for it—obviously, it's members' money and we're applying for a lot of ballots, so it's important that we use the AEC'.[55]

In addition, bargaining representatives pointed to the AEC's 'recognized authority', which provides confidence in the legitimacy of the vote. For example, one interviewee observed that 'we prefer to use the State [the AEC] because that's seen as clean and above board'.[56] Another stated that: 'from our point of view, we like the credentials and the regard that the AEC is held in'.[57] The AEC's role as a 'neutral third party'[58] was also considered to reduce the risk of employer challenge to the conduct of pre-strike ballots. Union representatives observed that there is 'less chance of an argument with an employer if you use the AEC';[59] and that 'employers have no problem with them [the AEC], it's one of those things that we can get an agreement on without too much dispute'.[60]

Ballot mode is a further important consideration in choosing a ballot agent. Electronic voting is available only if an independent ballot agent other than the AEC is used. Nine of the ten ballots in the Study conducted by ballot agents other than the AEC were electronic ballots. This suggests that the predominant

[52] FW Act ss 464–465. According to the Productivity Commission 2015: 870, in the 2013–2014 financial year the conduct of ballots cost the Commonwealth Government roughly $863,000 at an average cost of $1,500 per ballot.
[53] Interview 60, Union.
[54] Interview 49, Union.
[55] Interview 2, Union.
[56] Interview 60, Union. However, such views were not universal with one union representative observing that 'union elections should not be run by the government', Interview 8, Union.
[57] Interview 41, Union.
[58] Interview 12, Union.
[59] Interview 8, Union. Similar comments were expressed in Interview 30, Union.
[60] Interview 20, Union.

reason that unions chose to use a ballot agent other than the AEC was to access electronic voting. In the words of one interviewee, the cost incurred as a result of using a ballot agent other than the AEC was just 'part of doing business'.[61] However, other union respondents who wanted the option of electronic balloting considered the associated cost to be 'prohibitive'.[62] Several union participants expressed dissatisfaction at the AEC's inability to offer electronic balloting. It should be noted in this context that there is no legal reason why the AEC could not conduct electronic ballots. However, in an interview conducted for this Study, AEC officials indicated that it had determined not to use electronic ballots for reasons related both to resourcing and concerns over the integrity of electronic balloting methods.[63]

In terms of ballot mode and the choice between the two ballot modes offered by the AEC—postal or attendance ballot—some bargaining representatives expressed frustration that the AEC did not accommodate their ballot preference. The AEC was perceived to have 'rules' over pre-strike ballots that dictate when an attendance vote will be provided, and respondents suggested that attendance ballots were not available at particular times of the day, in particular locations, or in larger enterprises, especially if geographically dispersed. Typical comments included:

> [L]ast time I wanted a protected action ballot for a large site with three shifts I think the response from the AEC was that they didn't have the personnel to cover an attendance ballot on all of those shifts.[64]
>
> [The AEC] don't want to go to sites in the middle of nowhere at 5:00 am.[65]
>
> [G]iven the nature of where our ballots take place, i.e. regional and remote areas, it would be very difficult if not impossible [to obtain an attendance ballot].[66]

Concern was also expressed by some interviewees that the AEC was susceptible to pressure from employers, who could effectively veto an attendance ballot by indicating that they would not co-operate in its conduct. For example one union respondent observed:

61 Interview 41, Union.
62 Interview 49, Union; Interview 26, Union.
63 Stakeholder Interview 13.
64 Interview 63, Union.
65 Interview 61, Union.
66 Interview 8, Union. However, this view was not consistent across all interviewees with one union representative recalling having no problems getting attendance votes at sites in Ballarat (116 km from Melbourne) and Mildura (542 km from Melbourne): Interview 63, Union.

> I think [the AEC is] susceptible to pressure from the employers, if the employers say, okay, we don't want an attendance ballot on our sites . . . we've had some arguments with them in the past, particularly where employers have not wanted to facilitate having an attendance ballot and despite our arguments the AEC has decided to conduct a postal ballot at the employer's request.[67]

Whilst there was a common perception that it was difficult to secure the AEC's agreement to attendance ballots in certain locations or at certain times, one interviewee commented upon the willingness of the AEC to make adjustments to accommodate certain worksites:

> [T]he other difficult thing with the whole ballot process was the AEC now only ballots between 7am and 7pm and of course, we have a night-shift which starts at 10pm and finishes at 6am . . . Speaking to the local AEC they actually bent the rules a bit and they actually balloted [from] 6am . . .[68]

The existence of any hard and fast rules on when postal or attendance ballots would be used was denied by AEC officials interviewed in the Study. Instead, they emphasized that the role of the AEC was to provide 'everyone with the opportunity to participate in the ballot' and explained that there was a range of factors that impacted the final decision as to whether to conduct a postal or an attendance vote in any particular ballot.[69] In particular they commented that the industrial election officers try to accommodate the requests of bargaining representatives if possible, but cannot always do so in practice.

According to the AEC officials, the factors that may influence choice of ballot mode include: the characteristics of the employees (number, location, industry, working patterns); the importance of maximizing the opportunity of all employees to participate; AEC workload; and concern about 'the expenditure of Commonwealth money . . .'.[70] They acknowledged that determining ballot mode often involves walking a 'fine line' between satisfying the applicant's preferences and minimizing disruption to the employer. For example, where an attendance ballot is scheduled at an industrial site, the AEC will try to provide flexibility over the timing of the ballot to avoid interfering with the production schedule and to ensure that the arrangements are 'fair all around'.[71]

[67] Interview 61, Union.
[68] Interview 48, Union.
[69] Stakeholder Interview 13.
[70] Stakeholder Interview 13. Postal ballots incur costs associated with printing and postage, however attendance ballots require the AEC to have staff available to attend the workplace.
[71] Stakeholder Interview 13.

Analysis of ballots in the Study confirms that the AEC most commonly uses postal balloting. Of the ballots conducted by the AEC during the reference period, 84 per cent (n = 1,003) were by post and 16 per cent (n = 191) were by attendance.

In summary, the AEC was the most popular choice of ballot agent, in part due to the fact that the cost of using the AEC is borne by the Commonwealth Government, whereas the cost of using another independent ballot agent is borne by the ballot applicant. However, the AEC does not provide electronic balloting as an option, and does not guarantee choice of ballot mode. This was a particular source of concern to union representatives who were unhappy at the fact that they were unable to obtain attendance ballots when desired. The findings highlight that resources and other constraints on the AEC limit its ability to provide ballot applicants with their preferred ballot mode, which in turn reduces applicants' prospects of reaching quorum since postal ballots have less chance of reaching quorum than attendance ballots.

Associated administrative burdens

The ballot regime imposes administrative burdens on unions seeking to engage in protected industrial action. Typically, it is not making the PABO application itself that is particularly onerous. As one union interviewee noted, 'it's a pretty well-trodden path for us, you know, our affidavits . . . the rest of the material that's in the application that we need to put to the Commission is all essentially a template'.[72] Instead, the administrative and practical challenges for most unions, where an employer is not engaging in litigious delaying tactics, are focused on ensuring that quorum is achieved, that the ballot is successful, and strategizing around an uncertain timeframe.

It is not enough that the bargaining team consult members before applying for a PABO, and then make an application. Rather, the FW Act effectively requires unions to dedicate resources to ensuring that the members who are to be balloted: (i) understand the nature of the ballot and the importance of casting a valid ballot; (ii) actually do vote; (iii) vote in favour of the proposed industrial action; and (iv) have provided the union with up-to-date membership information so that they can be included on the roll of voters.

[72] Interview 55, Union.

Educating members, encouraging voter participation, and support for action

Part of the union workload involves educating members about the ballot process so that they understand the significance of voting. Unions need to explain to members the legislative requirements and the significance of the ballot itself, as distinct from the decision to take industrial action. Otherwise, members may fail to recognize the importance of participating in the vote or fail to distinguish between voting to approve the option of taking industrial action and voting actually to take industrial action.[73] As one union representative explained:

> [O]ur members predominately, unless they're very, very highly educated in the bargaining framework (because they've done it many, many times) you know, for them if they want to take industrial action they feel like, well they've made that decision, they can do it. They don't see the clear connection or the importance of the ballot as a process. The ballot is a legal technical thing that they have to do . . . The meeting that authorises the union to make the protected action ballot application is really important because people are actively making a decision. The ballot is kind of seen as a fait accompli, it's just a process we have to go through—and that's what people are a bit apathetic about . . . I think people go, 'Oh well, it's just a technicality, if I don't vote it doesn't matter'.[74]

Many union representatives described taking efforts to distinguish between the vote to authorize proposed action and the actual decision to strike which comes later:

> [A] lot of members there don't understand the process, so I sort of explain to them that legally the only position you have under an enterprise agreement or any action you can take when you come to this, [is] that you've got to do this [ballot]: it doesn't mean we have to take action, it just means that we need a strong 'Yes' vote to endorse action, which then gives myself and the delegates more, I'd almost say the word—well, it is work-bargaining power—at the table . . . So, I normally do an overall 'Vote Yes' letter . . . and I . . . hand that

[73] See further Chapter 6.
[74] Interview 47, Union.

> to the members and I ask them to try and update [their contact] details within a certain date.[75]

To ensure that members vote, unions generally engage in an education process to explain the legislative requirements to their members. The larger and more diffuse the membership, the longer this process is likely to take. For instance, in one negotiation involving a large number of employees spread across different locations State-wide, it took the union 'a couple of months' to 'go and educate the members about what is a PABO and why we do this' before the union could 'then go back out and seek endorsement from the members to do the PABO'.[76]

Arguably the 'delay' that the ballot requirements impose on unions includes the statutorily imposed time it takes to apply for a PABO and to organize and conduct a ballot, any time associated with an employer contesting the ballot, *and* the time it takes to fulfil the *de facto* requirement of educating members and conducting an internal poll or other process to ascertain member support. The greater the number of employees to be balloted, and the more geographically dispersed those employees are, the longer the lead time required to pursue industrial action.

Further, unions normally undertake a member-engagement strategy during the period between the initial decision to apply for a PABO and the conduct of the vote. In particular, the requirement that half of all enrolled voters cast a vote means that unions must invest resources in ensuring that members remain committed and motivated to participate in the ballot.[77] As one bargaining representative explained, with reference to the outcome of a failed ballot:

> We've sent out more communications and we've made sure an official is at the facility at the time of the ballot, which we didn't do last time—we just had trust in our leaders at the workplace to make sure that people would vote . . . that didn't work last time so this time we've made sure we have at least one official there during the voting hours to be in the lunchroom telling people, 'Remember, we've got to vote now, [have] you voted?,' that kind of stuff. And that will mean the turnout will be a lot higher.[78]

The quorum requirement influences union messaging. Union representatives described frequently having to 'reassure' members that a further vote will be

[75] Interview 58, Union.
[76] Interview 70, Union.
[77] See further Creighton et al 2019b.
[78] Interview 47, Union.

conducted later should the negotiations fail to progress after the ballot has been conducted. The following quotes from two different bargaining representatives exemplify the kind of messaging that is typically used:

> We've got an inbound and outgoing call centre and I actually put together a script for them and sent it and they called most of the members. And the basis of the script was: we're still negotiating, they've really not come at anything. We've . . . put this out to a ballot which was approved by members and now to make the biggest possible impact and to give the company the biggest possible scare, we need to all to vote yes for everything. And another reminder that a vote could help to access protected action, not a vote to take it, and a reassurance that taking action would be a separate vote that everyone could contribute to at a later date should negotiations not progress and should we get the actions through.[79]
>
> [O]ur messaging usually is—'Really, really important that you vote and you vote "Yes" on all questions. Whether or not we take action, well we'll make that decision after the ballot. So, this ballot is about your right to take action.' So, we want to be really, really clear with people that the two things are separate. So when we vote in this ballot, it doesn't mean we're going out on strike or taking any kind of industrial action, it just means that we give ourselves that right and then we'll be democratic about any decisions after that. And so . . . people hopefully understand that. So, the ballot's about having the right to do that.[80]

However, different messaging may be used depending on the circumstances, as one union interviewee explained:

> Oh look, it probably depends on the workplace. I mean, sometimes obviously protected action ballots are just used as a tool to put a little bit more pressure on the company. So, it probably depends on the mood of the workers at the time. Sometimes, you know to be honest, we'll say—'Vote on it now, we'll decide on action later,' some it's upfront, you know—'We intend to take action' or the members endorse taking that sort of action and, you know, it's made clear from the get-go. So, I think it varies based on the site.[81]

[79] Interview 56, Union.
[80] Interview 47, Union.
[81] Interview 24, Union.

As discussed above, the legislative requirements in relation to voting method and ballot agent also influence union bargaining strategy and resource allocation—notably the fact that if the AEC is used to conduct the ballot, the cost is borne by the State, whereas if another ballot agent is used, the applicant bears the full cost.[82] This pushes ballot applicants towards the AEC, a choice which has consequences in terms of the voting method used.

While choosing to use the AEC is cost-effective, it does not guarantee ballot applicants their preferred choice of ballot mode, and does not presently offer electronic voting, even though this option is available under the FW Act. These constraints impose a burden on unions. The fact that the AEC does not offer electronic balloting means that in order to use electronic voting, unions must pay the full cost of the ballot. A similar problem arises if unions do not want to take the risk of failing to achieve quorum in a postal ballot, and this is all that the AEC can offer in the circumstances. Here the union can either pay for an attendance ballot, or accept a postal ballot through the AEC and take steps to mitigate the risk of failure to attain quorum. In each case, the union must expend resources to maximize the prospects of successfully navigating the ballot process.

Maintaining membership records

As noted above, preparation of the electoral roll is the responsibility of the ballot agent who conducts the ballot. Due to the quorum requirement, coupled with the fact that the ballot result will reveal the level of union density at the enterprise, it is incumbent on unions to ensure that the ballot agent has access to a complete list of all of the members who are eligible to participate in the ballot, and that the address and contact details for those members is up to date for the purposes of preparing the roll and notifying eligible employees of their right to participate.

It should be noted that unions are unable to check the accuracy of the AEC electoral roll. Instead, individual voters must ensure that the AEC has their correct details. Inaccuracies in the roll affect voting outcomes because, as noted earlier, abstentions effectively count as 'no' votes. To overcome this, unions need to prompt members to update their details in advance of the roll being prepared.[83] The following quote from a union representative speaks to the need

[82] FW Act ss 464–465.
[83] Interview 58, Union; Interview 47, Union.

to educate members to ensure that they maintain up-to-date membership records, and to mitigate the risk of failing to attain quorum:

> A lot of the work has to get done initially by me but there's a lot of responsibility on the individuals to make sure that their address and all their information is correct because when the electoral roll sends this out if you don't receive your paper you need to contact the electoral roll. I can't do it. It's up to the individual. This is where a lot of them to be honest with you, it's the first time they've taken industrial action [then they think] oh well if there's only one [less] vote it won't really matter. But if three or four of them had the same thought process . . . then it's three votes and those three votes cost us.[84]

Variation in union experiences

Analysis of the union interviews reveals that some unions are better able to navigate the ballot requirements than others. For example, achieving quorum may be more difficult for a ballot applicant where there are a large number of employees to be balloted—especially where they are spread across multiple worksites. For some unions there is a need to devote significant effort to demystify and explain the ballot process to ensure that members remain engaged as the process unwinds. This is more complicated and requires a more concerted effort to obtain membership approval than would be the case if the union could manage its own ballot process and then take industrial action if a majority agreed in accordance with the rules of the union.

Given its complexity, the ballot regime favours 'repeat players' who are well-resourced and skilled in navigating the regulatory requirements. The delay created by the PABO process, and associated resource burden, were seen as a source of difficulty by some union interviewees:

> It's made so difficult and tiresome, this is the process. It is hard and long—whereas years ago we could walk in, show of hands, yep, bang, go in and see the boss and say right, they're ready for protected action. They're going to take action tomorrow . . . now this process has come in and it ties you all up.[85]
>
> It's a bureaucratic cumbersome waste of resources . . . the traditional process of people being able to vote by a show of hands, or being able to vote by a

[84] Interview 70, Union.
[85] Interview 28, Union.

> union conducted ballot is a much more appropriate [method] . . . this is just a process of regulating labour to slow down people's right to take industrial action. So, you know, it can slow it down significantly, and, yeah, in our view's a waste of the public resources too.[86]
>
> I think it's a bit cumbersome to make the application to the Commission then nine-times-out-of-ten the employer doesn't object anymore because, you know, it's quite a low threshold to get a protected action ballot order. Still have to go through the process, provide a statutory declaration; I mean, it just seems a bit cumbersome to me for something that's, you know, essentially a right of employees to take during collective bargaining.[87]

It should be noted that not all union respondents found the ballot process disadvantageous or difficult to navigate. One bargaining representative stated: 'in the general sense we like the ballot. Like there's a lot of unions who don't like the ballot, we like the ballot, we think it's a great campaign opportunity for us'.[88] Another union representative stated that they did not find the ballot requirements to be onerous:

> It doesn't actually, from my own point of view, it doesn't bother me too much that we do have to go through a few steps before [industrial action] can be employed. I think the process from the Commission has been reasonable in terms of them listing it within a short period of time.
>
> I don't think personally they are too onerous but they obviously I think it should be, as it is, if you've done the particular steps and that I don't think it should be made more onerous. You've certainly got to, you've got to put your . . . the ducks in place and have the steps and all that . . . But I think the steps at the moment are fairly reasonable.[89]

Ultimately, ballot applicants in certain industries or sectors may find it easier to go through the PABO process than their counterparts in other industries or sectors due to the relative likelihood of an employer taking steps to obstruct subsequent industrial action:

> [In this industry] for us to do a four-hour stoppage it might literally cost them hundreds of thousands of dollars . . . they're subcontracted to [companies] up

[86] Interview 59, Union.
[87] Interview 24, Union.
[88] Interview 55, Union.
[89] Interview 49, Union.

> the chain, so there's a lot of pressure on them from the contractors to avoid any stoppages of work because it literally costs so much money . . . these are employers who have deep pockets to fund significant legal challenges to the PABO. When I was at [a different union] we might be talking about [redacted] workers wearing stickers that say 'I'm low paid'. That was the kind of industrial action that we'd take. So the employers, they had less money, they had less of an interest in stopping the action potentially, it was more reputational damage rather than commercial damage.[90]

Taking protected industrial action post-ballot: issues in practice

Once a union has successfully navigated the ballot requirements, and proposed industrial action is authorized by a ballot, the bargaining representative and the employees represented can take protected industrial action provided that they continue to comply with the legislative requirements that were discussed in Chapter 4.[91] Any failure in this respect could be challenged by the employer, and any industrial action which had not been approved in the prescribed manner would be unprotected. This in turn means that bargaining representatives and employees need to remain vigilant to ensure that errors are not made and the rules are followed.

The most significant of the post-ballot requirements are that the action that is taken must be *the* action that was authorized in the ballot, and that each form of action that is authorized by the ballot must commence within thirty days (or up to sixty if extended by the FWC) of the declaration of the ballot result (the 'thirty-day rule').[92] Each requirement will be discussed in turn.

Action must be 'industrial action' and the action approved in the ballot and of which notice is given

To be 'industrial action' that is protected under the FW Act, any action by the bargaining representatives or employees must fall within the definition of 'industrial action' in s 19(1) of that Act, and must be the industrial action

[90] Interview 62, Union.
[91] See Chapter 4 at 104–22.
[92] FW Act s 459(1).

authorized by the ballot and notified to the employer in any relevant notice of industrial action under s 414. The importance of this is reflected in the fact that in several instances employers have sought orders from the FWC or injunctions in the Federal Court where they have asserted that the action taken by the employees did not constitute industrial action within the meaning of s 19 or that it did not conform to the description of the action that was approved in the ballot. The difficulties here are twofold.

First, the precise scope of the definition of industrial action in s 19(1) remains uncertain in a number of respects. For example, there are ongoing questions over whether or not a picket can constitute industrial action under s 19(1),[93] whilst there is also a lack of clarity as to the status of more 'exotic' forms of industrial action, such as wearing union t-shirts, communicating with the media or business clients, or taking lunch breaks in management offices.[94] For this purpose it does not matter if the action has been set out in the PABO or approved in the ballot of relevant employees. If the action is not industrial action within the meaning of s 19(1) it cannot be 'protected' for purposes of the FW Act.

The continuing lack of clarity concerning the scope of the definition of industrial action in s 19(1) means that unions and employees acting in reliance upon ballot results may find themselves faced with applications for injunctions or other forms of relief, and employees may face disciplinary action. For example, in *Ambulance Victoria*,[95] the union (United Voice) obtained a PABO which included a question seeking approval for proposed industrial action which contemplated the release of ambulance response times to the public. The proposed action was subsequently approved by the balloted employees, and in due course United Voice served notice on the employer that it proposed to release data to the media as contemplated by the ballot question. The employer then sought a Federal Court injunction to restrain the action on the grounds that the proposed release of the data did not constitute industrial action under s 19(1). The injunction was granted, with the consequence that the industrial action could not lawfully proceed. Had the action commenced before the injunction was granted, it would have been found to have been unprotected industrial action which could have led to the employer seeking damages/compensation

[93] The Federal Court in *David's Distribution v NUW* (1999) 91 FCR 463 found that picketing was not industrial action for the purposes of the definition in the WR Act. Cf *CEPU v Laing* (1998) 159 ALR 73 at 88; *Transfield Construction Pty Ltd v AMWU* [2002] FCA 1413 and the robust critique of *David's Distribution* in Creighton et al 2017: 402–4.

[94] See, eg *United Firefighters Union of Australia v Easy* [2013] FCA 763; *Ambulance Victoria v United Voice* [2014] FCA 1119.

[95] *Ambulance Victoria v United Voice* [2014] FCA 1119.

in tort or under the FW Act, whilst the employees could have been subject to disciplinary action within the terms of their contracts of employment or relevant industrial instruments. All of this despite the fact that the proposed action was included in the PABO, set out in the ballot paper, and approved in the ballot itself.

The second source of difficulty derives from the fact that once a proposed form of industrial action has been included in a PABO and approved in a ballot there is still room to question whether or not any subsequent action taken in reliance on the ballot actually *is* the action that was authorized in the ballot. This is ultimately a question of fact, and one that can be challenged by the employer by seeking a FWC order or Federal Court injunction against the conduct on the basis that it is not the action authorized in the ballot. If the action is not that which is authorized in the ballot, the action will be unprotected.

The problems associated with this requirement are demonstrated by *Esso Australia v The Australia Workers' Union*.[96] This case involved a dispute at a natural gas plant in the State of Victoria. At various times, equipment at the plant was taken offline for maintenance, a process known as 'isolation' of the equipment. To bring it back online, the equipment was 'de-isolated'. The Australian Workers' Union (AWU) sought and obtained a PABO which included industrial action in the form of 'bans on de-isolation of equipment'. This proposed form of action was approved in the ballot and in due course the AWU notified the employer of industrial action in that form. A dispute then arose between the union and the employer over exactly what 'de-isolation of equipment' meant, with the union contending that it included all the steps necessary to de-isolate the equipment, but the employer contending that it only included the last step—that of turning the equipment back on (literally turning on the switch!). The employer sought an order from the FWC against the alleged 'unprotected industrial action' which was granted. The AWU continued to assert that the industrial action undertaken was de-isolation of equipment, and sought to have the order set aside by the Federal Court.[97] The Court upheld the order, and the matter was further appealed to the Full Federal Court, where again the order was upheld.[98] However, the Full Court was divided in relation to the factual question as to what constituted 'de-isolation of equipment' for purposes of the ballot and the notice. Two members of the Court agreed with

[96] (2017) 263 CLR 551. The history of this litigation is set out in Creighton & McCrystal 2017.
[97] *Esso Australia Pty Ltd v Australian Workers' Union* (2015) 253 IR 304.
[98] *Esso Australia Pty Ltd v Australian Workers' Union* (2016) 258 IR 396, [130]–[145].

the employer, whilst one agreed with the union, with the consequence that the union and its members were found to have taken unprotected industrial action.

The *Esso* case is an example of how employers can successfully challenge and delay union industrial action over a whole range of matters including competing interpretations of the types of industrial action that the union proposes to take and that were approved in the ballot. However, it has even more significance due to the fact that s 413(5) of the FW Act provides that protected industrial action cannot be taken where a bargaining representative has contravened an order of the FWC or a Court during bargaining for an agreement. In this case the AWU continued its bans in the face of a FWC order to stop engaging in unprotected industrial action—because the AWU continued to believe that the action was protected and therefore that the order did not apply. The effect of the Federal Court decisions was that in continuing the action, the AWU had breached the FWC order, and it was subsequently determined by the High Court of Australia that s 413(5) had the effect that the AWU could not take any further industrial action during the negotiations for the enterprise agreement.[99] This effectively removed access to industrial action for AWU members until the next round of agreement negotiations in what was likely to be three or four years.[100]

The experience of the AWU provides a sobering illustration of how pre-strike ballot provisions interact with other aspects of the regulation of industrial action and can produce unintended consequences. The AWU sought permission to ballot its members to take a certain form of industrial action—where it and its members had a common understanding of what that meant. The ability of the employer to intervene and challenge that understanding led to extensive litigation, with the High Court ultimately accepting the employer's perspective. Further, because of a genuine disagreement over a question of fact, the AWU ended up breaching a FWC order and being prohibited from taking any further protected industrial action during the life of the then-current negotiations. In late 2019 the Australian Rail, Tram and Bus Industry Union (RTBU) suffered a similar fate to that of the AWU. In this instance, the Union had failed properly to post notices on various websites and at railway stations as required by an interlocutory injunction which had been issued by the Federal Court on the ground that certain industrial action proposed by the RTBU was arguably

[99] *Esso Australia v The Australia Workers' Union* (2017) 263 CLR 551; see further McCrystal 2019.

[100] Note however the view of Gostencnik VP in a subsequent case arising out of this litigation that the employees concerned could take protected industrial action again during the agreement negotiations if they replaced their bargaining representative with another one that had not engaged in conduct that would offend s 413(5)—*Esso Australia Pty Ltd T/A Esso v AWU; CEPU; AMWU* [2019] FWC 6143.

unprotected in terms of the FW Act.[101] On the basis of the *Esso* principle, this failure had the consequence that the Union lost the capacity to take any further protected industrial action in the context of negotiations for a new enterprise agreement to apply to the Melbourne metropolitan rail network.[102]

The thirty-day rule

As indicated above, each form of action that is authorized by the ballot must commence within thirty days (or up to sixty if extended by the FWC) of the declaration of the ballot result (the 'thirty-day rule').[103]

The ability to take any form of action that is not commenced in that period is lost, and then the employees and unions concerned must repeat the entire approval process if they wish to take that form of action in relation to those negotiations.[104] In addition, if the union wants to re-use any form of industrial action, the ballot must have approved multiple occurrences of that action.

These requirements compromise unions' capacity to take industrial action even after the ballot results have been declared due to the fact that they make it more likely that a trade union will make a mistake in the timing of industrial action, thereby leaving any action that is taken open to challenge.

The thirty-day rule affects access to industrial action in several ways. The rule influences how bargaining agents draft ballot papers because if a paper contains multiple forms of action set out as different questions, each proposed action must be separately approved in a ballot and one of each form of action must be taken in the first thirty days to ensure that the action remains available to the union thereafter.[105] Where multiple forms of action are included in

[101] *Metro Trains Melbourne Pty Ltd v RTBU* [2019] FCA 1265.

[102] *Metro Trains Melbourne Pty Ltd v RTBU* [2019] FCA 2034.

[103] FW Act s 459(1). The CFA has determined that a requirement to re-ballot if industrial action has not commenced within three months of the conduct of a ballot 'does not constitute an infringement of freedom of association'—ILO 2018: [814]. This suggests that the thirty-day rule would be acceptable in ILO terms, although conceivably the shorter period within which action must be taken would be regarded as rendering the re-ballot requirement unacceptable. The Australian requirement may be contrasted with the British provisions discussed in Chapter 3 at 83 which set an outer limit on the mandate of the ballot of six months (or nine months with the agreement of the employer)—irrespective of whether the action has commenced within that time. In a Direct Request to the British Government in 2019 the CEACR indicated that to the extent that this re-ballot requirement serves to limit the duration of industrial action once commenced, it is not consistent with art 3 of Convention No 87.

[104] FW Act s 459; *United Collieries Ltd v CFMEU* (2006) 153 FCR 543; *Energy Australia Yallourn Pty Ltd v CFMEU* (2014) 218 FCR 316. For discussion of the 'thirty-day rule', see Denvir & McCrystal 2017: 173–5.

[105] In Australia the bargaining representative can choose the form of the questions in the ballot (single catch all question or set out as separate questions). This contrasts with the position in the United Kingdom where if a union proposes to seek approval for both strike action and action short of a strike in a ballot, the actions must be put to the voters as separate questions: TULRCA s 229(2); see

a single rolled up question, it has also been determined by the FWC that each separate action in the rolled up question must be taken in the thirty-day period for the action to retain the mandate of the ballot.[106] Analysis of a sample of 400 PABO applications during the Study period revealed that all but one application proposed more than one type of industrial action: on average, ballot papers in the sample proposed seven types of action although there were applications which listed many more types of action.[107] To ensure that all of these different kinds of industrial action remain open to unions and employees after the first thirty days, unions often 'tweak' the wording of ballot questions in a strategic manner to enable industrial action to be taken concurrently rather than consecutively.[108] For example, the ballot papers almost always asked voters to approve action that takes place 'separately, concurrently or consecutively', such that if four-hour, eight-hour, twelve-hour and twenty-four-hour strikes are approved, workers can give notice of all four types of strike at the same time and take them concurrently.[109] In this way the legislative regime drives behaviour, sometimes forcing unions to adopt unnecessarily complicated ballot wording and to pursue industrial action in a manner that is more directed at satisfying the legislative requirements than achieving bargaining objectives.

This impact was confirmed in interviews with union representatives. In the words of one union interviewee:

> I can say that's been driven from a legal perspective more than anything rather than an organising or campaign sort . . . that approach is not my preferred approach from an organising perspective . . . if I can be frank I think that all of that's a waste of time and I'd just prefer to . . . get to a system where it's just really clear what the action is and people just do it.[110]

Many union interviewees referred to the difficulty of complying with the thirty-day rule, particularly in cases where the notice period has been extended by the FWC to five or seven working days—especially in light of the fact that, as

further Chapter 4 at 113–14, and note the different questions that were put in the English rail case study in Chapter 1.

[106] *James Cook University v NTEU* [2017] FWC 4976—in this case a question authorized the taking of stoppages of different lengths (ten minutes; one hour, and twenty-four hours). The FWC found that engaging in one of the stoppages did not activate the two other stoppages which could only retain the mandate of the ballot if they were also taken during the thirty-day period.

[107] Denvir & McCrystal 2017: 173. See also the Victoria Police ballot described at 121.

[108] Denvir & McCrystal 2017: 174.

[109] Denvir & McCrystal 2017: 174.

[110] Interview 4, Union.

noted earlier, this equates to seven or nine days in practice.[111] Where a longer period of notice is required it could eat up one quarter of the thirty-day period, making it even more difficult to complete the steps necessary to take industrial action and engage in all approved forms of industrial action before the closing of the thirty-day window. As other interviewees explained:

> Well, what happens is the ballot's approved and we've got to use that ballot in 30 days, so in a four-week period, okay? Now, we've got to give notice of that so if the employer is able to extend out your notice that you have to give to the employer, then that lessens your ability to take the protected industrial action in the 30 days . . . So, that means you only have, like [employer] were able in their negotiations and in their—when we made our application—they were able to convince the Commission to make it six days, okay? And when I say six days, that six Monday to Friday so that means you lose, it takes you nine days technically, or ten days, to give notice. So that means it only gave us two opportunities to take protected action in the first 30 days.[112]
>
> [M]y biggest concern is the notice period and having to apply for the extension. So from the date that the ballot results are out to when you have to have initiated all of the actions on your protected action ballot unless you apply for that extension is really extreme when you take into account the need to get consensus from the members and start putting into action the timetable and then to give the written notice. You actually get a really tiny period . . . So I think that that is really problematic and probably doesn't help either party.[113]

This introduces a level of technical artifice into the operation of the statutory provisions, forcing employees to take one instance of all approved action in the first thirty days or lose the ability to use it, and have to re-ballot with attendant cost and delay.

Employers have argued that the thirty-day rule leads to a 'rush' by unions to take protected industrial action within the thirty-day period in circumstances where the action may not have been taken if the rule did not apply.[114] Several union interviewees acknowledged this. For example:

[111] See Chapter 4 at 120.
[112] Interview 16, Union.
[113] Interview 57, Union.
[114] Suggested in employer submissions to the Productivity Commission Inquiry into the Workplace Relations Framework, see Productivity Commission 2015.

> [B]eing able to use it or lose it is the only real area of issue for us. If that was a little longer it would make it . . . it would be a bit more sensible. Because what that has meant in the past is for instance with our negotiations in [redacted employer] some time ago we were in the position of having to say to . . . to the sort of senior HR management well, look, unfortunately we seem to be making progress, but seeing as we don't really want to have to ballot our members again we're going to have to take some action, we're going to have to take our action, and we went around and around and around, they understood with the circumstances that we were in, they didn't want us to take action, but even if they hadn't objected . . . it wouldn't have made any difference, we still would have lost our capacity because one of their customers could have complained or the Fair Work Commission itself could have intervened. So that's a bit of a stupid quirk then, that doesn't help anybody [.][115]

However, other union participants stated that they did not try to use all forms of industrial action specified in the ballot within the thirty days, commonly because they had reached an agreement with the employer before exhausting all of the types of action that were available.

In some instances, employer negotiating tactics were cited as a reason for unions' failure to take action within the thirty days. In the words of one union interviewee:

> Certainly I've had ballots up in the past whereby actions have been endorsed and then the company will string out negotiations and I think it's 30 days that you get to take an action, that just runs through your fingers like water if the company is basically just stringing you along during that time period and then you've got to go through the whole thing all over again. It's in good faith, you think you're negotiating and the company's just stringing you along that 30 days goes in the blink of an eye, it's amazing. And then no-one wants to have to reapply for it because by then your members are a bit disheartened and wondering why it's taking so long in the first place and you lose credibility.[116]

Some union respondents described the need to have an 'enlivenment' strategy, in which a process was in place to ensure that each form of industrial action was taken within the thirty-day period and as a consequence remained 'live'

[115] Interview 55, Union.
[116] Interview 63, Union.

for subsequent use. In addition to the strategies described above, this could also involve identifying single individuals to take each form of action during the thirty-day period, such that one member might give notice of an indefinite strike (which the member then would take for a short period of time and then stop), another member might take a short strike and a third impose short work bans. While one person taking industrial action is unlikely to have any effect in practice, this allows unions to spread the burden of 'enlivenment' around members (all of whom take a short personal cut in pay) while retaining the right of all members to strike beyond the thirty-day period. Many interviewees described this. For example:

> [B]efore we apply for the PAB[O] we also make sure that there's an enlivenment plan developed to make sure that we don't get the PAB[O] up and then run around thinking about how to do it within the 30 day use it or lose it rule. So before we do the PAB[O] application first of all the team has to confer with members about the questions, identify the people who are most likely going to take the action, and identify the employer's response . . . [we] need to make sure that for enlivenment at the very least . . . [we] have people who have committed to take that particular action.[117]
>
> We've just commenced, so we've enlivened the actions, so in the [union] we actually enliven them before we go straight into . . . so we make sure that, you know, we take them all within one month so they're valid . . . We have a full plan[.][118]

The only forms of industrial action that may be taken in reliance upon a ballot are those that were approved in the original ballot, which clearly inhibits employees' and unions' capacity to adapt their tactics in response to the progress of the bargaining process. This requirement also creates an incentive for 'inflated' ballot applications in order to provide as much flexibility as possible in the bargaining process.

Ultimately, in practice the thirty-day rule operates to limit union bargaining power. As the following union interviewee explained:

> If you think of it as it's just a lever that you have to put pressure on the employer well, it's either been—you're having that lever either severely shortened or taken away from you. You're limited with how you can use it because of

[117] Interview 43, Union.
[118] Interview 3, Union.

> the Act and the Act is designed that way. It is designed to limit—it shifts the power away from a collective bargaining sense, from the employees, to the employers. It takes that leverage away from you.[119]

ILO compliance

As noted in Chapter 2, ballot requirements, like other pre-strike procedural requirements, are not necessarily incompatible with ILO standards relating to the right to strike. However to be acceptable in ILO terms any such requirements: 'should be reasonable'; should not be 'such as to place a substantial limitation on the means of action open to trade union organisations'; and 'should not be so complicated as to make it practically impossible to declare a legal strike'.[120]

As also noted in Chapter 2, the requirements set out in Division 8 of Part 3-3 of the FW Act sails very close to the wind in relation to all three criteria. Indeed, in 2010 in *Case No 2698 (Australia)* the Committee on Freedom of Association (CFA) recalled:

> . . . recalls that the conditions that have to be fulfilled under the law in order to render a strike lawful should be reasonable and, in any event, not such as to place a substantial limitation on the means of action open to trade union organisations. Furthermore, the requirement of a decision by over half of all the workers involved in order to declare a strike is excessive and could excessively hinder the possibility of carrying out a strike, particularly in large enterprises.[121]

In an Observation published in its 2012 Report, the Committee of Experts on the Application of Conventions and Recommendations (CEACR) stopped short of expressing the view that the ballot provisions in the FW Act were inconsistent with art 3 of Convention No 87, but did 'request' the Government 'to ensure that the exercise of the right to strike in practice is not restricted by unduly challenging and complicated ballot procedures', and also asked the Government 'to continue

[119] Interview 66, Union.

[120] ILO 2018: [789], [790]. See also the discussion in Chapter 2 at 55–8.

[121] CFA, Report No 357, [168]–[229], [225]. See also [229(f)]. McCrystal 2011: 171 notes that in 2009 the United Nations Committee on Economic, Social and Cultural Rights had recommended the removal of the Australian ballot requirements by reason of its concerns over the quorum requirements: CESCR, *Concluding Observations*, Australia, 22/5/09, UN Doc No E/C. 12/AUS/CO/4, [19] and [29].

providing statistics on the number of protected action ballots authorized out of a total number of applications, as well as to any important or excessive delays resulting from this procedure'.[122] Apart from a 2017 Direct Request acknowledging receipt of the requested data on the number of ballots that were authorized between 1 April 2013 and 31 March 2016, the CEACR has not made any further comment on the ballot requirements in the FW Act, whilst the CFA has had no occasion to comment on these provisions since 2010.[123] This apparent lack of detailed consideration of the Australian provisions by the CEACR is unfortunate. It means that the only formal finding by the Supervisory Bodies in relation to the ballot requirements in the FW Act (and its predecessor) is that of the CFA in *Case No 2698* to the effect that 'the requirement of a decision by over half of all the workers involved in order to declare a strike is excessive'.[124] This suggests, therefore, that the Supervisory Bodies consider that all of the other FW Act requirements are consistent with the principles of freedom of association and with art 3 of Convention No 87. Viewed in isolation this may be true. What the CEACR has conspicuously failed to do, however, is to look to the combined effect of the statutory requirements. As the findings of the Study show, the cumulative effect of the requirements in Division 8 of Part 3-3 of the FW Act is severely to inhibit the capacity of workers in Australia lawfully to take industrial action to protect and to promote their economic and social interests. As the discussion at the start of this section demonstrates, the principles developed by both the CFA and the CEACR clearly permit them to look at the total effect of ballot requirements and other procedural requirements in order to ascertain whether they constitute a *de facto* interference with the right to strike. The failure of (especially) the CEACR to do this in its consideration of Division 8 of Part 3-3 is a clear example of the tendency to lose sight of the wood due to an excessive concern with studying the trees that was noted in the concluding section of Chapter 2.

Conclusions

The findings discussed in this chapter provide an illustration of Bogg's observation that the suppression of strikes 'can be achieved through legal techniques

122 ILO 2012c: 60.

123 For the CEACR's views on the quorum requirements in the British legislation, see Chapter 2 at 55–8.

124 The CEACR directed a significant number of Observations and Direct Requests to the Commonwealth Government in the period between the introduction of the Work Choices amendments in 2006 and their repeal (and in some instances re-enactment) in 2009, but none of them related to the pre-strike ballot requirements. The 2012 Observation was the first communication directly to refer to these provisions.

that are formally permissive but practically insurmountable'.[125] In the abstract, the imposition of compulsory pre-strike ballots on trade unions appears relatively benign, and as experience in both Britain and Australia demonstrates, is difficult to challenge in political terms. However, in both countries, the simple idea that unions should ballot members before taking strike action has resulted in the creation of complex, formalistic, and highly technical legal regimes, and these regulatory choices have the effect of making strike action more and more difficult to organize and to take in practice.

The chapter has empirically examined key features of the Australian pre-strike ballot system: procedural and process limitations, including the majority and quorum requirements, ballot mode, and choice of ballot agent; the administrative burdens that unions incur by engaging in the ballot process; and the difficulties the ballot regime continues to create when employees and their representatives seek to take industrial action. Through this examination, the chapter shows that the cumulative effect of the regulatory arrangements in practice has a negative impact upon what is ostensibly a democratic process. The aggregate effect of these provisions inhibits the capacity of workers to exercise their rights. A number of key findings emerge.

The fact that employers can contest ballot applications is used by some of them to delay the taking of protected industrial action and to compromise unions' capacity to ensure that industrial action can be taken when it would have maximum impact. Further, the law has had a shadow effect, encouraging Australian unions to agree to give employers a longer notice period of up to seven business days (which amounts to nine days in practice) for the taking of industrial action in exchange for the employer agreeing to allow the application to proceed without further opposition. This additional delay has two further consequences: (i) it may diminish the effectiveness of the industrial action as it affords employers the opportunity to take measures intended to reduce its impact; and (ii) agreeing to a longer notice period, combined with the thirty-day rule, reduces the timeframe within which action can be taken.

It is clear that quorum requirements lead to a significant number of ballots failing to meet the requirements for a legally efficacious vote. This is borne out by the fact that 22 per cent of the cases in the sample were unsuccessful due to failure to reach quorum, even though in almost all instances a majority of those employees who cast a valid ballot voted in support of industrial action.[126]

[125] Bogg 2016a: 325–6.

[126] Only 14 per cent of non-quorate ballots failed to produce a majority vote in favour of at least one form of industrial action included on the ballot paper.

Australian union members rarely vote against industrial action: the problem for unions is ensuring that sufficient numbers of members vote in the first place. To overcome this, unions need to devote considerable time and resources to maintaining member lists and to member communications concerning balloting, with particular emphasis on the fact that the pre-strike ballot establishes the capacity lawfully to take the proposed industrial action, rather than constituting a decision actually to take it. Holding separate ballots at separate enterprises (as required in Australia) can make it easier to achieve quorum, but can also mean that union resources are thinly spread, especially where numerous ballots are run simultaneously.

The mode of ballot used has an impact on the likelihood of reaching quorum. Union representatives commonly perceived postal votes as being less likely to reach quorum than attendance ballots, and this is borne out by statistical analysis which shows that attendance ballots are associated with a significantly improved chance of reaching quorum. However, cost drivers and workforce variables profoundly impact union decision-making in this respect. In Australia, because use of the AEC is free, unions more often use this service, even though the AEC does not offer electronic balloting, and more frequently conducts postal ballots than attendance ballots. Consequently the ballot regime does not guarantee unions their preferred choice of ballot mode, and the high costs associated with engaging a ballot agent other than the AEC render electronic balloting (and potentially, attendance balloting) off-limits for most unions.

The qualitative findings reveal that in order to pursue protected industrial action unions must invest significant time and resources in ensuring that the legislative requirements are met, in particular, that a sufficient number of employees vote in the ballot, and that those employees vote in favour of taking industrial action. As a precursor to this, unions need to communicate with members to encourage them to maintain up-to-date membership records so that they are included on the voter list, and more generally, unions need to educate members so that they understand the significance of ballot participation. Further, where postal balloting is used, unions may develop strategies to combat the risk of postal ballot papers being forgotten, lost, or accidentally discarded. Such actions are seen as integral to meeting the quorum requirement.

The ballot regime places significant restrictions on when and how protected industrial action can be taken. Employees are limited to taking only the types of industrial action expressly approved in the ballot: this may inhibit unions' and workers' capacity to modify their tactics in response to developments in the course of negotiations. The forms of action available to unions are also constrained by the lack of clarity as to what constitutes 'industrial action' for purposes of the FW Act, with a consequent risk that the lawfulness of industrial action may be open to challenge, even though it has been endorsed by a PABO and a subsequent ballot, without challenge by the employer. Coupled with this, the thirty-day rule imposes a tight timeframe for taking industrial action, which may be reduced further by any extension of the notice period. In effect these rules force unions to adopt unnecessarily complicated ballot wording in order to have a range of escalating actions that can be 'activated' as need arises.

Having considered the interaction between a series of interrelated ballot requirements in this chapter, and empirically explored the capacity of the ballot regime to frustrate and impede the ability to organize and to take industrial action, Chapter 6 considers whether these disadvantages are to any extent offset by the potential for unions to use the ballot process strategically to signal the threat of industrial action without necessarily needing actually to take such action. It describes employers', unions', and stakeholders' overall perceptions of the PABO regime, and their suggestions to reform the perceived problems with the regime, including the issues—quorum, employer challenges, the notice period and the thirty-day rule—examined in this chapter.

6

Bargaining Leverage and Stakeholder Perceptions

Introduction

Chapter 5 examined the interaction and operation of the various ballot requirements, and empirically demonstrated the capacity of the ballot regime to frustrate and impede unions' ability to organize and to take industrial action. This chapter considers whether these consequences are to any extent offset by the potential for unions to use the ballot process strategically to signal the threat of industrial action without necessarily needing actually to take such action.

The research on pre-strike ballots in the United Kingdom, described in Chapter 1, demonstrated that in addition to the negative impacts of mandatory pre-strike ballots on access to the right to strike for workers, they can also have potentially positive consequences for union administration and operation, and associated collective negotiations. In particular, the ballot requirement had driven efficiencies within unions, leading them better to maintain member records, adopt more streamlined decision-making processes, and take steps to ensure voter turnout. It also led to better lines of consultation and communication between union officials and members.[1] The evidence from the British studies also suggests that pre-strike ballots had the effect of legitimating decisions to take industrial action, thereby countering suggestions from employers or other stakeholders that unions make industrial action decisions without consulting their members.[2] This had the flow-on effect of enabling trade unions to use the threat of strike action more credibly in bargaining negotiations, where such threat was backed up by the demonstrated resolve of the membership.[3]

The British findings are reinforced by recent Australian research showing that a range of factors can influence power relations between parties in collective bargaining, such as competitive pressures on the employer, the history

[1] Elgar & Simpson 1996: 20, 26; Undy et al 1996: 215–16.
[2] Martin et al 1991: 202.
[3] Undy et al 1996: 230; Martin et al 1991: 202; Elgar & Simpson 2017.

Strike Ballots, Democracy, and Law. Breen Creighton, Catrina Denvir, Richard Johnstone, Shae McCrystal, Alice Orchiston, Oxford University Press (2020).
DOI: 10.1093/oso/9780198869894.001.0001.

of the negotiations, and whether or not the relationship between the parties is cooperative or antagonistic in character.[4] In Australia, the structure of the regulatory regime, the enterprise focus,[5] and the shift to employer control over initiation of bargaining and agreement-making processes all shape power dynamics affecting decision-making.[6] How pre-strike ballots impact collective bargaining processes, and whether the findings of the British studies are reflected in the Australian system, is the subject of this chapter, along with an exploration of stakeholder perceptions of the Australian pre-strike ballot regime.

The chapter analyses whether the *Fair Work Act 2009* (Cth) (FW Act) pre-strike ballot provisions enable unions to gain leverage in collective bargaining by using the ballot as an opportunity to threaten industrial action without necessarily having to take it. The chapter then examines related tactical considerations for unions, before considering employer responses and the capacity of employers to use the legislation to their advantage. It then explores stakeholder perceptions of the ballot regime, drawing on analysis of the qualitative interview data collected in the Study. The chapter concludes by considering whether the disadvantages discussed in Chapter 5 are to any significant extent offset by the potential for unions to use the ballot provisions strategically; and with a discussion of suggestions made by employer, union, and stakeholder interviewees as to how the rules and processes governing the Protected Action Ballot Order (PABO) system might be reformed to address difficulties raised in this and the previous chapter.

Opportunities for bargaining power

As noted in Chapter 1, under the logic of voluntary collective bargaining, access to industrial action provides unions and their members with industrial leverage or bargaining power as a counterweight to the inherent advantages employers derive from managerial prerogative and control of private property. As Weiler observes, it is 'the strike that determines which side will find it more painful to disagree, which party will be forced to make the major moves toward compromise'.[7] However, it is clear from the findings of the Study that

[4] See further Pekarek et al 2017.

[5] Townsend, Wilkinson, & Burgess 2013: 113; Creighton 2012b: 283; Peetz 2012b: 246–7; Briggs 2001: 38.

[6] See generally Gahan & Pekarek 2012a; Cooper & Ellem 2017; Creighton 2018; Read 2018; Tracy 1987.

[7] Weiler 1980: 49.

mandating a series of publicly accountable steps before industrial action can occur creates new opportunities for unions to exert pressure in bargaining.

Analysis of the interview data reveals that a PABO application can be an effective means for unions to increase leverage (via escalating the 'threat' of industrial action), without necessarily having to resort to industrial action. This is because a successful ballot outcome signals industrial strength and accelerates the 'countdown' towards industrial action.

In general, the union representatives interviewed for the Study perceived the decision to *apply* for a PABO (with a subsequent ballot) and the decision to *take* industrial action as separate and distinct steps in escalating pressure in negotiations.[8] However, respondents expressed a range of different views as to just how much leverage a PABO application and/or subsequent industrial action would provide.

Some union representatives explained the power of a PABO application with reference to the risk of 'disruption' that employers would face from any industrial action that could logically follow a successful ballot.[9] Other representatives described a successful ballot result as a strategic signal of collective strength. For example:

> It's factored as a message . . . the conversation I had with the members is, look to be honest even if you disagree with taking industrial action have a think about voting yes for it anyway because it is the message that counts . . . in the formal process the employer sees employees vote yes because they will be looking at that and seeing how strong you are.[10]

For some union representatives, the prospect of media coverage, either of the ballot outcome or subsequent industrial action, and the opportunity to 'get the employer's name in the paper', were seen as further potential advantages of initiating the PABO process.[11] For example, one union interviewee said that once the ballot results were announced 'it actually made the papers', and this helped to shift the negotiations in the union's favour because of the employer's desire to avoid 'bad press'.[12] These sentiments were echoed by the employer representative from the same negotiation:

[8] See the discussion of the three decisions in the process of taking strike action introduced in Chapter 1, and discussed further in Chapters 4 and 7.

[9] Interview 49, Union.

[10] Interview 73, Union.

[11] Interview 22, Union; Interview 28, Union; Interview 49, Union; Interview 56, Union; Interview 67, Union; Interview 70, Union.

[12] Interview 22, Union.

> We have an employer brand. We don't want to be splashed all over the media and . . . we don't want that out there because I don't think it's a positive look.[13]

The threat of media coverage can create pressure on employers in situations where industrial action could disrupt production or service delivery. For instance, one employer representative referred to a PABO application that was timed to coincide with negotiations for a major business contract, and indicated that if the customer found out about the threat of industrial action they would 'probably cease negotiations' with the company.[14]

Interviews revealed that some unions are able successfully to threaten industrial action (via the application for a PABO), even where they have no intention of actually taking any action. As one union representative explained:

> I have to confess one of the greatest things the Liberals [conservative] ever did for us soft unions was that really lengthy and painful process to take a protected action ballot. That's actually been one of the greatest advantages for us . . . in the olden days you couldn't bluff about industrial action; you took it or you didn't take it. You were out the gate or you were not out the gate. This lengthy process of both and application and objection and things like that, it's just been a godsend for us because you can bluff the whole way through it. Even if there's no intention of taking action you can look like you're going to take action. Whereas before the ballot process and all the lengthy things the first thing the company knew about action was people were marching past the bloody manager's office out the gate.[15]

However, the ability to 'bluff' in this manner was highly sector and negotiation specific. For instance, one bargaining representative said that making a PABO application did not have the same effect as it had 'a few years ago' due to a 'downturn' in the sector of the economy in which the employer operated.[16] It also relied on the union being able to get its members to vote for industrial action in the ballot, even if they would not be prepared to take the action. Another union interviewee said that a PABO application was not an effective

[13] Interview 21, Employer.

[14] Interview 19, Employer. Note that the employer added: 'we really don't mind if we lose this contract, we're not making any money out of it', and that the employees have 'more to lose' because without the contract, the employer would not be able to pay them.

[15] Interview 56, Union.

[16] Interview 8, Union.

threat because the employer could easily call the union's bluff: 'if you're using it as a bargaining chip, a bluff, you'll be found out eventually'.[17]

For the majority of union interviewees, the PABO process in itself was insufficient to bring the bargaining process to an end or to gain a major concession from the employer. Instead, it was perceived as a step in 'ramping up' pressure, and a prelude to industrial action:

> [Applying for a PABO is a] stage of taking industrial action . . . when faced with the threat of taking industrial action each of those steps [including a PABO application] ramps up the pressure, and . . . certainly there has been occasions where the threat of an application for [a PABO] has been enough to move the employer.[18]

Accordingly, many interviewees observed that they would not pursue a PABO application unless they were confident that the members were actually committed to taking industrial action, and that taking the industrial action was the only way to legitimize what was otherwise an empty threat. For example:

> [T]he conversations that we have with the [bargaining] team . . . is that they need to make sure that . . . even before we go to the PABO application itself, they have people who have committed to take that particular action.[19]

In summary, sometimes a PABO application in itself was enough to break a deadlock in the negotiations or achieve a beneficial outcome for the union. This was also the case in relation to the conduct of the ballot, particularly where there was strong endorsement of the proposed action. However, there were also situations where there was no change in the employer's bargaining behaviour until after a union engaged in industrial action. Of course, as with industrial action, the effect of a PABO application and ballot will depend on the prevailing economic conditions, along with the capacity and willingness of any specific employer to resist such pressure.[20]

[17] Interview 66, Union.
[18] Interview 48, Union.
[19] Interview 43, Union.
[20] The broader factors that dictate the effectiveness of industrial action in the course of bargaining negotiations lie beyond the scope of this book but include: the degree of cooperativeness in the bargaining relationship, the degree of experience of participants, economic and reputational costs, delay costs, and incentives to make concessions. See Cramton & Tracy 2003: ch 4; Montgomery & Benedict 1989: 380; Tracy 1987: 149.

Follow-up data were collected from the union interviewees in order to ascertain the extent to which employees went on to take industrial action after a successful ballot. Data were recorded for forty-nine ballots conducted during the reference period, with single interest authorization ballots excluded.[21] Analysis of this dataset shows that industrial action was taken in 63.3 per cent of ballots (n = 31); or put differently, industrial action was not taken in 36.7 per cent (n = 18) of ballots. This confirms that the majority of successful ballots lead to industrial action, which suggests that the ability for unions successfully to 'bluff' is limited.[22]

Opportunities for recruitment and engagement

Analysis of the qualitative interviews also revealed that the PABO process could, at least on occasion, be used for the benefit of unions in building their relationships with their members. Some interviewees suggested that the process provided an opportunity to recruit members and/or to engage existing members:

> We would always go to negotiations before we started the ballot process, because I think members would wonder why we were sort of putting the cart before the horse.[23]
>
> The good thing about it is that it gets the members involved and they feel like they're actually doing something to better their own EBA. . . . It actually increases membership at times as well. . . . They want to have their say and they suddenly come, oh, if I'm not a member I've got to come to work for the industrial actions. So sometimes in some areas, not all areas, it's increased the membership.[24]
>
> From a recruitment point of view and walking your members through the process is actually very useful to be honest, the whole ballot process. . . . that

[21] Some research participants did not respond to requests for follow-up information. Single interest authorization ballots were excluded as they constituted a significant number of ballots conducted during the reference period and would therefore have compromised the representativeness of the sample. See further Chapter 4 at 106–8 and the Appendices.

[22] It is not possible to extrapolate from this dataset the reason(s) why 36.7 per cent of the successful ballots did not culminate in industrial action. Obtaining concessions from the employer is one possible explanatory factor. Equally, employees might have been deterred from taking industrial action due to fatigue (associated with the delay created by the PABO timeline), and/or employer scare tactics, and/or changed economic circumstances.

[23] Interview 55, Union.

[24] Interview 40, Union.

> big speech about if you want to have the vote, if you want to vote in this industrial action you need to be a member is just gold.[25]
>
> I think in this particular context what's been good about this was that it's allowed the workers at that facility to do some kind of really, really basic and simple collective action they've just never had the ability or the right to do before and so it's been a bit of an education for them about the processes that are available to them. . . . So for these people it was a very, very new experience, we think that's led to increased or heightened workplace activism and more involvement and interest in the union which has been a good thing for us over the last few weeks.[26]

In addition, one union interviewee commented that the delays in the ballot process were helpful, 'because it was about building the campaign and thinking about your engagement, that just gave us more time to do another engagement so it wasn't that problematic'.[27]

Tactical considerations

While a PABO application is a necessary precondition for taking protected industrial action, or escalating the threat of industrial action, engaging with the regulatory system carries with it inherent risk for applicants. There was a general consensus among interviewees that an unsuccessful ballot could damage the union's bargaining position and undermine its credibility. As one union representative put it, the harm caused by a failed ballot is '[g]uaranteed, because it shows . . . that the [workers] aren't prepared to take any industrial action'.[28]

Importantly, interviewees did not distinguish between ballots that were unsuccessful due to a failure to meet the quorum requirement and ballots that failed because the proposed action was not approved. In both instances there was a perceived adverse impact upon the union's bargaining position. However, the extent of such impact depended on the circumstances.

In some contexts, a failed ballot may completely undermine the position of the bargaining representative, leading to an employer breaking off negotiations

[25] Interview 60, Union.
[26] Interview 6, Union.
[27] Interview 70, Union.
[28] Interview 28, Union. The issues discussed in this section are explored at length in Orchiston et al 2019.

and putting their preferred agreement to a vote. For example one union representative described the significance of a failed ballot in the following terms: 'It destroys the credibility. I don't know how you pick yourself up from that'.[29] Several employer respondents stated that a failed ballot signalled that the membership had lost faith in the union's bargaining team and indicated that employees might be ready to 'vote up' the employer's agreement instead of holding out. For example:

> If the employees don't vote for a protected industrial action then you'd have to say that this was an action driven entirely by the bargaining representatives. That then means they're not what the employees sought. And what we try then is you would have to think that maybe our agreement, if we put it back with . . . a revised offer, in fact may get voted up as well.[30]

However, in some negotiations, a failed ballot simply delayed protected industrial action. For example, one union representative described an unsuccessful ballot as 'annoying', because 'everything works on the assumption that the ballot will get up'; but then added that it 'wasn't a huge problem' as their bargaining strategy could be revised post-ballot, and that negotiations with the employer were ongoing.[31]

A second tactical consideration is that if the ballot succeeds, the lower the level of voter turnout or support for industrial action, the less persuasive the ballot will be in escalating pressure on the employer. This came across strongly in both union and employer interviews, and is illustrated by the following comments:

> [T]he speech I give is, 'guys, if this is going to be anywhere near close 50/50, don't bother. The employer knows you're not interested in industrial action, we know we're not interested in industrial action so why would we bother [applying for a] PAB[O]?'[32]
>
> I think the results of the ballot, whereas 57%, and that equates to 25% of our total number of staff voted for industrial action. That tells us there's not much heat out there on these issues . . . If it was that bad, then you would have 80% of the staff . . . voting to go on strike but we haven't got that.[33]

[29] Interview 63, Union.
[30] Interview 34, Employer. Similar comments were expressed in Interview 16, Union.
[31] Interview 47, Union.
[32] Interview 73, Union.
[33] Interview 31, Employer.

As discussed in Chapter 5, in order to guard against the risk of low turnout and encourage a convincing 'yes' vote in support of the proposed forms of industrial action, unions have to expend considerable resources educating their members about the significance of participation (in respect of quorum) and the strategic benefits of voting in favour of the proposed forms of action.

A third consideration is that conducting a ballot exposes the level of union density in the workplace to the employer. The results of the ballot show how many employees were balloted, which equates to the number of employees who would be covered by the proposed agreement who are members of that union. This plays an important role in determining whether unions pursue a ballot application. As one union interviewee explained:

> And the other biggest thing is that it exposes your density. So as part of the ballot process you have to provide a list to the Australian Electoral Commission—the standard ballotter—and they [the employer] provide a list of employees. And they don't get the list of members which is really good so there's no identities given but they get the numbers. So they know that they have 54 employees and that at the time that the ballot was held there was 31 who were able to vote. So you don't take the decision lightly because density and employer not knowing density can sometimes very much be in your favour. So if for example we had 30% density at the site I doubt we would take the measure because then the employer knows, well, you don't really have much pull here.[34]

Several union representatives stated that they would not even consider a PABO application unless they had a certain level of density at that enterprise. For example, one union interviewee said: 'I always say to the organisers don't give me a protected action ballot to make, or an order application to me if you haven't got 70 per cent'.[35]

Employer responses

Employer responses to PABO applications feed into tactical considerations and the regulatory burden, and provide insight into how the legislation is operating from the perspective of the party whom it was designed to shield from

[34] Interview 57, Union.
[35] Interview 12, Union.

'unnecessary' industrial action.[36] The interviews also reveal how employers have adapted to the regime and how they have responded to maximize their own advantage.

Employer responses to a PABO application vary according to the likely benefits to them of the outcome, and external factors such as vulnerability to industrial action, public image, and resources. Three specific employer strategies deployed in response to PABO applications were identified by the analysis: forestalling industrial action; undermining momentum in order to frustrate the union's ability to use protected industrial action at a specific time; and creating fatigue so as to reduce employees' appetite for industrial action and force concessions.

Undermining support for industrial action

Some employers utilize the time-lapse between the PABO application and the vote taking place to discourage support for industrial action: for example, by flooding union members with communications designed to scare the employees off taking industrial action:

> Our members are getting flooded with toolbox meetings and letters from the boss and they're here all the time, so they really ramp up the propaganda of our membership when this sort of stuff happens. And you know, when you've got the boss in your ear 24/7, sometimes you start to believe them.[37]

Several employers alluded to doing this. For instance, one employer representative described sending the following message in order to diminish employee support and undermine the likely success of the ballot:

> I also need to flag, if you go down this path of protected action, it's absolutely fine—that's your prerogative, no problem whatsoever—however, we will need to know in advance. We'll have to have you taken off the after-hours roster because you can't go and support our customers seven days a week, 24 hours a day if you're not prepared to work overtime, and there'll also be an impact on [redacted client]. Now, [redacted client] for us is an important service customer, it's not our biggest service customer, but all the work we do for

[36] See discussion in Chapter 1.
[37] Interview 51, Union.

> [redacted client] is very lucrative for them. So as soon as they started hearing, oh my goodness, that means I'm not going to get my 200-odd dollars a week if I'm on the roster for after-hours, I won't be able to work at [redacted client], that's a problem.[38]

The legislation in effect creates a 'moving' timeline which makes it more difficult for unions to plan when to use industrial action. The PABO regime provides opportunities for employers to throw off the union's timeline, undermining momentum and member support for the proposed course of action. This contributes to the administrative burden that the legislation imposes on unions because ensuring participation and support for industrial action becomes more difficult the longer the process takes. A decision to pursue a PABO may be entirely democratic, but when faced with interruptions and tactics to induce fatigue, or simply the length and complexity of a large postal ballot, support may wane, and members may disengage. An ACTU representative explained this as follows:

> Number one, the delay is fatal because you can expect the employer to actively campaign against what the union is trying to organise. And the longer the process takes, the more opportunity there is for the 'no' campaign, the counterinsurgency, to be run and won. So unions want it to be quick, is one consideration.[39]

Deterring ballot participation

As observed earlier, the method of voting has an impact on ballot outcome, because attendance ballots are more likely to reach quorum than postal ballots.[40] A representative from the AEC confirmed that the AEC does not guarantee ballot applicants their preferred choice of ballot mode, and acknowledged that the AEC must walk a 'fine line' between satisfying the applicant's preferences and minimizing disruption to the employer.[41] In practice, this provides an

[38] Interview 29, Employer.
[39] Stakeholder Interview 9.
[40] See Chapter 5 at 135–8; and see further Creighton et al 2019a.
[41] Stakeholder Interview 13.

opportunity, and an incentive, for employers to object to the conduct of an attendance ballot at the work premises.[42]

According to union representatives, some employers are aware of the difference between a postal and attendance ballot in respect of ballot outcomes, and try to make it more difficult for the union to achieve a successful ballot outcome by opposing an attendance vote:

> Well, a lot of companies will go postal votes hoping that the lads haven't updated their addresses and stuff, because a lot of people move around from house to house and stuff. Attendance votes I like because they're the blokes actually on the job.[43]

One union interviewee described the reverse situation, where on two occasions employers had urged that the ballot be an attendance ballot, but then sent the employees to be balloted to work at another location so that they would be absent when the ballot took place:

> [S]ome companies have turned around and said the vote's got to be here: 'sorry I've got a job away; I just sent 10 or 15 blokes interstate or into a remote area'. That happened a couple of times and we got caught out. So . . . we'd say that all these people that are on the list must attend this date. The boss doesn't have the right to send them away somewhere else. If he does, he has to notify the AEC say probably two hours before he makes his decision, at least offer the guys to either ring in or put in a postal vote.[44]

Although it was clear from many employer interviews that employer representatives are aware that ballot mode impacts on quorum, none of the employer representatives interviewed for the Study explicitly referred to taking steps to deter employees from participating in ballots, whether by opposing an attendance ballot, or by directing eligible voters to work at another location where they could not be present for an attendance ballot.

[42] Note that to attain their preferred choice of ballot mode, it is open to a ballot applicant to elect to use a protected action ballot agent other than the AEC. However, the cost and inconvenience of doing so militates against this in many instances, Creighton et al 2019b: 369.

[43] Interview 28, Union.

[44] Interview 28, Union.

Stakeholder perceptions of the PABO regime

This part of the chapter considers stakeholders' overall perceptions of the pre-strike ballot regime in order to evaluate whether the opportunities for leverage and the potential for recruitment and engagement, discussed in this chapter, offset the negative impact, examined in Chapter 5, of the ballot requirements on unions' ability to organize and to take protected industrial action.

Some union respondents pointed out that many of the difficult issues with the PABO system had been mitigated by court and FWC decisions, and by their own experience in working out how to navigate the system. For these reasons they expressed a neutral view of the legislative regime, indicating that they did not regard it as unduly onerous:

> My personal view is the protected action ballot process is basically a dead letter these days, there's limited grounds on which the employer can object, . . . and there were a number of decisions [in 2009, just after the FW Act was introduced] . . . exploring how you met the test, but all of those issues have been resolved so it's a . . . in my view it's a very low bar to jump over. You know, all that's left is the question of genuinely trying to reach an agreement, . . . if you've been bargaining for a reasonably long period of time it's a pretty easy test to meet. . . . I think what you'd probably find is probably nine out of 10 employers don't object and that's because there's no grounds to object.[45]
>
> So then in terms of the statutory process well it's no great problem to us, . . . it's a pretty well-trodden path for us, you know, our affidavits, . . . the rest of the material that's in the application that we need to put to the commission is all essentially a template.[46]

Other union respondents took a mixed view of the impact of the legal regime, contrasting positive (discussed in this chapter) and negative features (outlined in Chapter 5) of the ballot regime. For instance:

> I mean sometimes the very act of applying for a PABO is enough to get an employer to move. So prior to the Fair Work Act you had to formally initiate a bargaining period which is a procedure under the Act and then once you were in a bargaining period then you could move towards taking industrial action. So I think all those steps, even though they're

[45] Interview 8, Union.
[46] Interview 55, Union.

> bureaucratic and they slow you down and they create barriers, they also create pressure points that you can leverage from . . . the application for a PABO sometimes is enough to get some movement, not in our industry . . . but when I was at the [redacted union] that was definitely the case. But it also obviously is bureaucratic, it takes away resources. I mean, as I said before, if the parties had put as much into the actual bargaining as they've put into applying and defending PABO, bargaining order, Federal Court applications then maybe we would have actually got somewhere on the bargaining.[47]

Most union representatives interviewed regarded the ballot regime as disadvantageous due to the delay it creates in unions' ability to take protected industrial action and the difficulty which this imposes on the timing of effective industrial action:

> And then, I guess, one of the, probably the most critical aspect for us here, is also the timeframes that you then have in terms of taking action and what kind of action are you going to be able to do or commence within that timeframe that's going to have any impact . . . So we know that from when we sort of start talking about moving to industrial action you're looking at probably six to eight weeks really, by the time we talk to everyone, you've got to get all the members together, the delegates from each area, work on what the questions are going to be and cross reference that with the other union then take it to the lawyers and redraft it.[48]
>
> And I guess the only other thing is that . . . you know, you make the application, get the order a few days later, then there's a ballot three or four weeks later, it's a long period of time. Especially in negotiations where you can only make the application 30 days before the expiry date of the agreement. You know, it's essentially a four-week process; that's a long time just to be able to exercise your right to take industrial action.
>
> The protected action application is really just an administrative bureaucracy that has to be dealt with . . . If you have to delay [industrial action] for eight weeks for some sort of administrative process to occur it's very challenging.[49]

[47] Interview 62, Union.
[48] Interview 71, Union.
[49] Interview 74, Union.

The opportunity for employers to contest, and unforeseen delays, contribute to the difficulties in navigating the process and organizing to take industrial action:

> So, yes, there's a lot of mechanical issues that have to be worked through, you know, not sort of crying into my beer about it but when we're doing it, it's very long days for us here, just to make sure you get all the paperwork right, because you don't want to be in a position of sending something to [the FWC] that's wrong and having to correct it. This last time around, well actually on both of them, the application, both applications for PAB[O]s, the Act said the Commission should hear it, if possible, if at all possible within two days and we factored that into our planning but because the employers objected to the initial one . . . we had to have a hearing, we had to then . . . the Commissioner took about two days to write the decision, so that actually blew out the timeline a little bit, and then this most recent one . . . the employer representative had that terrible fluey thing that was going around, the two days would have been the Friday, the person was crook, couldn't do it, so it was put off, it didn't actually happen until the Tuesday of the following week, so again, we lost two days, and we've factored in, in our planning, that we think this will take two days when it takes four days, you then have to, okay, in this case, go to the AEC and say, look, you know, can we crib a day out of the timeline here and crib a day here and that sort of stuff.[50]

Some union representatives, however, regarded the delay as beneficial. Again, this was context-specific and was linked to leverage:

> . . . there's one way of pressuring a company is the protected action ballot process because it is such a long drawn out process. It's not just about walking off the job, it's a long drawn out process and it takes a month to get an order for instance. By the time you make the application it is about a month to get the order then of course you've got another month to take the action. So within that period of just making the application usually—and my experiences are—that we usually reach agreement before any action is taken . . . It's useful to try and put pressure on the employer, definitely. Because they have time to think about it.[51]

[50] Interview 32, Union.
[51] Interview 67, Union.

The three-working-day (seventy-two-hour) notice requirement[52] was perceived as another significant disadvantage with the ballot regime:

> The thing about protected industrial action, the process you have to do under [the FW Act], the timeframes, the voting and all this and then you've got to put in the bans and the hours and then you've got to make sure you give them seven days' notice and it's a nightmare. To be perfectly honest with you, if I ever did it again I reckon I'd just put in an indefinite strike. I wouldn't mess around with anything because what you've got to do is ridiculous . . . And I think also it's lost its effectiveness in general because of the notice period because you could call a stop work meeting and then decide then that you weren't going back to work. So it takes away the strength that the employees would have had previously.[53]

One union representative pointed to the unfairness of employers having no notice period before they could take industrial action themselves, in the form of a lockout:

> Well look, the idea of, you know, the employer—once we take industrial action—can lock us, their position is they can lock us out at a minute's notice. So, what's the difference? It should be the same for both sides, you know?[54]

In conclusion, while in some circumstances and contexts unions do gain some degree of leverage through skilful use of the ballots process, overall these advantages are overshadowed by the demands imposed on unions by the PABO process, as described in Chapter 5. These include the challenges of achieving quorum, the burden (human resources, cost, and time) on unions in working through the process, the significant delays resulting from employer challenges, and the restrictions (including the notice period and the thirty-day rule) on when and how protected industrial action can be taken. All of these impediments institutionalized in the PABO requirements have imposed significant compliance costs on unions and have had a negative impact on unions' ability to take timely and effective industrial action. The evidence of the Study suggests that the PABO process is not 'fair', and it shifts the balance of industrial power away from unions, and to employers. Chapter 7 will examine whether,

[52] As noted in Chapter 4, the three days does not include either the day the notice is given or the actual day on which the action commences, so that in reality the action cannot commence until the fifth day at the earliest.
[53] Interview 64, Union.
[54] Interview 16, Union.

and how, it promotes or impedes genuine democracy in the decision-making processes leading to industrial action.

Stakeholder views on possible reforms to the system

Stakeholders made a number of suggestions as to how the system—particularly its structure and the substantive requirements—should be reformed to ensure that it functioned more efficiently and/or fairly, at least from the perspective of the stakeholder. These proposals emanated principally from union representatives, and focused on: the thirty-day rule; the seventy-two-hour notice period; and, especially, the ballot process—including the quorum requirement and ways of authenticating which employees were entitled to participate in the ballot. Employers and some FWC members had different concerns and proposals. In particular, there were concerns that it was too easy for unions to go to ballot, and that in consequence the 'bar' for successfully applying for a PABO should be raised.

Despite the strong criticisms of the quorum requirement expressed by unions, one employer was concerned that the quorum requirement was too low, and should be increased.

> [T]hey [the union] had 102 on the list, 51 voted, the other 51 union members didn't bother to vote, so we had at least 50% voted and then out of that they had just over half that voted yes. So to me, how fair is that? . . . there's 200 staff there, so you've got a very small percentage, the minority of people, voting to go on strike, whereas the majority of your staff either couldn't care or weren't interested. This is really unfair, the way that is.[55]

Not surprisingly, unions suggested simple reforms to reduce what they saw as the inequities of the quorum requirement: 'It should be fifty per cent of those who vote, the same as what an [enterprise] agreement process would be'.[56]

An employer association was concerned that there should be a way of authenticating which employees were entitled to participate in the ballot:

> One of the big problems is that the employer doesn't see the list of people entitled to participate in the ballot which is a major problem because they have no idea in a partially unionised workplace which employees are entitled

[55] Interview 33, Employer.
[56] Interview 40, Union.

> to take industrial action and which aren't. So you might have a 60% unionised workforce, no one rolls up for work. If the ballot succeeds and industrial action is taken, 40% of those people are taking unlawful industrial action but they have no idea what 40%. So that's constantly raised as a problem and unions argue, well, you can't see that list because you then know who the union members are.... [W]e think the employer should see the list but if they can't then there needs to be another way of dealing with the issue so that it's quite clear who's entitled to take industrial action and who's not.... Well, the employer provides a list to the Electoral Office and the union provides a list and then the ballot process occurs. And then we got a result of the ballot.[57]

Consistent with criticisms that the ballot process was too slow, some union and FWC interviewees argued that the process could and should be quicker.

> But going through the [AEC] or through [the FWC] is a slow process and I think that if you've had two or three meetings with the company and you know you're going nowhere then it should be a lot quicker to say, 'Well, we've had our three meetings, we're not going anywhere, give us the right to have the ballot.'[58]
>
> I think as a general rule [the system should aim for] three weeks to conduct a ballot and whilst I understand the resource issue I think it is an inordinate amount of time for a process which starts off with ... as a general rule you should make a determination within two days. But then we've got to wait 21 days at least before the ballot is finished and then a few more days for the declaration so ... That would be the most, if, we're talking about putting aside the policy issue, whether or not there should be such a requirement at all or whether or not you make it a bit easier for employers to object to ballots. They're policy considerations but in terms of the process, as I say the conduct of the ballot is the biggest drag on the efficiency.[59]

One proposal to speed up the ballot process, made by a FWC member, was that it should be easier to choose a party other than the AEC to conduct the ballot:

> but if you accept that ... protected industrial action is a legitimate form of action during bargaining to place pressure on the employer, then the process needs to be as efficient as possible. And one of the inefficiencies in the process is that the Australian Electoral Commission as a general rule wants 21 days in

[57] Stakeholder Interview 10.
[58] Interview 51, Union.
[59] Stakeholder Interview 3.

which to conduct the ballot. And as a general rule we make our orders so as to enable that. Which means, in effect, there's at least a three week delay plus another week potentially before a result is known. So that, it's not a legislative mechanism it's just a resource issue means that ballots can't happen as quickly as perhaps applicants would like. So if you're going to make a legislative change to accommodate that I think you need to make it easier for there to be an alternative ballot agent appointed.[60]

Union interviewees offered a number of proposals for the reform of the rule requiring approved industrial action to be taken within thirty days. Most of these involved abolition of the rule:

I think it would be better if you didn't only have [strike action] available for 30 days. . . . when you make an application, you're going to only make it available during period of negotiation, that once you make a protected action ballot and once a declaration of results confirms a majority support for those actions being taken, you shouldn't have to activate them within 30 days. You should be able to [take specific strike action] until negotiations are completed. . . . They should revise that section so as long as it's approved by membership, those actions are indefinitely available at least until the end of negotiations.[61]

Until the bargaining period has stopped or there's a replacement agreement, once you've done a ballot for industrial action, it should never die.[62]

They should revise that section so as long as it's approved by membership, those actions are indefinitely available at least until the end of negotiations.[63]

There was also a proposal that the rule be extended to 'somewhere around the six-week mark but . . . it could depend on the workplace and the industry and how one model probably doesn't fit all'.[64] Another proposal was that the rule be extended to:

60 days and then the ability to apply for the extra 60 days. . . . [The FWC] is quite willing to give the extension. But it's just sort of a waste of time that within that 30 day period you have to apply for the extension.[65]

60 Stakeholder Interview 3.
61 Interview 20, Union.
62 Interview 40, Union.
63 Interview 57, Union.
64 Interview 66, Union.
65 Interview 60, Union.

Employers, on the other hand, favoured a more restrictive approach to the thirty-day rule. One supported a Federal Court decision to the effect that that each form of approved action has to be taken in thirty days: [66]

> [B]ecause it's a use it or lose it proposition. On the basis of that Federal Court decision if you say that we want the right to take an overtime ban, a paperwork ban, a two day strike or an indefinite strike and they don't put an overtime ban on then when you get to the 30 days; they can't have an indefinite strike. So that, to us, is a very significant protection for employers.[67]

There were mixed proposals to reform the length of the notice required to be given before industrial action could be taken. The view of one FWC member was that:

> I don't know, whether you extend the notification. You could still have that as a separate process. You could have a default notification period of 72 hours and then . . . if the employer wants to have a longer requirement they can ask for one.[68]

An employer association interviewee was concerned about:

> how much specificity you've got to have when you actually give notice, the 72 hours' notice, we would want specificity at the notice stage and we want specificity at the ballot stage so that employers can defend against the industrial action. . . . If you've just got this completely open ended thing even if you've got the 72 hour requirement that's not a lot of time if you're a Qantas or Telstra or whatever and you've got to put in major contingency plans and you've only got 72 hours' notice you're entitled to know at the ballot order stage what you're potentially facing in the different types of industrial action so that you can adequately defend against it.[69]

But union interviewees simply recommended either reducing the notice period or abolishing it entirely:

> It would be beneficial for us if there was no, or if it was 24-hours' notice or something.[70]

[66] *United Collieries Ltd v CFMEU* (2006) 153 FCR 543.
[67] Stakeholder Interview 10.
[68] Stakeholder Interview 7.
[69] Stakeholder Interview 10.
[70] Interview 22, Union.

> [Unions] should not have to give notice. Once people have the ability to take their industrial action, we should be able to put it on when we feel like it because they've agreed to take it. The company knows, the company knows that the blokes have agreed to take it, you know? What the Act's designed to do is to limit the employees from advancing their claims by us, by them giving notice to their employer; so, that gives the employer as much opportunity as anything to be in a position to counter the industrial action that we are going to take. Now my view is that we don't want them to have that ability; that limits our, that limits our pressure-point, as you might say. The employers probably say the opposite to what I've just said.[71]

One FWC member suggested that 'it would be useful to legislate when the notification time ends. That would be good'. [72]

Some employers and FWC members, concerned that the PABO process could be used as leverage in the industrial relations process, and that it was too easy for unions to go to ballot, suggested that the 'bar' for successfully applying for a PABO should be higher.

There were a range of proposals for making it more difficult to get a PABO. These included increasing the time during which employers could challenge a PABO application; limiting the grounds upon which unions could argue that they had genuinely tried to reach agreement; and ensuring that industrial action could only be taken as a 'last resort'.

Some employers suggested that the timeframe for contesting a PABO application was too short: 'it was effectively something like about 48 hours'; 'in the broader scheme of things that tightness of that 48 hours or whatever was interesting compared to how long and languid other things are in the process'.[73] An employer association representative suggested that 'very few challenge it because it happened so quickly so we'd like to see a lot more at the front end'.[74] One employer explained that two days was not enough time because:

> [W]e had to get all this information together, in regards to the good faith bargaining argument [requirement that the applicant be genuinely trying to reach agreement], we knew that probably wasn't going to get up but . . . we had to get all of this information. Our site manager here had to do this massive witness statement . . . So we were really rushed for time to get that done in

[71] Interview 16, Union.
[72] Stakeholder Interview 4.
[73] Interview 54, Employer.
[74] Stakeholder Interview 10.

> order for that hearing, so that was a really tight timeframe. But interestingly, we then submitted the witness statement . . . but then the union were a bit caught off guard because they hadn't had enough time to even to go through the witness statement. Even if he hadn't done the witness statement [and instead] he went into the box, they still wouldn't have had their questions prepared and things like that. So I mean it's complete opposite to most of the failings in the court system where you feel like it's always dragged out . . . [75]
>
> The ballot orders are issued far too early in the process. In our view, there should be a higher bar to get a ballot order. You know, you should have to put in more effort to genuinely try to reach agreement, you should not be pursuing non-permitted matters and there should be tighter tests around those things. . . . [I]f you take the view that industrial action should be [permitted], we'd like it to be seen as a last resort. But the unions often apply for a ballot as a tactic . . . [and] a very high proportion of ballots never lead to any industrial action . . . And we see that as a problem because there . . . is a requirement to genuinely try to reach agreement before you can get your ballot.[76]

Many employers supported the call for more rigorous scrutiny of whether there had been 'genuine bargaining' before a PABO could be sought.

> There has to be at least three or four months' worth of genuine discussions for starters before they can put an application in; you know, that you have to go before the commission and demonstrate that there's been genuine bargaining before you're entitled to [an order] . . . [A]ll they do now is just fill out a stat[utory] dec[laration], we had three meetings and talked about this, and, you know, sign it off. . . . So there needs to be a timeline, and also, you know, another provision to stop or cease the industrial action, you know, is when it comes to significant harm.[77]
>
> You shouldn't have the right to take industrial action until you genuinely try to reach agreement which is the test but the test at the moment is applied in an inconsistent way by different members of the Commission. And there's not enough direction from Parliament about what needs to occur.[78]

Others argued that a union should only be allowed to apply for a ballot after the FWC has had the opportunity to assist the parties in their negotiations. One

[75] Interview 1, Employer.
[76] Stakeholder Interview 11.
[77] Interview 9, Employer.
[78] Stakeholder Interview 10.

employer considered that 'there should be more emphasis on driving a process to assist organisations and unions to reach agreement'.[79] Another employer's view was that:

> But there are . . . certain very minor changes you could make . . . the suggestion I made . . . was that you require the Commission to conciliate before you go through the process of the ballot order being issued I think that's a fairly minor reform that might actually assist the process.[80]
>
> There needs to be some process that both sides need to go through before they go down the path of protected industrial action. . . . [I]f the union thinks the employer's being unreasonable, they should be able to apply for some conciliation but there needs to be, and this is the difficult part, there needs to be some onus of responsibility on the outcomes and the . . . you know, you just can't walk away from that, say, well . . . that was a great meeting, I know the Commissioner said this but that doesn't suit us so we're not going to abide by it.[81]

Another suggestion was that the PABO process only be initiated if the parties were at an 'impasse':

> I think the Commission needs to . . . determine whether a ballot should be conducted by assessing whether the parties had reached an impasse.[82]

Conclusions

The discussion in this chapter has explored how the pre-strike ballot regime helps shape bargaining dynamics and influences employee and employer bargaining behaviour.

The findings confirm that applying for a PABO, and the conduct of the subsequent ballot, can be an effective means for unions to increase leverage by escalating the 'threat' of industrial action, without necessarily having to resort to industrial action to gain that leverage. A successful ballot outcome signals potential industrial strength and accelerates the 'countdown' towards industrial action. The findings also show that some

79 Interview 17, Employer.
80 Interview 7, Employer.
81 Interview 17, Employer.
82 Interview 19, Employer.

unions are able to use the PABO process as an opportunity for recruitment and engagement.

At the same time, however, the findings show that an unsuccessful ballot outcome, whether by a failure to achieve quorum, or due to insufficient voter support for taking industrial action, signals weakness, significantly de-escalates the threat of industrial action, and shifts the balance of power in the negotiations in favour of the employer. In addition, the Study confirms that some employers use the pre-strike ballot regime to their strategic advantage—for instance by capitalizing on the extended timeline created by the PABO regime and exercising opportunities to undermine employee support for industrial action. In some instances employers are taking steps to deter eligible employees from voting in order to reduce the likelihood that the ballot will reach quorum.

While the PABO system has produced unexpected benefits for unions, these benefits come at a substantial cost. As discussed in Chapter 5, in order to maximize the strategic 'benefit' of a PABO, unions must invest time and resources in ensuring that a sufficient number of employees vote in the ballot, and that those employees vote in favour of taking industrial action. In some instances, this most likely offsets the signalling effect that has been argued to be a 'positive' of the ballot process for unions.[83] The interviews with union representatives also revealed that the PABO system has a 'shadow' effect on bargaining and access to the right to strike, because some unions choose not to go to ballot due to concerns about exposure of union density or to the risk of not achieving quorum. Even where industrial action is approved, low voter turn-out or a narrow majority may signal weakness to an employer.

The constraints of the Study meant that it was not possible to quantify this effect due to the fact that only union representatives that had actually made a PABO application were interviewed. To assess the shadow effect accurately would be methodologically difficult, and would require interviews with union officials who had decided *not* to apply for a PABO. It seems reasonable to suppose, however, that such an impact would be significant. This is borne out by recent research by Stanford on the decline of strike disputation in Australia which suggests a direct link between increased regulation of the right to strike, decreased levels of strike action, and wage stagnation.[84] The potential deterrent

[83] Orr & Murugesen 2007: 285.
[84] Stanford 2018.

effect of the PABO regime on unions seeking to test member support for industrial action may form part of this picture.

Analysis of stakeholder interviews shows that unions expressed a variety of views on whether the current regulatory approach is working effectively. While a small number of union respondents saw the ballot regime overall as neutral, or as a minor inconvenience, many more union interviewees regarded the ballot regime as disadvantageous, particularly in the way in which it prolongs the process of seeking a PABO, imposes significant human resource and financial burdens on the unions, and impedes the taking of timely and effective industrial action. The findings confirm that stakeholders do not view the beneficial aspects of the regime as sufficient to offset the negative impacts with respect to the ability to organize and to take protected industrial action when it is most effective.

The chapter also describes stakeholder proposals for reform of the PABO process. Union proposals included: making the quorum requirement 50 per cent of those who actually vote; abolishing the rule requiring approved industrial action to be taken within thirty days; and abolishing, or at least reducing, the requirement to give seventy-two-hours' notice before taking industrial action. Employers and some FWC members, on the other hand, suggested a range of proposals for making it more difficult to get a PABO, including: increasing the time during which employers could challenge a PABO application; limiting the grounds upon which unions could argue that they had genuinely tried to reach agreement; and ensuring that industrial action could only be taken as a 'last resort'.

The findings in this and the previous chapter suggest, however, that such technical 'micro' reforms are unlikely to promote more democratic union decision-making about industrial action in a way that is fair and efficient. Rather, they suggest that a better balance could be struck between the public interest in ensuring democratic decision-making and the legitimate interests of organized labour by allowing unions to conduct their own ballot process within an appropriate regulatory framework without having first to apply for a PABO, face a potential delay whilst the FWC deliberates, and then wait for a protected action ballot agent such as the AEC to conduct a ballot. A key factor in pursuing this argument is whether there is evidence that the PABO process impedes, rather than promotes, genuine democratic practice in trade unions. As noted in earlier chapters, the language of democracy has consistently been harnessed by legislators and policy-makers as a shield against otherwise legitimate criticisms of mandated pre-strike ballot requirements—the very idea that a process should be 'democratic' is one with which it is very hard to disagree in principle. Chapter 7 explores the form of 'democracy' fostered by the existing Australian pre-strike ballot requirements. Chapter 8 reflects on the findings of the Study, and proposes a regulatory model that would more effectively institutionalize democratic union decision-making about taking industrial action.

7
Democratic Rationales for Pre-Strike Ballots

Introduction

> Legislation on ballots poses major tactical difficulties for the trade union movement. It is impossible to oppose ballots in principle: they are undoubtedly a democratic mechanism.[1]

As the discussion in previous chapters shows, democracy and democratic process are commonly invoked by policy-makers and legislators to justify the introduction of compulsory pre-strike ballots. For example, in 1983 in the United Kingdom the Thatcher Government's Green Paper *Democracy in Trade Unions* emphasized that the strike weapon should be 'used sparingly, responsibly and democratically'.[2] In Canada, the Sims Report noted that:

> Unions, as democratic organizations, customarily take their mandates from their members, particularly on crucial questions like the decision to take industrial action. A visible and proximate reaffirmation of that fact is healthy because it reinforces the legitimacy of the union's position in the eyes of the employer, the employees and the public at large.[3]

In Australia, 'democracy' was built into the law itself, with the 2005 compulsory ballot provisions stating that their object was 'to establish a transparent process which allows employees directly concerned to choose, by means of a fair and *democratic* secret ballot, whether to authorise industrial action' [emphasis added].[4]

[1] Undy & Martin 1984: 215.
[2] Department of Employment 1983. The history of the introduction of strike ballots in Britain is outlined in Chapter 3 at 76–80.
[3] Sims Task Force 1996 cited in Slinn & Tucker 2016: 180. The history of the introduction of strike ballots in the federal jurisdiction in Canada is outlined in Chapter 3 at 72–5.
[4] *Workplace Relations Act 1996* (Cth) (as amended 2005) s 449(1).

Strike Ballots, Democracy, and Law. Breen Creighton, Catrina Denvir, Richard Johnstone, Shae McCrystal, Alice Orchiston, Oxford University Press (2020). © Breen Creighton, Catrina Denvir, Richard Johnstone, Shae McCrystal, Alice Orchiston.
DOI: 10.1093/oso/9780198869894.001.0001.

The imposition of additional legislative constraints on trade unions is justified in public discourse by reference to the 'rights and privileges' vested in unions and exercised through strike action, along with the need to ensure that the allegedly more 'moderate' union membership can have a say on proposed industrial action to rein in the impulses of their more 'militant' leadership. When compulsory pre-strike ballots were first introduced in Britain in 1984, it was claimed that unions were unresponsive to their members, that union leaders were more militant than their members, and that strike ballots act as a moderating impact on union leaders.[5] In Australia, a ministerial discussion paper released in 1998 proposing secret ballots observed that ballots would 'strengthen the accountability and responsiveness of unions to their members',[6] ensuring that industrial action was legitimized only where the union 'had the genuine support of its members'.[7] While such claims have been subject to robust challenge by many observers,[8] they still appear from time to time—for example, in Britain in 2015 in the context of amendments to the pre-strike ballot laws to impose restrictive quorum requirements.[9]

For regulators, such justifications have the advantage of harnessing the language of democracy for what may well be undemocratic ends. As Fredman has observed, any criticisms 'can simply be labelled as "anti-democratic" and dismissed'.[10] However, the type of democracy that is fostered by a legal requirement to hold a pre-strike ballot, and how any resultant democratic process is shaped by the context of contestation in which such ballots arise, remain unaddressed.

This chapter will consider the kind of 'democracy' that results from a legal requirement to hold a pre-strike ballot in the context of enterprise bargaining under the *Fair Work Act 2009* (Cth) (FW Act). A pre-strike ballot is unlike other union electoral processes because it takes place in the context of active contestation with an employer during enterprise bargaining negotiations which may involve the exposure of sensitive information to an employer around union density and internal union divisions, and that in consequence may have a significant impact on the progress of those negotiations. Further, despite the complex legal requirements surrounding pre-strike ballots, and the associated

[5] Department of Employment 1983. The Thatcher Government position is described in Smith et al 1993: 366; Fredman 1992.

[6] Reith 1998: 1.

[7] Reith 1998: 1.

[8] See, eg, Fredman 1992; McCallum 1976; Ewing, Hendy, & Jones 2016; Ford & Novitz 2016; Dukes & Kountouris 2016.

[9] In what became the *Trade Union Act 2016* (UK); see Ford & Novitz 2016; Dukes & Kountouris 2016: 348.

[10] Fredman 1992: 24.

administrative processes, the pre-strike ballot does not result in any decision on the part of the union actually to take industrial action—that decision comes later, once the ballot results have been declared. This injects a degree of artifice into the ballot process which necessarily affects the form of 'democracy' that is fostered by the balloting rules.

Consideration of the form of democracy fostered by the pre-strike ballot requirement under the FW Act draws upon the discussion of democracy in Chapter 1, in particular the differences between representative, participatory, and deliberative democracy, and the discussion of how democracy translates in the industrial context when considering the internal decision-making practices of trade unions.

As noted in Chapter 1, various models of union democracy have been identified in the literature. Characteristically, they measure democracy by reference to factors such as the responsiveness of leaders to union members, the existence and toleration of opposition, and the degree and quality of member participation in union activities.[11] Some models mimic parliamentary democracy, advocating the protection of member interests through representative elections. In this approach, it is the ballot itself that ensures democratic imperatives are met, which Fairbrother argues means 'put baldly voting equals secret individual ballot equals democracy'.[12] By contrast, Fairbrother's own view of union democracy requires membership participation in decision-making, 'characterised by a continuous dialogue between members and delegates'.[13] Another view, proposed by Undy & Martin, is that the role of democracy in unions is to increase the influence of members in decision-making (democracy) and restrict the ability of leaders to implement their own individual visions of the goals of the unions (oligarchy).[14] Undy & Martin suggest that democracy in unions can be measured by exploring the degree to which the following governance factors promote or permit oligarchy or democracy:[15]

- the degree of participation of members in elections and the degree of competition between candidates for office;
- the existence of opposition factions and parties where national officials and policy-makers are challenged by internally organized opposition;

[11] See, eg, Davis 1987: 4–9; Lipset, Trow, & Coleman 1956; Summers 1958.
[12] Fairbrother 1984: 25. For further discussion of the 'parliamentary' model of union democracy, see Tracey 1985: 178–82.
[13] Fairbrother 1984: 23–4.
[14] Undy & Martin 1984: 187.
[15] Undy & Martin 1984: 190–240.

- the internal division of powers and associated checks on oligarchy;
- the level of internal bargaining between leaders and members; and
- the decentralization of decision-making whereby the lower the level of decision-making in a union structure, the more democratic the union.

While not all of these governance factors are directly relevant to pre-strike ballots, they provide a useful picture of the considerations that are relevant when exploring democratic practice in trade unions. Recurring themes are: active participation in decision-making by members; the responsiveness of leaders to members; the opportunity to present opposing viewpoints (and the degree to which doing so is tolerated); and the decentralization of decision-making. In this last respect, Undy & Martin observe that local autonomy is taken as vital 'if not synonymous with union democracy'.[16]

The discussion in this chapter will examine the pre-strike ballot decision-making process under the FW Act by reference to the extent to which union decision-making in the process of taking industrial action involves active participation by members, a responsive leadership, the opportunity to present opposing viewpoints, and decentralization. It will also consider whether these processes resemble a form of representative democracy or preference aggregation, or perhaps a more complex form of participatory or deliberative democracy.

As outlined in Chapter 4, the legislative scheme under the FW Act creates a series of 'decision points' for unions in deciding whether to take industrial action. Before any member of a union can engage in protected industrial action, three key decisions must be made: to apply for a Protected Action Ballot Order (PABO); to approve proposed industrial action in the pre-strike ballot; and to take industrial action once the legal pre-requisites have been satisfied. It is only the second of these decisions that is the subject of a mandatory ballot requirement: the other two decisions, while equally important to the right of members to take protected industrial action, are subject only to the internal rules of the union. In effect they are left entirely to the unions to undertake through processes of self-governance. This means that the processes that apply to the making of those decisions provide a useful contrast to the process that applies to the pre-strike ballot itself, which is entirely taken out of the hands of the union.

To consider the type of democracy that is engaged when unions make decisions about taking strike action, it is important first to understand

[16] Undy & Martin 1984: 204.

the legal context within which Australian unions operate The following discussion sets out how the legal rules in Australia dictate democratic processes within registered unions, particularly in respect of union rules and the relationship between the union and its members, before describing and discussing what the qualitative data in the Study reveal about democratic practice and strike decisions in practice.

The legal context

As outlined in Chapter 4, Australia has a long history of the external regulation of the internal affairs of trade unions.[17] Dating from the earliest days of the conciliation and arbitration system in the early part of the twentieth century, unions were subject to intrusive regulation of their membership rules, including in the admission or expulsion of members, the conduct of elections, and internal governance. This regulation was the price that the union movement was required to pay for privileged access to the conciliation and arbitration system—both as institutional players and as representatives of working people more broadly.[18] In general, they were, and remain, prepared to pay that price even though the degree of regulation involved means that Australian trade unions are subject to one of the highest levels of external regulation anywhere in the world.[19] Interestingly, the Supervisory Bodies of the International Labour Organisation (ILO) have expressed only very limited concern about this—probably on the basis of the convenient fiction that registration under the federal legislation is optional.[20]

When unions lost their centrality to the industrial relations system from the early 1990s onwards, there was no consequent reduction in levels of regulation of their internal affairs. On the contrary, as the privileges that had formerly been accorded to unions were removed, the degree of regulation of their internal affairs has not only been maintained, but has increased quite markedly in certain respects.[21] While much of this regulation focuses on the financial

[17] Traditionally British unions were subject to a much lesser degree of external regulation than their Australian counterparts. However levels of external regulation have increased very significantly since the enactment of the *Trade Union Act 1984* (UK), and now approaches those of Australia. For a brief summary of the relevant legislative developments, see Deakin & Morris 2012: 985–7.

[18] Creighton, Ford, & Mitchell 1993: 923; Portus 1958: 115; Healey 1972.

[19] Boulton 1982.

[20] This was the basis upon which ILO Conventions Nos 87 and 98 were ratified in 1973. For a detailed description of this process, and of some of the internal contradictions to which it has given rise, see Creighton 1998: 259–61, 267, and 276–8.

[21] Stewart et al 2016: 814–21.

affairs of unions, there also continues to be significant regulation of the conduct of elections, and of the membership decisions that unions can take.[22]

The law regulating trade unions is now principally to be found in the *Fair Work (Registered Organisations) Act 2009* (Cth) (FW(RO) Act) and in the associated Fair Work (Registered Organisations) Regulations 2009 (Cth).

Chapter 7 of the FW(RO) Act is titled 'Democratic Control', and sets out detailed rules for the conduct of elections for office in registered organizations and branches thereof.[23] Such elections must be conducted by the Australian Electoral Commission (AEC) unless an exemption from this rule has been granted by the Registered Organisations Commission (ROC). Chapter 6 of the FW(RO) Act, meanwhile, deals with membership, and entitles anyone who falls within the scope of the eligibility rules of a union to membership of that union, unless the person is of 'bad character'.[24] There are detailed provisions governing membership, including resignation, financial status of members, membership disputes, and the capacity to litigate membership matters in the Federal Court of Australia.[25]

As concerns the capacity of unions to discipline their members for any failure to abide by collective decisions, the FW(RO) Act provides that a member is entitled to remain a member of an organization provided that the person 'complies with the rules of the organisation'.[26] However, this must be read in the context of those provisions of the FW Act which prevent a union from taking action against any of its members for certain industrial activities and decisions. In particular, no adverse action, including the imposition of any penalty, forfeiture, or disability of any kind can be taken by a union against a member of the union in response to the exercise by that member of their 'workplace rights' or their engaging in 'industrial activity'.[27] Those rights and activities include any decisions that the member takes about industrial action, including a decision not to participate in a ballot, or in industrial action, even though it has been approved by ballot and initiated by the union in accordance with all relevant requirements. This means that a member cannot lawfully be disciplined for such non-participation,[28] even though the rules of the union might otherwise

[22] See generally Stewart et al 2016, ch 24.

[23] Chapter 2 of the FW(RO) Act deals with the registration of unions (and employer associations), whilst Chapter 5 deals with their rules.

[24] FW(RO) Act s 166.

[25] Such litigation was commonplace from the 1950s until the 1980s—largely as a consequence of ideological and sectarian fissures within the labour movement. Whilst not entirely unknown, such litigation is now much less common than in the past.

[26] FW(RO) Act s 166(1)(b).

[27] FW Act ss 340 and 346.

[28] FW Act ss 341 and 347. See, eg, *Fair Work Ombudsman v Australian Workers' Union* [2020] FCA 60, where the respondent union was fined a total of $18,000 (out of a maximum of $102,000) for initiating

require participation in a strike ballot or compliance with the decision of the majority to take strike action.[29]

The process of authorizing and conducting a pre-strike ballot under the FW Act is overwhelmingly externally regulated, such that the only scope for the exercise of discretion or autonomy by unions is: whether to apply for a PABO; whether to seek the appointment of a person other than the AEC as a ballot agent; and whether actually to take industrial action once such action has been authorized by ballot. All other matters relating to the decision to take industrial action are taken out of the hands of the union.

To inform understanding of the context in which these decisions about industrial action take place, the rules of all federally registered trade unions were reviewed to determine the extent to which democratic processes concerning industrial action decision-making were prescribed by those rules. It is, of course, clear that irrespective of what the rules might say, registered unions cannot take or organize industrial action without first securing authorization through the mandatory ballot procedure. The rules of the union could, however, deal with other industrial action issues, including the decision to apply for a PABO or actually to strike.

As noted earlier, all federally registered trade unions are required to have rules,[30] and those rules are publicly accessible on the website of the FWC. There are currently forty-five federally registered trade unions. For purposes of the review, the rules of all forty-five were searched using the terms 'strike', 'industrial action', 'industrial dispute', and 'ballot'.

Only three unions had provisions specifically requiring a member vote in a decision to take industrial action,[31] whilst a further three had rules requiring any decision to take industrial action to be a decision of the members with no prescription as to how that decision is to be made.[32] Of the remaining

disciplinary proceedings (which were subsequently withdrawn) against two members who had refused to participate in a (lawful) two-hour work stoppage.

[29] The CEACR has expressed concern about this issue in a series of Direct Requests starting in 2001 in which it called upon the Government to amend those provisions of the (then) *Workplace Relations Act 1996* (Cth) (ss 298R(a) and (b) and 298U) which prevented a union from disciplining, or adopting rules providing for the disciplining, of a union member for (*inter alia*) refusing to join in industrial action. Despite at least seven further Direct Requests (most recently in 2011) to the same effect, Governments of all persuasions have declined to address the matter. Curiously, however, the Committee has never seen fit to elevate its 'dialogue' with the Government on this issue to the level of an Observation. See McCrystal 2010: 44.

[30] FW(RO) Act s 140.

[31] Australian Education Union (clause 29(E)); Musicians' Union (clause 97(n)); and Union of Christmas Island Workers (clause 26(b)(i)).

[32] Australian Federation of Air Pilots (rule one, 17(a)); Qld branch of the Australian Services Union—clause 49(c)(B)(3); and Civil Air Operations Officers' Association of Australia—rule 22(6), the latter

thirty-nine unions, five had rules providing for the authorization of industrial action by union officials, branch committees, or the national executive.[33] There is no mention of industrial action or strikes in the rules of the remaining twenty-six unions, which is well over half of those that are federally registered.

Despite this, the rules review disclosed substantial evidence of a commitment to democratic processes within unions. Some, for instance, had specific rules governing the processes applicable to the taking of member decisions at meetings,[34] whilst a majority had rules providing for member-initiated plebiscites on any question, and extensive provisions governing the conduct of union elections by secret postal ballot.

Overall, however, little can be gleaned from the rules of registered unions about the nature and extent of democratic practice in relation to decisions concerning the taking of industrial action. Put differently, the rules reveal an ongoing commitment to democratic practices in internal processes but very little as to what this actually means in the context of industrial action. One explanation for the absence of more specific rules concerning this issue is the legislative framework itself. While unions are required to have rules, the degree of regulation of their internal practice through the FW(RO) Act and the FW Act means that they have not needed to maintain the currency of their rules or to include detailed prescription of decision-making. Many of the rule books that were reviewed were significantly out of date, often referring to repealed legislative provisions and to concepts that have little relevance under the current system of industrial regulation. In particular, the overwhelming majority of federally registered trade unions have not updated their rules to take account of the range of decisions that unions must make in the context of enterprise bargaining, and specifically by reference to the PABO process. In consequence, an understanding of democratic processes in decision-making about industrial action is not materially enriched by examination of union rules. Evidence of union practices in relation to this issue is likely to be more helpful.

rules providing, eg, that 'in all matters of industrial action the national executive shall first determine to the greatest extent possible, the wishes of the members'.

[33] Australian Meat Industry Employees Union (clause 26.9); Australian Nursing and Midwifery Federation (clause 41.1); Construction, Forestry, Maritime, Mining and Energy Union (clause 31(g)); Health Services Union (clause 29(a)(ii)); and National Union of Workers (clause 53A).

[34] For example, the Bacon Factories' Union of Employees Qld requires member decisions to be by secret ballot on request of ten members and the Flight Attendants' Association of Australia requires that all decisions at meetings of members be taken by a show of hands unless a resolution is carried which determines that the question be submitted to a secret ballot.

Democratic union practices and industrial action decision-making

As part of the semi-structured interviews conducted for the Study, union bargaining representatives were asked about their decision-making processes in the decision to apply for a PABO, and in the decision to take industrial action if and when the action had been authorized in a ballot. The interviews explored how these decisions were made, with an emphasis on the degree to which they were member-initiated. When focusing on the industrial action ballot itself, the interviews explored the interactions between union officials and members in connection with the ballot, the messaging to members about the ballot, and the vote itself.

The discussion above identified the following relevant factors that can be considered in assessing whether union decision-making practices tend towards democracy or oligarchy:

- active participation in decision-making by members;
- the responsiveness of leaders to members;
- the opportunity to present opposing viewpoints (and the degree to which this is tolerated); and
- the decentralization of decision-making.

The discussion will consider these factors in the context of industrial action decision-making by unions as described by union interviewees in the course of the Study. This discussion is broken down into the three decisions preceding industrial action: (i) the decision to apply for a PABO; (ii) the protected industrial action ballot; and (iii) the decision actually to take industrial action.

The decision to apply for a PABO

As explained in Chapter 4, before a protected industrial action ballot can be conducted, the bargaining representative(s) who wants to organize industrial action must first obtain a PABO from the FWC. Assuming the bargaining representative is a union, the union must first have decided to apply for that PABO.

As discussed in preceding chapters, that decision can be taken only in the context of negotiations for a new enterprise agreement between the employer and employee bargaining representatives. The decision to apply for a PABO is not neutral—rather, it will be shaped by a range of legal, tactical, and practical factors. For example, to obtain a PABO the applicant must be able to show that negotiations for an agreement have commenced and that the applicant is genuinely trying to reach an agreement.[35] The decision to apply for a PABO will also be influenced by the fact that the union would not want to make an application if there was a real likelihood that it would be denied and/or that a ballot subsequent upon the making of an Order would be unsuccessful. Further, making a PABO application signals to the employer that the union is considering industrial action, and as discussed in earlier chapters, if successful will provide the employer with strategic information about the level of union membership at the workplace, and the extent of support for proposed action on the part of the membership. As appears in Chapter 6, this signalling function can have both advantages and disadvantages from a union perspective, but the point for present purposes is that it is a factor to be taken into account in making decisions about whether or not to apply for a PABO.

A common theme in the union interviews was how the issue of taking industrial action was frequently raised by union members at an early stage in agreement negotiations, with the consequence that conversations around tactics, issues of legality, and the potential for industrial action occurred continually throughout a campaign. Some interviewees described members as having been 'itching for a fight',[36] and described themselves as needing to 'talk people down'[37] from taking industrial action too early. Many of the interviewees described a push for industrial action that was unequivocally member-driven, rather than initiated or driven by union officials or union processes. There was little evidence of industrial action being something that was initiated only by union officials. Rather, it appeared that across the unions involved in the Study, the impetus for industrial action was provided principally by the membership.

Turning to the decision to apply for a PABO, interviewees consistently described the decision as one part of an ongoing conversation between union officials (paid union officers), union delegates,[38] and the union members at the enterprise. That conversation very often started as early as the development of the claims to be pushed by the union in negotiations, and continued through meetings concerning the commencement and progress of negotiations. Many of the interviewees indicated that this dialogue between members,

[35] FW Act s 443.
[36] Interview 71, Union.
[37] Interview 43, Union.
[38] These are employees from an enterprise acting for the union in negotiations at that enterprise. They can properly be seen as the Australian equivalent to shop stewards in the British context, although workplace representatives in Australia are also referred to as shop stewards in some contexts.

delegates, and officials occurred directly at members' meetings where members of the union from the enterprise who would be covered by the proposed agreement had the opportunity to participate. However, in some negotiations covering very large enterprises or dispersed workplaces, interviewees described a representational model where delegates representing individual sites attended delegates' meetings to represent the views of their members.

While the decision to apply for a PABO operates as part of a broader conversation between union officials, delegates, and members, someone acting in that process has to make the decision based on an understanding of the legal framework, the state of play of the negotiations, and potential member support for industrial action. The union bargaining representatives interviewed overwhelmingly indicated that the decision was usually initiated by union officials and delegates in the relevant bargaining team based upon the considerations outlined above, and in some instances after being signed off by a relevant official or legal officer. Many interviewees were at pains, however, to point out that the final decision to apply for a PABO was made by the membership, not by officials or delegates. Some indicative comments are:

- 'members pass a resolution that directs the branch secretary to apply for a PABO'[39]
- 'members vote to endorse the decision to make the application'[40]
- 'the union acts entirely on the instruction of members'[41]

One interviewee noted that in some instances the decision to apply for a PABO would be initiated by members, 'from the floor' at member meetings.[42] Another interviewee described returning from a period of leave to a phone call from union members effectively demanding that a PABO application be made.[43] However, these were exceptions rather than the rule. Generally, the PABO process was initiated by delegates and officials followed by some form of member decision-making process.

While the majority of union interviewees indicated that the PABO decision was made by the membership, not every union involved in the Study operated on this model. In one interview, it was indicated that the PABO decision was taken or endorsed by a delegates' council because the membership was

[39] Interview 69, Union.
[40] Interview 73, Union.
[41] Interview 20, Union.
[42] Interview 22, Union.
[43] Interview 63, Union.

dispersed over a number of different sites.[44] In another, it was indicated that union delegates and officials took the decision, which was then discussed with members by delegates,[45] and in a third, it was indicated that it was the union that made the decision.[46]

In discussing the member decision-making process, most interviewees referred to 'member endorsement' or 'member vote' at a member meeting, generally conducted through a show of hands. However, some bargaining representatives described more formal processes, or processes adapted to the needs of a particular enterprise or site. One interviewee indicated that all PABO decisions in their union were made through the conduct of a secret ballot of members,[47] and another indicated that their union conducted 'advisory ballots' at each separate work site to authorize a PABO application.[48] Another interviewee stated that their approach to PABO authorization varied depending on work-site and workplace culture, using both mass member meetings and more informal organized conversations with smaller groups of members,[49] whilst yet another described a highly consultative, individual approach which began well before such a decision was taken:

> We do a lot of background work . . . we phone people and ask them directly, members, whether they think, you know, the negotiations are going well, do they think industrial action is appropriate, that sort of thing, well before we even think seriously about making an application for a PABO.[50]

Interviewees consistently said that the decision to apply for a PABO was made by the membership, on the advice and sometimes at the instigation of, union officials and delegates. The evidence gathered in the Study suggested that in most unions there was active participation in the PABO decision-making process by those union members who chose to be involved by attending member meetings, whilst in other unions, the membership was consulted individually through one-on-one conversations. There was substantial evidence that union leaders were responsive to the membership and to member concerns, and that the decision-making process was characterized by frequent communication between members and delegates and officials in respect of progress in

[44] Interview 70, Union; Interview 16, Union.
[45] Interview 55, Union.
[46] Interview 41, Union.
[47] Interview 14, Union.
[48] Interview 32, Union.
[49] Interview 48, Union.
[50] Interview 43, Union.

negotiations and potential industrial action. The processes that were described were also almost uniformly decentralized, with direct member meetings appearing to be the norm, while representative meetings were less common (but necessary in some cases for geographical or practical reasons).

The data do not provide a clear indication as to the extent to which there was opportunity for opposing viewpoints to be heard when deciding whether to apply for a PABO. It seems reasonable to assume that member meetings and the occasional use of internal union-administered ballots to make the decision to apply for a PABO provide opportunities for expressions of dissent, although it was not possible in the Study to test the extent to which this was true in practice. Further, it was also clear that union officials were aware of the tactical implications of seeking a PABO, and maintained control over whether the question of whether to apply could even be put to members. Two interviewees in particular described a process where the union first needed to be convinced that there was sufficient member support for industrial action before a PABO application could be canvassed. One of these interviewees described using a petition model to garner support amongst members for industrial action before a PABO application could be made:

> the last step before we even file for a protected action ballot order is I want our members to sign a petition, and the petition that I have is very similar to the one that we have to file with the Australian Electoral Commission . . . I want to know how many guys, and I said [to the delegates] you need to have the conversation with them [the members] are you prepared to take industrial action?[51]

The second interviewee described the conversations that were had with union delegates at the relevant sites to determine whether industrial action was even something that could be considered in an industrial campaign from the outset:

> I will have a number of teleconferences with them [the delegates] and I will say I want the mapping, get out and map those yards, you tell me how many employees are there and how many members we've got and we will discuss that information. So before I even walk into the room for the first meeting I will know we are never going to be able to take protected action here, we just don't have the strength.[52]

[51] Interview 58, Union.
[52] Interview 12, Union.

These examples clearly show that making PABO applications (and any pre-strike ballot) are part of the union's tactical arsenal and, if deployed without any realistic prospect of success, may harm the negotiating position of the union. Therefore, while the decision to make a PABO application may be pursued in a democratic manner, it is likely that in many instances the option of applying for a PABO is simply not put to the membership where there are concerns about the likelihood of success or the chances of sufficient numbers being prepared actually to take industrial action, even assuming a successful ballot outcome. This effect is likely to be much greater than the Study data suggest due to the fact that by definition bargaining representatives who were interviewed had submitted PABO applications. The data do not make it possible to determine how often and in what circumstances the question of whether to make a PABO application and/or to take industrial action following a successful ballot is withheld from members by union officials without extensive (or any) member consultation.

The protected industrial action ballot

Once the FWC makes a PABO, the ballot itself must be conducted in accordance with the terms of the Order and the provisions of the FW Act. As outlined in earlier chapters, the ballot must be conducted by an independent ballot agent who will be either the AEC or another agent appointed by the FWC at the suggestion of the PABO applicant.[53] Overwhelmingly, pre-strike ballots are conducted by the AEC.

Because the ballot process is conducted in accordance with the provisions of the FW Act, there is no scope for decision-making by unions in this context, except in a decision to cancel a ballot after an Order has been made. Such a decision may be taken by reference to the impact at the bargaining table of a successful PABO application, and while decisions to cancel a ballot were not specifically discussed in the interviews, the impression given by some interviewees was that such decisions would usually be taken at a members meeting.

All ballots conducted under the statutory scheme are part of a democratic process, albeit one essentially involving preference aggregation. An electoral roll is established by reference to union and employer records. All those on the electoral roll are given the opportunity to vote for or against proposed forms of industrial action in a secret ballot conducted by postal, attendance, or

[53] FW Act s 443(4).

electronic means. The results are collated by the independent ballot agent, and the outcome is declared and published on the FWC website.

While the process itself may serve the purpose of ensuring that all affected members of a union get an opportunity to 'have a say' on proposed industrial action, it is not necessarily the case that the official ballot itself is the forum in which the genuine views of the membership are expressed. The importance of the ballot in fulfilling the legal requirements to take lawful industrial action under the FW Act, and the public nature of the ballot where the results are published on the FWC website, necessarily influence how the ballot is viewed by unions, and the messaging that is conveyed to union members.

Union officials and delegates are acutely aware of the signalling effect of the ballot and the potential impact of the ballot outcome on ongoing negotiations. In practice, this affects the messaging that unions provide to members in preparation for the ballot. Three very strong themes about union messaging emerged from the interviews.

First, unions appear consistently and repeatedly to stress the fact to their members that the formal ballot is not a ballot actually to take industrial action. Instead, union messaging emphasizes that the ballot is a necessary pre-requisite to taking lawful industrial action, and that any decision actually to take industrial action would be made after the ballot results were declared. Interviewees consistently repeated that members were told that the actual decision would be made later and that they would have an opportunity at that point to have a say on whether the action should be taken. Examples of this approach are:

> And then we say, 'Will I have to take the action if I vote "Yes?" The answer is "No", you know what I mean? The vote only authorises . . . industrial action. If and when any action is taken, this will be decided in the normal way: Your union representatives will call meetings, we'll discuss the issues and a decision on what protected industrial action to take is made'.[54]
>
> And we will have another vote after this when it actually comes to the crunch in putting in the notice of industrial action what we're going to do and when we're going to do it.[55]
>
> So when we vote in this ballot, it doesn't mean we're going out on strike or taking any kind of industrial action, it just means that we give ourselves that right and then we'll be democratic about any decisions after that.[56]

[54] Interview 16, Union.
[55] Interview 73, Union.
[56] Interview 47, Union.

Second, the messaging that the ballot itself is not a vote actually to take industrial action often included intimations that it was important for members to vote 'yes', even if they were not sure whether they would subsequently support taking industrial action. This was because of the message that a strong yes vote would send to the employer and the potential impact this could have on negotiations. For example:

> The conversation I had with the members is, 'look to be honest even if you disagree with taking industrial action have a think about voting yes for it anyway because it is the message that counts'. [57]
>
> What we explain to members is that for you to vote in a protected action ballot is not you voting to take industrial action. What it is it's you voting to put pressure on the employer that you may take action at a later date.[58]
>
> So this is what I say to members always, there are two separate steps, one step is the actual ballot process itself and at this point the critical issue is that in order to be successful members have to vote and vote yes to all the options that are there, that's step number one. The outcome of the ballot is significant because the employer understands the strength of the members' feelings about the issues under negotiation through how many returned the ballot and the answers to each question, that's step number one.[59]
>
> We always say, 'Look, it's really, really important that you vote "Yes" and it's a really, really strong turnout and a really, really strong "Yes" vote because that shows everyone that we're united and acting together'.[60]

A third theme was the need to convey to members the fact that the ballot process was one that was mandated by the FW Act, and that the process was necessary to fulfil the requirements under that Act so that industrial action could remain available as an option for members in respect of negotiations. For example:

> Please vote yes to all the actions. And it doesn't mean that you have to take the actions. There will still be votes and decisions made later but if you vote yes to all the actions then that gives you the authority to take those actions if and when you want to.[61]

[57] Interview 73, Union.
[58] Interview 60, Union.
[59] Interview 46, Union.
[60] Interview 47, Union.
[61] Interview 57, Union.

> I put out a flyer to our . . . members, okay so, and then in that flyer we, well I say, 'You must vote "Yes" to all the questions. Why vote yes? Under the [FW Act] there must be a secret ballot before unions can even threaten industrial action against your employer for a new agreement. If there's a "No" vote your union representatives will face up to your employer and be unable even to threaten any industrial action'.[62]

Connected to this was an understanding of the importance of meeting quorum and the potential impact that abstaining from voting could have on the ballot outcome. One interviewee, for example, described conversations with union members who were reluctant to take industrial action, where they were encouraged to vote, even if only to vote no, in order to achieve quorum.[63] Another described similar messaging to members used through the union's call centre to remind members that an abstention would count as a no vote:

> [T]he clear message we send, and we generally get people on the phone just ringing members to remind them to vote, we generally say look, given that you've got to hit 50 per cent not voting is like voting no so, you know, if your intention is to vote yes you've got to vote.[64]

In contrast to the emphasis placed by interviewees on the role of the membership in industrial action decision-making, when considering the ballot itself they consistently focused on union-member communication and member education about process and impact. The general impression given by interviewees was that the legal framework surrounding the ballot dictated in practice that the ballot played a less significant role in the conversations unions had with their members about industrial action, and was secondary to the union's own decision-making practices. There was also a sense that this could make members less, rather than more, engaged in the process. One interviewee described the disconnect in their union between mass meetings of the membership where actual decision-making around industrial action occurred, and the ballot itself, about which their membership could be 'apathetic':

> The ballot is a legal technical thing that they have to do that they perhaps don't treat as seriously as something like a mass meeting where we would

[62] Interview 16, Union.
[63] Interview 26, Union.
[64] Interview 55, Union.

> make a democratic decision to engage in industrial action. That's the key, that's the key thing: So, to turn up to a meeting like that would be really important where people discuss it, make a decision and make the decision about what kind of action they want to take—that's really important. The meeting that authorises the union to make the protected action ballot application is really important because people are actively making a decision. The ballot is kind of seen as a fait accompli it's just a process we have to go through—and that's what people are a bit apathetic about.[65]

In practice this could mean that if members psychologically 'switch off' from the balloting process and see it as a formality or technicality, they may not remember to vote, which can potentially affect the capacity to reach quorum—a problem that this interviewee had faced in the context of their most recent ballot.

Overall, with very few exceptions, union interviewees described communication with members in the weeks leading up to the ballot vote in similar terms. Almost invariably, they described messaging to members that highlighted that:

- the ballot was a formality necessary to fulfil the requirements under the Act;
- members should vote yes even if they did not support industrial action in order to ensure that the union had the right to take industrial action and as a show of strength in the bargaining process; and
- members would have an opportunity to vote for or against the actual taking of industrial action at a later date once the formal processes were completed.

Such messaging downplays the role of the ballot as a tool of democratic decision-making: instead of ensuring that a democratic process is followed, it emphasizes the legalities, the power dynamics, and the significance of the bargaining outcomes in the process.

As a democratic process, the pre-strike ballot provides a mechanism for the aggregation of member preferences and decentralized decision-making. However, there is little evidence that the ballot itself facilitates more meaningful democratic engagement.

Union messaging to members indicates that many are encouraged to vote, not in accordance with their preferences, but to strengthen their bargaining

[65] Interview 47, Union.

position in the associated negotiations, to comply with the legal requirements, and to send a message of strength to employers. This is accompanied by assurances that the 'real' decision to take industrial action will be made subsequently, once the legal hurdles have been cleared.

There is little evidence in the data that the actual ballot process involved active participation in decision-making by members, beyond casting a vote, which is in direct contrast to the other decision-making processes associated with taking industrial action. The overwhelming majority of pre-strike ballots in the Study were conducted by postal vote, a process providing little opportunity for engagement between members and leaders through constructive debate. Further, the public nature of the ballot and the declaration of the results of the ballot, provide a positive disincentive to the expression of opposing viewpoints. Opposition may well be expressed in member meetings, and indeed may be welcomed, but in the context of the formal ballot process, most unions appeared to encourage members to vote yes, irrespective of the individual member's personal views.

The decision actually to take industrial action

The third decision that requires consideration is the decision actually to give notice of protected industrial action, and to take one or more forms of the action that was approved in the ballot. This decision is taken after the PABO has been sought and obtained, and the action has been approved in the subsequent ballot. The FW Act does not regulate this third decision in any way. Provided each form of action taken by a union has been approved in a ballot conducted in accordance with the Act, the actual decisions as to which action will be taken, by whom, and when are entirely in the control of the union, acting in accordance with its rules. As noted earlier in this chapter, very few union rule books actually contain provisions expressly dealing with the decision to take, or not to take, industrial action.

In their messaging to members about the ballot vote, union officials frequently emphasized that members would have an opportunity to participate in the decision actually to take industrial action if it was approved in the ballot. The understanding that members make the decision to take industrial action and the forms of industrial action that may be taken was strongly in evidence across the interviews. The decision was variously described as member-driven, member-endorsed, or a decision of the members. As one interviewee stated, 'it's not my decision, it's the members' decision'[66]—a sentiment echoed by

[66] Interview 73, Union.

another interviewee who observed that 'the union, with respect to matters of industrial action, acts entirely on the instruction of membership'.[67] It was also clear that member decisions might not necessarily correspond with the perceptions or expectations of union officials. One interviewee, for example, described being surprised by a member decision to take further industrial action during a long campaign, having thought the members were too fatigued and would not support it.[68]

In common with their description of the decision-making processes to make a PABO application, interviewees referred to a range of different mechanisms used by unions to engage their membership in the process of making the decision actually to take industrial action. Most said that the decision was made following a discussion at members' meetings, either through a show of hands or a more formal balloting process. Other forms of member consultation and decision-making described by interviewees included small group conversations, one-on-one member consultation, and formal delegate structures for geographically dispersed or larger enterprises. For example, one interviewee described the different processes used by the union depending on the enterprise involved. For sites with twenty to thirty members, meetings at which members would be 'happy to speak up' were utilized, whereas at bigger sites where there were perhaps 100 plus members, members were telephoned individually.[69] This interviewee observed that 'the call centre is essential because people don't speak up. Even the shyer ones get a chance to feel like they haven't been railroaded and have a chance to talk'.[70]

As with the decision to apply for a PABO, interviewees repeatedly observed that the industrial action decision was informed in practice by tactical considerations related to negotiations, and that these were commonly discussed through members' meetings. In that context, interviewees described: outlining the 'pros and cons' to members;[71] having discussions with members about the range of industrial action options available and the best tactics for implementing that action;[72] and returning to members after the decision to take action has been made to review the decision in light of developments at the bargaining table.[73] The processes described were highly consultative and responsive to developments in bargaining.

[67] Interview 20, Union.
[68] Interview 57, Union.
[69] Interview 56, Union.
[70] Interview 56, Union.
[71] Interview 57, Union.
[72] Interview 59, Union.
[73] Interview 20, Union.

One of the problems with this analysis is that it is based on the perceptions of union representatives, rather than of union members. It is possible, for example, that union members do not experience these processes in the same consultative and responsive manner as has been described. The idea that members could potentially be 'railroaded' at members' meetings was a risk identified by some union interviewees. As mentioned above, one interviewee described the use of individual consultations through call centres to overcome that risk, giving all members the opportunity to be heard.[74] Another described a situation 'where a show of hands vote has been used to bully and harass', in consequence of which the interviewee had formed the view that secret ballots or voting by email were a better way to obtain member consent, and ensure that members had the opportunity to 'think about it'.[75] There was, however, also an understanding amongst those interviewed that members simply would not take industrial action if they did not support it or had not authorized it. As one interviewee explained, if industrial action decision-making was not member-led, 'people start asking the question, well who put you in charge, why are you making these decisions?',[76] whilst another observed that it was 'impossible' to take members out on strike against their will, 'you can't make people go on strike. Yes, it's democratic but it's the only way you can run it'.[77]

The practices for authorizing industrial action described by interviewees in the Study demonstrate that industrial action decisions are commonly made through processes that involve: active participation in decision-making by members; responsiveness of union leadership to member views; opportunities to present opposing viewpoints; and decentralized decision-making. All of these factors suggest that unions use processes that are more democratic than oligarchic in nature. However, a substantial limitation of the analysis is the absence of the perspective of union members themselves, who, as indicated, may not always experience these processes in as democratic a manner as generally described by interviewees.

Conclusions

This chapter describes three decision-making processes in relation to taking industrial action. All three of those decisions occur in the context of negotiations

[74] Interview 56, Union.
[75] Interview 18, Union.
[76] Interview 69, Union.
[77] Interview 73, Union.

for a new agreement during enterprise bargaining where the interests of unions and their members on the one hand, and those of employers on the other, may be finely balanced. Two of those decisions were made internally by unions, without any requirement for permission from an outside body, and without public dissemination of the outcomes of the decision-making process. The third decision is, however, one that is legislatively mandated, externally controlled, and involves public dissemination of the outcomes.

The evidence and analysis presented in this chapter demonstrates that there is a significant distinction between the forms of democracy fostered by these different decision-making processes, and that this is very much driven by the regulatory and bargaining context in which the decisions are taken. For this purpose, it is necessary to separate the public decision of union members to *authorize* the possible taking of industrial action through a legislatively mandated and externally controlled pre-strike ballot from internal union decisions to *apply for* a PABO, and to *take* industrial action once such action has been authorized through the ballot process.

It seems clear from the analysis that the mandatory pre-strike ballot requirement under the FW Act does not foster any form of democracy other than one that simply aggregates preferences—preferences which may not even reflect the genuine views of the members. The public nature of the ballot and the signalling effect of the ballot outcome in the context of associated negotiations at the bargaining table places pressure on unions to secure the requisite level of voter turnout and a strong yes vote for the proposed forms of industrial action. Maximizing the level of turnout is also impelled by the quorum requirement—especially in light of the fact that abstentions effectively count as votes against. It is against the interests of the union and its members to encourage a more fulsome democratic or deliberative process in respect of the manner in which union members vote in the mandatory pre-strike ballot. Public debate and encouragement of dissent in public forums, or through the casting of a no vote in a ballot, undermines the union's position at the bargaining table if the employer becomes aware that there is dissent in the union ranks. In many instances, the impact of industrial action flows as much from the existence of a credible threat of action, as from such action itself. Active, public, dissent can clearly detract from the credibility of any such threat.

Union messaging to members about pre-strike ballots demonstrates that union members are not encouraged to voice their dissent through that process. Rather, members are encouraged to vote tactically, with an understanding that the ballot does not actually constitute a decision to take industrial action, but rather that the purpose of the exercise is to comply with 'legal formalities', and that the outcome of the ballot constitutes a 'show of strength'. The public nature of the ballot and the element of risk involved for unions in respect of the disclosure of membership levels and of member views on proposed action clearly subvert any suggestion that pre-strike ballots as enacted in the FW Act are about encouraging or facilitating democratic decision-making by unions. There is an inherent tension between a conception of democracy which encourages dissent and ensures that all viewpoints can be aired, and the context in which pre-strike ballots take place under the FW Act, which places a premium on the suppression of dissent.

This lends support to the proposition that the process for conducting pre-strike ballots under the FW Act undermines, rather than promotes, 'real' democracy. Because of the role that the pre-strike ballot plays in the context of collective bargaining negotiations, the goal of the union and the members has to be to get as many people as possible to vote, and to vote in favour of proposed industrial action, rather than to engage in a truly democratic decision-making process. Such a process would require that competing views be discussed and debated, and an outcome agreed by means to be determined by the union in accordance with its rules. If these processes are conducted in public, the union's negotiating position must inevitably be compromised.

Paradoxically, the results of the Study show that the other key decisions that need to be taken in the context of industrial action under the FW Act—to apply for a PABO, and actually to take industrial action subsequent to a ballot—*are* generally arrived at in a truly democratic manner where competing views are canvassed and outcomes agreed by members without the involvement of employers or regulators. The integrity of these democratic processes is, however, compromised by the regulatory environment within which they operate. This includes the need to seek the permission of a regulator (the FWC) in order even to ask their members whether they might wish to take industrial action at some point in ongoing negotiations, and that employers have the right to intervene in proceedings concerning what surely ought to be a union's internal decision-making processes.

Anti-democratic as the current pre-strike ballot requirement may be, it does at least do something to foster union/member communication and engagement. The analysis in this chapter describes ongoing conversations between unions and their members about issues such as voting in ballots and voting 'yes' irrespective of the member's true preferences. This may be a perverse form of democracy, but it does at least promote discussion and communication between the union and members about issues such as the union's rules and processes, the statutory requirements associated with taking industrial action, and the current state of negotiations. Unions variously use call centres, emails, informative flyers and pamphlets, and member meetings to engage collectively and individually with members in relation to these issues. Further, unions use the promise of a further opportunity to vote on the proposed action—another democratic opportunity—for members to express their true views, to encourage a yes vote in the formal ballot. This suggests that the public balloting process has a flow-on effect into the internal decision-making processes of the union, where the union must commit to further democratic processes and must make a concerted effort to educate and inform their membership. This process ensures that future decision-making is likely to be better informed and potentially of higher quality.

As indicated, unlike the mandated pre-strike ballot process, the analysis demonstrates that union practice in internal decision-making is largely based around direct democratic practice where possible, with representative democracy being utilized in larger and/or geographically dispersed enterprises. While it is not possible to evaluate these processes directly through the perspective of participatory or deliberative styles of democracy because internal union practices by their very nature lack the involvement of the plurality of societal interests, it is possible to consider how the processes fare by reference to the aims of participatory democracy.

As explored in Chapter 1, the goal of such democracy is to ensure that citizens participate in decision-making, and in that process receive education on the issues involved and are better able to understand and accept collective decisions. The processes for internal union decision-making for industrial action described in this chapter appear to meet this goal. In the majority of cases in the Study, interviewees described a process that potentially enabled all union members to participate in decision-making through a variety of forums, where it appears that opportunities for dissent and challenges to the views of union leaders are provided, and decisions are informed by both individual and collective discussion. While ultimately decisions are made by a majority determination (there was no indication of the kind of consensus-based decision-making that is the goal of deliberative democracy), underpinning this approach was a commitment amongst the union interviewees to continuing member dialogue, education, and engagement, to the extent possible in the sometimes fraught circumstances of an industrial campaign.

Overall, it can be said that, on the basis of the evidence in this chapter, internal union decision-making in the process of deciding to take industrial action tends, in practice, more towards democracy than oligarchy. Union practices facilitate active participation in decision-making by members;

demonstrate the responsiveness of union leaders to members; appear to tolerate opposing viewpoints, providing opportunities for their expression; and largely devolves decision-making to those who will be asked actually to take any industrial action that may be approved. To the extent that the processes reflect any particular form of democratic practice, they appear to encourage a form of participatory democracy.

There are, however, limitations to these conclusions. In particular, it remains unclear to what extent the ability to initiate decisions in respect of industrial action may be affected by union bureaucracy and decision-making conventions and rules. It is very likely that the risks associated with a PABO application and the eventual ballot have the effect in many instances of shutting down any prospect of taking industrial action. This reflects the fact that it is impossible accurately to measure the shadow effect of the legal provisions. Further, it is important to bear in mind that the data do not reflect the perspective of union members themselves. It is possible, therefore, that they may experience internal union practices in a manner different to that understood by union bargaining representatives who were interviewed for the purposes of the Study.

Ultimately what the analysis demonstrates is that unions have a real commitment to forms of democratic practice in their internal decision-making processes. External ballot requirements do not necessarily change this, although paradoxically they may both inhibit and encourage it.

8

Reflections on the Australian Pre-Strike Ballot Model

Introduction

Although the Australian *Fair Work Act 2009* (Cth) (FW Act) provisions for pre-strike ballots are ostensibly intended 'to establish a fair, simple and democratic process to allow a bargaining representative to determine whether employees wish to engage in protected industrial action',[1] the provisions, as discussed in detail in Chapter 4, are not fair, not simple, and not democratic other than in a somewhat simplistic sense.

The original 2005 provisions, enacted as amendments to the *Workplace Relations Act 1996* (Cth) (WR Act),[2] were, theoretically at least, motivated by concerns with freedom of choice, ensuring that industrial action is only taken with the support of the employees concerned, and making trade unions more responsive and accountable to their members. The rationale for the current provision appears to be limited to providing a process for determining whether employees wish to engage in particular protected industrial action for purposes of negotiating a proposed enterprise agreement. As the wording of s 436 makes clear, in the Australian pre-strike ballot model, the stated purpose of the pre-strike ballot process is to ensure that protected strike action is only taken after a ballot of members (the 'democratic imperative'), and only as part of broader work processes, involving the negotiation of future working conditions through enterprise bargaining. As discussed in Chapter 4, protected industrial action, for various reasons, is the exception rather than the norm for most employees.

Interviews with stakeholders for the Study suggested that many of them were aware of other underlying motivations for the pre-strike ballot provisions, particularly when first enacted in 2005. These included delaying the taking of industrial action ('to slow down the process') and placing hurdles in the path of

1 FW Act s 436.
2 WR Act s 451. See the discussion of these provisions in Chapter 4.

Strike Ballots, Democracy, and Law. Breen Creighton, Catrina Denvir, Richard Johnstone, Shae McCrystal, Alice Orchiston, Oxford University Press (2020).
DOI: 10.1093/oso/9780198869894.001.0001.

doing so ('to enable objection . . . to industrial action . . . during bargaining').[3] Another stakeholder interviewee suggested that a key motivation was to 'rid Australia of a *reputation* for being a strike prone country'.[4]

How does the Australian pre-strike ballot system measure up to these various objectives in action? And how does it reflect these publicly expressed motivations and private understandings of its aims?

This final chapter of the book addresses these questions. It reflects upon whether the Australian pre-strike ballots model does indeed establish a fair, simple, and democratic process to determine whether employees wish to take industrial action, or whether the underlying motivations of impeding and frustrating the taking of industrial action in fact predominate. The chapter begins with an overview of the Australian model in practice. It then considers the overall impact of the pre-strike ballots process, and in particular, its consequences for employers, unions, and, most important, for 'democracy' at work.

After reviewing employer, union, and tribunal member reflections on the operation of the system, and proposals for reform of the system, the chapter concludes with a number of simple proposals for reform of the Australian system, and reflects on the implications of the Study for pre-strike ballot models in other, comparable, countries—particularly the United Kingdom.

An overview of the Australian model in practice

The pre-strike ballot requirements in Division 8 of Part 3-3 of the FW Act involve three stages: a bargaining representative—usually a trade union—must apply to the Fair Work Commission (FWC) for a ballot; the FWC must order a ballot; and the ballot must be conducted in order to authorize the proposed action. Chapter 4 draws on qualitative and quantitative empirical data to provide a profile of the operation of this process in practice.

The total number of Protected Action Ballot Order (PABO) applications lodged annually with the FWC is usually between 500 and 1000 applications, and averages just under 900 applications a year.[5]

The FWC is required to approve a PABO application if: it is made in accordance with the requirements of the Act; bargaining for a new enterprise agreement has commenced; and the bargaining representative has been genuinely

[3] Stakeholder Interview 3, first quoted in Chapter 4.
[4] Stakeholder Interview 12.
[5] See Chapter 4, Table 4.1.

trying to reach an agreement with the employer. The Study shows that negotiations for an enterprise agreement were generally well underway when applications for PABOs were made. There was little evidence of any 'rush' to take premature strike action.

The FWC has determined that employers are entitled to be heard when it is considering a PABO application. During the Study period, employers contested applications in 21.4 per cent of cases: their most common objection was that there had been a failure to meet the requirement genuinely to try to reach agreement, and the most common request was for a longer notice period before taking protected strike action.[6] Only six employer challenges to an application were successful: four on the basis of the genuinely try to reach agreement requirement.

Interviews with FWC members suggested that they did not take a consistent approach to dealing with PABO applications—some conducted formal hearings 'either in person or by telephone or by video',[7] whilst others simply made orders 'on the papers', usually after contacting the employer to see if the employer objected to the application. In practice, the FWC approves PABO applications in almost all cases, and the vast majority of approved applications proceed to ballot. This is borne out by the fact that during the Study period the FWC approved 96.3 per cent of applications, and did not approve 0.5 per cent. Proposed ballot questions were changed in only 1.2 per cent of cases. Of the 1,253 applications that were approved by the FWC in the Study period, 1,203 proceeded to ballot—the remainder were withdrawn before the ballot was conducted.

Bargaining representatives sought approval for a wide range of forms of strike action in the PABO applications submitted during the Study period:[8] overtime and job function bans were common; and strike action of shorter duration was more often proposed than strike action of longer or indefinite duration.

Once a PABO has been made, the next stage is the ballot itself. The mode of ballot must be secret, and may be carried out by postal, attendance, or electronic means.[9] In practice, almost all ballots (99.2 per cent in the Study period) are conducted by the Australian Electoral Commission (AEC). The main reason for this was that the union does not have to pay for an AEC-run ballot, and does not have to devote resources to organizing and conducting the ballot.

[6] The requirements for notice are discussed in detail in Chapters 4 and 5.
[7] Stakeholder Interview 6.
[8] See Chapter 4, Table 4.3.
[9] These provisions and their implementation are also discussed in Chapter 5.

If the AEC conducts the ballot, it has the final decision on the voting method. It does not offer electronic balloting, and approves many more postal ballots than attendance ballots: 84 per cent of ballots conducted by the AEC in the Study were conducted by post.

The Study found great variation in the rate of voter turnout when a ballot was conducted: in just under a fifth of ballots, the voter turnout was 80–100 per cent; and in another fifth it was between 50 and 60 per cent. Just over 76 per cent of pre-strike ballots in the Study reached quorum and approved at least one form of proposed action. Ballots conducted by attendance and electronic modes were much more likely to secure a higher voter turnout than postal ballots; and at least four times more likely to achieve a quorum. Only 3.8 per cent of ballots failed to approve *any* strike action. Analysis of ballots where voters were asked to indicate support for action separately shows that long strikes and stop work meetings were less often supported than other forms of action.

During the Study period, the average interval between lodging a PABO application and the declaration of the result of the ballot was 37.4 days (ie just over five weeks): on average just over 6.5 days from the date of application until an order by the FWC, and 31.1 days from the date of the PABO until the declaration of results. On average, postal ballots took much longer (33.4 days) than attendance ballots (19.2 days). The other factor causing significant delay was ballot objections by employers.

Once the results of successful ballots are declared, employees must decide whether or not to take strike action. The bargaining representative and/or employees must give three days (or up to seven days, if the FWC so requires or the bargaining representative so concedes) notice of strike action to the employer: in the Study just over 27 per cent of approved PABO applications involved a longer notice period.[10] Strike action must be taken within thirty days (or sixty days if so determined by the FWC).

By the end of 2018, three quarters of enterprise bargaining negotiations in the Study had resulted in agreement being reached and an enterprise agreement had been submitted to the FWC for approval.[11] Of those cases where strike action was approved in a ballot, 84.4 per cent went on to reach agreement; whilst

[10] As noted in Chapter 4 at 120, the actual number of days' notice is, at minimum, five (and up to nine) due to the statutory definition of 'working day'.

[11] The research team stopped checking for the lodgment of new agreements with the FWC in December 2018—eighteen months after collection of PABO data itself ceased. The eighteen-month buffer period was instigated by the research team due to the length of time ordinarily taken to reach agreement, produce and vote on a formal agreement document, send this document to the FWC, and await the FWC's approval.

agreement was reached in 85.7 per cent of cases where strike action was not approved in a ballot and/or the quorum was not reached. Of those cases where agreement was reached, 85.5 per cent involved a ballot which approved strike action; and of those where agreement was not reached, 87 per cent involved a ballot which approved strike action. Of those cases that reached agreement, 23.7 per cent involved no action, 47.5 per cent involved action, and for 23.7 per cent the ballot was withdrawn.[12]

Overall impact: consequences for employers, unions, and democracy

Chapter 1 outlined the three key research sub-questions that the Study sought to answer. This part of the chapter briefly summarizes the Study findings that address each of these sub-questions.

Do pre-strike ballot requirements inhibit the ability of unions and their members to take strike action in support of their claims during collective bargaining?

The inclusion of a legislative requirement for a pre-strike ballot within a regime regulating access to legally protected strike action can *appear* to be neutral in effect. As the discussion in Chapter 5 demonstrates, however, a pre-strike ballot requirement, and the content of the rules imposed to govern the conduct of those ballots, may *not* be neutral in practice. Although each part of the pre-strike ballot regime, considered separately, may seem neutral in its impact, the rules may, on a cumulative basis, have practical consequences that were not apparent on the face of the legislation—or a shadow effect—and may drive behaviours in a way that is not immediately obvious from the text of the individual provisions. The data from Chapter 4, summarized earlier in this chapter, suggest that this may be the case with the Australian pre-strike ballot provisions. They show that the combined effect of the rules governing pre-strike ballots in Division 8 of Part 3-3 of the FW Act is to prolong the process for taking strike action—the average time from the PABO application to the declaration

[12] This figure excludes some PABOs where there were multiple ballots in the context of single interest employers. For a further 1.7 per cent, industrial action was not approved in a vote, and for 3.4 per cent, quorum was not reached.

of the ballot was about five weeks. The analysis in Chapter 5 demonstrates that, in practice, the combined effect of the pre-strike ballot provisions under the FW Act is to inhibit the capacity of unions to organize industrial action, and to impede their capacity to use industrial action in the most strategically effective manner.

Chapter 5 examined the impact of the first formal step for Australian unions that want to take protected industrial action: seeking a PABO from the FWC to permit the conduct of a pre-strike ballot. Of all the pre-strike ballot requirements in the FW Act, this requirement is the one that is least obviously directed to ensuring democratic practice by unions. It does not require unions to act democratically in their processes for deciding that permission will be sought, and the legislative tests for determining whether a PABO will be granted focus on whether the procedural requirements for the application have been met and on the behaviour of the applicant in the associated enterprise negotiations. The true purpose of this requirement is not to promote democratic decision-making, but rather to police the behaviour of unions as participants in voluntary enterprise bargaining, and to limit access to protected industrial action to those participants who are focused solely on negotiations at the relevant enterprise.

Further evidence that the PABO requirement is a mechanism to police union bargaining behaviour prior to industrial action is furnished by the fact that it provides an opportunity for employers strategically to use legal tactics to delay the conduct of ballots, and consequently the taking of protected industrial action. While the number of employers who actively contest PABO applications (just over 21 per cent in the Study period) is not high, those who do contest were shown to use the process largely as an opportunity to raise technical challenges to applications in order to slow the momentum of the union campaign, and to delay access to industrial action. The chapter demonstrates that even a technical objection to the correctness of the name of the employing entity on a PABO application can delay a PABO order by two weeks—considerably longer than the two days stated within the FW Act framework for the determination of a PABO by the FWC. This shows that the statutory requirement for PABOs to be made within two days of lodgement of an application means little in practice because proceedings can be drawn out for periods of up to several weeks.

An aspect of employer opposition to PABO applications that is more difficult to ascertain from the formal statistics is the way that employers deploy threats to oppose applications in order to obtain concessions from unions. These include concessions on the length of time that the ballot will be open and the length of notice to be given to an employer before starting industrial action, both of which have the effect of delaying the commencement of industrial action and giving employers a greater opportunity to organize their resources to mitigate the effect of subsequent action. In around one third of the ballots in the Study, the employer withdrew any objection to the PABO, or promised not to object, provided that the ballot stayed open for a longer time, or notice of industrial action was extended. Further, in some industries, these kinds of employer tactics have produced standard notice periods that are longer than the minimum statutory notice period. This means that the statutory timelines should not be taken at face value: in practice, in a significant proportion of cases, the notice periods will be longer than those specified in the statute.

Once a PABO is made, the conduct of the ballot itself is also shaped by the statutory regime. The FW Act mandates a secret ballot conducted by an independent ballot agent with a quorum requirement of 50 per cent and a majority requirement of 50 per cent of those voting. It also offers three balloting methods to bargaining representatives—postal, attendance, and electronic. None of these options are, on their face, objectionable as a requirement for the conduct of a democratic ballot, and indeed may appear to operate in a neutral manner. Chapter 5, however, demonstrates how each component of this process impedes access to protected industrial action, and how in combination they make it difficult to take action in practice.

First, the quorum requirement is not neutral in effect, because it can deny motivated workers access to industrial action in situations where other workers simply do not vote. The statistical analysis in Chapter 5 demonstrates that union members generally do not vote *against* taking industrial action, but that they do frequently *fail to vote*. In the Study, abstentions defeated proposed industrial action more effectively than did members' voting against industrial action.

Second, failure to meet quorum is not simply a product of members deliberately choosing not to vote. The research shows that postal ballots fail to reach quorum around 20 per cent of the time; whereas attendance ballots only fail to meet quorum around 8 per cent of the time. This can be attributed to a range of factors, including: incorrect addresses; post being ignored or lost; members failing to understand the postal ballot; and an 'out of sight out of mind' consideration.

Third, the system provides positive incentives to use postal ballots rather than attendance and electronic ballots. While electronic ballots are, in principle, available, a union has to pay for an independent ballot agent to conduct any such ballot—the Commonwealth Government only pays for the AEC to run ballots and, as noted earlier in this chapter, the AEC does not offer electronic balloting. Further, the AEC generally prefers postal ballots to attendance ballots: in the Study, 84 per cent of AEC-run ballots were postal, compared with only 16 per cent of attendance ballots. Furthermore, all but ten successful PABO applicants used the AEC, and of those ten, nine of the ballots were conducted electronically.

While appearing to incorporate 'neutral' provisions governing quorums and ballots, the PABO system, in practice, positively incentivizes the form of balloting that is least likely to reach quorum; and failure to reach quorum is the major reason for the vast majority of unsuccessful ballots.

Another aspect of the ballot regime that is not obvious on the face of the legislation is the level of administrative burden that the provisions place on unions to comply with the rules and to ensure that they are able to meet quorum. Union representatives interviewed for the Study reported that they had to devote significant financial and human resources to ensure compliance with the technical requirements of the legislation, and to respond to employer opposition and delaying tactics. Unions must also devote considerable resources to educating members about the PABO process, and in particular to explaining that neither the PABO itself, nor the outcome of the ballot, are decisions actually *to take* strike action. The ballot process, and the inevitable delays associated with it, can be confusing to members, and can lead to frustration and apathy. Conversely, the union must also devote resources to ensuring that members do not act unlawfully. As a result of these complexities, the ballot regime favours repeat players who are well resourced and skilled in complying with the regulatory requirements, and in maintaining high levels of member communication. Unions with little experience of the system may not fare so well—which suggests that the regime likely has a significant shadow effect in denying access to strike action to those who are unable to navigate the system or are too intimidated by it in practice.

Chapter 5 shows that even where unions are able to meet the requirements of the complex regulatory regime, and union members authorize proposed strike action, other elements of that regime have the capacity to trip up even experienced players. The most significant of these are the thirty-day rule and the need to ensure that any industrial action taken was the action that was authorized in the ballot and contained in the notice. This latter requirement can be particularly challenging in practice where there is doubt over whether conduct falls within the definition of industrial action, or where there is dispute over what the proposed and notified industrial action actually entails. Such issues can lead to a loss of protection even in cases where unions and their employees have been vigilant in ensuring compliance with the legislative framework.

The apparently neutral thirty-day rule—which requires that industrial action be commenced within thirty days of the declaration of the ballot result—has been interpreted in a way that means that unions must deploy each form of strike action authorized in the ballot within a reasonably short period at least once in order to be able to use that action again.[13] This rule has made it easier for unions to make a mistake and lose access to the capacity to engage in some or all of the forms of action authorized in the ballot. It also drives technical artifice in the taking of strike action itself: instead of focusing on the associated negotiations for an enterprise agreement, unions must ensure that each form of action is deployed at least once. This can, for example, lead to situations where unions arrange for small numbers of employees (even just one) to take a given form of industrial action simply to keep alive the capacity to access that form of action at a later stage in the bargaining process.

The cumulative effect of these features of the ballot regime provides support for the view that the FW Act balloting regime is not consistent with international labour standards on the right to strike. Chapter 5 shows that the overall effect of each seemingly neutral and otherwise acceptable ballot requirement is to produce a regime that is so complex that it is very difficult to navigate; incentivizes forms of balloting that are less likely to authorize industrial action; provides multiple avenues for employers to intervene to challenge access to industrial action and cause delay; and contains many traps for the unwary. Both for unions that use the provisions routinely, and for inexperienced players, the provisions place hurdles in the way of authorizing industrial action that are not justified by any clear regulatory imperative. As discussed in Chapter 6 and later in this chapter, interviews with unions in the course of the Study, confirmed that the PABO requirements imposed very significant compliance burdens upon unions, and significantly delayed the timing, and the effectiveness, of industrial action.

How do pre-strike ballot requirements impact upon the internal democratic processes of trade unions?

The central theme of this book, the extent to which pre-strike ballots foster democratic practice in trade unions, was explored in Chapter 7. As noted in earlier chapters, the language of democracy has consistently been utilized by

[13] *United Collieries Ltd v CFMEU* (2006) 153 FCR 543; *Energy Australia Yallourn Pty Ltd v CFMEU* (2014) 218 FCR 316.

legislators and policy-makers as a shield against criticism of mandated pre-strike ballot requirements—the notion that a process like initiating industrial action should be 'democratic' is one with which it is very hard to disagree as a matter of principle.

Pre-strike ballot requirements are, however, imposed on trade unions in a very different context when compared with other forms of political or industrial contests. In most contexts where balloting procedures are involved, different parties actively compete for positions of power, and the ballot operates as a mechanism to resolve the contest. Where, however, pre-strike requirements are imposed, the active contest is not between members of the union, or between members of the union and union officials. Rather, it is between the union and the target of the concerns of union members, that is, the employer, and the context is active bargaining for a new enterprise agreement not some more or less abstract industrial or political environment. Active contests between union members that involve open debate and opposition—elements that would usually feature as part of a healthy democratic process—can harm the union and its members at the bargaining table, and can be counterproductive, revealing weaknesses in the union's position that an employer may subsequently be able to exploit in the bargaining context. There is, therefore, tension between a full conception of democracy that encourages dissent and the expression of differing points of view, and the public context in which pre-strike ballots take place, where dissent cannot be encouraged without potential adverse consequences for unions in the bargaining process.

As noted at several points in the book the legal and industrial frameworks for pre-strike ballots in Australia require unions and their members who are contemplating the possibility of engaging in industrial action to take three interrelated, but different, key decisions: (i) the decision to *apply* for a PABO; (ii) the decision to *approve* proposed industrial action; and (iii) the decision to *take* approved industrial action. Each of these decisions occurs within the context of the legal and industrial relations framework, and the democratic processes involved are inevitably shaped by those frameworks.

The evidence from the Study clearly suggests that the first and third decisions—made by unions internally and without external scrutiny or the public release of balloting results—are generally conducted in a manner that allows for participatory democratic processes. When unions make the decision to *apply* for a PABO from the FWC, or make the decision *actually to strike*, the decision-making is member-led, involves active and participatory processes, and appears to provide opportunities for active and tolerated dissent. The Study findings suggest, however, that when union members vote in a ballot following the making of a PABO, there is little evidence of the kinds of practices that typically characterize a participatory democratic model. Instead, union engagement with members is focused on educating them about the legal requirements, and the consequences of abstention or a no-vote in associated bargaining, rather than on the arguments for and against the proposed industrial action.

This second decision—to authorize proposed industrial action in a pre-strike ballot—is heavily regulated by the FW Act, and in practice is part of the 'theatre' of enterprise bargaining because it is conducted in public by an independent ballot agent, and the results are in the public domain. The relationship that this public process has with the associated enterprise bargaining negotiations means that it cannot in practice operate as a source of participatory or deliberative democratic practice—it can play no substantive role beyond preference aggregation. Further, the public nature of this preference aggregation means that it cannot represent a genuine reflection of union members' views on proposed industrial action, as union messaging to members during this process usually urges members to 'vote yes, even if you don't intend to take industrial action'. As proponents of the legal theory of autopoesis (or systems theory) would observe,[14] the legal rules governing pre-strike ballots fail to mesh with—and do not translate into—the kind of democracy nurtured by industrial relations processes, and severely 'irritate' (or distort), and perhaps even destroy, industrial democratic processes within unions.

By contrast, the first decision—to apply for a PABO—and the third—actually to take industrial action—appear to involve meaningful democratic processes of a participatory nature precisely because they are not heavily regulated by the FW Act, and what regulation there is 'steers' union decision-making towards participatory democracy. They involve internal deliberations in which dissent and robust discussion can be tolerated because nothing about the decisions, and the processes that led to them, will be published to the employer and the world at large. Where unions have been able to craft their own approaches to decision-making without concern that their internal deliberations can be used against them at the bargaining table, the evidence presented in Chapter 7 in respect of internal union decision-making suggests that those processes are highly participatory and responsive to the needs of particular workplaces and member groups. Of course, the two different kinds of decisions—the second, and the first and third—are interrelated. The necessity for member

[14] See Luhmann 2004; Teubner 1993; Rogowski 2013; Lodge & Wegrich 2012: 35; Stewart et al 2016: 28–9.

communication and education that arises in the pre-strike ballot process itself means that unions have developed sophisticated strategies for member engagement in these processes—which feeds into the discussions leading to the decisions to apply for a PABO and actually to take industrial action. These are, however, side effects, not direct results, of the pre-strike balloting rules in the FW Act, and do not provide credible support for the proposition that the formal pre-strike ballot rules actively foster democratic process.

Overall, Chapter 7 demonstrates that internal union decision-making about strike action exhibits the characteristics of participatory forms of democratic practice. Union practices in this context facilitate active participation in decision-making, demonstrate the responsiveness of union leaders to members, appear to tolerate opposing viewpoints and largely devolve decision-making to those who will be asked actually to take any industrial action. Where, however, balloting occurs through FW Act mandated rules and in public, the process used positively undermines democratic practice, suppresses dissent and debate, and potentially leads to ballot outcomes that are intended not to reflect the genuine wishes of the membership, but to signal (genuinely or otherwise) the readiness of the membership to take industrial action.

What impact do mandatory pre-strike ballot requirements have on associated collective bargaining negotiations?

The analysis of internal union processes and of bargaining dynamics in Chapter 6 suggests that the PABO process can provide unions with some benefits, or advantages, in the enterprise bargaining process. First, the compulsory and public process of *applying* for a PABO, and the conduct of a subsequent successful ballot, can be an effective means for unions to increase leverage by escalating the 'threat' of industrial action without necessarily having to *take* the approved action to gain that leverage. A successful ballot outcome can signal industrial strength, accelerate the 'countdown' towards industrial action and/or disadvantage the employer through receiving negative publicity, especially when it suggests that the employer's production or service delivery could be adversely affected. Whether or not effective 'bluffing' using these kinds of leverage is possible depends on: the prevailing sector-specific economic conditions; the state of the negotiations; the ability of the union to get its members to vote in the first place, and then to indicate a preparedness to take industrial action; and the ability of the employer to call the union's bluff and resist the pressure signalled by applying for a ballot and/or its outcome. For most unions, this kind of leverage is seen as a step in ramping up pressure as part of the wider bargaining process, rather than as a tactic to win significant concessions from the employer in itself. Many union interviewees observed that actually taking industrial action was the only way to validate what might otherwise be seen as an empty threat: unions reported situations where there was no change to the employer's approach to negotiations until industrial action was taken. In the Study period, of those ballots where it was possible to follow up the rate of industrial action taken, industrial action was not taken after just under 37 per cent of successful ballots, suggesting that most unions do need to take industrial action to have an impact, and the 'bluff' element has only a limited effect in practice.

The Study also found that the PABO process, in some circumstances, benefits unions by providing an opportunity to engage existing members in the bargaining campaign, and/or to recruit new members. However, it also suggests that engaging with the PABO process is not without risk for unions. The findings show, for instance, that an unsuccessful ballot outcome—whether because of failure to achieve quorum or insufficient voter support for taking industrial action—can have a number of adverse impacts for a union. It can, for instance, severely compromise its credibility; evidence a weak bargaining position; significantly reduce the likelihood of industrial action occurring; and advantage the employer in the negotiating process. A failed ballot could delay the taking of industrial action and/or require the union to revise its strategy, and in some instances could entirely derail the union campaign. The findings also suggest that even where there is a successful ballot, if the level of voter turnout and/or support for industrial action is low the pressure on the employer will be reduced.

It follows that, in order to maximize the strategic 'benefit' of a PABO, unions generally need to invest considerable time and resources to ensure that a sufficient number of members vote in the ballot, and that those employees vote in favour of taking industrial action. Some unions will avoid balloting altogether if the process or outcome may disclose low levels of membership density to an employer and/or a limited commitment to taking industrial action (especially where there is a failure to achieve quorum).

Interviews with employers showed that employers responded in one or more of three ways to the lodging of a PABO application. Some used the time between the PABO application and the actual ballot actively to try to discourage support for industrial action, by, for example, implementing a communication strategy to scare employees off supporting or taking industrial action. Some tried to disrupt the momentum of the union's campaign—for example by prolonging negotiations and/or challenging ballot applications. Not only could this delay the union's capacity lawfully to take industrial action, it could also distract the union by causing it to have to focus on trying to maintain member support. It could also help generate member fatigue, reduce their appetite for taking industrial action, and lead to member disengagement. Other employer tactics included formally opposing attendance ballots and/or trying to undermine them—for example by allocating employees to work away from the workplace at which the attendance ballot was conducted.

This overview of the finding of the Study leaves at least two important questions unanswered: overall, how did employers and unions perceive the pre-strike ballot regime?; and did unions consider that the potential to gain bargaining leverage from applying for PABOs and/or conducting a ballot, and the potential to enhance recruitment and membership engagement, in any way balance out the disadvantages of the system—in particular, its tendency to impede and delay industrial action?

Stakeholder perceptions of the pre-strike ballot provisions and their impact on enterprise bargaining negotiations

Not surprisingly, employers and unions had different perceptions of the PABO process in this context.

Employer perceptions

Most employers interviewed for the Study considered the PABO process to be fair, because it served the democratic imperative: 'I think it's fairer for everyone to have their voice heard' and 'the voting process puts more accountability in place'.[15] One employer particularly liked electronic ballots because it meant workers could vote without being subject to peer pressure.[16]

Current and former employer association representatives were satisfied with the PABO process:

> My perception is that they [the PABO provisions] have generally worked in a satisfactory manner. Certainly there's no external industrial or labour market

[15] Interview 13, Employer.
[16] Interview 15, Employer.

> or economic reasons why we could say that they haven't contributed to a continuing trend of low levels of industrial disputes in Australia.[17]
>
> You can't organise a strike across an industry anymore because you've got to go through all the fairly rigorous application process and balloting process at the enterprise level. . . . And I think the history now shows that . . . it's had a massive positive effect on the level of industrial action and I think that's a great benefit of course to employees as well as employers and the broader community.[18]

Employers mostly considered the PABO process to be beneficial for them. For example, some noted that the notice period removed the element of surprise and enabled them to find out what industrial action was planned, and 'when it's going to start' and when it is 'going to stop'.[19] It allowed them

> enough time to plan and put . . . our contingency plans in place . . . And because you can only have the actions that you have put in the ballot, you can't do other things, that's actually allowed us to knock back and disqualify some of the notices that they have put in . . . because they haven't met the requirements'.[20]

Some employers considered that, while they derived some benefits from the PABO process, it also had benefits for workers—in particular because it made employers see the depth of their workers' feelings about the issues. For example, one employer stated that while 'the voting process' gives 'an organisation a little bit more time—about three or four weeks—to actually prepare for possible issues' arising from industrial action, it also had benefits for workers because 'an organisation can actually see how employees voted is helpful as well and puts pressure, I think, on organisations to actually understand, you know, the depths of the feeling that their employees have around the issues involved'.[21]

On the other hand, some employers pointed out that whatever the in-principle merits of the PABO process, it was 'too easy' for unions to obtain a PABO, and that 'it is very difficult for an employer to oppose an order if the

[17] Stakeholder Interview 12.
[18] Stakeholder Interview 10.
[19] Interview 7, Employer.
[20] Interview 41, Employer.
[21] Interview 13, Employer.

union wants to get an order that they can engage in industrial action'.[22] 'The unions seem to think these are automatic orders'.[23]

Some employers argued that the PABO process is 'perfunctory' and 'very much a "tick-the-box" exercise',[24] especially after the unions had 'ironed out' their mistakes in the process for making orders in the six months after the FW Act came into force:

> The intention of those who brought it in—not the Labor Party when the Fair Work Act was written, but the one previous, Work Choices—was to somehow stymie industrial action, so if that was the intent they've got that wrong, because it doesn't do that. What it does is . . . in a strong workforce they just vote it up anyway, in a jittery workforce what they say to them is they say oh, no, no, this isn't a vote to take industrial action this is a vote that gives us the right to take industrial action at a later time and we'll give you another vote on that. So why would you not say yes to that?[25]

This employer concluded that 'the ballot process is a falsehood because . . . it's not a vote to take action at a particular time at a particular day, it's a vote so you can have another vote' as to whether to take the industrial action.

This same employer observed that the PABO can also impede negotiations because unions become so preoccupied with complying with the legal requirements that they are distracted from the negotiations:

> The other thing I find that happens, interestingly enough, is because the union is trying to get that organised they stop speaking to us. . . . Because they've got to go and organise the guy . . . or the girl, or whoever it is that they're getting to do it, they've got to organise the AEC, they've got to have a thing with them, and they've got to organise with them, and they've got to pay them, and they've got to do a whole range of other stuff. Or, you know, they don't have to pay the AEC but if they've got their own person they do. And so what they do they're liaising with them now, they're not liaising with me anymore, they're liaising with them to try and arrange a day with them and get them sorted out, so they're not talking to me so it doesn't help.[26]

[22] Interview 19, Employer.
[23] Interview 34, Employer.
[24] Interview 7, Employer.
[25] Interview 7, Employer.
[26] Interview 7, Employer.

A union interviewee confirmed this:

> [U]nfortunately what happens is when you're dealing with one part of it then you sometimes have to let down the others because there's only so many resources. So where there are times when we were trying to work things out strategically between the unions then the members on the ground weren't feeling communicated with enough. Or when we were doing the legal processes of applying for the protected action ballot order or for the extension to be able to keep taking the action and take different actions then of course that then takes your resources that way. And we find some of our members and delegates are saying to us, 'Let's just get back to the table and keep negotiating'.[27]

Union perceptions of the PABO process

Did the opportunities for leverage and potential for member engagement and recruitment provided by the Australian pre-strike ballot regime, and outlined in Chapter 6, offset the disadvantages imposed on unions by the PABO process, as discussed in Chapter 5? This section summarizes unions' and their peak body representatives' overall perceptions of the process.

Most union interviewees expressed strong dissatisfaction with the PABO regime, and explained how it impeded their efforts to take strike action. As noted in Chapters 5 and 6, the main criticisms were that it imposed heavy burdens upon unions in their efforts to comply with the ballot process requirements, and caused significant delays in the timing of strike action, which reduced its effectiveness.

Union interviewees repeatedly pointed out that the process of applying for a PABO was extremely cumbersome, bureaucratic, resource intensive, 'difficult and tiresome . . . long and hard'.[28] '[I]t takes a good two or three weeks often just to get the application actually ready to submit, to file and serve.'[29] The process led to significant delays in taking protected industrial action—which were further exacerbated if there were postal ballots, which took 'so many weeks'[30]—so that unions, in many cases, were prevented from taking industrial action at a time when it would be most effective. The delay in the vote had other adverse consequences for unions: during the delay, workers' opinions could

27 Interview 57, Union.
28 Interview 28, Union.
29 Interview 71, Union.
30 Interview 51, Union.

be influenced against supporting industrial action by the employer, other workers, and the workers' families. One union interviewee emphasized that negotiations for enterprise agreements are

> time sensitive and so is the mood of the members . . . people will potentially have their families in their ear . . . sowing the seeds of fear about how they answer those questions. It's not a good process.[31]

This does not, however, mean that *all* unions are significantly adversely affected by the PABO provisions. Trade union peak body representatives pointed out that the weaker unions were the most affected:

> Well for strong unions it's largely an irrelevancy, because they go into the bargaining from a position of strength, and it doesn't trouble them. But for weaker unions representing low paid workers, it's a problem, or it can be a problem, as you say, if the employer wants to use the various delays and other opportunities presented to campaign against the action. Because if there's low density, for instance the argument can be run that the action will be futile if only three people out of 100 go on strike. There's just that time and space to bring pressure to bear on people. So I think it does have a chilling effect on some negotiations.[32]

As explained in Chapter 6, some union officers with extensive experience of the PABO process who were interviewed for the Study took a fairly sanguine view of the regime, indicating that they did not regard it as unduly onerous because there were limited grounds upon which employers could object, and they had developed templates and routine processes to comply with the PABO requirements.

A few unions reported mixed experiences, and, consistent with the findings described in Chapters 5 and 6, noted that there were positive and negative features of the ballot process. Some union interviewees pointed out that the process provided an opportunity to recruit members and/or to engage existing members. One suggested that the delays in the ballot process were positively helpful, 'because it was about building the campaign and thinking about your engagement—that just gave us more time to do another engagement so it wasn't that problematic'.[33] Other interviewees expressed similar views.

[31] Interview 51, Union.
[32] Stakeholder Interview 9.
[33] Interview 70, Union.

Some union interviewees remarked that the PABO regime had, to some extent, neutralized employer claims that unions did not act democratically. They pointed out that, practically, and despite employer claims that union officers called their members out on strike without member support, unions have always had to make decisions in consultation with their members:

> You can't make people go on strike, if they don't want to it's not going to happen. So you have that conversation and sure, some of the conversations can be pretty strenuous, pretty wild for sure but in the end you've got to have a majority of people wanting to go on strike for it to happen, end of story.[34]

In that sense at least, the ballots regime has reinforced unions' existing democratic practices, albeit by imposing a public and bureaucratic process. Despite the critique of the operation of the PABO process in Chapter 5, and the union criticisms noted in Chapter 6, some union interviewees acknowledged that the process served the democratic imperative in a way that could advance union interests, by forestalling employer criticism of union industrial action decisions and removing any questions over member support:

> Personally, I think the protected action stuff does not serve the purpose it was claimed to be serving when it was brought in. It seems to be the belief that unions can—and maybe it's true in some industries, I don't know—that unions can somehow make their members do what they don't want to do. We've always had state-wide meetings to determine what action we take and when we stop taking it and then we increase it and we continue to do that. The protected action application is really just an administrative bureaucracy that has to be dealt with. The timing of taking industrial action is very much a part of the bargaining process more so than the requirement to have a ballot.[35]
>
> I suppose the biggest issue is that the provision was introduced obviously as a means of frustrating workers from taking protected action . . . So the Conservatives brought it in because they thought, look, the unions stand over their members, they don't properly represent their interests, force people to go on strike against their will, so let's have a secret ballot and what that will mean is there'll be less industrial action. That's proven to be completely incorrect. And what it does show I think in a lot of instances is there is a democratic [endorsement] from the employees to take protected action . . . it does

[34] Interview 73, Union.
[35] Interview 74, Union.

> show that it's a secret ballot, it's democratic, and it does show the will of the workers.[36]

The irony, of course, is that, as pointed out in Chapter 7, the PABO process itself promotes a formalistic, public, preference aggregation model of democracy, which does little to encourage genuine democracy, but does help counter employer criticism of lack of union democracy.

As noted in Chapter 6, there were some unintended consequences of the ballots process, some of which benefited unions, at least in some contexts.

Some union interviewees explained that one unintended consequence was that, because of the length of time the process takes, it drove some unions to go to ballot a considerable time before there was an impasse in negotiations:

> I know that's a risky thing for me to say because there's a belief that you shouldn't be able to make the application until it gets to an impasse. But you can appreciate that's going to be six or eight weeks, it would be just illogical and especially in an environment where you're fighting with government wages policy that works in a contrary direction, you're better off the sooner you reach agreement. If you have to delay it for eight weeks for some sort of administrative process to occur it's very challenging.[37]
>
> I guess the amount of time that it can take to be firstly granted to the PABO, and secondly the ballot to be conducted means that, yes, it does need to be applied for prior to when you necessarily want to take it, and I guess indicated . . . that's kind of indicative of the fact that often we are applying for extension, three day extension.[38]

Most importantly, as discussed at length in Chapter 6, union interviewees pointed out that sometimes the PABO process enabled unions to increase leverage by escalating the 'threat' of strike, which enabled them to signal industrial strength, to accelerate the 'countdown' towards industrial action, and to disadvantage the employer through receiving negative publicity:

> [Y]ou hear reports from unions that like to call themselves organising unions, that they actually see it as an opportunity, and a rallying point, and a reason to organise people. And the fact that it's given some formal status in the system

36 Interview 8, Union.
37 Interview 74, Union.
38 Interview 2, Union.

> might even assist in that regard, in that people are told, like at a national election: this is your opportunity to decide, to draw a line in the sand. So there are some reports that it's useful in that way . . . It's certainly a signal to the employer that the union means business, and that because of the structure of the Act, at that point industrial action is imminent, if you've got the ballot. . . . [I]t probably is useful that way. [39]

Tribunal members agreed that the PABO process could provide unions with leverage in the enterprise bargaining process:

> Well I think it does [give unions some leverage in the bargaining process] in two respects. One, the lead times [sic] of it was a bit like the sword of Damocles hanging over the employer. There's the application that's made which is effectively serving notice that the ante is going to be upped, then the ballot and once the ballot is declared then there's the positive reinforcement that industrial action is likely. So that places pressure on the employer. But then there's also the tactical move by unions during that period, particularly the 30 day period within which they must take industrial action. And it was not uncommon for unions to give notice and then not carry through with it. . . . And so that then disorients the employer into taking steps to mitigate the effect of the notified industrial action . . . So it does give them an additional strategic tool to use during the bargaining. . . . It's not infrequent.[40]
>
> In the main the unions know their members. They know they can turn them out. If they need to turn them out, they can turn them out. One or two go down, but they'll go down by not very much if they do go down. . . . I think that what the unions can do now and the smart ones do now, is they use the timing of the application as leverage in the bargaining process.[41]

Employers were well aware of the way in which unions could use the PABO process for leverage. An employer association interviewee noted that:

> when the issue of ballots first came on the agenda . . . one school of thought was that if you ballot people it would lock them in more to industrial action and it would be harder to get them back to work, that was a view.[42]

[39] Stakeholder Interview 9.
[40] Stakeholder Interview 3.
[41] Stakeholder Interview 2.
[42] Stakeholder Interview 10.

Another observed that '. . . I do believe that unions are using the protected action process as a way to achieve an outcome . . . '[43] A third reflected that in arguing for the ballot process:

> we underestimated the significance of the threat of taking industrial action as distinct to the taking of industrial action. That the processes by which unions could notify of intention to take industrial action and effectively set the system up for a prestrike secret ballot, that those processes weren't given as much attention as they probably should have in terms of understanding how that would play out in the distribution of industrial and economic power in the enterprises concerned. . . . And that the attempt to curtail union officials exercising some unilateral or non-representative economic power over a company or a supply chain, which we thought would be achieved by compulsory prestrike ballots, is diminished somewhat by the fact that the union officials can effectively set up for a strike action. And that then changes company behaviour. Because the company then is effectively in the process by which it's exposed to a strike. Which obviously forces operations management and those in charge to try to mitigate risk. So that's probably my major observation about how they've operated in practice.[44]

Overall, however, the advantages to unions provided by the ballots process are overshadowed by the resource demands and impediments the PABO process imposes on unions. For all but the strongest unions—and particularly those that had built up significant experience in, and effective routine processes for complying with, the PABO processes—the PABO requirements have imposed significant compliance costs (time, money, and human resources) and have had a negative impact on unions' ability to take timely and effective strike action. This suggests that it is not a 'fair' process, and that it shifts the balance of industrial power away from unions and in favour of employers. This is not to deny that, in the right circumstances, unions can, as Chapter 6 and the preceding pages suggest, gain a measure of tactical advantage from some aspects of the ballots process. However these advantages are significantly outweighed by the costs and delay associated with the ballots process.

43 Stakeholder Interview 11.
44 Stakeholder Interview 12.

Reform of the system: stakeholder views

Chapter 6 outlined a number of possible 'micro' reforms to the legal rules governing the PABO process. Union representatives, in particular, focused largely on remedying the problems posed by the ballot process (including the quorum requirement and ways of authenticating which employees were entitled to participate in the ballot), the thirty-day rule and the three-day notice period. The findings in Chapter 7 suggest that these proposed reforms might marginally speed up the PABO process, but would do little to turn the PABO requirement into one which promotes anything more democratic than a flawed means of preference aggregation.

At a more 'macro' level, stakeholders made some sweeping proposals to remove the ballot system altogether and replace it with a return to the conciliation and arbitration system; or with a full blooded right to strike.

Some tribunal members, for example, were strongly of the view that the ballot system ought to be abolished and that there should be a return to the 'old' system where the tribunal did more to prevent industrial disputes:

> My personal view is that I don't like the system because of the divergence . . . It seems to me this system helps the industrially strong and does nothing for the industrially weak. . . . I would prefer to see the industrially strong getting a little less and the industrially weak getting evened up. I like the old school stuff back in the days where the Commission's function was to prevent industrial disputes. . . . I think the whole argument that underpinned this is the American proposition about the way this works. Too many of the American elements are in it. The majority support determination and the idea of getting enough on the site up into the union and then the whole processing following that pathway I don't like. I preferred the old historically Australian system where the Commission did intervene. The Commission did assist the industrially weak and it did, in things like pay rates awards and so forth, constrain the industrially strong and pulled them back. That's just a personal view. Economic rationalists and so forth will just scoff at me but I preferred that.[45]
>
> [B]ut the whole legislation is in my view . . . it's orientated towards taking the industrial action in the first place, rather than having the Commission intervene at an earlier point and saying, '. . . we'll impose the outcome on you here for a variety of reasons . . .[46]

[45] Stakeholder Interview 1.
[46] Stakeholder Interview 1.

On the other hand, one union interviewee had a simple and far-reaching solution—one that gave expression to an unconditional and unconditioned 'right to strike':

> we should recognise the right to strike and that our workers should be able to activate industrial action, not just during negotiations but during any period of workplace dispute, it shouldn't just be during negotiations.[47]

This proposal, of course, does not address the question of democratic union decision-making in the taking of industrial action—but its implementation would certainly be consistent with International Labour Organisation (ILO) standards concerning the right to strike as described in Chapter 2.

A third set of suggestions did address democratic decision-making. These proposals were consistent with the conclusions in Chapter 7—that internal union decision-making about industrial action exhibits the characteristics of participatory forms of democratic practice; and that balloting through legislatively mandated rules and in public actively undermines democratic practice, suppresses dissent and debate, and potentially leads to ballot outcomes that are intended not to reflect the genuine wishes of the membership but rather to signal the readiness of the membership to take industrial action.

Interviewees from all stakeholder groups suggested that the key question for reform is whether there should be a statutory and public PABO process. Unions, some FWC members, and even one employer considered that the PABO process was unnecessary, and that the process of ensuring that members decide whether to take industrial action should simply be determined by secret ballot without FWC supervision or the need for an independent ballot agent. For example, one employer suggested that:

> I'd be far happier . . . if all they had to prove was they'd taken a valid vote of employees on site for a range of actions . . . a secret ballot, whatever, on site. Most sites can organise that. You know, we put all the votes in it, we gave everybody this thing, we pushed them all into a room, they did this, this is what we've got approval for, because it's the notice that's important for us.[48]

[47] Interview 20, Union.
[48] Interview 7, Employer.

Some unions argued that the PABO process was unnecessary and a waste of money:

> [M]y personal view is that I think [the requirement] to apply for a PAB[O] is a ridiculous one. If you look at the results of [ballots], they always get up . . . well there's 99.9% of the time they get up, and then for a union like ours, where we are seeking endorsement from members before we take any action . . . before they take any action, I think there's enough internal processes in place and members . . . in any event don't have to take part in any action . . . I just think that the AEC ballot process is unnecessary, probably it's a waste of taxpayers' money too.[49]

Some interviewees pointed out that unions had institutionalized democratic practices in the decisions about taking strike action before and after the PABO process—they activate the PABO process only after a vote of their members, and then only take strike action after a vote of their members. In general, since the debates over ballots in the late 1990s and early 2000s, unions have, explicitly or implicitly, acquiesced in the rhetoric of the democratic imperative:

> so long as they were in control of the process, and it was not designed to delay or obstruct the taking of the action, then that was entirely appropriate. So we moved from being oppositional to saying it was a matter of internal union democracy, and that was an appropriate thing, but other people should stay out of it. So that shift occurred during the Work Choices time. It was probably in part a pragmatic shift, in that it was a bit hard to fight against democracy. . . . pragmatically you would never call a strike or put on a ban without testing the support amongst your workforce anyway. So . . . as long as the process wasn't cumbersome, the concept wasn't offensive. It was actually consistent with their philosophy and their practices.[50]

Union officials suggested that a union-run (or even a union/employer-run) secret ballot would be more appropriate than the current regime:

> The other point I'd make about these protected action ballots is the ridiculousness of the Australian Electoral Commission being involved in vote counting for industrial action ballots which was only introduced by [former Prime Minister] Howard. It's a bureaucratic, cumbersome waste of resources.

[49] Interview 2, Union.
[50] Stakeholder Interview 8.

> The Electoral Commission doesn't enjoy it, they think it's a waste of resources too, and it was specifically designed by Howard to slow down industrial action and it's something that should be changed. . . . [T]he traditional process of people being able to vote by a show of hands, or be able to vote by a union conducted ballot is a much more appropriate manner in my opinion. . . . [B]-efore we lodge an application for a protected action ballot at the Fair Work Commission we have a vote of the members as to whether they want to do that or not. So that vote itself is not run by the Electoral Commission it's run by the union, and it's broadly accepted that . . . it is a fully reasonable way to do it. And then the next stage is once the Electoral Commission has had a vote about the industrial action you can take and tabulate the numbers with scrutineers from the union of the employer, all the votes that are taken subsequently about what industrial action you're going to take based on that ballot are all conducted by the union. . . . The actual agreement-making vote is not conducted by the Electoral Commission, so again there's another important plank in the framework of industrial relations that does not require the Electoral Commission, so the question has to be asked well why is it for industrial action but not for formalisation of ballots [for making an enterprise agreement], because clearly they know that people can have an effective and efficient ballot which is not funded by the tax payer for agreement making itself. . . . the basic points are the Electoral Commission should not be involved in ballots for protected action like they're not involved in ballots for enterprise agreements.[51]

This interviewee proposed that the ballot be 'conducted either by the union, or by the employer, or by the two of them together, whether it's by a secret ballot or a show of hands that's specified on the notification for the ballot'.[52]

One tribunal member agreed that the FWC did not need to be involved in the ballot process:

> You could easily say for industrial action to be protected there must have been a ballot that met these requirements. You don't have to have an order. . . . I don't think Commission role adds much, to be honest. . . . I think it's just an extra bloody hurdle that is bureaucratic than anything else, quite frankly.[53]

[51] Interview 59, Union.
[52] Interview 59, Union.
[53] Stakeholder Interview 7.

In contrast, another tribunal member was of the view that 'the regulated process be retained', but that it be 'less prescriptive':

> I think there is benefit in having a regulated process because without that you are likely to have arguments over the integrity of the process that was applied. . . . I would probably change some things around the edges. I think the detail relating to what has to go in the application is probably a little bit too prescriptive and there ought to be some greater flexibility available to side step some of those requirements to avoid an application having to be repeated simply because it didn't meet one of those administrative hurdles.[54]

The FW Act regime and industrial democracy

The findings of the Study clearly demonstrate that the ballot requirements in Division 8 of Part 3-3 of the FW Act inhibit the capacity of Australian workers lawfully to take industrial action to protect and to promote their occupational interests, and entirely deny them the capacity to take such action to protect their broader social and economic interests.

The problems start from the fact that Australian law, like that of the United Kingdom, does not recognize anything resembling a free-standing right to strike. Instead, the FW Act, like its British counterpart, starts from the premise that all industrial action is unlawful at either or both common law and statute. As was shown in Chapter 1, this was true historically and remains true today. It has the consequence that the capacity lawfully to take industrial action in both countries depends upon providing legal protection against a pre-existing liability rather than upon the exercise of a right—as is the case in countries where the right to strike is enshrined in the national constitution.

Put differently, the capacity lawfully to take industrial action in Australia and the United Kingdom is a privilege rather than a right. Being a privilege, it is only to be expected that that privilege will be conditional. In Britain, for example, the capacity lawfully to take industrial action is conditioned by the requirement that the action be taken 'in contemplation or furtherance of a trade dispute'. In Australia, action can be protected only if it is 'organised or engaged in for the purpose of supporting or advancing claims in relation to the agreement that are only about, or are reasonably believed to only be about,

[54] Stakeholder Interview 5.

permitted matters'.[55] In both jurisdictions, action can be protected only if it has been approved in a ballot conducted in accordance with the relevant provisions of the Australian FW Act and the British *Trade Union and Labour Relations (Consolidation) Act 1992* (UK) (TULRCA).

As explained earlier in this chapter, the Australian provisions are exceedingly complex, and operate in such a manner as significantly to impair the capacity of Australian workers lawfully to take industrial action. Furthermore, the findings of the Study suggest that the PABO provisions under the FW Act operate to suppress strike action in a range of ways that are not immediately obvious from a simple reading of the relevant statutory provisions. Further, the legal regime itself has a significant inhibiting shadowing effect in that the risk of exposing levels of union density in the course of preparing an electoral roll, or of failure to achieve quorum causes some unions to forbear even applying for a PABO. This must inevitably have the effect of reducing access to strike action for workers in industries with low levels of union density and/or lack a tradition of industrial militancy.

This in turn suggests that in order adequately to assess the degree to which pre-strike ballot requirements constrain access to strike action for workers protected by the principles of freedom of association, the supervisory bodies of the ILO need to look at pre-strike ballot requirements in a more holistic manner than is presently the case. This should certainly include examining the letter of the relevant statutory provisions, but should also include considering the impact of those provisions in practice. As noted earlier, the Supervisory Bodies have consistently emphasized the importance of ensuring that 'the conditions that have to be fulfilled under the law in order to render a strike lawful should be reasonable and in any event not such as to place a substantial limitation on the means of action open to trade union organisations'.[56] As a statement of principle, this is entirely unexceptionable; however, neither the Committee of Experts on the Application of Conventions and Recommendations (CEACR) nor the Committee on Freedom of Association (CFA) appears to observe this principle in practice—as evidenced by their persistent failure to look at the substantive effect of the relevant Australian and British provisions concerning pre-strike ballots, as well as their form.

[55] FW Act s 409(1)(a). According to s 172(1) 'permitted matters' include: (a) 'matters pertaining to the relationship between an employer that will be covered by the agreement and that employer's employee who will be covered by the agreement'; (b) matters pertaining to the relationship between employers and unions covered by the agreement; (c) deductions from wages authorised by an employee covered by the agreement; and (d) 'how the agreement will operate'.

[56] ILO 2018: [789]. See also the discussion at 55–8.

The Study also suggests that policy-makers, stakeholders, and regulators need to maintain a healthy scepticism in relation to the use of the language of democracy to justify the imposition of pre-strike ballot requirements, or to justify increasing the layers of regulation attached to an existing pre-strike ballot regime. The findings of the Study demonstrate that the method used to implement mandatory pre-strike balloting rules can, as in Australia (and the United Kingdom), enshrine an impoverished form of democratic practice, particularly where simple preference aggregation is equated to a democratic outcome, and the entire process is conducted under the 'supervision' of the State and interested employers. It is also clear that the express rationale of democracy can commonly be understood as a proxy for a desire to reduce levels of industrial action in practice through the creation of complex and time-consuming balloting models, thereby disempowering workers and their unions.

The Study suggests that reformers should ensure that legal requirements for pre-strike ballots do not distort spontaneous democratic practice within unions, but instead should support, strengthen, and otherwise institutionalize existing participatory and deliberative democratic approaches. Further, political and industrial elections cannot be equated with pre-strike ballots that take place as part of a contested collective bargaining process. Pre-strike ballots are conducted in an industrial context in which employers have a stake in the outcome —they will not be subject to strike action if the ballot does not authorize the action. This context necessarily affects the way in which a trade union will approach and, if permitted, conduct a pre-strike ballot. Where the pre-strike ballot process is State-controlled and is conducted in public, from a union perspective democratic considerations will be significantly less important than the need clearly to signal to the employer the level of employee support for the proposed action in order to demonstrate union strength and the members' willingness to take strike action. Here, democratic considerations must necessarily be sacrificed to tactical ones.

A programme for reform

There is no realistic prospect of the law in either Australia or the United Kingdom being changed so as to recognize a free-standing right to strike in the foreseeable future. It must also be recognized that, at a superficial level, the rhetoric of 'democracy' is a compelling one—even though it can mean vastly different things to different stakeholders at different times and in different places.

However compromised the rhetoric of democracy may be, there is scarcely any greater prospect of ballot requirements being abolished in either Australia or Britain than there is of formal legal recognition of a right to strike: indeed the findings of the Study disclose surprisingly little demand for abolition of the Australian requirements—despite the labour movement's fierce opposition to their introduction in 2005.

If abolition is not a realistic option, the question then becomes one of determining what can and should be done in order to make the Australian, and by inference the British, ballot requirements a more legitimate means of promoting 'democratic' decision-making in relation to taking industrial action.[57]

An obvious starting point is to abolish the requirement that unions that want to give themselves the capacity lawfully to take industrial action at some point in a negotiating process must first obtain the permission of a State instrumentality even to ask their members whether they would like, at some point in the future, to decide to take industrial action. Stated in these terms, the preposterous character of the PABO requirement becomes clear.

Whilst the merits or legitimacy of doing so is far from axiomatic, it is one thing to stipulate that workers must ballot before they decide to take industrial action—it is quite another to require that they ballot before they can even decide whether they want to take industrial action. Even the highly intrusive British provision does not do this.

The anomalous character of the PABO requirement is thrown into stark relief by the fact that there is no requirement under the Australian provision for the decision actually to take industrial action to be approved by ballot or any other democratic means. The findings of the Study show that in practice post-ballot decisions to take industrial action *are* almost invariably taken by democratic means: the point is that the law does not require that to be the case.

On no credible view of the democratic imperative can the PABO requirement be justified. As pointed out in Chapter 4, the Howard Government did not provide any clear rationale for what is now the PABO requirement when introducing the ballot requirement in 2005—although as also noted in Chapter 4, there was a precedent in the form of provision first introduced in Western Australia in 1979.[58] None of the jurisdictions reviewed for purposes

[57] At various points throughout the text there is discussion of specific aspects of the operation of the ballot provisions in the FW Act, and suggestions as to how they ought to be changed—for example in relation to the operation of the thirty-day rule and the notification requirements for the taking of industrial action. The present discussion concentrates on 'big picture' issues, including the continuing role of the PABO requirement.

[58] As indicated, this provision was repealed in 2002, but was still in place when the Coalition was formulating its legislative proposals in the 1990s.

of Chapter 3 (except the Canadian Province of Alberta) had any requirement of this character.

Indeed, it is hard to see what legitimate purpose the PABO requirement serves, even on its own terms. It certainly does nothing meaningfully to promote democratic decision-making, even on a crude aggregation model of democracy. The Study data show that in the overwhelming majority of cases the proposed action is approved. Where it is not approved, it is almost invariably because of failure to achieve quorum. Leaving aside for the moment the appropriateness or otherwise of the quorum requirement, the same effect could be achieved in a mandatory ballot on the taking of industrial action, as opposed to authorizing the possible taking of industrial action. Only in a tiny minority of cases in the Study period was proposed action defeated on its merits, or lack thereof. Again, if proposed action truly lacked the support of the workers concerned, it could be defeated in a ballot on the taking of industrial action, as opposed to a ballot to authorize the possible taking of industrial action. These factors strongly suggest that the true purpose of the PABO requirement is to make it as difficult as possible for unions lawfully to take industrial action rather than to serve any higher democratic purpose.

The indefensible character of the PABO requirement is compounded by the fact that employers are permitted to intervene in the application of that process. It is true that there is no express legislative warrant for this. Indeed, in passing the FW Act in 2009, the Parliament deliberately changed the former provision which expressly made the employer a party to ballot proceedings. Nevertheless, as noted earlier, the tribunal at a very early stage in the life of the legislation recognized the employer's right to intervene in PABO applications. This is entirely inappropriate. The decision whether actually to take industrial action is properly a matter for those who will take that action—and indeed, as noted above, the FW Act does leave that decision to the workers concerned, just as it leaves the decision whether or not to lock out employees to the employer. *A fortiori*, and without accepting the legitimacy of the PABO process, the decision whether to authorize the possibility of deciding to take protected industrial action should clearly be a matter for those who may subsequently be asked by their union to decide whether they want actually to take industrial action. The employer has no legitimate role in that process. If workers choose to take industrial action that is unlawful—for example because it does not meet appropriate procedural or substantive standards—then the employer concerned can legitimately challenge the lawfulness of that action. But there is no proper basis for permitting employer involvement in union decision-making in relation to taking industrial action in the first place—any more than there is a legitimate role for worker involvement in employer decision-making about locking out employees or other responses to employee industrial action.

Implicit in the foregoing is an assumption that the lawfulness of industrial action can properly be made subject to a requirement that the action be approved by a ballot of the workers concerned. As noted earlier, this is not axiomatic. As pointed out in Chapter 7, it can legitimately be said that the decision to take industrial action is properly a matter for the union concerned acting in accordance with the rules adopted by its members—just as it should be a matter for unions to determine whether they wish to discipline members who decline to participate in democratically endorsed industrial action.[59] As experience in the United States shows, it can confidently be anticipated that most unions would adopt ballot requirements of their own volition. There is, nevertheless, merit in the Canadian approach where unions are positively required to have rules providing for the conduct of pre-strike ballots. Given the long tradition of external regulation of the internal affairs of unions in Australia,[60] this would not involve any significant culture shock in that country.

Under the Canadian system, any failure to ballot in accordance with the rules can be dealt with in the same manner as any other breach of the rules—the lawfulness or otherwise of the action itself does not turn on whether it was approved by ballot. It can be appreciated that this might be a bridge too for any Australian or British Government in the foreseeable future. This suggests that the appropriate approach would be to stipulate that union rules must contain provision for the approval of industrial action by ballot of members of the union who are to participate in the proposed action, and that the lawfulness of any subsequent action would be conditional upon its having been approved in such a ballot.

There does not appear to be any legitimate role for a quorum requirement in this context. If the democratic will of the affected union members who choose to vote favour the taking of the proposed industrial action then that should be the end of the matter. If proposed action is approved only by a small number of the affected members, then it is unlikely that the action will have any significant practical impact, but the point is that the decision will have been taken by the democratically expressed will of the membership.[61] Ironically, that is

[59] See the discussion at 194–5, nn 28–9.

[60] See the discussion at 193–5.

[61] The FW Act contemplates the making of enterprise agreements without any union involvement. The merits or otherwise of that approach are beyond the scope of this book. It is, however, unlikely that non-unionized workers would wish to take protected industrial action in the course of negotiations for an agreement—but if they do, it would be perfectly possible to require that the workers represented by the bargaining representatives concerned should be required to approve the taking of such action by ballot.

how the final decision to take or not to take industrial action is normally made under the current Australian regime. The quorum requirement applies only to the entirely superfluous PABO requirement. It is also the way in which this issue was determined in the United Kingdom prior to the introduction of the quite egregious and manifestly undemocratic 2016 amendments.

Legislative changes along the lines outlined in this section would provide a basis for meaningful, democratic decision-making in relation to the taking of industrial action. It would do little more than accord formal recognition to the non-legislated democratic processes which the Study shows are already the norm in Australia. But it would at least constitute a repudiation of the hypocritical posturing that underpins the current provision in Australia (and Britain) which uses the rhetoric of democracy to deprive workers of their democratic right to take industrial action to protect and to promote their legitimate social and economic interests.

APPENDIX 1

Study Methods

Overview

The data for the empirical study (the Study) in this book were collected during a project entitled 'Protected Action Ballots and Protected Industrial Action under the Fair Work Act: The Impact of Ballot Procedures on Enterprise Bargaining Processes', funded by an Australia Research Council (ARC) Discovery Grant.[1] The Study was designed to provide the first empirical account of the Australian Protected Action Ballot Order (PABO) process[2] and its effect on enterprise bargaining behaviour.

The Study received approval from the University of Sydney's Human Research Ethics Committee.[3] This approval followed a rigorous procedure in which all interview tools and documentation provided to participants underwent detailed scrutiny.

The Study was designed to explore three specific dimensions of the PABO process, namely:

1. whether bargaining representatives *escalate decisions* about protected industrial action during enterprise bargaining in order to accommodate the statutory process and associated timeframes;
2. whether (and if so, how) bargaining representatives use PABO applications in a *strategic* manner to influence progress in enterprise bargaining negotiations; and
3. whether (and if so, how) the PABO process affects the length of time between a decision to pursue action and the taking of that action.

These issues were explored through a 'point-in-time' examination of how the PABO system operated in practice. The Study used a mixed methods approach with quantitative and qualitative components. The quantitative data were largely used to provide a frequency count of the number of PABO applications, and frequency distributions of PABO applications by state and by industry, and of the different kinds of industrial action proposed in PABOs and actually taken. Chapter 5 includes a multilevel binary logistic regression model to predict 'reaching the quorum' on the basis of ballot mode, the city in which the ballot application was lodged, and the length of the voting period. The qualitative data comprised two sets of semi-structured interviews exploring the 'lived experience' of (i) union and employer participants in the PABO process; and (ii) persons responsible for conducting ballots, tribunal members hearing PABO applications, and representatives of peak industrial associations. Both sets of interviewees were also asked to reflect on the PABO system, and to propose possible reforms.

[1] DP140100902. The Chief Investigators were Professors Shae McCrystal, Breen Creighton, and Richard Johnstone.

[2] The PABO process is discussed in detail in Chapter 4.

[3] Project ID Number 2014/369.

This appendix describes the research methods adopted for each of the quantitative and qualitative components of the research project.[4]

Quantitative Study design

Data sources and coding

The quantitative component of the Study involved descriptive and inferential statistical analysis of information about the PABO system collected in a database developed by the authors. The database captured information relating to all enterprise agreement negotiations that led to a PABO application being submitted to the Fair Work Commission (FWC) during the Study period from 1 July 2015 to 30 June 2016 (n = 1,302). The information used to create the database was drawn from five main documentary sources:

1. ballot applications submitted to the FWC;
2. applications submitted to the FWC to vary or withdraw an order;
3. ballot decisions and orders made by the FWC in relation to orders;
4. ballot vote outcomes; and
5. records of new enterprise agreements registered for approval with the FWC.

Applications for PABOs are in the public domain and hard copies of applications are available at FWC registries. To streamline the data collection process, the FWC agreed automatically to forward, by email, all applications (including applications to withdraw or vary) to the research team. Ballot decisions, orders, and vote outcomes, as well as new enterprise agreements registered for approval, are also in the public domain and are published on the FWC website. For each PABO application made, the research team gathered the associated decision/order and vote outcome statement from the FWC website and monitored the website to determine whether any enterprise agreement arising out of the negotiations had been approved. The approval of a new agreement signals the conclusion of negotiations, but it may take some time after the initial PABO application for an agreement to be approved. For this reason, the research team continued monitoring newly approved agreements from the conclusion of the initial data collection period of 30 June 2016, until January 2019 (a period of thirty months).

Some quantitative data was also extracted from interview transcripts: in particular, data on the use of industrial action in the worksites that were the subject of PABOs, and where action was taken, the frequency and form of action taken.

Table A1.1 summarizes the variables for which quantitative data was collected and the details of the data source.

One of the most challenging issues in building the database was the great variety and number of different forms of industrial action put to employee vote in the ballots themselves.

In order to streamline the recording of proposed industrial action, the following forms of bans were recorded cumulatively as count variables:[5]

- job function bans;
- overtime bans; and
- bans on recalls/call backs/weekend work/shift changes.

[4] Reporting of qualitative methods is designed to accord with the Consolidated Criteria for Reporting Qualitative Research (COREQ) requirements, following Tong, Sainsbury, & Craig 2007: 349–57.

[5] Count variables are non-negative (discrete) integers, eg 0, 1, 2.

Table A1.1 Data captured

Variable	Type	Details
PABO application		
Ballot lodgement jurisdiction	Categorical	Vic, WA, SA, Tas, NSW, QLD, ACT
Industry	Categorical	
Interpreter required	Categorical	Yes, no
Special assistance required	Categorical	Yes, no
Name of enterprise agreement	Text	
Date of enterprise agreement expiry	Date	dd/mm/yy
Date negotiation commenced	Date	dd/mm/yy
Date PABO application submitted	Date	dd/mm/yy
Statement on GTRA	Text	
Forms of IA proposed	Categorical	See below
Form of ballot question	Categorical	Single, rolled-Up
Question/s listed on ballot	Text	
Ballot agent	Categorical	AEC, other
Applicant organization	Text	
Applicant trade union	Categorical	
Respondent organization	Text	
Respondent State	Categorical	Vic, WA, SA, Tas, NSW, QLD, ACT
Representative organization	Text	
Representative State	Categorical	Vic, WA, SA, Tas, NSW, QLD, ACT
EBAs registered for approval		
EBA submitted	Categorical	Submitted, approved
Name of new enterprise agreement	Text	
Date agreement approved by FWC	Date	dd/mm/yy
Ballot variations/withdrawal requests		
Order withdrawn	Categorical	
Reason given for withdrawal	Text	
thirty-day extension given	Categorical	Yes, no, n/a
Application for ballot variation	Categorical	Yes, no
Variation details	Text	
Ballot vote		
Mode of ballot	Categorical	Person, postal, electronic

Continued

Table A1.1 Continued

Variable	Type	Details
Number voters on roll	Count	
Number of valid votes	Count	
Number of votes	Count	
Percentage on the roll voting	Percentage	
Number of votes in favour of action	Count	
Number of votes against action	Count	
FWC decisions/orders		
Commissioner	Text	
Ballot approved	Categorical	Yes, no, not found
Hearing type	Categorical	Person, telephone, on papers
Length of ballot vote in days	Count	
Change of notice period (at hearing)	Categorical	Yes, no, n/a
Length of notice period change (at hearing)	Count	Days
Change of questions (at hearing)	Categorical	Yes, no, n/a
Ballot contested (at hearing)	Categorical	Yes, no
Grounds of contest	Text	
Decision on contest (at hearing)	Categorical	Upheld, rejected
Qualitative interview		
IA occurred	Categorical	Yes, no, n/a
Form of IA occurring	Categorical	See below

Stop work meetings were recorded as yes/no categorical variables.[6] Strike action (in the sense of a total stoppage of work) or stop work action proposed was coded as yes/no against the following durations:

- less than one hour;
- one hour;
- two hours;
- three hours;
- four hours;
- six hours;
- eight hours;
- ten hours;
- twelve hours;

[6] Categorical variables are assigned 'names' or 'labels' and represent groupings such as Yes/No. In this case, where stop work meetings were proposed, the label 'yes' was assigned under the variable 'stop work meetings'. Where stop work meetings were not proposed, 'no' was assigned under the variable 'stop work meetings'.

- seventy-two hours;
- shift length;
- indefinite;
- week long; and
- time unspecified.

Where a ballot application proposed a duration different to those described above, the time was rounded up to the nearest hour in which a time category already existed. 'Time unspecified' strikes/stop work were recorded separately from 'indefinite' strikes/stop work, as the latter specified that the stoppage would be indefinite, whereas the former specified no timeframe at all. Ballot vote outcomes were recorded as count data.

A small number of derived variables were created to represent the length of time from the commencement of negotiations to the submission of a PABO, and from PABO submission to decision outcome.[7] Additional derived variables were produced to record whether the ballot was a suspected 'original ballot' or a 're-ballot'.

Matching a ballot to an agreement approved by the FWC was not always straightforward. The researchers had to deal with many minor, and occasional major, variations in the agreement title as new agreements were made to replace an old agreement. Minor variations were obvious and generally involved updating the year of the agreement.[8] Occasionally, however, the research team could find no new agreement to match the existing agreement title, and had to search for and verify whether an agreement with a different title might represent a match. Suspected matches were verified by cross-reference to existing information in the Study database (eg site name, trading name) and the 'known' existing agreement was compared with the 'possible' new agreement in order to confirm the match.

The end of the Study period in July 2016 marked the end of the main data extraction process, with the exception of agreement tracking which continued up until January 2019.

Analytical strategy

The database was hierarchical in nature with PABO applications nested within 'negotiations' for single-enterprise agreements. In order to impose a hierarchy, each PABO application, each proposed enterprise agreement, and each worksite was given a unique identification number. Enterprise agreement numbers were similar across ballot applications in instances where a single-enterprise agreement negotiation gave rise to more than one ballot application, whilst worksite numbers enabled the hierarchy to account for applications submitted as re-ballots under the same agreement at the same site, as well as accounting for applications relating to an enterprise agreement which covered more than one site.

The 1,302 PABO applications that were made during the Study period covered approximately 397[9] enterprise agreement negotiations involving approximately 917 worksites.

[7] Derived variables are the product of calculations performed upon existing variables. For example, in the database one variable recorded the date the ballot was submitted to the FWC, whilst another variable recorded the date the PABO vote concluded. From these two variables it is possible to derive a new variable recording the length of time in days between these two dates. This variable would represent the length of time in days between submission and vote outcome.

[8] For example 'Smith Metalworks enterprise agreement 2013' would be recorded as 'Smith Metalworks enterprise agreement 2016'.

[9] This figure is estimated as it requires an inference to be drawn as to the likely connection between PABO applications that are submitted separately by different ballot representatives or resubmitted by the same ballot representative (eg where two different unions submit PABO applications in respect of

They included five sets of negotiations, which between them generated 741 ballots. This is because the applications involved 'single interest employers' who had obtained single interest employer authorizations. 'Single interest employers' are defined in *Fair Work Act 2009* (Cth) (FW Act) s 172(5) as employers engaged in a joint venture or common enterprise; employers that are related bodies corporate; or employers specified as such in a single interest employer authorization. Single interest employer authorizations can be made by the FWC under s 249 or by the minister under s 247, and enable employers who wish to bargain together to do so, even though they would not otherwise constitute a single interest employer for the purposes of s 172(5).

More specifically:

- 496 applications related to the Catholic Employing Authorities Single Enterprise Agreement Collective Agreement—Diocesan Schools of Queensland 2012 negotiation;
- 43 related to the Catholic Employing Authorities Single Interest—South Australian Catholic Schools Enterprise Agreement 2013 negotiation;
- 144 related to the Nurses and Midwives (Victorian Public Sector) (Single Interest Employers) Enterprise Agreement 2012–2016 negotiation;
- 35 related to the Victorian Public Health Sector (Health Professionals, Health and Allied Services, Managers and Administrative Officers) Multiple Enterprise Agreement 2011–2015 negotiation;[10] and
- 23 related to the Victorian Public Mental Health Services Enterprise Agreement 2012–2016 negotiation.

Limitations of the data

The data collected was cross-sectional and did not allow for consideration of how the number of PABO applications may fluctuate over longer time periods. The approach was chosen to facilitate the tracking of PABO applications in real time, and to ensure that memory decay amongst interview participants did not impede the quality of the data collected. The disadvantage of this approach was that it excluded industries or occupations that did not engage in enterprise bargaining for new agreements during the twelve-month Study period. However, a review of PABO applications across time suggested that there had been no significant shifts in the characteristics of applications since they were introduced in 2006.

As shown in Table 4.1 in Chapter 4, over the life of the FW Act (excluding the Study period), PABO applications have varied from a high of 1,011 in 2011–2012 to a low of 627 in 2013–2014. These variations may be due to a range of factors, including the occurrence, and progress, of bargaining rounds in particular industries in any given year. This is particularly true of the Study period 2015–2016 in which the high number of PABOs lodged (1,302) can be attributed to the large number of negotiations occurring in relation to single interest authorizations. For example, if the single interest authorization PABOs were not counted

the same negotiation). This figure has previously been reported as 399 (see Creighton et al 2018, 2019, 2019a; Orchiston et al 2019).

[10] FW Act s 413(2) provides that industrial action must not relate to a proposed multi-enterprise agreement. However, the fact that multiple employers are pursuing a multi-enterprise agreement does not prevent the relevant employees pursuing a single-enterprise agreement at each site, and applying for a PABO in respect of each separate enterprise,

as individual ballots (n = 741) but as single ballots (n = 5) then the numbers for 2015–2016 come down to 566 ballots lodged, 517 ballots approved (91.3 per cent), with 467 votes conducted (90.3 per cent of ballots approved). These rates of approval and votes conducted align more closely with figures reported over the previous six years.

It is important to note that the nature of data collected during the Study significantly increased the complexity of the recording and analysis process. For several variables, the research team had to make inferences about links between the data or inferences based on incomplete data and this was particularly true of derived variables. For example, deciding whether a ballot was an 'original ballot' or a 're-ballot' required triangulation between a number of data points, including: (i) the date the PABO was submitted; (ii) the name of the ballot representative; (iii) the name of the worksite; (iv) the title of the proposed enterprise agreement; and (v) the ballot outcome for the suspected 'original ballot'. Similarly, there was some complexity in matching database records against new enterprise agreements lodged with the FWC, as is discussed above.

In addition, the data were not static in nature and the length of the agreement-making process spanned a number of years, which meant that initial coding variables assigned to a record were occasionally subject to later amendment upon receipt of additional information or clarification. This accounts for minor variations in the raw numbers reported in previous publications, none of which affected the findings in percentage terms.[11]

Methods and models of analysis and model outputs

Most of the statistical analysis of quantitative data in Chapters 4 and 5 is simple, and largely comprises frequency counts (Table 4.1) and frequency distributions (Tables 4.2 and 4.3, and Figures 4.1, 4.2, and 5.1). Chapter 5, did, however, include some regression analysis involving the use of one model fitted using MLwiN.

Models fitted

The model used multilevel binary logistic regression and employed Markov Chain Monte Carlo (MCMC) methods with deviance information criteria (DIC)[12] presented below the table.[13]

This model[14] is used to predict the likelihood that the quorum requirements will be met on the basis of vote mode and length of vote (Table A1.2 below). The model assesses whether

[11] For example, clarifications have resulted in small downward shifts in the number of 'negotiations' the database was reported to cover, from 399 (as reported in Orchiston et al 2019; Creighton et al 2018, 2019) down to 397; and small amendments to the number of PABOs reported as approved by the FWC, from 1,254 to 1,253. In the latter case, the discrepancy arose because a challenge to a PABO resulting in the matter being remitted to Commissioner Williams for a decision, was coded as approved, although no record of either withdrawal or approval was found as of November 2018: see further *MUA v Maersk Crewing Australia Pty Ltd* [2016] FWCFB 1894 (B2015/1574). This had a flow-on effect to the number of PABOs reported as 'withdrawn after approval but before the vote took place' (fifty-one down to fifty).

[12] The deviance information criterion is a hierarchical modelling generalization of the Akaike Information Criteria. It combines measures of model accuracy and complexity, with lower values indicating the best trade-off between the two; see Spiegelhalter et al 2002.

[13] Those wishing to understand more about MCMC Bayesian approaches in contrast to likelihood-based frequentist methods (IGLS and RIGLS) are referred to Browne 2017: 1–19.

[14] Discussed in Chapter 5 at 133–5.

Table A1.2 Multilevel binary logistic regression model predicting the likelihood of reaching the quorum on the basis of ballot mode, lodgement city, and length of vote

Predictor	Level	Estimate	Standard error
Constant		0.50	0.64
Mode	Postal	0.00	–
	Attendance	1.04**	0.33
Lodgement city	Sydney	0.00	–
	Melbourne	0.11	0.38
	Brisbane	−0.86*	0.36
	Adelaide	−0.11	0.50
	Hobart	−0.76	0.54
	Perth	1.84	1.32
Length of vote		0.06*	0.03
Random effects			
	Enterprise agreement level variance	0.57	0.25
	Site within enterprise variance	0.00	0.00

Notes: Deviance = 1,055.0, DIC = 1,100.5
****p<0.001, **p<0.01, *p<0.05*

particular factors (eg mode of vote) are associated with an increase or decrease in the likelihood of achieving certain outcomes (eg quorum).

The regression model used is multilevel in order to account for the hierarchical structure of the dataset. As noted above, in the dataset ballot results are nested within sites, which are nested within negotiations. All PABO applications arose within the context of negotiations for an enterprise agreement. PABO applications may be submitted at multiple sites as part of the same negotiations. The model uses a random intercept method that allows the probability of achieving the quorum to vary across sites, and across negotiations.

Table A1.2 shows the output of the multilevel binary logistic regression model predicting the likelihood of the quorum being reached in a ballot on the basis of the mode, lodgement city, and the length of the ballot vote (days).

As can be seen from the table, attendance voting was associated with a greater likelihood that the quorum requirement would be satisfied in a ballot when compared to ballots undertaken by post (the reference category). This was statistically significant;[15] in practice, this equates to there being a 79.7 per cent chance of reaching the quorum in a postal ballot, compared to an attendance ballot where the chance stands at 91 per cent.

The city in which the initial PABO application was lodged produced an impact on the likelihood that the quorum would be reached in a ballot. When compared to the reference

[15] $\beta = 1.04, \chi^2_1 = 10.29, p<0.01$.

category (Sydney), for applications submitted in Melbourne, ballots were slightly more likely to reach quorum (87.5 per cent chance of reaching quorum in Melbourne, compared to 86.1 per cent in Sydney); this did not, however, reach statistical significance. For applications lodged in Brisbane, the ballots were slightly less likely to reach the quorum, and this finding reached statistical significance.[16]

The likelihood of the quorum being reached in a ballot increased as the length of the voting period increased.[17] Further, the model output reported in Table A1.2, suggests that there is clustering by enterprise agreement negotiation. Where multiple ballots were conducted in the context of one set of agreement negotiations, there was a similar likelihood that a quorum would be reached.[18] In order to explore whether industry had an impact on reaching the quorum, an industry variable was added to the model. This distinguished between ballots taking place in white-collar and blue-collar industries. Findings were not significant. As the model yielded a slightly higher DIC, the industry variable was removed from the model in favour of the more parsimonious model.

Qualitative Study design

The qualitative element of the Study involved two groups of participants. Part A participants were applicants and respondents to PABO applications submitted to the FWC from July 2015 to June 2016. Part B participants included those involved in conducting ballot votes, those charged with making PABOs, those involved in the legislative changes brought about by the FW Act, and those with an interest in the operation of the system (eg, peak representative bodies).

Part A—PABO interviews

The PABO applicant/respondent interview questions were designed to explore:

- factors influencing decisions to apply for PABOs;
- stakeholder perceptions of the state of negotiations at the time of the application;
- stakeholder perceptions of why applications and consequential pre-strike strike ballots are successful or unsuccessful;
- factors influencing the number of pre-strike ballots which lead to industrial action; and
- factors influencing the time between an application to the FWC, the conduct of a pre-strike ballot, and any subsequent industrial action.

Participant recruitment and selection

Participants were drawn from a database of applicants and respondents listed in PABO applications submitted to the FWC during the period from July 2015 to June 2016. PABO applicants were union officials or union legal officers, who were either: (i) directly involved in the negotiations with an employer for an enterprise agreement (that gave rise to the PABO application); or (ii) union legal officers who were less involved in the negotiations, but who took responsibility for submission of the PABO application and the legal process governing

16 $\beta = -0.86, \chi^2_1 = 5.71, p<0.05$.
17 $\beta = 0.06, \chi^2_1 = 4.84, p<0.05$.
18 Enterprise agreement negotiation-level random effect, $\beta = 0.57, \chi^2_1 = 5.02, p<0.05$.

the granting of a PABO (including appearing at a FWC hearing to determine the outcome of the application where necessary). PABO application respondents were employer representatives (typically HR Managers or small business owners) involved in negotiations with union officials for an enterprise agreement.

As discussed above, during the period from July 2015 to June 2016 the FWC forwarded each PABO application it received to the research team. Applicant and respondent names were drawn from these applications and the resulting list formed the basis of the sample from which potential participants were drawn. Contact details for participants were acquired only from publicly available information.

Prior to contacting potential participants, the research team took steps to generate awareness of the Study by contacting a number of key stakeholder groups, including the Australian Industry Group (a peak representative body of a wide range of Australian employers) and the Australian Council of Trade Unions. Both of these organizations sent out information on behalf of the research team to promote knowledge of the project amongst unions and employers.

Participants were contacted via email in the first instance. Where an interview on one side of a PABO application had been secured, additional effort was made to engage the other side via additional email and phone contact. That is to say, where an interview with the respondent of a particular PABO application had been secured, further steps were taken to encourage the participation of the applicant.

The interview sample was recruited in three waves. In the first wave, the research team sought to 'pair' applicant and respondents (employer and union representatives). Pairing was not possible in some cases: there were three outright refusals to participate (by the 'pair' to Interviews 37, 45, and 46) and a slightly larger number of silent refusals (as indicated by continued non-response) (n = fourteen). At the end of the first wave in November 2015, the research team evaluated the interviews conducted until then for thematic saturation, industry, and State/Territory coverage and size of business. At this point, further recruitment of participants (as part of a second wave) was undertaken to recruit PABO applicants (unions) in a small number of industries and States/Territories that were underrepresented in the interview sample. Additional efforts were also made to recruit employers (respondents) in Government. In May 2016, following evaluation of the interviews already undertaken, the research team decided to conduct a third wave of recruitment to enable the team to capture data relating to an important change in the law occurring in December 2015 that had ramifications for ballot processes. The change, brought about by the *Fair Work Amendment Act 2015*, imposed a new requirement for PABO applications before an order could be granted. Under the change, a PABO application could only be brought to the FWC if a 'notification time' had passed, and bargaining for a proposed agreement had commenced. Interviews conducted in the period from May 2016 to August 2016, as part of this third wave of recruitment, enabled the research team to explore the impact (if any) of this change in the law.

Data collection

Contact with participants made it clear that the objectives of the research were designed to:

> Explore the impact that [the PABO requirement] has on decisions made by bargaining representatives during enterprise bargaining negotiations and the challenges and/or advantages that may arise as a result of the protected action ballot order requirement.

Participants were provided with a participant information statement, which made clear the voluntary nature of their participation and their ability to withdraw from the Study at any point in time. Participants were provided with assurance as to the confidentiality and anonymity of their data.

Interviews were semi-structured and based on an interview guide developed by the research team. Data collection was piloted in May 2016 with three pilot interviews. Slight modifications were made to the interview guide based on the pilot interviews, and pilot participants were invited to offer feedback on the interview questions. The interview guide gave participants the opportunity to elaborate on any issues of particular importance to them at the end of the interview.

Data were collected via phone (n = forty-four) and face to face (n = thirty). The majority of face-to-face interviews took place at the workplace of the participant —only one participant expressed a preference to be interviewed at the University of Sydney. In all cases, the only people present in the interview were the interviewee/s and the interviewer/s. Where permission was granted (in all but three interviews), interviews were recorded via digital voice recorder. All audio recordings were later transcribed in full for analysis and made available to members of the research team (following the requirements of the project's ethical clearance). Interviews were generally of approximately forty minutes' duration.

Sample

In total, and excluding data captured during the pilot, seventy-four interviews were conducted, comprised of thirty-two 'paired interviews', one triple pair (in which two representatives of two unions and one employer were interviewed in relation to the same enterprise agreement negotiation), nine single employer interviews, and thirty single union interviews.

Although seventy-four interviews were conducted, the interview discussions related to approximately 719 ballot applications submitted from July 2015 to June 2016. As noted above, the FWC received a total of 1,302 ballot applications during this period, meaning that the seventy-four interviews conducted covered 55 per cent of ballot applications submitted.[19] This coverage arises because applications are nested within 'negotiations' for an enterprise agreement—the 1,302 applications submitted during the Study period pertained to only 397 enterprise agreement negotiations and approximately 917 employment sites. Interviewees, particularly employee representatives, typically spoke 'globally' about negotiations (which may have given rise to more than one PABO application) rather than confining their comments to specific PABO applications. In total, the interviews covered fifty-five enterprise agreement negotiations or 13.8 per cent of the total number of negotiations for which one or more PABO application was submitted during the July 2015–June 2016 period.

Table A1.3 indicates the percentage of interviews from different States achieved in interview compared to the percentage of ballot applications received by the FWC during the data collection period.

[19] This figure is approximate given that ballot discussions sometimes touched upon earlier unsuccessful ballots captured in the Study period, or later re-applications for ballots that had expired. Researchers made attempts to locate, cross-reference, and link these ballot applications to the interview, though this process of manual data-matching necessarily introduced a degree of human error. In previous publications reporting on this data, this number was referred to as 713. This total counts only one ballot per employee interview. However, there were a number of employee interviews involving ballots submitted jointly by unions coordinating their actions. If more than one ballot per employee interview is counted, this number rises to 719. It should be noted that in percentage terms, the impact of this increase in terms of the proportion of ballots covered by the interviews, is minimal (54.8 per cent versus 55.2 per cent).

Table A1.3 Percentage of interviews in each State alongside percentage of ballot applications in each Jurisdiction.[1]

	% of all unique ballot applications	% of interviews
Sydney (NSW)	23.1	33.8
Perth (WA)	7.3	5.4
Melbourne (Vic)	45.1	44.6
Hobart (Tas)	4.1	1.4
Canberra (ACT)	1.5	1.4
Brisbane (QLD)	11.6	5.4
Adelaide (SA)	7.31	8.11

[1] Excludes pilot data. Excludes duplication brought about by separately balloting sites under a single interest authorization meaning 740 ballots are counted as five separate applications.

Table A1.4 shows that the interviews covered thirty-one of a possible fifty-three industries in which ballots were submitted to the FWC during the Study period.

Post-interview follow up

In order to minimize the impact of memory failure, the research team contacted potential interviewees soon after the submission of a PABO application with a view to conducting interviews as soon as possible. This often meant that, at the time of interview, negotiations leading up to the enterprise agreement had not always finished. To ensure capture of as much data as possible the research team undertook a process of follow up until the end of the qualitative data collection period in August 2016. Participants were invited to participate in

Table A1.4 Interview industry coverage.

	% of all unique ballots submitted	% of ballots covered by interviews
Health	7.8	20.3
Food production and manufacturing	9.8	0.6
Transport and maritime	14.1	1.5
Building, construction, and labour	11.6	0.8
Manufacturing and engineering	20.9	1.8
Public services and utilities	14.9	2.9
Education	2.0	69.3
Other services	11.6	1.4
Metal, mining, oil, and gas	7.3	1.4

follow-up contact and were approached via email on a semi-regular basis in order to provide an indication of the progress of negotiations since the interview. Most interviewees participated in follow up, although one interviewee (Interview 39) did not respond to researcher contact. At the end of the qualitative data collection period (end of August 2016) the majority of negotiations had been completed, with only thirteen negotiations—out of fifty-five—still ongoing. As discussed above, these data were reconciled with data drawn from the FWC website listing the registration of new agreements. By the end of January 2019, the outcome of the negotiations was known for all but three negotiations included within the interview sample.

Analytical strategy

To enable coding consistency, one member of the research team coded all interview data. Major and minor themes were identified in advance using the interview topic guide as a basis, with further themes identified via an inductive grounded theory approach.[20] The research team also used content analysis, with key word searches (orientated around the identified themes) undertaken in order to ensure thorough coding of the interview material against the identified (major and minor) themes. The research team used Nvivo Software to carry out the coding. The coding framework used in the Study is shown in Appendix 2, with a short descriptive sentence explaining the nature of the code.

Interview data were analysed inductively to develop the key research findings emerging from the Study. Direct quotation of participants was used: to provide direct support for claims made; as a means by which to give 'voice' to interviewees; as a means of illustrating emerging themes; and as a method of providing greater context to emerging themes by highlighting depth of feeling and emotion verbally expressed.[21] Where direct quotation of participant data was used to illustrate research findings, the source of the quotation was anonymized and referred to only by interview number.

Major and minor themes identified in advance (via the coding framework) and identified naturalistically ('in-vivo') during the process of coding and qualitative analysis are reported on in this and other publications. Reporting reflected both the overarching positions expressed by participants, as well as the views that ran counter to the majority.

Part B—Stakeholder interviews

In late 2015 the research team decided to add an additional component to the Study by undertaking further qualitative interviews with stakeholders engaged in the PABO regime. These interviews would enable the research team to acquire important contextual information about the rationale underpinning the PABO regime and the interactions between PABO applicants and stakeholders charged with responsibility for certain elements of the PABO process. Stakeholders included: (i) the AEC; (ii) FWC members; (iii) those involved in the legislative changes brought about by the FW Act; and (iv) and those with a vested interest in the operation of the system (eg peak representative bodies).

The interview with the AEC focused on:

- how a ballot is actioned and tasks assigned to relevant staff members;
- the preparations undertaken in advance of a ballot;

[20] Glaser & Strauss 1967.
[21] See further Corden & Sainsbury 2006.

- the factors (internal/external) influencing the mode of ballot selected;
- how disagreements between parties over the conduct of a ballot are managed (voting roll, mode, location, timeframes, etc); and
- the availability of electronic balloting.

Interviews with FWC members focused specifically on:

- the motivations underpinning the introduction of the ballot regime;
- the experience of deciding upon PABO applications;
- the way in which the PABO process influences collective bargaining behaviours;
- the resources required to determine PABO applications; and
- what reforms to the system, if any, are required.

Stakeholders were asked about:

- the introduction of compulsory ballots in 2005 and the prevailing political context at the time;
- the role their organization played, or the position they took, in relation to the introduction of compulsory ballots and the motivations underpinning that role/position;
- the wider motivations underpinning the regime; and
- their experience of the compulsory ballot system, and what reforms, if any, were necessary to enhance the operation of the regime.

Participant recruitment and selection

Recruitment for the stakeholder interviews was purposive. The research team members identified a possible sample of participants by drawing on their existing knowledge of stakeholders involved in: conducting PABO ballots; approving PABO applications at the FWC; and the development of the FW Act. The pool of potential interviewees responsible for making decisions about PABO applications (FWC members) was refined after looking at information contained in the ballot database prepared for the quantitative element of the Study. This allowed the research team to identify the FWC members most involved in ballot decision-making during the Study period. As members are typically assigned applications in industry-specific areas, the research team tried to ensure that those approached for interview represented a mix of industry coverage.

An invitation to participate in an interview was circulated, via the FWC General Manager, to a shortlist of FWC members, and invited interested parties to contact the research team via phone or email. FWC members who expressed an interest in participating in the Study were contacted by the research team, provided with additional information, and an interview time was arranged. Stakeholders from the Australian Electoral Commission (AEC), Australian Council of Trade Unions (ACTU), Australian Industry Group (AIG), and Australian Minerals and Mining Association (AMMA) were directly invited to participate in the Study by the research team, drawing on research team members' existing contacts within those organizations. These stakeholder interviewees were selected strategically in order to ensure a balance of perspectives (and in particular a balance of union and employer affiliated organizations).

Data collection

Data collection largely followed the same processes as used for Part A participants. Contact with potential participants in Part B of the Study made it clear that the objectives of the research were to:

> facilitate a better understanding of the impact of protected industrial action ballot order provisions on enterprise bargaining behaviour and trade union decision-making concerning protected industrial action.

Participants were provided with a participant information statement similar to that provided for Part A participants. Whilst participants were advised that their organization would be identified in the Study, they were given the option to identify themselves or remain anonymous. All elected to remain anonymous.

Interviews were semi-structured and orientated around an interview guide. Data were collected via phone or face to face. In all cases, the only people present in the interview were the interviewee/s and the interviewer/s, and permission was granted to record the interviews using a digital voice recorder. All audio recordings were later transcribed in full for analysis and made available to members of the research team. Where requested, interviewees were granted access to interview transcripts for the purposes of comment and/or correction. This option was exercised only by the AEC. Most interviews were approximately forty minutes in duration.

Sample

In total, the stakeholder interview sample consisted of data collected from two AEC representatives (in a joint interview), seven FWC Commissioners, two representatives from the ACTU, one representative from AIG, one representative from AMMA, and one individual with relevant experience.

Analytical strategy

As with the interviews in Part A, to enable coding consistency, one member of the research team coded all stakeholder interview data collected in Part B, using Nvivo Software. Major themes were identified in advance using the interview topic guide as a basis, with further minor themes identified inductively during the process of coding. The coding framework used in the Study is shown in Appendix 2, along with a short descriptive sentence explaining the nature of the code.

Interview data collected in Part B provided valuable explanations of the purpose and operation of the FW Act in practice. These data were used to support, validate, and, in some cases, help to explain key research findings emerging from the Study from the analysis of material in Part A.

As with the analysis of interview data collected in Part A, direct quotation of participants was used: to provide direct support for claims made; as a means by which to give 'voice' to interviewees; as a means of illustrating emerging themes; and as a method of providing greater context to emerging themes by highlighting depth of feeling and emotion verbally expressed.[22] Where direct quotation of participant data was used to illustrate research findings, the source of the quotation was anonymized and referred to only by interview number.

Findings reported in this book, and in other publications that have emerged from the research project, derive from the major and minor themes identified in the interview data. These themes were identified in advance and naturalistically ('in-vivo') during the process of coding. Reporting reflected both the overarching positions expressed by participants as well as the views that ran counter to the majority.

[22] See further Corden & Sainsbury 2006.

APPENDIX 2

Interview Coding Frameworks

Interview coding framework for Part A (employer/bargaining representative) interviews

NODE	SUB-NODE	DESCRIPTION
BACKGROUND FOLDER		
Background	*Background to dispute*	Information pertaining to background of an enterprise agreement (EA) that gave rise to the application for a Protected Action Ballot Order (PABO)
	Bargaining representatives and other unions	Bargaining representatives and other unions involved in negotiating the enterprise agreement (EA)
	Greenfields	Reference to Greenfields agreements in the history of the EA negotiations
	History of union involvement	History of union involvement at the worksite and within the context of the EA negotiations
	Industry	The industry in which the PABO has been lodged and the job functions of the group of employees applying for protected industrial action
	Joint enterprises	Comments related to the history of an EA in circumstances where the employer is engaged in a joint enterprise with other employers
	Length of previous agreement	The length of previous EBAs
	Previous unprotected action	Evidence relating to any previous unprotected action at the site
	Single interest authorization	Discussions relating to the existence of a single interest authorization (SIA) in the context of the EA negotiations
	Size	Size of the employee group applying for protected industrial action
BALLOT AGENT AND VOTING		
Ballot agent	*Australian Electoral Commission (AEC)*	Use of the AEC as a ballot agent
	Other ballot agent	Use of other ballot agents
Voting process	*Communications*	Material relating to communications between the union and membership base in relation to voting on the PAB
	Getting 50 per cent	Comments relating to the impact of the quorum
	Member lists	Discussion related to the compilation of voter lists
	On site	Comments relating to the conduct of protected industrial action ballots at the employer site, ie 'on site'

NODE	SUB-NODE	DESCRIPTION
COMMUNICATION		
	Employer to employees *Employer to union* *Union to employer* *Union to union members*	Sub-headings relating to communications between certain parties about the EA, the PABO, the protected industrial action ballot, taking industrial action, and the agreement vote
EMPLOYER		
Coordination of unions across businesses		Discussion related to action coordinated by unions across businesses when there is a supply chain involved and negotiations are occurring further up or lower down the chain
Coordinating with other unions	*In negotiations*	Comments related to cooperation and non-cooperation between unions involved in the EA negotiations
	In PABO application	Comments related to cooperation and non-cooperation between unions involved in simultaneous PABO applications
Issues specific to employer	*Bargaining autonomy*	Issues around capacity of employer representatives at the table to bargain and agree to matters without higher authority
	Bargaining team	Construct of EA bargaining team and characteristics of union/employer representatives
	Economic climate	Role of economic climate as a factor influencing EA negotiations
	Emotional investment	Extent of emotional investment of employers/employer representatives in EA negotiations
	Local knowledge	Extent of local knowledge of members in bargaining teams
	Organizational changes	(Employer) organizational changes and the impact on EA negotiations
	Resources	Resource intensity of EA negotiations
	Revealing union density	Capacity for protected industrial action ballot to reveal union density to employer
	Union membership in human resources team	Extent to which union membership of employer representatives (HR representatives) does/does not change bargaining dynamic
EMPLOYER REACTION		
Employer reaction	*Challenges by employer*	
	Buying time No contest subject to certain conditions Pointlessness of contesting	Discussions related to any legal challenges/objections submitted by an employer in relation to the PABO application as well as motivations (real and perceived) driving any legal challenges
	Effect on bargaining	Impact of the PABO application/ballot result on EA negotiations
	Employers perception of PABO motive	How employers perceived the motives underlying the PABO application made

NODE	SUB-NODE	DESCRIPTION
	Ramifications of taking industrial action	Impact of industrial action on workplace relationships, supply chains, and employees themselves
	Reaction of external parties	Observed reactions and impact of reactions by external parties, eg contracting organizations, Government ministers/departments, and media/public opinion
	Undermining industrial action	Evidence of underhand tactics (real or perceived) that may detract from a protected industrial action ballot vote or the success of industrial action
Retaliatory action	*Lock out* *No pay*	Employer reaction to industrial action
FORMS OF ACTION		
Equity of impact of industrial action on workers		Comments relating to importance of ensuring that the impact of industrial action is fairly shared across all members voting for/agreeing to take action
Forms of Action	*Thirty-day rule*	Discussions relating to the impact of thirty-day rule on taking industrial action
	Action taken	Details of the actions taken where action was taken during course of dispute
	Decision-making	*How the decision to take industrial action is made and by whom*
	Employer perspective on action	How employers perceived industrial action (real or threatened)
	Escalation	Extent to which industrial action proposed/voted on is designed to allow for escalation in severity
	Intention to use Bluffing Vote as intention to undertake Vote as retaining option	Extent to which action is intended to be used when the PABO application is made. Discussions relating to use of PABO as a bluff/option to retain the right to take action
	Notifying	Issues around the requirement to notify an employer of scheduled industrial action
	Readiness to use *Enlivement Plan*	Comments relating to readiness to undertake industrial action in the event a protected industrial action ballot is successful and the use of enlivenment plans
	Wording	Wording of the forms of actions proposed on the protected industrial action ballot and design of wording
Secondary vote to authorize action		Ballot as a two-stage process in which stage (i) involves the formal vote to approve action and stage (ii) involves an informal (or formal) vote to actually undertake authorized action

NODE	SUB-NODE	DESCRIPTION
FAIR WORK COMMISSION (FWC) AND FEDERAL COURT		
FWC mechanisms	*Section 240 and conciliation*	Role of conciliation/applications under s 240 in EA negotiations
	FWC Prep	Extent of preparation required for PABO hearings
	Section 418	Applications under s 418 to stop industrial action
Federal Court		Use of Federal Court injunction to stop industrial action
GOOD FAITH		
Good faith	*Employer on employer* *Employer on union* *Union on employer* *Union on union*	Employer and union perceptions regarding the extent to which they and the other party were negotiating in good faith
ISSUES IN DISPUTE		
Domino effect		Effect that can occur when conceding (by either an union or employer) to one item in a log of claims could lead to a domino effect, setting precedents across the industry
Issues in Dispute	*Ascertaining issues* Survey	How union logs of claims are compiled and the methods unions employ to canvass the issues/concerns of members including use of surveys to gather information from members
	Building code *Conditions* *Finances* *Income protection* *Labour hire* *Productivity gains* *Scope* *Workplace recognition*	The range of issues in dispute during the EA negotiations
Pattern bargaining		Discussions directly pertaining to pattern bargaining or comments which implied pattern bargaining
MODE OF BALLOT		
Mode of ballot	*Attendance* *Electronic* *Postal*	The mode of the ballot and associated issues/opinions/motivations for selecting a particular mode
NEGOTIATIONS		
Negotiations	*Authorisation to sign off*	Comments/perceptions pertaining to the extent to which employer representatives at the bargaining table have the authority to sign off on various claims
	Bargaining personalities	Impact that personality/attitudes of members of the negotiating team had on EA negotiations

NODE	SUB-NODE	DESCRIPTION
	Changes to bargaining team staff	Extent to which changes to the negotiating team impacted on EA negotiations
	Impact of failed ballot	Impact of a failed protected industrial action ballot vote
	Information asymmetry	Issues relating to lack of trust in the information provided by the other side/misperceptions arising during bargaining as a result of information asymmetry
	Length	Duration of EA negotiations, number of meetings, etc
	Local knowledge	Role that knowledge or lack of knowledge of the nature of the workforce, the environment, and the local community had in the EA negotiations and understanding the log of claims
	Nature	Nature of EA negotiations: friendly, professional, hostile, antagonistic, etc . . .
	Stage Impasse	Stage that the EA negotiations had reached at the point at which the application for a PABO was made, including whether negotiations had reached impasse
	Teleconference	Impact of distance/technology in EA negotiations in which much negotiation occurred via teleconference and not face to face
	Undermining negotiations	Comments regarding behaviour (on both sides of the EA negotiations) which were perceived to undermine the negotiation process
	Vote agreement	Comments relating to an employer putting an agreement out to vote during the current EA negotiations
OPINIONS		
Opinions	*Enterprise bargaining* *FWC* *On employer behaviour* *PSBF*	General opinions pertaining to the enterprise bargaining system, the FWC, and employer behaviour during the course of negotiations and the Public Sector Bargaining Framework (PSBF)
	Views of legislation Benefits for employer Benefits for union Impact for employer Impact for members Impact for union	Specific opinions on the PABO application including any benefits/impact that arise as a result of having to adhere to the legislative process
PABO APPLICATION		
Diminishing appetite for industrial action		Extent to which the appetite for industrial action diminishes over time, ie industrial action fatigue in relation to a particular EA negotiation

NODE	SUB-NODE	DESCRIPTION
PABO application	*Internal PABO decision-making* Factors influencing Process Collaborative Top down	The process by which a decision is made to apply for a PABO including the process, the nature of the process, (eg collaborative, top down) and factors influencing the decision to apply
	Motivation for PABO	Comments regarding (real or perceived) motivations for applying for a PABO
	Other issues with PABO process	Other issues associated with the PABO application process
	Previous PABOs	Previous PABOs made in relation to the same set of EA negotiations
PERCEPTIONS		
Agreement in perception **Misperceptions in other actors' behaviour**		Extracts from transcripts where both sides of an EA (union and employer) were interviewed and where comments suggest an alignment or misalignment in the perception of events by the parties
POST-APPLICATION		
Post-application	*Status of negotiations*	Current status of EA negotiations at the time of interview
	Possible unprotected action	Suggestions of unprotected industrial action occurring in the context of the current EA negotiations or the current PABO
	Industrial action	Whether industrial action had occurred in relation to the EA negotiations/PABO at the time of the interview
	Ballot success	Whether the ballot was successful
	Ballot change	Impact of ballot in bringing about change
	Agreement	Whether or not parties had reached agreement at the time of interview
PUBLIC SECTOR		
Public sector bargaining framework	*Australian Public Service Commission (APSC) approval process*	Discussions pertaining to the APSC approval process
	Content	Extent to which content of public sector EBAs is restricted by the PSBF
	Extending length of negotiations	Role of the PSBF and APSC approval process in extending the length of time taken to reach agreement
	Inflexibility	Comments relating to the restrictions imposed by the PSBF and APSC and impact of this on EA negotiations
	Pay	Impact of PSBF pay restrictions on EA negotiations
	Political dynamic	Impact of political dynamic at play in public sector EA negotiations

NODE	SUB-NODE	DESCRIPTION
STRATEGY		
Strategies		Strategy relates to use of certain tactics or techniques used by one party in the course of EA negotiations to promote their ssbargaining agenda
	Achieving wider goals	Use of EA negotiations as a means by which to achieve wider union/industry/employee/employer goals
	Conceding to prevent industrial action	Conceding to certain log of claims concessions in order to avoid industrial action and reach agreement
	Controlling the dialogue	Efforts to exert control over the negotiation dialogue
	Delaying	Use of delay mechanisms/stalling to induce bargaining fatigue
	Hard tactics	Perceived use of 'hard bargaining' tactics and nature of said tactics
	Keeping members 'in the dark'	Withholding information from employees/members
	Leveraging off contract renegotiations	Leveraging contract renegotiations as a means by which to incite fear/concern
	Manoeuvring around legislation	Efforts to work around the restrictions imposed by the legislation
	Mentioning and preparing industrial action early on	Flagging willingness to use industrial action early in negotiations
	Padding LOCs	Inclusion of additional non-central and non-crucial claims in the LOCs to provide a sacrificial buffer
	Set up of meetings	Organization of meetings/negotiating team hierarchy as a means (perceived or real) by which to frustrate the EA negotiation process
	Smear campaign	Use of comments intended to present one side of the negotiations in a certain light
	Timing of PABO or industrial action	Strategizing around the timing of industrial action so as to optimize its efficacy
	Understanding underlying needs	Going beyond the log of claims to understand the needs of employees/members as a means by which to introduce greater flexibility in the negotiating process
THIRD PARTY AND SUPPLY CHAIN		
Third party and supply chain		Role of third (contracting) parties and the supply chain on EA negotiations and industrial action
UNDERSTANDING		
(Mis)understanding of process	*Union* *Member* *Employer*	Comments which directly or indirectly speak to the way in which certain stakeholders misperceive the PABO process

NODE	SUB-NODE	DESCRIPTION
UNION		
Issues specific to unions	*Union rulebooks*	Extent to which union rulebooks specify requirements pertaining to the PABO application process
	Union requirements	Internal union processes (formal or informal) guiding PABO applications
	Poaching and increasing membership	Comments relating to perceived poaching of members between unions, and incentives around increasing membership
	Overarching motives Wider specific campaign Wider general campaign Protections going forward Preserving dignity Parity Boost or justify membership	Discussions relating to union objectives that may influence EA negotiations, including claims directed at wider union campaigns, preserving employment conditions/protections, preserving the support of members, increasing membership, and achieving parity of conditions between employees and across employers within an industry
	Election of delegates	Election process for union delegates involved in EA negotiations
	Democratic representation	Comments (direct and indirect) relating to democratic processes employed by unions in EA negotiations/protected industrial action

Interview coding framework for Part B (stakeholder) interviews

CODE	SUB-NODE	DESCRIPTION	INTERVIEW GROUP		
			1	2	3
HISTORY					
Fair Work Act (FW Act)	*History*	Context of/involvement in passage of FW Act		✓	✓
	Origins	Origins/motivations underpinning emergence of the PABO legislation		✓	✓
	Work choices	Work choices legislation			✓
Rationale	*Debates for/against*	Debates for and against introduction of ballot legislation			✓
	Curbing union behaviour	Perceptions of legislation as directed at curbing unions pushing action with member support			✓
Drafting	*International Labour Organisation (ILO) provisions*	Cognizance of the ILO provisions in drafting ballot legislation			✓
VOTING PROCESS					
Voting	*AEC*	Use of AEC as a ballot agent		✓	
	AEC processes	Steps taken by the AEC when conducting a ballot	✓		
	Voter roll	How the roll of voters is compiled	✓		
	Electronic balloting	The use and availability of electronic balloting	✓	✓	
	Postal ballots timeframes	Postal service timeframes—implications for postal vote returns	✓		
	Mode of ballot	Selection of mode of ballot	✓		
	Ballot agent	Choice of agent/use of AEC		✓	
OPERATION OF LEGISLATION					
Operation	*Thirty-day rule*	Impact of the thirty-day rule		✓	
	Notice period	Issues emerging regarding the extension of the notice period		✓	
	Bedding down	Adapting to the introduction of the FW Act/initial 'teething' problems	✓		
	Extension of notice period	Applications/decisions to extend the notice period		✓	
	Genuinely trying to reach agreement (GTRA)	Determining whether parties are genuinely trying to reach agreement and threshold for meeting GTRA requirement		✓	

CODE	SUB-NODE	DESCRIPTION	INTERVIEW GROUP	
	Notification time	Operation of the notification time requirement	✓	
	Mode of hearing	Choosing between a decision on the papers or holding a hearing	✓	
	Problems/ difficulties	Potential problems with the PABO process and suggestions for reform	✓	✓
Impact	*PABO process*	Impact of the PABO process on collective bargaining	✓	✓
	Quorum requirement	Impact of the imposition of quorum	✓	✓
Strategy	*Opposing applications*	Employers opposing PABO applications	✓	✓
	Leverage	Use of PABO application as leverage in collective bargaining negotiations	✓	✓
	Submitting a PABO	How unions approach PABO applications	✓	

Bibliography

Adams, GW 1993 *Canadian Labour Law*, 2nd ed Looseleaf, Canada Law Book, Aurora.

Adlercreutz, A & Nystrom, B 2015 'Sweden' in Frederick Hendrickx (ed) *International Encyclopaedia for Labour Law and Industrial Relations*, Wolters Kluwer, Kluwer Law Online.

Agomo, CK 2016 'Nigeria' in Frederick Hendrickx (ed) *International Encyclopaedia for Labour Law and Industrial Relations*, Wolters Kluwer, Kluwer Law Online.

AIRC (Australian Industrial Relations Commission) 2005 *Annual Report of the President of the Australian Industrial Relations Commission and Annual Report of the Australian Industrial Registry 2004—2005*, Commonwealth of Australia, Canberra.

Alston, R 2004 'Core Labour Standards and the Transformation of the International Labour Rights Regime' 15(3) *European Journal of International Law* 457.

Alston, R 2005 'Facing up to the Complexities of the ILO's Core Labour Standards Agenda' 16(3) *European Journal of International Law* 467.

Alston, R & Heenan, J 2004 'Shrinking the International Labour Code: An Unintended Consequence of the 1998 ILO Declaration on Fundamental Principles and Rights at Work?' 36 *New York University Journal of International Law & Politics* 101.

Anton, FR 1961 *Government Supervised Strike Votes*, CCH Canadian Ltd, Toronto.

Arudsothy, P 2001 'Malaysia' in Frederick Hendrickx (ed) *International Encyclopaedia for Labour Law and Industrial Relations*, Wolters Kluwer, Kluwer Law Online.

Auerbach, S 1990 *Legislating for Conflict*, Clarendon Press, Oxford.

Baylas, A 2010 'Collective Action in Spain' in Edoardo Ales & Tonia Novitz (eds) *Collective Action and Fundamental Freedoms in Europe*, Intersentia, Antwerp, pp 109–34.

Bellace, JR 2014 'The ILO and the Right to Strike' 153(1) *International Labour Review* 29.

Bellace, JR 2016 'Back to the Future: Freedom of Association, the Right to Strike and National Law' 27(1) *King's Law Journal* 24.

Bellace, JR 2018 'ILO Convention No. 87 and the Right to Strike in an Era of Global Trade' 39(3) *Comparative Labor Law & Policy Journal* 495.

Ben-Israel, R 1988 *International Labour Standards: The Case of Freedom to Strike*, Kluwer, Deventer.

Benjamin, P & Cooper, C 2016 'Pre-strike Ballots in South Africa' 29(2) *Australian Journal of Labour Law* 210.

Bercusson, B 1978 *Fair Wages Resolutions*, Mansell, London.

Bessette, JM 1980 'Deliberative Democracy: The Majority Principle in Republican Government' in Robert A Goldwin & William A Schambra (eds) *How Democratic is the Constitution?*, AEI Press, Washington DC, pp 102–16.

Blondal, E & Sigurdardottir, RM 2012 'Iceland' in Frederick Hendrickx (ed) *International Encyclopaedia for Labour Law and Industrial Relations*, Wolters Kluwer, Kluwer Law Online.

Bogg, A 2016a 'Beyond Neo-Liberalism: The Trade Union Act 2016 and the Authoritarian State' 45(3) *Industrial Law Journal* 299.

Bogg, A 2016b 'Common Law and Statute in the Law of Employment' 69(1) *Current Legal Problems* 67.

Bogg, A & Novitz, T 2012 'Investigating Voice at Work' 33(3) *Comparative Labor Law and Policy Journal* 323.

Bohman, J & Rehg, W 1997 *Deliberative Democracy: Essays on Reason and Politics*, MIT Press, Cambridge MA.

Boulton, AJ 1982 'Government Regulation of the Internal Affairs of Unions' in Kathryn Cole (ed) *Power, Conflict and Control in Australian Trade Unions*, Pelican, Melbourne, pp 216–36.

Briggs, C 2001 'Australian Exceptionalism: The Role of Trade Unions in the Emergence of Enterprise Bargaining' 43(1) *Journal of Industrial Relations* 27.

Brodie, D 2003 *A History of British Labour Law 1867-1945*, Hart Publishing, Oxford and Portland.

Brooks, B 2017 'South Pacific' in Frederick Hendrickx (ed) *International Encyclopaedia for Labour Law and Industrial Relations*, Wolters Kluwer, Kluwer Law Online.

Browne, WJ 2017 *MCMC Estimation in MLwiN, v3.01*, Centre for Multilevel Modelling, University of Bristol.

Butler, M 2018 'Great Britain' in Frederick Hendrickx (ed) *International Encyclopaedia for Labour Law and Industrial Relations*, Wolters Kluwer, Kluwer Law Online.

Campolieti, M, Hebdon, R, & Dachis, B 2014 'The Impact of Collective Bargaining Legislation on Strike Activity and Wage Settlements' 53(3) *Industrial Relations: A Journal of Economy and Society* 394.

Carter et al 2000 'Canada' in Frederick Hendrickx (ed) *International Encyclopaedia for Labour Law and Industrial Relations*, Wolters Kluwer, Kluwer Law Online.

Chandran, R 2017 'Singapore' in Frederick Hendrickx (ed) *International Encyclopaedia for Labour Law and Industrial Relations*, Wolters Kluwer, Kluwer Law Online.

Cheadle, H 2015 'Constitutionalising the Right to Strike' in Bob Hepple, Rochelle le Roux, & Silvana Sciarra (eds) *Laws Against Strikes. The South African Experience in an International and Comparative Perspective*, Milano, FrancoAngeli, pp 67–86.

Collins, H, Ewing, KD & McColgan, A 2019 *Labour Law*, 2nd ed, Cambridge University Press, Cambridge.

Colvin, A 2016 'Strike Ballot Law and Practice in the United States: Order Without Law in Labour Relations' 29(2) *Australian Journal of Labour Law* 243.

Cooper, R & Ellem, B 2017 'Cold Climate: Australian Unions, Policy and the State' 38(3) *Comparative Labor Law & Policy Journal* 415.

Corden, A & Sainsbury, R 2006 *Using Verbatim Quotations in Reporting Qualitative Social Research: Researchers' Views*, Social Policy Research Unit, University of York.

Costello, K 2015 'Ireland' in Frederick Hendrickx (ed) *International Encyclopaedia for Labour Law and Industrial Relations*, Wolters Kluwer, Kluwer Law Online.

Cramton, P & Tracy, J 2003 'Unions, Bargaining and Strikes' in John T Addison & Claus Schnabel (eds) *International Handbook of Trade Unions*, Edward Elgar, pp 86–117.

Cramton, P, Gunderson, M, & Tracy, J 1999 'The Effect of Collective Bargaining Legislation on Strikes and Wages' 81(3) *The Review of Economics and Statistics* 475.

Craver, CB 2014 'The Right to Strike: United States of America' in Bernard Waas (ed) *The Right to Strike: A Comparative View*, Kluwer Law International, Alphen aan den Rijn, pp 567–84.

Creighton, B 1991 'Enforcement in the Federal Industrial Relations system: an Australian Paradox' 4(3) *Australian Journal of Labour Law* 197.

Creighton, B 1997 'The Workplace Relations Act in International Perspective' 10(1) *Australian Journal of Labour Law* 31.

Creighton, B 1998 'The ILO and the Protection of Fundamental Human Rights in Australia' 22(2) *Melbourne University Law Review* 239.

Creighton, B 2012a 'Government Procurement as a Vehicle for Workplace Relations Reform: The Case of the National Code of Practice for the Construction Industry' 40(3) *Federal Law Review* 349.

Creighton, B 2012b 'Impacts of Enterprise Bargaining on Unions and Employers: Discussants Comments' 22(3) *Labour & Industry* 275.

Creighton, B 2014 'Freedom of Association' in R Blanpain (ed) *Comparative Labour Law and Industrial Relations in Industrialised Market Economies*, XIth ed, Wolters Kluwer, Alphen aan den Rijn, pp 315–60.

Creighton, B 2018 'Getting to the Bargaining Table: Coercive, Facilitated and Pre-Commitment Bargaining' in Shae McCrystal, Breen Creighton, & Anthony Forsyth (eds) *Collective Bargaining under the Fair Work Act*, Federation Press, Sydney, pp 25–44.

Creighton, B, Denvir, C, & McCrystal, S 2016 'Pre-Strike Ballots and the Law in Australia' 29(2) *Australian Journal of Labour Law* 154.

Creighton, B, Denvir, C, & McCrystal, S 2017 'Defining Industrial Action' 45(3) *Federal Law Review* 383.

Creighton, B & McCrystal, S 2016 'Pre-Strike Ballots and the Law in Comparative Perspective' 29(2) *Australian Journal of Labour Law* 121.

Creighton, B & McCrystal, S 2017 'Before the High Court—Esso Australia Pty Ltd v the Australian Workers' Union: Breaches of Orders, Coercion and Protected Industrial Action Under the Fair Work Act 2009 (Cth)' 39(2) *Sydney Law Review* 233.

Creighton et al 2018 'Protected Industrial Action Ballots: An Empirical View' 60(1) *The Journal of Industrial Relations* 53.

Creighton et al 2019a 'The Role of the "Genuinely Try to Reach Agreement" Requirement in the Protected Industrial Action Regime under the Fair Work Act 2009' 31(3) *Australian Journal of Labour Law* 279.

Creighton et al 2019b 'Pre-Strike Ballots and Collective Bargaining: The Impact of Quorum and Ballot Mode Requirements on Access to Lawful Industrial Action' 48(3) *Industrial Law Journal* 343.

Creighton, WB, Ford, WJ, & Mitchell, RJ 1983 *Labour Law: Materials and Commentary*, Law Book Co, Sydney.

Creighton, WB, Ford, WJ, & Mitchell, RJ 1993 *Labour Law: Text and Materials*, 2nd ed, Law Book Co, Sydney.

Curthoys, M 2004 *Governments, Labour, and the Law in Mid-Victorian Britain: The Trade Union Legislation of the 1870s*, Clarendon Press, Oxford.

Dahl, R 1956 *A Preface to Democratic Theory*, University of Chicago Press, Chicago.

Darlington, R & Dobson, J 2015 *The Conservative Government's Proposed Strike Ballot Thresholds: The Challenge to Trade Unions*, Institute of Employment Rights, Liverpool.

Davies, P & Freedland, M 1993 *Labour Legislation and Public Policy: A Contemporary History*, Clarendon Press, Oxford.

Davies, P & Freedland, M 2007 *Towards a Flexible Labour Market: Labour Legislation and Regulation Since the 1990s*, OUP, Oxford.

Davis, EM 1987 *Democracy in Australian Trade Unions*, Allen & Unwin, North Sydney.

Deakin, S & Morris, GS 2012 *Labour Law*, 6th ed, Hart Publishing, Oxford and Portland.

Deinert, O 2010 'Collective Action in Germany' in Edoardo Ales & Tonia Novitz (eds) Collective Action and Fundamental Freedoms in Europe, Intersentia, Antwerp, pp 53–76.

Denvir, C & McCrystal, S 2017 'Researching Labour Law in Practice' in John Howe, Anna Chapman, & Ingrid Landau (eds) *The Evolving Project of Labour Law: Foundations, Development and Future Research Directions*, Federation Press, Sydney, pp 161–75.

Department of Employment 1983 *Democracy in Trade Unions*, Cmnd 8778.

Department of Trade and Industry 1969 *In Place of Strife: A Policy for Industrial Relations*, Cmnd 3888.

Dereli, T 2015 'Turkey' in Frederick Hendrickx (ed) *International Encyclopaedia for Labour Law and Industrial Relations*, Wolters Kluwer, Kluwer Law Online.

Despax, M, Laborde, J, & Rojot, J 2017 'France' in Frederick Hendrickx (ed) *International Encyclopaedia for Labour Law and Industrial Relations*, Wolters Kluwer, Kluwer Law Online.

Dicey, AV 1964 *Introduction to the Study of the Law of the Constitution*, 10th ed, Macmillan & Co Ltd, London.

Dimitriu, R 2016 'Romania' in Frederick Hendrickx (ed) *International Encyclopaedia for Labour Law and Industrial Relations*, Wolters Kluwer, Kluwer Law Online.

Donovan, Lord 1968 *Royal Commission on Trade Unions and Employers' Associations, 1965-1968*, Cmnd 3623.

Douka, VS & Koniaris, VT 2015 'Greece' in Frederick Hendrickx (ed) *International Encyclopaedia for Labour Law and Industrial Relations*, Wolters Kluwer, Kluwer Law Online.

du Toit, D 2014 'The Right to Strike: South Africa' in Bernard Waas (ed) *The Right to Strike: A Comparative View*, Kluwer Law International, Alphen aan den Rijn, pp 477–94.

Dukes, R 2010 'The Right to Strike Under UK Law: Not Much More Than a Slogan?' 39(1) *Industrial Law Journal* 82.

Dukes, R & Kountouris, N 2016 'Pre-strike Ballots, Picketing and Protest: Banning Industrial Action by the Back Door?' 45(3) *Industrial Law Journal* 337.

Edwards, J, McCallum, R, & Moore, M 2012 *Towards More Productive and Equitable Workplaces—An Evaluation of the Fair Work Legislation*, Commonwealth of Australia, Canberra.

Elgar, J & Simpson, B 1993 'The Impact of the Law on Industrial Disputes in the 1980s' in David Metcalf & Simon Milner (eds) *New Perspectives on Industrial Disputes*, Routledge, London, pp 70–114.

Elgar, J & Simpson, B 1996 *Industrial Action Ballots and the Law*, Institute for Employment Rights, London.

Elgar, J & Simpson, B 2017 'The Impact of the Law on Industrial Disputes Revisited: A Perspective on Developments Over the Last Two Decades' 46(1) *Industrial Law Journal* 6.

Elias, P 1990 'Law and Union Democracy: The Changing Shape' in Patricia Fosh & Edmund Heary (eds) *Trade Unions and their Members: Studies in Union Democracy*, MacMillan, London, pp 29–51.

Elias, P 1994 'The Strike and Breach of Contract: A Reassessment' in KD Ewing, CA Gearty, & BA Hepple (eds) *Human Rights and Labour Law: Essays for Paul O'Higgins*, Mansell, London, pp 257–66.

Elias, P & Ewing, K 1987 *Trade Union Democracy: Members' Rights and the Law*, Mansell Publishing Ltd, London.

Evans, S 1987 'The Use of Injunctions in Industrial Disputes May 1984-April 1987' 25(3) *British Journal of Industrial Relations* 419.

Evatt, HV 1937 and 2009 *Injustice within the Law: A Study of the Case of the Dorsetshire Labourers*, Law Book, Sydney [Re-published as *The Tolpuddle Martyrs: Injustice within the law*, Sydney University Press, Sydney].

Ewing, KD 1991 *The Right to Strike*, Clarendon Press, Oxford.

Ewing, KD 1999 'Freedom of Association and the Employment Relations Act' 28(4) *Industrial Law Journal* 283.

Ewing, KD 2004 'Laws Against Strikes Revisited' in Catherine Barnard, Simon Deakin, & Gillian S Morris (eds) *The Future of Labour Law: Liber Amicorum Sir Bob Hepple*, Hart Publishing, Oxford and Portland, pp 41–61.

Ewing, KD, Hendy, J, & Jones, C (eds) 2016 *A Manifesto for Labour Law: Towards a Comprehensive Revision of Workers' Rights*, Institute of Employment Rights, Liverpool.

Ewing, KD, Hendy, J, & Jones, C (eds) 2018 *Rolling out the Manifesto for Labour Law*, Institute of Employment Rights, Liverpool.

Ewing, K & Rees, W 1984 'Industrial Conflict and the Meaning of Trade Dispute' 13(1) *Industrial Law Journal* 60.

Fair Work Commission 2010 *Annual Report 2009-2010*, Commonwealth of Australia, Canberra.

Fair Work Commission 2011 *Annual Report 2010-2011*, Commonwealth of Australia, Canberra.

Fair Work Commission 2012 *Annual Report 2011-2012*, Commonwealth of Australia, Canberra.

Fair Work Commission 2013 *Annual Report 2012-2013*, Commonwealth of Australia, Canberra.

Fair Work Commission 2014 *Annual Report 2013-2014*, Commonwealth of Australia, Canberra.

Fair Work Commission 2015 *Annual Report 2014-2015*, Commonwealth of Australia, Canberra.

Fairbrother, P 1984 *All those in Favour: The Politics of Union Democracy*, Pluto Press, London.

Fenwick, C 2002 'Minimum Obligations with Respect to Article 8 of the International Covenant on Economic, Social and Cultural Rights' in Audrey Chapman & Sage Russell (eds) *Core Obligations: Building a Framework for Economic, Social and Cultural Rights*, Intersentia, Antwerp, pp 53–86.

Ford, M & Novitz, T 2016 'Legislating for Control: the Trade Union Act 2016' 45(3) *Industrial Law Journal* 277.

Forster, K 1971 'Strikes and Employment Contracts' 34(3) *Modern Law Review* 275.

Forsyth et al 2017 'Establishing the Right to Bargain Collectively in Australia and the UK: Are Majority Support Determinations under Australia's Fair Work Act a More Effective Form of Union Recognition?' 46(3) *Industrial Law Journal* 335.

Fredman, S 1992 'The New Rights: Labour Law and Ideology in the Thatcher Years' (1992) 12(1) *Oxford Journal of Legal Studies* 24.

Freedland, M & Prassl, J (eds) 2014 *Viking, Laval and Beyond*, Hart Publishing, Oxford and Portland.

Fudge, J 2007 'The New Discourse of Labor Rights: From Social to Fundamental Rights?' 29(1) *Comparative Labor Law & Policy Journal* 25.

Fudge, J & Jensen, H 2016 'The Right to Strike: The Supreme Court of Canada, the Charter of Rights and Freedoms and the Arc of Workplace Justice' 27(1) *King's Law Journal* 89.

Gahan, P & Pekarek, A 2012 'Collective Bargaining and Agreement Making in Australia: Evolution of the Legislative Framework and Practice' in Breen Creighton & Anthony Forsyth (eds) *Rediscovering Collective Bargaining: Australia's Fair Work Act in International Perspective*, Routledge, New York, pp 21–45.

Gahan, P & Pekarek, A 2012a 'The Rise and Rise of Enterprise Bargaining in Australia, 1991—2011' 22(3) *Labour and Industry* 195.

Gall, G 2012 'Quiescence Continued? Recent Strike Activity in Nine Western European Economies' 34(4) *Economic and Industrial Democracy* 667.

Gall, G 2017 'Injunctions as a Legal Weapon in Collective Industrial Disputes in Britain 2005-2014' 55(1) *British Journal of Industrial Relations* 187.

Gernigon, B, Odero A, & Guido, H 2000 *ILO Principles Concerning the Right to Strike*, ILO, Geneva.

Glaser, B & Strauss, A 1967 *The Discovery of Grounded Theory Strategies for Qualitative Research*, Sociology Press, Mill Valley.

Gomes, JMV & Carvalho, CDO 2011 'Portugal' in Frederick Hendrickx (ed) *International Encyclopaedia for Labour Law and Industrial Relations*, Wolters Kluwer, Kluwer Law Online.

Gorbacheva, ZA 2019 'Russian Federation' in Frederick Hendrickx (ed) *International Encyclopaedia for Labour Law and Industrial Relations*, Wolters Kluwer, Kluwer Law Online.

Gravel, E, Duplessis, I, & Gernigon, B 2001 *The Committee on Freedom of Association: Its Impact over 50 years*, ILO, Geneva.

Griffin, JI 1939 *Strikes: A Study in Quantitative Economics*, Columbia University Press, New York.

Habermas, J 1996 *Between Facts and Norms: Contributions to a Discourse Theory of Law and Democracy*, Cambridge MA, MIT Press.

Hardy, T 2018 'The State Strikes Back: Supervision and Sanctioning of Unlawful Industrial Activity by Federal Government Agencies in Australia' in Shae McCrystal, Breen Creighton, & Anthony Forsyth (eds) *Collective Bargaining under the Fair Work Act*, Federation Press, Sydney, pp 182–205.

Harris, J 2006 'Federal Collective Bargaining After Electrolux' 34(1) *Federal Law Review* 45.

Healey, B 1972 *Federal Arbitration in Australia*, Georgian House, Melbourne.

Hendrickx, F (ed) 2018 *International Encyclopaedia for Labour Law and Industrial Relations*, Wolters Kluwer, Kluwer Law Online.

Higgins, HB 1913 'A New Province for Law and Order' 29(1) *Harvard Law Review* 13.

Hilmer, JD 2010 'The State of Participatory Democratic Theory' 32(1) *New Political Science* 43.

Hornung-Draus, R 2018 'The Right to Strike in the ILO System of Standards: Facts and Fiction' 39(3) *Comparative Labor Law & Policy Journal* 531.

Howard, WA 1980 'Democracy in Trade Unions' in GW Ford, JM Hearn, & RD Lansbury (eds) *Australian Labour Relations: Readings*, 3rd ed, The MacMillan Company, South Melbourne, pp 162–78.

Hutton, J 1984 'Solving the Strike Problem: Part II of the Trade Union Act 1984' 13(1) *Industrial Law Journal* 212.

ILO (International Labour Organisation) 1983 *Freedom of Association and Collective Bargaining: General Survey by the Committee of Experts on the Application of Conventions and Recommendations*, 69th Session, Report III (Part 4B), ILO, Geneva.

ILO (International Labour Organisation) 1994 *Freedom of Association and Collective Bargaining*, General Survey of the Reports on the Freedom of Association and the Right to Organise Convention (No. 87), 1948 and the Right to Organise and Collective Bargaining Convention (No. 98), 1949, Report III (Part 4B), International Labour Conference, 81st Session, ILO, Geneva.

ILO (International Labour Organisation) 2001 *Report of the Committee of Experts on the Application of Conventions and Recommendations*, ILC, 89th Session, Report III (Part 1A), ILO, Geneva.

ILO (International Labour Organisation) 2010a Official Bulletin Vol XCIII, Series B, No 2, Report 357, ILO, Geneva.

ILO (International Labour Organisation) 2010b *Report of the Committee of Experts on the Application of Conventions and Recommendations*, ILC, 99th Session, Report III (Part 1A), ILO, Geneva.

ILO (International Labour Organisation) 2012a *Giving globalisation a human face: General Survey on the fundamental Conventions concerning rights at work in light of the ILO Declaration on Social Justice for a Fair Globalisation, 2008*, ILC, 101st Session, Report III (Part 1B), ILO, Geneva.

ILO (International Labour Organisation) 2012b *Record of Proceedings*, ILC, 101st Session, No 19 (Part 1), ILO, Geneva.

ILO (International Labour Organisation) 2012c *Report of the Committee of Experts on the Application of Conventions and Recommendations*, ILC, 101st Session, Report III (Part A), ILO, Geneva.

ILO (International Labour Organisation) 2016 *Application of International Labour Standards 2016(1), Report of the Committee of Experts on the Application of Conventions and Recommendations*, ILC, 105th Session, Report III (Part 1A), ILO, Geneva.

ILO (International Labour Organisation) 2017 *Report of the Committee of Experts on the Application of Conventions and Recommendations*, ILC, 106th Session, Report III (Part A), ILO, Geneva.

ILO (International Labour Organisation) 2018 *Freedom of Association: Compilation of decisions of the Committee on Freedom of Association*, 6th ed, ILO, Geneva.

ILO (International Labour Organisation) 2019a *Report of the Committee of Experts on the Application of Conventions and Recommendations*, ILC, 108th Session, Report III (Part A), ILO, Geneva.

ILO (International Labour Organisation) 2019b *Rules of the Game: an introduction to the standards related work of the International Labour Organisation*, Centenary Edition, ILO, Geneva.

ILO (International Labour Organisation) 2019c *Monitoring compliance with International Labour Standards: The key role of the International Labour Organisation's Committee of Experts on the Application of Conventions and Recommendations*, Centenary Edition, ILO, Geneva.

Jacobs ATJM 1986 'Collective Self-Regulation' in Bob Hepple (ed) *The Making of Labour Law in Europe: A Comparative Study of Nine Countries up to 1945*, Mansell, London, pp 193–241.

Jacobs ATJM 2009 'Collective Labour Relations' in Bob Hepple & Bruno Veneziani (eds) *The Transformation of Labour Law in Europe: A Comparative Study of 15 Countries 1945-2004*, Hart Publishing, Oxford, pp 201–32.

Jacobs ATJM 2014 'The Law of Strikes and Lockouts' in R Blanpain (ed) *Comparative Labour Law and Industrial Relations in Industrialised Market Economies*, XIth ed, Wolters Kluwer, Alphen aan den Rijn, pp 731–96.

Kahn-Freund, O & Hepple, B 1972 *Laws Against Strikes*, Fabian Society, London.

Kalula, E & Zulu, D 2009 'Zambia' in Frederick Hendrickx (ed) *International Encyclopaedia for Labour Law and Industrial Relations*, Wolters Kluwer, Kluwer Law Online.

Karp, JA & Banducci, SA 2000 'Going Postal: How All-Mail Elections Influence Turnout' 22(3) *Political Behavior* 223.

Kerr, A 2013 *The Trade Union and Industrial Relations Acts*, 4th ed, Round Hall Ltd, Dublin.

Kerr, A 2014 'The Right to Strike: Ireland' in Bernard Waas (ed) *The Right to Strike: A Comparative View*, Kluwer Law International, Alphen aan den Rijn, pp 303–16.

Knight, K 2017 *Electronic Balloting Review: The Report of the Independent Review of Electronic Balloting for Industrial Action*, Department for Business, Energy and Industrial Strategy, presented to the UK Parliament pursuant to s 4 of the Trade Union Act 2016.

Kousser, T & Mullin, M 2007 'Does Voting by Mail Increase Participation? Using Matching to Analyze a Natural Experiment' 15(4) *Political Analysis* 428.

Kovacs, E 2005 'The Right to Strike in the European Social Charter' 26(4) *Comparative Labor Law & Policy Journal* 445.

Kryvoi, Y 2017 'Belarus' in Frederick Hendrickx (ed) *International Encyclopaedia for Labour Law and Industrial Relations*, Wolters Kluwer, Kluwer Law Online.

Kuwamura, Y 2014 'The Right to Strike: Japan' in Bernard Waas (ed) *The Right to Strike: A Comparative View*, Kluwer Law International, Alphen aan den Rijn, pp 351–68.

La Hovary, C 2013 'Showdown at the ILO? A Historical Perspective on the Employers' Group's Challenge to the Right to Strike' 42(4) *Industrial Law Journal* 338.

La Hovary, C 2017 'Article 37 of the ILO Constitution: An Unattainable Solution to the Issue of Interpretation?' 38(3) *Comparative Labor Law & Policy Journal* 337.

Langille, B 2005 'Core Labour Rights—The True Story (Reply to Alston)' 16(3) *European Journal of International Law* 409.

Leader, S 1992 *Freedom of Association: A Study in Labour Law and Political Theory*, Yale University Press, New Haven and London.

Leary, VA 1996 'The Paradox of Workers' Rights as Human Rights' in Lance Compa & Stephen Diamond (eds) *Human Rights, Labour Rights and International Trade*, University of Pennsylvania Press, Philadelphia, pp 22–47.

Lee, H & Ko, ZK 2015 'South Korea' in Frederick Hendrickx (ed) *International Encyclopaedia for Labour Law and Industrial Relations*, Wolters Kluwer, Kluwer Law Online.

Lipset, SM, Trow, M, & Coleman, JS 1956 *Union Democracy*, Free Press, New York.

Lodge, M & Wegrich, K 2012 *Managing Regulation: Regulatory Analysis, Politics and Policy*, Palgrave Macmillan.

Luhmann, N 2004 *Law as a Social System*, OUP, Oxford.

Lyutov, N 2014 'The Right to Strike: The Russian Federation' in Bernard Waas (ed) *The Right to Strike: A Comparative View*, Kluwer Law International, Alphen aan den Rijn, pp 451–66.

Macaraya, BM 2017 'Philippines' in Frederick Hendrickx (ed) *International Encyclopaedia for Labour Law and Industrial Relations*, Wolters Kluwer, Kluwer Law Online.

Macintyre, S 1989 'Neither Capital nor Labour: The Politics of the Establishment of Arbitration' in Stuart Macintyre & Richard Mitchell (eds) *Foundations of Arbitration: The Origins and Effects of State Compulsory Arbitration 1890-1914*, OUP, Melbourne, pp 178–202.

Macintyre, S & Mitchell, R (eds) 1989 *Foundations of Arbitration: The Origins and Effects of State Compulsory Arbitration 1890-1914*, OUP, Melbourne.

Mansbridge, JJ 1980 *Beyond Adversary Democracy*, Basic Books, New York.

Mantouvalou, V 2014 'Democratic Theory and Voices at Work' in Alan Bogg & Tonia Novitz (eds) *Voices at Work: Continuity and Change in the Common Law World*, OUP, Oxford, pp 214–31.

Markey, R 1989 'Trade Union, the Labor Party and the Introduction of Arbitration in New South Wales and the Commonwealth' in Stuart Macintyre & Richard Mitchell (eds)

Foundations of Arbitration: The Origins and Effects of State Compulsory Arbitration 1890-1914, OUP, Melbourne, pp 156–77.
Marlow, J 1971 *The Tolpuddle Martyrs*, Andre Deutsch, London.
Martin et al 1991 'The Decollectivisation of Trade Unions? Ballots and Collective Bargaining in the 1980s' 22(3) *Industrial Law Journal* 197.
Matthews, The Honourable Justice 1946 'A History of Industrial Law in Queensland with a Summary of the Provisions of the Various Statutes', The Historical Society of Queensland Inc, Brisbane.
Mathur, AN 2008 'Nepal' in Frederick Hendrickx (ed) *International Encyclopaedia for Labour Law and Industrial Relations*, Wolters Kluwer, Kluwer Law Online.
Maupin, F 2005 'Revitalisation Not Retreat—The Real Potential of the 1998 ILO Declaration for the Universal Protection of Workers' Rights' 16(3) *European Journal of International Law* 439.
McCallum, RC 1976 'Mystique of Secret ballots: Labour Relations Progress v Industrial Anarchy' 2(2) *Monash University Law Review* 166.
McCallum, RC 1984 'Federal Controls Upon Trade Unions: The Australian Enigma' in DW Rawson & Chris Fisher (eds) *Changing Industrial Law*, Croom Helm Australia, Sydney, pp 174–223.
McCarry, G 1994 'Sanctions and Industrial Action: The Impact of the Industrial Relations Reform Act' 7(2) *Australian Journal of Labour Law* 198.
McCrystal, S 2006 'Smothering the Right to Strike: Work Choices and Industrial Action' 19(2) *Australian Journal of Labour Law* 198.
McCrystal, S 2009 'A New Consensus: The Coalition, The ALP and the Regulation of Industrial Action' in Anthony Forsyth & Andrew Stewart (eds) *Fair Work: The New Workplace Laws and the Work Choices Legacy*, Federation Press, Sydney, pp 141–63.
McCrystal, S 2010 *The Right to Strike in Australia*, Federation Press, Sydney.
McCrystal, S 2011 'Fair Work in the International Spotlight: The CEPU Complaint to the ILO's Committee on Freedom of Association' 24(2) *Australian Journal of Labour Law* 163.
McCrystal, S 2012 'The Relationship between Protected Industrial Action, Recognition and Bargaining in Good Faith under the Fair Work Act 2009 (Cth)' in Breen Creighton and Anthony Forsyth (eds) *Rediscovering Collective Bargaining: Australia's Fair Work Act in International Perspective*, Routledge, New York, pp 114–34.
McCrystal, S 2019 'The Right to Strike and the 'Deadweight" of the Common Law' 50(2) *Victoria University of Wellington Law Review* 281.
McCrystal, S & Novitz, T 2012 '"Democratic" Pre-conditions for Strike Action: A Comparative Study of Australian and UK Labour Legislation' 28(2) *International Journal of Comparative Labour Law and Industrial Relations* 115.
Merritt, AS 1982 'The Historical Role of Law in the Regulation of Employment—Abstentionist or Interventionist?' 1(1) *Australian Journal of Law and Society* 56.
Minister for Workplace Relations and Small Business 1998 *Pre-Industrial Action Secret Ballots*, Ministerial Discussion Paper, Parliament of Australia, Canberra.
Mitchell, R 1989 'State Systems of Conciliation and Arbitration: The Legal Origins of the Australasian Model' in Stuart Macintyre & Richard Mitchell (eds) *Foundations of Arbitration: The Origins and Effects of State Compulsory Arbitration 1890-1914*, OUP, Melbourne, pp 74–103.
Mitchell, R & Stern, E 1989 'The Compulsory Arbitration Model of Industrial Dispute Settlement: An Outline of Legal Developments' in Stuart Macintyre & Richard Mitchell (eds) *Foundations of Arbitration: The Origins and Effects of State Compulsory Arbitration 1890-1914*, OUP, Melbourne, pp 104–34.

Montgomery, E & Benedict, ME 1989 'The Impact of Bargainer Experience on Teacher Strikes' (1989) 42(3) *Industrial and Labor Relations Review* 380.

Morgando-Valenzuela, E 2015 'Chile' in Frederick Hendrickx (ed) *International Encyclopaedia for Labour Law and Industrial Relations*, Wolters Kluwer, Kluwer Law Online.

Mrachkov, V 2017 'Bulgaria' in Frederick Hendrickx (ed) *International Encyclopaedia for Labour Law and Industrial Relations*, Wolters Kluwer, Kluwer Law Online.

Mthombeni, R 1990 'The Right or Freedom to Strike: An Analysis from an International or Comparative Perspective' 23(3) *Comparative International Law Journal of South Africa* 337.

Nekrosius, I & Andriuskeviciute, J 2007 'Lithuania' in Frederick Hendrickx (ed) *International Encyclopaedia for Labour Law and Industrial Relations*, Wolters Kluwer, Kluwer Law Online.

Ngcukaitobi, T 2013 'Strike Law, Structural Violence and Inequality in the Platinum Hills of Marikana' 34 *Industrial Law Journal (SA)* 836.

Norris, P 2005 'E-voting as the Magic Ballot for European Parliamentary Elections? Evaluating E-voting in Light of Experiments in UK Local Elections' in Alexander H Trechsel & Fernando Mendez (eds) *The European Union and E-Voting: Addressing the European Parliament's Internet Voting Challenge*, Routledge, London, pp 60–90.

Novitz, T 2003 *International and European Protection of the Right to Strike*, OUP, Oxford.

Novitz, T 2010 'Collective Action in the United Kingdom' in Edoardo Ales & Tonia Novitz (eds) *Collective Action and Fundamental Freedoms in Europe: Striking the Balance*, Intersentia, Antwerp, pp 173–212.

Novitz, T 2016 'UK Regulation of Pre-Strike Ballots and Notices—Moving Beyond 'Democracy'?' 29(2) *Australian Journal of Labour Law* 226.

Novitz, T & Fenwick, C 2010 'The Application of Human Rights Discourse to Labour Relations: Translation of Theory into Practice' in Colin Fenwick & Tonia Novitz (eds) *Human Rights at Work: Perspectives on Law and Regulation*, Hart Publishing, London and Portland, pp 1–40.

Olea, MA, Rodriguez-Sanudo, F, & Guerrero, FE 2018 'Spain' in Frederick Hendrickx (ed) *International Encyclopaedia for Labour Law and Industrial Relations*, Wolters Kluwer, Kluwer Law Online.

Orchiston et al 2019 'Pre-Strike Ballots and Enterprise Bargaining Dynamics: An Empirical Analysis' 42(2) *Melbourne University Law Review* 593.

Orr, G & Murugesan, S 2007 'Mandatory Secret Ballots before Employee Industrial Action' 20(3) *Australian Journal of Labour Law* 272.

Orth, JV 1991 *Combination and Conspiracy: A Legal History of Trade Unionism 1721-1906*, Clarendon Press, Oxford.

Oxnam, DW 1973 'The Incidence of Strikes in Australia' in JE Isaac & GW Ford (eds) *Australian Labour Relations Readings*, 2nd ed, Sun Books, Melbourne, pp 19–58.

Palmer, EE 1969 *Responsible Decision-Making in Democratic Trade Unions*, Task Force on Labour Relations, Ottawa.

Parliament of the Commonwealth of Australia 1993 House of Representatives, Industrial Relations Reform Bill 1993, Explanatory Memorandum, Commonwealth of Australia, Canberra.

Parliament of the Commonwealth of Australia 2008 House of Representatives, Fair Work Bill 2008, Explanatory Memorandum, Commonwealth of Australia, Canberra.

Pascucci, P 2014 'The Right to Strike: Italy' in Bernard Waas (ed) *The Right to Strike: A Comparative View*, Kluwer Law International, Alphen aan den Rijn, pp 331–50.

Pateman, C 1970 *Participation and Democratic Theory*, Cambridge University Press, Cambridge.

Peetz, D 2012a 'Industrial Conflict with Awards, Choices and Fairness' in Breen Creighton & Anthony Forsyth (eds) *Rediscovering Collective Bargaining: Australia's Fair Work Act in International Perspective*, Routledge, New York, pp 159–81.

Peetz, D 2012b 'The Impacts and Non-Impacts on Unions of Enterprise Bargaining' 22(3) *Labour & Industry* 237.

Peetz, D 2016 'Industrial Action, the Right to Strike, Ballots and the Fair Work Act' 29(2) *Australian Journal of Labour Law* 133.

Pekarek, A et al 2017 'Old Game, New Rules? The Dynamics of Enterprise Bargaining under the Fair Work Act' 59(1) *Journal of Industrial Relations* 44.

Piron, J & Le Roux, P 2001 'South Africa' in Frederick Hendrickx (ed) *International Encyclopaedia for Labour Law and Industrial Relations*, Wolters Kluwer, Kluwer Law Online.

Pollock, F 1908 *Law of Torts*, 8th ed, Stevens & Sons, London.

Portus, JH 1958 *Development of Australian Trade Union Law*, Melbourne University Press, Melbourne.

Prassl, J 2014 'The Right to Strike: United Kingdom' in Bernard Waas (ed) *The Right to Strike: A Comparative View*, Kluwer Law International, Alphen aan den Rijn, pp 551–6.

Productivity Commission 2015 *Workplace Relations Framework*, Final Report, Commonwealth of Australia, Canberra.

Quinlan, M 1989 '"Pre-Arbitral" Labour Legislation in Australia and its Implications for the Introduction of Compulsory Arbitration' in Stuart Macintyre & Richard Mitchell (eds) *Foundations of Arbitration: The Origins and Effects of State Compulsory Arbitration 1890-1914*, OUP, Melbourne, pp 25–49.

Read, R 2018 'The Role of Trade Unions and Individual Bargaining Representatives: Who Pays for the Work of Bargaining' in Shae McCrystal, Breen Creighton, & Anthony Forsyth (eds) *Collective Bargaining Under the Fair Work Act*, Federation Press, Sydney, pp 69–92.

Reith, P 1998 *Pre-industrial Action Secret Ballots*, Ministerial Discussion Paper, Minister for Workplace Relations and Small Business.

Rogowski, R 2013 *Reflexive Labour Law in the World Society*, Edward Elgar, Cheltenham and Northampton.

Rood, MG et al 1986 *Fifty Years of Labour Law and Social Security*, Kluwer, Deventer.

Rudd, K & Gillard, J 2007 Forward with Fairness: Labor's Plan for Fairer and More Productive Australian Workplaces.

Rycroft, A 2015a 'Strikes and the Amendments to the LRA' 36(1) *Industrial Law Journal (SA)* 1.

Rycroft, A 2015b 'The Role of Trade Unions in Strikes' in Bob Hepple, Rochelle le Roux, & Silvana Sciarra (eds) *Laws Against Strikes. The South African Experience in an International and Comparative Perspective*, Milano, FrancoAngeli, pp 109–26.

Sanchez Sanchez, A 2014 'The Right to Strike: Mexico' in Bernard Waas (ed) *The Right to Strike: A Comparative View*, Kluwer Law International, Alphen aan den Rijn, pp 403–12.

Sandbrook, D 2010 *State of Emergency: The Way We Were: Britain, 1970-1974*, Allen Lane, London.

Sandbrook, D 2012 *Seasons in the Sun: The Battle for Britain, 1974-1979*, Allen Lane, London.

Sayles, LR & Strauss G 1972 'Are Unions Democratic?' in JM Shepard (ed) *Organisational Issues in Industrial Society*, Prentice Hall, New Jersey, pp 207–19.

Senate Employment, Workplace Relations, Small Business and Education Legislation Committee 1999 *Consideration of the Provisions of the Workplace Relations Amendment (More Jobs, Better Pay) Bill 1999*, Parliament House, Canberra.

Servais, J-M 2015 *International Labour Law*, 4th ed, Wolters Kluwer, Alphen aan den Rijn.

Servais, J-M 2017 'The Right to Take Industrial Action and the ILO Supervisory Mechanism Future' 38(3) *Comparative Labor Law & Policy Journal* 375.

Schumpeter, J 1942 *Capitalism, Socialism and Democracy*, Harper, New York.

Simon, D 1954 'Master and Servant' in John Saville (ed) *Democracy and the Labour Movement*, Lawrence & Wishart, London, pp 160–200.

Simpson, B 2002 'Trade Disputes and Industrial Action Ballots in the Twenty-First Century' 31(3) *Industrial Law Journal* 270.

Simpson, B 2005 'Strike Ballots and the Law: Round Six' 34(4) *Industrial Law Journal* 331.

Simpson, B 2013 'The Labour Injunction and Industrial Action Ballots' 42(1) *Industrial Law Journal* 270.

Sims Task Force 1996 *Canada Labour Code, Part 1, Review: Seeking a Balance*, Public Works and Government Services Canada, Ottawa.

Slinn, S & Tucker, E 2016 'Canadian Strike Ballot Laws: Barely a Tempest in a Teapot' 29(2) *Australian Journal of Labour Law* 171.

Smith et al 1993 'Ballots and Union Government in the 1980s' 31(3) *British Journal of Industrial Relations* 365.

Spiegelhalter DG et al 2002 'Bayesian Measures of Model Complexity and Fit' (2002) 64 *Journal of the Royal Statistical Society* 583.

Stanford, J 2018 *Historical Data on the Decline in Australia of Industrial Disputes*, The Australia Institute, Centre for Future Work.

Stewart et al 2016 *Creighton & Stewart's Labour Law*, 6th ed, Federation Press, Sydney.

Sturmthal, A 1969 'Canadian Industrial Relations—The Task Force Report' 24(3) *Industrial Relations* 489.

Summers, C 1958 'The Usefulness of the Law in Obtaining Union Democracy' 81(3) *Monthly Labor Review* March.

Suttawet, C 2018 'Thailand' in Frederick Hendrickx (ed) *International Encyclopaedia for Labour Law and Industrial Relations*, Wolters Kluwer, Kluwer Law Online.

Swepson, L 2014 'Crisis in the ILO Supervisory System: Dispute Over the Right to Strike' 29(2) *International Journal of Comparative Labour Law and Industrial Relations* 199.

Sykes, EI 1960 *Strike Law in Australia*, Law Book Company, Sydney.

Sykes, EI 1982 *Strike Law in Australia*, 2nd ed, Law Book Company, Sydney.

Teubner, G 1993 *Law as an Autopoetic System*, Blackwell, London.

Thomson, AWJ & Engleman, SR 1975 *The Industrial Relations Act: A Review and Analysis*, Martin Robertson, London.

Tong A, Sainsbury P, & Craig J 2007 'Consolidated Criteria for Reporting Qualitative Research (COREQ): A 32-item Checklist for Interviews and Focus Groups' 19(6) *International Journal of Quality Health Care* 349.

Townsend, K, Wilkinson, A, & Burgess, J 2013 'Is Enterprise Bargaining Still a Better Way of Working?' 55(1) *Journal of Industrial Relations* 100.

Tracy, JS 1987 'An Empirical Test of an Asymmetric Information Model of Strikes' 5(2) *Journal of Labour Economics* 149.

Tracey, RRS 1985 'The Legal Approach to Democratic Control of Trade Unions' 15(2) *Melbourne University Law Review* 177.

Trechsel, AH 2007 'E-voting and Electoral Participation' in Claes H de Vreese (ed) *The Dynamics of Referendum Campaigns: An International Perspective*, Palgrave Macmillan, Basingstoke, pp 159–84.

Treu, T 2016 'Italy' in Frederick Hendrickx (ed) *International Encyclopaedia for Labour Law and Industrial Relations*, Wolters Kluwer, Kluwer Law Online.

Tucker, E 2014 'Can Worker Voice Strike Back? Law and the Decline and Uncertain Future of Strikes' in Alan Bogg & Tonia Novitz (eds) *Voices at Work*, OUP, Oxford, pp 455–74.

Undy, R & Martin, R 1984 *Ballots and Trade Union Democracy*, Basil Blackwell, Oxford.

Undy et al 1996 *Managing the Unions: The Impact of Legislation on Trade Unions' Behaviour*, Clarendon Press, Oxford.

Vaillancourt, L 2000 'Amendments to the Canada Labour Code: Are Replacement Workers an Endangered Species?' 45(3) *McGill Law Journal* 757.

Valticos, N & von Potobsky, G 1995 *International Labour Law*, 2nd ed, Kluwer, Deventer.

Velden, J (ed) 2007 *Strikes Around the World 1968-2005*, Aksant, Amsterdam.

Vodovnik, Z, Korpic-Horvat, E, & Ticar, L 2018 'Slovenia' in Frederick Hendrickx (ed) *International Encyclopaedia for Labour Law and Industrial Relations*, Wolters Kluwer, Kluwer Law Online.

Waas, B (ed) 2014a *The Right to Strike: A Comparative View*, Kluwer Law International, Alphen aan den Rijn.

Waas, B 2014b 'The Right to Strike: Germany' in Bernard Waas (ed) *The Right to Strike: A Comparative View*, Kluwer Law International, Alphen aan den Rijn, pp 235–58.

Wedderburn, Lord 1986 *The Worker and the Law*, 3rd ed, Penguin Books, Harmondsworth.

Wedderburn, Lord 1991 'The Right to Strike: Is there a European Standard?' in Lord Wedderburn (ed) *Employment Rights in Britain and Europe: Selected Papers in Labour Law*, Lawrence & Wishart, London, pp 276–353.

Weekes et al 1975 *Industrial Relations and the Limits of Law: The Industrial Effects of the Industrial Relations Act, 1971*, Basil Blackwell, Oxford.

Weeks, P 1995 *Trade Union Security Law: A Study of Preference and Compulsory Unionism*, Federation Press, Sydney.

Weiler, P 1980 *Irreconcilable Differences: New Directions in Canadian Labour Law*, Carswell, Toronto.

Weiss, M & Schmidt, M 2008 'Germany' in Frederick Hendrickx (ed) *International Encyclopaedia for Labour Law and Industrial Relations*, Wolters Kluwer, Kluwer Law Online.

Wilson, M 2016 'Strike Ballots: The New Zealand Experience' 29(2) *Australian Journal of Labour Law* 194.

Wisskirchen, A 2005 'The Standard-Setting and Monitoring Activity of the ILO: Legal Questions and Practical Experience' 144(3) *International Labour Review* 253.

Woods, HD 1967 'Federal Government Taskforce on Labour Relations' 22(1) *Relations Industrielles* 130.

Woods, HD 1968 *Canadian Industrial Relations: The Report of Task Force on Labour Relations*, Privy Council Office, Ottawa.

Index

Tables and figures are indicated by *t* and *f* following the page number. Footnotes are indicated by n. following the page number.